The Positive Psychology
of Personal Factors

The Positive Psychology of Personal Factors

Implications for Understanding Disability

Edited by Michael L. Wehmeyer
and Dana S. Dunn

LEXINGTON BOOKS
Lanham • Boulder • New York • London

Published by Lexington Books
An imprint of The Rowman & Littlefield Publishing Group, Inc.
4501 Forbes Boulevard, Suite 200, Lanham, Maryland 20706
www.rowman.com

86-90 Paul Street, London EC2A 4NE

British Library Cataloguing in Publication Information Available

Library of Congress Cataloging-in-Publication Data

Names: Wehmeyer, Michael L., editor. | Dunn, Dana, editor.
Title: The positive psychology of personal factors: implications for understanding disability / edited by Michael Wehmeyer and Dana Dunn.
Description: Lanham: Lexington Books, 2022. | Includes bibliographical references.
Identifiers: LCCN 2021044032 (print) | LCCN 2021044033 (ebook) |
    ISBN 9781793634658 (cloth) | ISBN 9781793634672 (paper) |
    ISBN 9781793634665 (ebook)
Subjects: LCSH: Positive psychology. | People with disabilities—Psychology.
Classification: LCC BF204.6 .U53 2021 (print) | LCC BF204.6 (ebook) |
    DDC 155.9/16—dc23
LC record available at https://lccn.loc.gov/2021044032
LC ebook record available at https://lccn.loc.gov/2021044033

In honor and recognition of the important contributions of the American Psychological Association's Committee on Disability Issues in Psychology and in memory of Roger Barker, Beatrice A. Wright, and Tamara Dembo, early positive psychologists and founders of rehabilitation psychology

Contents

Editors' Note

As comprehensively discussed in chapter 3, language plays an important role in shaping how disability itself is viewed by others and how disabled people view themselves. In this volume, we have adhered to the APA 7.0 recommendations with regard to disability-related language; that being, as stated in chapter 3, either disability identity language or person-first language is acceptable.

Chapter 1

Introduction and Overview of the International Classification of Functioning, Disability, and Health

Michael L. Wehmeyer and Dana S. Dunn

Müller and Geyh (2015) observed that although personal factors "are a part of the contextual factors within the bio-psycho-social framework of the World Health Organization's (WHO) International Classification of Functioning, Disability and Health . . . a precise conceptualization [of these personal factors] is missing" (p. 430). Similarly noting the absence of such a conceptualization, a number of authors have proposed taxonomies and frameworks for understanding and classifying personal factors (Leonardi et al., 2016; Geyh et al., 2011; Müller & Geyh, 2015; Simeonsson et al., 2014). The intent of this book relates neither to classification nor to the creation of a comprehensive taxonomy of personal factors. Instead, we are interested in exploring personal factors that fall under the general category of psychological personal factors and, more specifically, psychological personal factors that relate to constructs in positive psychology. Our intent is to synthesize what is known from research about these positive psychological personal factors so as to address a segment of the conceptualization gap that exists in the field and, through doing so, promote a strengths-based approach to supporting and enabling disabled people to participate fully in society. The intent of this chapter is to overview models of disability that emphasize interactions among and between persons and their environment, to describe the World Health Organization's (WHO) International Classification of Functioning, Disability, and Health (ICF) in the context of these models, and to examine the role of personal factors within the ICF and their relationship to strengths-based approaches. In chapter 2, we discuss positive psychology, its constructs and their application to the disability context, and how the field can contribute to a greater focus on strengths and abilities of people with disabilities.

Before proceeding, it is important to state that by focusing on personal factors, this book is not in any way proclaiming a priority for such factors in understanding disability or promoting full and active participation. We are conscious of and will briefly examine understandings of disability that viewed disability as a problem within the person to be fixed or cured (Dunn, 2015; Wehmeyer, 2013a). Our focus on positive psychological personal factors reflects the facts that personal factors are important for all people, that their inclusion in the ICF was not incidental, and that understanding such positive psychological personal factors can support strengths-based approaches that empower disabled people to fully participate in society. We are interested in identifying approaches drawn from strengths-based approaches and positive psychology that emphasize self-advocacy, autonomy, agency, and self-determination. Nor are we proclaiming that the ICF itself is a perfect model. With those caveats in mind, to understand the ICF and the role of personal factors in understanding disability, it is important to begin with an overview of social models of disability.

SOCIAL MODELS OF DISABILITY

Disability, as a construct, has been defined across multiple disciplines—law, education, psychology, rehabilitation, medicine, and so on—for multiple purposes. Across these disciplines, disability has, historically, been defined or constructed as a juxtaposition between normality and abnormality (Bach, 2017); people with disabilities were seen as atypical, subnormal, aberrant, pathological, incompetent, and so on; as somehow different from the rest of *us* (Wehmeyer, 2013b). Inevitably, how disability was understood directly influenced how society responded to disability. Interventions or treatments designed to address disability focused on curative aspects, remediation, mitigation, and protection. People with disabilities were segregated, sterilized, discriminated against, and marginalized.

In the late twentieth century, numerous forces converged that began to change perceptions of disability and, thus, societal responses to disability. Before the eighteenth century, legal conceptualizations of disability dominated (Wickham, 2013). After the eighteenth century, medical models of disability prevailed (Ferguson, 2013). By the time psychology emerged as a discipline distinct from philosophy in the early twentieth century, medical definitions and conceptualizations were the predominant lenses through which disability was understood (Noll, Smith, & Wehmeyer, 2013). So-called biomedical models conceptualized disability through medical lenses, with disability viewed as a pathology within the person, and the types and severity of disability were categorized through taxonomies of diseases and disorders.

In the 1970s, however, health-care professionals realized that viewing long-term conditions like disability through the lens of pathology had limitations. In 1980, the World Health Organization introduced the International Classification of Impairments, Disabilities, and Handicaps (WHO, 1980), or ICIDH. Instead of being a classification of diseases or disorders, the ICIDH was a means to classify the long-term *consequences* or *impact* of diseases and disorders (Wood, 1989). Though still seated firmly in biomedical models of disability, the ICIDH was an important step away from past taxonomies. Disability was defined as "any restriction or lack (resulting from an impairment) of ability to perform an activity in the manner or within the range considered normal for a human being" that might result in "a disadvantage for a given individual, resulting from an impairment or disability, that limits or prevents the fulfilment of a role that is normal (depending on age, sex, social, and cultural factors) for that individual" (WHO, 1980, pp. 27–29). The change seems subtle 40 years later, but the ICIDH shifted disability as understood only in terms of impairments (and classified as diseases and disorders) and placed it in a context of how the impairment impacted a person's activities and, eventually, participation.

These themes of activities and participation were expanded upon in the ICF (WHO, 2001). The ICF conceptualized disability within the context of the interrelationships among health, environmental, and personal factors and situated disability as part of, and not apart from, typical human functioning. The ICF was described as a biopsychosocial model of disability because it shifted the locus of disability from within the person to existing only, essentially, in the gap between the person's abilities and capacities and the demands of the environment (Buntinx, 2013), one that is consistent with the person-environment relation espoused by social psychologist Kurt Lewin (1890–1947) and those among his students who helped to found the field of rehabilitation psychology (e.g., Lewin, 1935; Wright, 1983). The ICF will be described in more detail subsequently, but for purposes of strength-based approaches to disability, the ICF provided a person-environment fit (or social-ecological) model with which to build interventions and supports that emphasized personal capacity, adaptations, and modifications to contexts and environments.

A second, and perhaps more important, movement was emerging as health professionals began to rethink biomedical models of disability: the disability civil rights movement. In the early 1980s, disabled people began to come together to create a global disability rights and self-advocacy movement (Driedger, 1989). One emphasis within this rights-based self-advocacy movement was the "advancement of a positive disability identity and culture" (Caldwell, 2011). Longmore (2003) termed the establishment of disability identity and culture as the second phase of the disability rights movement and argued that while public policy has sought to fashion disability as a generic category and attempted to impose that classification of people with an assortment of conditions, disability has never been a monolithic grouping. There has always been a variety of disability experiences. [These] experiences of cultural devaluation and socially imposed restriction, of personal and collective struggles for self-definition and self-determination—recur across the various disability groups and throughout their personal histories. (Longmore & Umansky, 2001, p. 4)

What leaders in the disability rights and self-advocacy movement emphasize is that by embracing disability identity, they recapture their personhood and lay claim to social justice, full citizenship, and participation. What emerged from this movement was what is referred to as a social model of disability, which views disability as arising "from the discrimination and disadvantage individuals experience in relation to others because of their particular differences and characteristics" (Bach, 2017, p. 40). Within a social model,

> the unit of analysis shifts from the individual to the legal, social, economic, and political structures that calculate value and status on the basis of difference. Informed by principles of human rights, and an equality of outcomes that takes account of differences, the social model does not reject bio-medical knowledge of impairments and research on individual rehabilitation. Rather, it celebrates impairment as part of the human condition, and looks at achieving equity for people with impairments in terms of the social, cultural, and political contexts. (Bach, 2017, p. 40)

Social-ecological or person-environment fit models of disability are situated within the broader context of social models. There is some tension among advocates who emphasize the identity aspects of disability and ascribe to a pure social model and the social-ecological models that evolved through the medical system. For one, the latter still include medical and health formulations with the equation of understanding disability. Bach (2017) noted that although the WHO changed the term "handicap" in the ICIDH to "impairment" in the ICF, based heavily on the efforts of the civil rights organization Disabled Peoples' International (DPI), the retention of the term "impairments" may be construed as reflecting "intrinsic limitations" (p. 40). Bach discussed the difficulty aligned with ignoring a person's so-called limitations, noting that certain social-relational models recognize that "physical or cognitive impairments can have real effects and limitations in a person's life," and that such models (e.g., social-relational models) "acknowledge the reality of impairment while challenging the assumptions that one person is given the status to define another as 'impaired' from some 'objective' criteria of 'normal' functioning" (Bach, 2017, p. 40).

We recognize the tightrope we must walk when discussing positive psychological personal factors in the context of social-ecological models, and we understand that "impairment is a lived and subjective reality, given meaning within the individual and collective narratives expressed by people with disabilities themselves" (Bach, 2017, pp. 40–41). That said, while these issues are critically important, there are many points of agreement among social and social-ecological models, the primary one being that one cannot understand disability without taking into account the person's strengths and abilities and the contexts in which people live, learn, work, and play. For the applied disciplines, such as psychology or education, whose purposes include the development of interventions to improve human functioning, social-ecological models provide a framework to approach intervention development in a strength-based manner. The WHO itself stated that "[t]he ICF provides a scientific, operational basis for describing, understanding and studying health and health-related states, outcomes and determinants" (WHO 2013, p. 6). With this in mind, we turn our attention to examining the ICF in more detail.

THE INTERNATIONAL CLASSIFICATION OF FUNCTIONING, DISABILITY, AND HEALTH

According to the WHO, the ICF "is a framework for organizing and documenting information on functioning and disability" (WHO, 2001). It "conceptualises functioning as a 'dynamic interaction between a person's health condition, environmental factors and personal factors'" (WHO, 2013, p. 5).

Within the ICF framework, human functioning and disability are understood "as umbrella terms denoting the positive and negative aspects of functioning from a biological, individual and social perspective. The ICF therefore provides a multi-perspective, biopsychosocial approach which is reflected in the multidimensional model", depicted in Figure 1.1 (WHO, 2013, p. 5). One of the empowering features of the ICF is that it "conceptualises functioning and disability in the context of health" (WHO, 2013, p. 6). Rephrasing this, we would say that it conceptualizes disability as a part of typical human functioning and health, and not apart from them; health and disability are not opposed.

There are a number of definitions in the ICF that are important to understand (from WHO 2001, pp. 212–213). In the *context of health*,

Functioning is an umbrella term for body functions, body structures, activities and participation. It denotes the positive aspects of the interaction between an individual (with a health condition) and that individual's contextual factors (environmental and personal factors).

Michael L. Wehmeyer and Dana S. Dunn

Health Condition
(disorder/disease)

Body
function&structure ←→ Activities ←→ Participation

Environmental
Factors

Personal
Factors

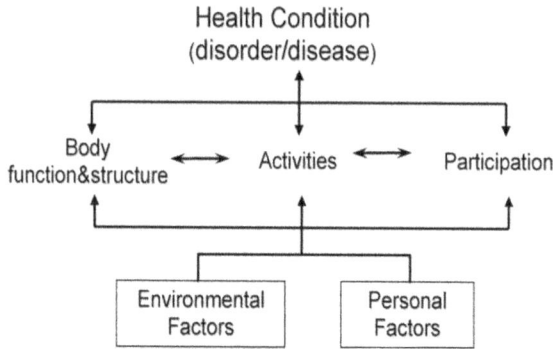

Figure 1.1   Interactions among and between the Components of the ICF. *Source:* From WHO, 2013, p. 18, in the Public Domain.

Disability is an umbrella term for impairments, activity limitations and participation restrictions. It denotes the negative aspects of the interaction between an individual (with a health condition) and that individual's contextual factors (environmental and personal factors).

Body functions—The physiological functions of body systems (including psychological functions).

Body structures—Anatomical parts of the body such as organs, limbs and their components.

Impairments—Problems in body function and structure such as significant deviation or loss.

Activity—The execution of a task or action by an individual.

Participation—Involvement in a life situation.

Activity limitations—Difficulties an individual may have in executing activities.

Participation restrictions—Problems an individual may experience in involvement in life situations.

Environmental factors—The physical, social and attitudinal environment in which people live and conduct their lives. These are either barriers to or facilitators of the person's functioning.

Personal Factors: Personal factors are the particular background of an individual's life and living and comprise features of the individual that are not part of a health condition or health states. These factors may include gender, race, age, other health conditions, fitness, lifestyle, habits, upbringing, coping styles, social background, education, profession, past and current experience (past life events and concurrent events), overall behaviour pattern and character style, individual psychological assets and other characteristics, all or any of which may play a role in disability at any level.

The WHO (2001) noted that "there is a dynamic interaction among these entities: interventions in one entity have the potential to modify one or more of the other entities" (p. 19). About personal factors specifically, the WHO (2001) noted that "these factors interact with the individual with a health condition and determine the level and extent of the individual's functioning" (p. 19).

As was noted at the onset, the WHO goes no further in trying to define personal factors. Geyh and colleagues (2011) conducted a systematic literature review on personal factors as situated within the ICF. From a pool of 353 papers, these authors narrowed the synthesis down to 79 papers. Almost 60 percent of the papers focused on one of three areas of disability: communication disorders, neurological disorders, and musculoskeletal conditions. From among the 79 papers, Geyh and colleagues (2011) extracted "238 examples of PFs [Personal Factors] not found in the ICF" (Geyh et al., 2011, p. 1098). Most of these 238 personal factors were mentioned only in one article, with motivation ($n = 7$), personality ($n = 7$), attitudes ($n = 5$), and depression ($n = 5$) the only such factors mentioned in five or more articles. It should be noted that although the WHO does not operationalize personal factors in the ICF, it does operationalize environmental factors, categorizing them as either facilitators or barriers to human functioning. Although this chapter has purposefully focused on positive psychological personal factors that, by definition, would serve as facilitators to more successful human functioning, as is demonstrated by the presence of depression among the four most frequently mentioned personal factors in the literature reviewed by Geyh et al., personal factors can be both facilitators and barriers to successful human functioning.

Geyh et al. (2011) specifically sought out examples of personal factors that were not found in the ICF, suggesting that there were some examples found in the ICF itself. Indeed, at a very broad level, the ICF mentioned fitness, coping styles, individual psychological assets, and other characteristics as examples of personal factors (WHO, 2001, p. 17). Müller and Geyh (2015) attempted to go beyond the very broad operationalization of personal factors in the ICF and the exceedingly large number of personal factors identified in the Geyh et al. (2011) review by describing extant categorizations of personal factors in the literature. This effort yielded eight categorizations, organized mainly in the disciplines or fields in which they appeared or the purpose they were developed to serve. These eight categorizations were (1) personal factors in audiological rehabilitation, (2) personal factors in work, (3) personal factors in individual sociomedical expertise, (4) subjective dimensions of functioning and disability, (5) personal factors for individual-centeredness, (6) inherent or acquired personal factors, (7) personal factors in motor neuron disease, and (8) personal factors as health-related habits and lifestyle. Müller and Geyh (2015) then mapped these eight categorization models against twelve *content topics* (sociodemographic factors, behavior/lifestyle, cognitive/psychological factors, social relationships, experiences/biography, coping, emotion, satisfaction, other conditions, biological/physiological factors, personality, and motivation).

Perhaps the highest level takeaway from this work is the complexity of conceptualizing personal factors and the fact that personal factors exist as much in the interaction with other elements of the ICF model as they do as standalone factors. That, of course, is something that research in positive psychology has made clear for understanding even this limited subset (e.g., positive psychological personal factors) of personal factors (Snyder, Lopez, Edwards, & Marques, 2021). Indeed, several authors have commented on the justification for personal factors as a component of the ICF given the "conceptual and taxonomic problems that are non-consistent with the requirements for a scientific classification" (Simeonsson et al., p. 2187). Among the concerns raised is that the "classification of PFs [Personal Factors] can be misused as a classification of the person" (Leonardi et al., 2016, p. 1327). As was noted previously, we are not interested in creating a classification or taxonomy system, but simply in identifying and describing one subcategory of personal factors (positive psychological personal factors) that may contribute to the development of strength-based interventions to promote optimal functioning for disabled people.

PARTICIPATION

There is another term within the ICF that deserves elaboration as part of a discussion of the application of positive psychological personal factors to strength-based approaches: *participation*. Whether an impairment (defined as problems in body function and structure) results in disability (defined as an umbrella term for impairments, activity limitations, and participation restrictions) is not a function of the presence of the impairment itself but a function of the interaction between personal and environmental factors that mediate the impact of the impairment on activity and participation. That is, in a concrete sense, disability itself exists only when participation is impacted. Within the ICF, *Activities* refer to a person's execution of a task or action. *Participation* is defined in the ICF as a person's involvement in life situations. While there is an intuitive understanding of activities as tasks or actions, the same is not true for participation as involvement in life situations. What constitutes involvement? What is meant by life situations? The ICF includes *Activities and Participation Domains* (discussed subsequently), but these are mainly generic areas in which activities occur and, presumably, participation is situated. If we are to understand disability as a function of limited participation, it would seem important to have a clear definition and understanding of participation.

Dean and colleagues (2016) conducted a scoping review of the participation construct in the literature from the field of intellectual disability. Dean et al. noted that within the broader disability literatures, participation has been defined as fulfilling social roles, as goal-focused action, and as autonomous functioning. One difficulty in defining participation is that has an individual element to it; that is, even when all barriers to full participation are removed, levels and types of participation will vary a great deal from individual to individual as a function of personal preferences, interests, or goals. Further, types and levels of participation are often context- or domain-specific. Dean and colleagues identified five themes that were raised consistently throughout the literature: (1) meaningful engagement, (2) choice and control, (3) personal and societal responsibilities, (4) access and opportunity, and (5) inclusion.

Drawing from this scoping review by Dean et al., we have conceptualized participation as a person's self-determined involvement in a pattern of life (i.e., roles, life situations, and activities). Participation occurs in and across contexts and is influenced by multiple personal and environmental factors. Placing participation within the idea of *patterns of life* recognizes the temporal aspect of participation. How participation looks varies not only by context but by one's stage of life, as it were. As such, participation is not static across life, but evolves with the person. Patterns of life represent the changing roles, life situations, and activities that comprise daily life; they represent the socially defined sets of behavior that support participation. The idea that participation refers to self-determined involvement brings in the issues of choice, control, goal orientation, preferences, and intentionality. People choose how they spend their time and their resources; participation can look very different from one person to the next because it is self-determined involvement in a pattern of life.

Considering participation as a function of a person's self-determined involvement in a pattern of life (e.g., participation) is important to strength-based approaches to disability in that this aligns with the person-environment fit nature of social-ecological models of disability. Not only do we identify the need for interventions and supports by the level of a person's participation, but that identification, in turn, aligns such interventions and supports with a person's preferences, interests, values, and goals. Systems of support are driven not by the need to fix or change a person, but by the need to support a person to engage in activities that lead to full participation.

As was mentioned previously, the ICF does provide *Activities and Participation Domains*. To understand these, it is worth considering the aims of the ICF, as stated by the WHO:

- to provide a scientific basis for understanding and studying health and health-related states, outcomes and determinants;
- to establish a common language for describing health and health-related states in order to improve communication between different users, such as health care workers, researchers, policy-makers and the public, including people with disabilities;
- to permit comparison of data across countries, health care disciplines, services and time;
- to provide a systematic coding scheme for health information systems. (WHO, 2001, p. 5)

To this point, we have discussed the ICF only in the context of social-ecological models of disability. But, as can be seen by these aims, the ICF allows for and describes a valid and reliable data collection and management process (Bickenbach, 2011). The ICF is a tool to "provide a consistent and comparable, international language of the lived experience of health to generate internationally comparable health and disability data" (Bickenbach, 2011, p. 2). Unlike the personal factors component within ICF, the participation component does have domains identified so as to facilitate data collection. Specifically, the *Activities and Participation Domains* are measured by both performance and capacity indicators and consist of the following areas:

- Learning and applying knowledge
- General tasks and demands
- Communication
- Mobility
- Self-care
- Domestic life
- Interpersonal interactions and relationships
- Major life areas
- Community, social and civic life. (WHO, 2001, p. 14)

CONVENTION ON THE RIGHTS OF PERSONS WITH DISABILITIES

Before closing this chapter with a discussion pertaining to strength-based approaches that have arisen from social-ecological models like the ICF, it is worth discussing one more international convention that guides our examination of positive psychological personal factors: the United Nations Convention on the Rights of Persons with Disabilities (CRPD; UN General

Assembly, 2007). The relevance of the CRPD to the intent of this book is readily apparent in the CRPD Article 3: General Principles:

(a) Respect for inherent dignity, individual autonomy including the freedom to make one's own choices, and independence of persons;
(b) Non-discrimination;
(c) Full and effective participation and inclusion in society;
(d) Respect for difference and acceptance of persons with disabilities as part of human diversity and humanity.

The themes of participation, dignity, autonomy, and choice and control that have been discussed as elements of social models and social-ecological models of disability are obvious in these general principles. Some authors have discussed the role of data from the *Activities and Participation Domain* of the ICF in providing a means to monitor the progress of countries toward the CRPD rights and to introduce greater accountability. Bickenbach (2011) mapped ICF Activities and Participation Domains with CRPD Articles, finding direct relationships between these domains and CRPD Articles on rights to living independently, personal mobility, freedom of expression, education, health, work, rehabilitation, and other areas (p. 6). Although there are no Personal Factors Domains within the ICF, Geyh et al. (2011) suggested that personal factors "might reflect the individual's 'needs and strengths,' as required for rehabilitation care in the United Nations' Convention on the Rights of Persons with Disabilities, Article 26" (p. 1099).

As was noted at the onset of this chapter, it is not the intent of this book to provide a classification or taxonomy system for personal factors. To that end, our focus is on the broader topic of thinking about and understanding disability, as embraced in both the ICF and CRPD, that emphasizes dignity and participation and that provides a means to align disability supports with positive psychology and strength-based approaches to disability. To that end, we close this chapter with a discussion of what is meant by strength-based approaches to disability.

STRENGTH-BASED APPROACHES TO DISABILITY

Strength-based approaches to disability are predicated on social models of disability, but the two are not synonymous. As discussed previously, social models of disability refer to an understanding of disability emphasizing lived experiences and the opportunities and barriers introduced by attitudes, structures, and environments in society. Strength-based approaches begin with the assumptions of the social model of disability and then translate them into

approaches to support or enable people with disabilities to function successfully in typical contexts.

As mentioned by Wehmeyer (2021), strength-based approaches are not
unique to the disability context. Practice social welfare, for example, introduced a strength-model in the late 1990s (Rapp, 1997). Rapp, Saleebey, and
Sullivan (2005) identified the "six hallmarks of strengths based practice" (p.
81) in social welfare as follows:

1. *Goal setting.* People who need supports have a meaningful role in setting
   goal related to their lives.
2. *Assessment of strengths.* Support provision begins with assessments of
   abilities and interests, and not deficits.
3. *Resource-rich environments.* Strengths-based approaches emphasize the
   critical role of environments and contexts in creating both opportunities
   for people and barriers to people achieving what they want to achieve.
4. *Goal attainment.* Not only are people who need supports actively
   involved in goal setting, they are also at the center of self-directed and
   self-regulated action to achieve these goals.
5. *Relationships create hope.* Strengths-based approaches are built on relationships based on trust and that promote hopefulness.
6. *Choice.* Strengths-based approaches emphasize the opportunity and
   importance of supporting people to make meaningful choices about all
   aspects of supports provision. (Rapp, Saleebey, & Sullivan, 2005, pp.
   81–82)

Strength-based approaches to disability operationalize social and person-
environment fit models that recognize that disability is not a problem within
the person, but a function of the complex, multifaceted interaction between
a person, their strengths and abilities, the supports that are provided that
enable them to function, and the demands of the environment. Strength-
based approaches build on advances in positive psychology to enable people
with disabilities to obtain optimal outcomes in their lives. The purposes and
focus of positive psychology and its application to the disability context are
discussed in chapter 2.

CONCLUSIONS

Historically, interventions designed to impact the lives of disabled people
were predicated upon deficit-based models of disability. This began to
change with the introduction of two World Health Organization frameworks, most recently the ICF, that emphasized that disability could only be

understood in the context of interactions among health, environmental factors, and personal factors and by examining the impact of such factors on a person's activities and participation. The ICF identified personal factors as among the elements of a social-ecological model of disability but did not provide an extensive taxonomy of what constitutes such factors. The intent of this book is to examine in greater detail personal factors that come from the field of positive psychology and, as such, to begin to identify and build strength-based approaches to promoting the full participation, dignity, and well-being of disabled people.

REFERENCES

Bach, M. (2017). Changing perspectives on intellectual and developmental disabilities. In M.L. Wehmeyer, I. Brown, M. Percy, K.A. Shogren, & W.L.A. Fung (Eds.), *A comprehensive guide to intellectual and developmental disabilities* (2nd ed.) (pp. 35–45). Baltimore: Paul H. Brookes.

Bickenbach, J.E. (2011). Monitoring the United Nation's convention on the rights of persons with disabilities: Data and the International Classification of Functioning, Disability and health. *BMC Public Health, 11*(Suppl 4): S8.

Dean, E.E., Fisher, K.W., Shogren, K.A., & Wehmeyer, M.L. (2016). Participation and intellectual disability: A review of the literature. *Intellectual and Developmental Disabilities, 54*(6), 427–439.

Dunn, D. S. (2015). *The social psychology of disability*. New York: Oxford University Press.

Ferguson, P.M. (2013). The development of systems of supports: Idiocy in middle modern times (1800-1899). In M.L. Wehmeyer (Ed.), *The story of intellectual disability: An evolution of meaning, understanding, and public perception* (pp. 79–116). Baltimore, MD: Paul H. Brookes.

Geyh, S., Peter, C., Müller, R., Bickenbach, J.E., Kostanjsek, N., Ustun, B.T., Stucki, G., & Cieza, A. (2011). The personal factors of the International Classification of Functioning, Disability and health in the literature-a systematic review and content analysis. *Disability and Rehabilitation, 33*(13–14), 1089–1102.

Leonardi, M., Sykes, C.R., Madden, R.C., Napel, H.T., Hollenweger, J., Snyman, S., Madden, R.H., De Camargo, O.K., Raggi, A., van Gool, C.H., & Martinuzzi, A. (2016). Do we really need to open a classification box on personal factors in ICF? *Disability and Rehabilitation, 38*(13), 1327–1328.

Lewin, K. (1935). *A dynamic theory of personality*. New York: McGraw-Hill.

Müller, R., & Geyh, S. (2015). Lessons learned from different approaches towards classifying personal factors. *Disability and Rehabilitation, 37*(5), 430–438.

Noll, S., Smith, J.D., & Wehmeyer, M.L. (2013). In search of a science: Feeblemindedness in late modern times (1900-1930). In M.L. Wehmeyer (Ed.), *The story of intellectual disability: An evolution of meaning, understanding, and public perception* (pp. 117–156). Baltimore, MD: Paul H. Brookes

Rapp, C.A. (1997). *The strengths model: Case management with people suffering from severe and persistent mental illness*. Oxford, UK: Oxford University Press.

Rapp, C.A., Saleebey, D., & Sullivan, W.P. (2005). The future of strengths-based social work. *Advances in Social Work, 6*(1), 79–90.

Simeonsson, R.J., Lollar, D., Bjorck-Akesson, E., Granlund, M., Brown, S.C., Zhuoying, Q, Gray, D., & Pan, Y. (2014). ICF and ICF-CY lessons learned: Pandora's box of personal factors. *Disability and Rehabilitation, 36*(25), 2187–2194.

Snyder, C.R., Lopez, S.J., Edwards, L.M., & Marques, S.C. (2021). *The Oxford handbook of positive psychology* (3rd ed.). Oxford, UK: Oxford University Press.

UN General Assembly, Convention on the Rights of Persons with Disabilities: resolution/ adopted by the General Assembly, January 24, 2007, A/RES/61/106, available at: https://www.refworld.org/docid/45f973632.html [accessed March 30, 2021].

Wehmeyer, M.L. (2013a). *Oxford handbook of positive psychology and disability*. Oxford, UK: Oxford University Press.

Wehmeyer, M.L. (2013b). *The story of intellectual disability: An evolution of meaning, understanding, and public perception*. Baltimore, MD: Paul H. Brookes

Wehmeyer, M.L. (2021). Positive psychology and strengths-based approaches to neurodiversity. In L.K. Fung (Ed.), *Neurodiversity: From phenomenology to neurobiology and enhancing technologies* (pp. 19–38). Washington, DC: American Psychiatric Association.

Wickham, P. (2013). The emergence of idiocy in early modern times (1500-1799). In M.L. Wehmeyer (Ed.), *The story of intellectual disability: An evolution of meaning, understanding, and public perception* (pp. 63–77). Baltimore, MD: Paul H. Brookes.

Wood, P. (1989). Measuring the consequences of illness. *World Health Statistics Quarterly, 42*(3), 115–121.

World Health Organization (1980). *International classification of impairments, disabilities, and handicaps. A manual of classification relating to the consequences of disease*. Geneva, Switzerland: Author.

World Health Organization (2001). *The International Classification of Functioning, Disability and Health (ICF)*. Geneva, WHO (http://www.who.int/classifications/icf/en/).

World Health Organization (2013). *How to use the ICF: A practical manual for using the International Classification of Functioning, Disability and Health (ICF)*. Geneva, Switzerland: WHO (https://www.who.int/docs/default-source/classification/icf/drafticfpracticalmanual2.pdf?sfvrsn=8a214b01_4).

Wright, B. A. (1983). *Physical disability: A psychosocial approach*. New York: Harper & Row.

Chapter 2

Positive Psychology and Disability

Focusing on Intrapersonal Strengths

Dana S. Dunn and Michael L. Wehmeyer

Positive psychology is a subfield of psychology that flourished at the end of the twentieth century (see Seligman, 1999, 2002) and is now a sustained and expanded area of scientific inquiry that is itself flourishing. Journal articles, books and handbooks, dedicated journals, and topical conferences appeared en masse and the first generation of positive psychologists quickly followed. Many psychologists who already identified as being social-personality, clinical, or rehabilitation psychologists, among other types, quickly shifted their research programs to include questions and issues tied to the strength-oriented framework of positive psychology. One portrayal of the impact of positive psychology is how it helps people to flourish in their daily lives; that is, to report high levels of positive well-being while experiencing low levels of mental illness (Keyes, 2009, 2013; see also, Keyes & Simoes, 2012). Languishing is flourishing's opposing psychosocial process, one where social, psychological, and emotional well-being as well as mental health are all low (see, for example, Keyes, 2013).

Like any successful new subfield in psychology, positive psychology has what we might refer to as a Velcro quality to it: its content "sticks to" or connects with many of the concepts, constructs, or settings to which it is linked. We know that individuals who are flourishing in their daily lives, finding meaning and purpose in living, enjoy beneficial social relations with other people, experience favorable levels of self-esteem, and hold optimistic outlooks for the future (e.g., Bolt & Dunn, 2016). Clearly, these are intrapersonal factors that affect interpersonal relations and interact with many situations or environmental factors.

In this chapter, we discuss the fundamental focus of positive psychology, some of its theories and constructs, and their application to understanding the experience of disability. Like the authors represented in this book, we are interested in how the field can contribute to a greater focus on strengths and enhancing the abilities and well-being of people with disabilities. Our emphasis is primarily on intrapersonal factors, as represented in the International Classification of Functioning, Disability, and Health (ICF) (WHO, 2001) model of disability, and how they can moderate the impact of health impairments on functioning and increase participation for people with a disability (see chapter 1, this volume). Of course, interpersonal and situational factors play a role as well. To begin, we discuss a list of perspectives shared between positive psychology and rehabilitation psychology, and then consider positive psychology's three levels of analysis: positive subjective states and experiences, positive individual traits, and positive institutions.

POSITIVE PSYCHOLOGICAL
PERSPECTIVES ON DISABILITY

Positive psychology can be defined in a variety of ways but at its core it goes about the business of establishing, building upon, or improving human strengths. By strengths, we refer to human capacities that can withstand internal and external stressors, thereby promoting optimal human functioning when facing unexpected problems or challenges posed by daily life. Positive psychological research is also said to rest on three pillars: positive subjective states, positive traits, and positive institutions. Because this book is about personal factors that promote well-being among disabled individuals, we are clearly dealing primarily with the first two pillars (although the third can potentially shape people's intrapersonal qualities, as, for example, when quality schools help people develop new skills).

Dunn (2015) identified some perspectives shared between positive psychology and rehabilitation psychology, where the latter field's purpose is to leverage research, practice, advocacy, and education to promote well-being among disabled individuals and people with chronic health conditions. These perspectives show that:

- *Individuals craft their personal and social worlds.* How people construe their personal and social experiences influences their health, well-being, and whether they believe they can act and exercise choice over their future lives. This "looking ahead" affects their outlook on their disabilities as well as their daily lives.
- *Individuals are shaped by the physical and the social world.* Our physical selves are determined in part by particular constraints—whether psychological or social—tied to their physical environments. Yet humans are more

than physiology, physique, or behavioral responses to given circumstances; what they can do or try to accomplish is more important psychologically than any activities that are precluded by any personal or environmental limits. Thus, psychosocial successes and coping responses matter more than any behavioral setbacks.

- *Emphasizing the development of human strengths and assets is essential to psychosocial well-being.* Regardless of disability, individuals are assumed to have positive strengths or the ability to learn them. Focusing on such positive characteristics will be more helpful in their own development and response to challenges than emphasizing any adversities present in their lives (e.g., Chou et al., 2009).

- *Positive perspectives are not novel but the focus on them and their potential might be.* Themes of positive strengths and how to acquire them run through Eastern and Western philosophy, as well as humanistic psychology and cognitive-behavioral approaches (e.g., self-efficacy) and therapies, among other areas of the discipline of psychology. Positive psychology is likely more than "old wine in new bottles," but many of its insights and messages about the nature of the or a "good life" are more of a reprise than something truly new. Where disability is concerned, positive rather than negative points of view have always been seen as more helpful for combatting stigma, prejudice, and ableism in general. (Dunn & Dougherty, 2005; see also, Livneh & Martz, 2016)

Relying on these and related perspectives, positive psychology explores, as noted previously, three levels of analysis: positive subjective states, positive individual traits, and positive institutions (e.g., Arewasikporn et al., 2019). We briefly review the scope of each level where strengths tied to disability are concerned.

Positive Subjective States and Experiences

Positive subjective states are favorable, but private, thoughts and feelings individuals have regarding themselves and the various events that occur in their lives. Greater frequency of positive states or experiences is tied to psychosocial success in personal relations (e.g., marriage, friendships), income, health, and personal accomplishments (e.g., Lyubomirsky, King, & Diener, 2005). Very often, the word happiness is used as a shorthand description to characterize positive subjective states and experiences (David, Boniwell, & Conley Ayers, 2013). Although we may view these subjective states and experiences as occurring in the present, they can also be recalled from memory, as when people call up feelings of joy associated with long-past holidays, vacations, or even key events from childhood. Familiar positive subjective states include positive or good moods (e.g., Isen, 2002), positive emotions (e.g.,

Tugade et al., 2014), optimal experience or flow (e.g., Czsikszentmihalyi, 2014), savoring (e.g., Bryant & Veroff, 2007), and mindfulness (e.g., Langer & Ngnoumen, 2018), among other possibilities.

Where disability is concerned, the status of positive subjective states following the onset of disability is the issue of focus (thus, whether an impairment is congenital or acquired can matter). If a disability is acquired via trauma, then a person's level of subjective well-being may be tested and even disrupted. Adaptation may occur across time but not necessarily to the level presumed by the classic hedonic treadmill model proposed by Brickman and Campbell (1971), as disability can shift self-reported positive states to significantly lower and thereafter relatively stable levels (e.g., Anusic et al., 2014; Diener, 2008; Diener et al., 2006). Individuals with spinal cord damage, for example, do report lower levels of happiness compared to the general population, and their subjective accounts tend to align with the severity of the acquired disability (e.g., Dijkers, 2005; Lucas, 2007a, 2007b). This lowered affect is likely due to the onset of secondary complications linked with spinal injuries, such as depression or depressive symptoms (see Elliott & Kennedy, 2004).

Research questions on subjective states and experiences are generally present-focused, that is, aimed at determining disabled individuals' current reported levels of life satisfaction, overall quality of life, and subjective well-being. Investigators might be motivated to track the course of positive emotions (and negative ones, as well) across time following a disabling event and rehabilitative efforts. The appraisal processes used by people with disabilities are also of interest: Do some individuals find positive meaning in their disability experience (e.g., Dunn, 1996) or do they attribute some favorable or "side" benefits to the disabling event? In turn, do positive moods or emotions enable individuals to look forward in optimistic ways to rehabilitative experiences as well as to their futures? Such positive perspectives imply the presence of positive traits, like optimism and hope, among other possibilities.

Positive Traits

In contrast to positive subjective states and experiences, positive traits entail individual dispositional qualities that explain why some people display higher levels of happiness and psychological health than do others. These positive traits or other distinguishing qualities guide people's choices, help them to see meaning and purpose in everyday experiences, and generally drive their behaviors across a variety of situations. Positive traits are individual difference factors that enable people to stand out from larger groups. These traits can appear as a response to the life circumstances—good and bad—that people encounter. One of the important features of positive traits is the working assumption that they can be learned and even taught (Peterson & Seligman, 2004; see also chapter 8, this volume). Traits and trait-like qualities include optimism (Bouchard et al., 2018), resilience (e.g., Ryff & Singer, 2003; see also chapter 8, this volume), hope (e.g., Cheavens & Ritschel, 2014; see also chapter 7, this volume), and gratitude (e.g., Ahrens & Forbes, 2014).

Disability is linked to positive traits and dispositions in a variety of ways. Martz and Livneh (2016) looked closely at the literature in positive psychology that was relevant to psychosocial adaptation to disability and chronic illnesses, identifying six trait-like constructs and intrapersonal factors: resilience, optimism, hope, benefit-finding, meaning-making, and posttraumatic growth. The investigators argued that these constructs are found to coincide with important adaptive outcomes, including higher reported quality of life and levels of well-being, as well as disability acceptance. At the same time, lower levels of depression, psychological upset, and anxiety were found. Focusing on the positive rather than negative aspects of clients' lives was associated with better adaptation to disabling events. However, Martz and Livneh noted inconsistencies where the measurement and definitional distinctions of these constructs were concerned, cautioning researchers to pay careful attention to both issues (for a discussion of issues tied to assessing and explicating resilience, see chapter 8, this volume).

One growing form of positive trait research is disability identity, which addresses feelings of affinity, camaraderie, solidarity, and understanding that people with disabilities have for one another (Dunn & Burcaw, 2013; Olkin & Pledger, 2003). Individuals with favorable disability identities harbor beneficial beliefs about their own disabilities, where those with low or even no disability identity do not view themselves as being disabled (despite awareness of or apparent evidence to the contrary). Disability identity is best characterized as being on a continuum (Dunn, 2015; Olkin, 1999). Bogart and Nario-Redmond (2018), for example, explored how self-categorization, identity, and pride tied to disability and disability culture can promote favorable self-images and understanding, as well as cultivate activism and resistance efforts to combat prejudice and discrimination linked to overt or covert ableism.

Other positive trait-related research questions include the study of personal values, value changes, and the broadening of values following the onset of and adjustment to disability (e.g., Wright, 1983). Examining goal-setting following trauma and rehabilitation experiences, too, is a way to determine how positive traits guide recovery and adaptation. Whether and how people with acquired disabilities leverage their existing assets—the broad array of resources (including personal traits or skills) that are distinct in each individual that can be used to cope with disability—or seek to acquire new ones (Dunn, 2015, see also chapter 8, this volume). Finally, researchers and practitioners will likely be interested in identifying ways to enhance or further develop positive traits that people with disabilities already possess. Niemiec et al. (2017), for example, examined how character strengths could be cultivated among people with intellectual and developmental disabilities (see also, Shogren et al., 2017). The potential malleability of such strengths and traits highlights their importance to positive psychology-based interventions (e.g., Smirnova & Parks, 2018).

Positive Institutions and Organizations

In contrast to positive subjective states or experiences and positive traits, positive institutions or organizations benefit the community rather than individuals per se (of course, people who reside in the community or who work for such organizations do reap positive rewards). Typifying a group-level of analysis, positive institutions promote civic virtues, thereby leading people to behave like good citizens and to seek the collective good. Schools, workplaces, organizations (including local government), and even families can be recognized as positive institutions. Within these institutions, the goal is a sort of "civic socialization" so that community members learn to be tolerant, responsible, and altruistic, thereby willing to acquire a good work ethic aimed at benefiting others.

At present, the least amount of empirical research and inquiry has focused on positive institutions. Still, it does not take a great deal of imagination to consider what sorts of community institutions and values could create positive environments where concern for the local citizenry could be fostered, including promoting the rights and welfare of people with disabilities. Positive institutions aimed at aiding disabled individuals could be community-based, national, or international. These institutions could be focused on rehabilitation, vocational training, organized for recreational or social purposes, or designed to provide other job opportunities for the disability community. Other institutions might engage in political or advocacy efforts, advancing legal as well as health interests of disabled persons, issues that were particularly challenging during the Covid-19 pandemic (see Andrews et al., 2021; Lund & Ayers, 2020).

Where established efforts aimed at ameliorating the experience of disability are concerned, the disability rights movement (Charlton, 1998) qualifies as a positive organization (or an assembly of smaller groups) with a scope that is often local or national, and sometimes international. In the United States, national legislative efforts, such as the Americans with Disabilities Act (ADA) of 1990 and the Individuals with Disabilities Educational Act of 1990, represent positive efforts designed to create positive change, including education and employment opportunities, in organizations at all levels for people with disabilities (see also Bruyere & O'Keefe, 1994; Pelka, 1997).

Dunn (2018) adapted a list of virtues tied to positive institutions from Peterson (2006) and the National Institute on Consumer-Directed Long-Term Services (1996). These virtues include:

- *Purpose*—The organization should offer a clear list of moral goals, perhaps embedded within a vision statement. Members of the organization are reminded of the nature of the goals through annual celebrations.
- *Humanity*—Individually and collectively, the members of the organization share care and concern for each other.
- *Safety*—Those who take part in the organization are duly protected from any exploitation, threat, or other forms of danger.
- *Expertise*—Members of the organization are treated as experts regarding their own disabilities as well as any relevant needs or services.
- *Fairness*—Equity is an important part of the institution's governance, so that both rewards and punishments are consistently exercised.
- *Dignity*—All members of the organization are seen as individuals, so that no one has undue advantage based on role or position.

Two of these virtues—humanity and dignity—are reminiscent of Wright's (1972, 1983) value-laden beliefs and principles, which shaped rehabilitation psychology into a compassionate service provider as well as a source of scientific research on disability. Purpose, fairness, and safety indicate ways that any positive organization can foster connections to its members. Expertise is important because it establishes the primacy of the affected individual as the de facto expert where caring and needs are concerned.

Dunn and Dougherty (2005) suggested avenues for research concerning positive institutions and organizations, some of which echo Olkin and Pledger's (2003) call for disability-focused research that involves people with disabilities as designers and co-investigators rather than exclusively as participants (much of the latter grows out of the efforts of the interdisciplinary field known as disability studies). Dunn and Dougherty's research suggestions are still relevant. Research that examines the culture and history of disability as well as cultural norms and institutions that promote the well-being of people with disabilities is highly desirable. Any scholarship that informs advocacy efforts aimed at removing the physical, social, legal, and economic barriers that disabled people and groups face is also very welcome. The study of positive strengths (and how to inculcate them) within positive institutions clearly fits here, as well.

LOOKING FORWARD

One of the primary purposes of this book is to identify and examine positive psychological personal factors that might be considered within the context of the ICF (see chapter 1). We believe that this is important as a means to both elaborate on the role of these personal factors, which are not extensively defined or elaborated on in the ICF itself, and to provide a foundation for disability researchers and policy-makers on a strength-based, positive approach that includes positive psychological personal factors. However, a desired outcome of the volume is its impact outside of the disability sphere. That is, we hope to bring attention to positive psychologists and researchers in this field the importance of including research and practice on disability in the broad scope of the field. There has, certainly, been a growth in attention to disability from positive psychology (Dunn, 2017; Shogren, Wehmeyer, & Singh, 2017; Wehmeyer, 2013). However, a focus on flourishing, well-being, and optimal human functioning for people with disability remains under-addressed in the field (Shogren, 2013).

For most of the history of the intersection of psychology and disability, as discussed in chapter 1, the latter has been conceptualized within deficit models emphasizing illness and pathology. Until recently, the field has not had a language with which to talk about disability in the context of optimal human functioning. There has, however, been a robust examination of quality of life as an organizing framework within disability supports (Schalock & Keith, 2016) and on promoting the self-determination of youth with disabilities (see Wehmeyer, this volume), and it is time to move the discussion about flourishing, well-being, and optimal human functioning for people with disability to the broader context of the field of positive psychology itself. The reality is that not only do people with disability constitute a sizeable percentage of the population, but understanding flourishing, well-being, and optimal human functioning for people with disability will, in turn, provide insight into these issues across the spectrum of the human condition.

REFERENCES

Ahrens, A. H., & Forbes, C. N. (2014). Gratitude. In M. M. Tugade, M. N. Shiota, & L. D. Kirby (Eds.), *Handbook of positive emotions* (pp. 342–361). Guilford.

Americans with Disabilities Act of 1990, Pub. L. No. 101-336, 104 Stat. 327 (1991).

Andrews, E. E., Ayers, K. B., Brown, K. S., Dunn, D. S., & Pilarski, C. R. (2021). No body is expendable: Medical rationing and disability justice during the COVID-19 pandemic. *American Psychologist, 76*(3), 451.

Anusic, I., Yap, S. C., & Lucas, R. E. (2014). Testing set-point theory in a Swiss national sample: Reaction and adaptation to major life events. *Social Indicators Research, 119*, 1265–1288.

Arewasikporn, A., Roepke, A. M., & Ehde, D. M. (2019). Positive psychology and disability. In D. S. Dunn (Ed.), *Understanding the experience of disability:*

Perspectives from social and rehabilitation psychology (pp. 286–299). Oxford University Press.

Bogart, K. R., & Nario-Redmond, M. R. (2019). An exploration of disability self-categorization, identity, and pride. In D. S. Dunn (Ed.), *Understanding the experience of disability: Perspectives from social and rehabilitation psychology* (pp. 252–267). Oxford University Press.

Bolt, M. A., & Dunn, D. S. (2016). *Pursuing human strengths: A positive psychology guide* (2nd ed.). New York: Worth.

Bouchard, L. C., Carver, C. S., Mens, M. G., & Scheier, M. F. (2019). Optimism, health, and well-being. In D. S. Dunn (Ed.), *Positive psychology: Established and emerging issues* (pp. 112–130). Routledge.

Brickman, P., & Campbell, D. T. (1971). Hedonic relativism and planning the good society. In M. H. Appley (Ed.), *Adaptation level theory: A symposium* (pp. 287–302). Academic Press.

Bruyere, S. M., & O'Keefe, J. (1994). *Implications of the Americans with disabilities act for psychology*. American Psychological Association.

Bryant, F. B., & Veroff, J. (2007). *Savoring: A new model of positive experience*. Erlbaum.

Charlton, J. I. (1998). *Nothing about us without us: Disability oppression and empowerment*. University of California Press.

Cheavens, J. S., & Ritschel, I. A. (2014). Hope theory. In M. M. Tugade, M. N. Shiota, & L. D. Kirby (Eds.), *Handbook of positive emotions* (pp. 396–410). Guilford.

Chou, C.-C., Lee, E.-J., Catalano, D. E., Ditchman, N., & Wilson, L. M. (2009). Positive psychology and psychosocial adjustment to chronic illness and disability. In F. Chan, E. Da Silva Cardoso, & J. A. Chronister (Eds.), *Understanding psychosocial adjustment to chronic illness and disability: A handbook for evidence-based practitioners in rehabilitation* (pp. 207–241). Springer.

Czsikszentmihalyi, M. (2014). *Applications of flow in human development and education: The collected works of Mihaly Czsikszentmihalyi*. Springer Science + Business.

David, S. A., Boniwell, I., & Conley Ayers, A. (2013). *Oxford handbook of happiness*. Oxford University Press.

Diener, E. (2008). Myths in the science of happiness, and directions for future research. In M. Eid & R. J. Larsen (Eds.), *The science of subjective well-being* (pp. 493–514). Guilford Press.

Diener, E., Lucas, R. E., & Scollon, C. N. (2006). Beyond the hedonic treadmill: Revising the adaptation theory of well-being. *American Psychologist, 61,* 305–314. doi: 10.1037/0003-066X.61.4.305

Dijkers, M. P. J. M. (2005). Quality of life if individuals with a spinal cord injury: A review of conceptualization, measurement, and research findings. *Journal of Rehabilitation Research and Development, 42,* 87–110. doi: 10.1682/JRRD.2004.08.0100

Dunn, D. S. (1996). Well-being following amputation: Salutary effects of positive meaning, optimism, and control. *Rehabilitation Psychology, 41,* 285–302.

Dunn, D. S. (2017). *Frontiers of social psychology: Positive psychology: Established and emerging issues.* New York: Routledge.

Dunn, D. S. (2018). Positive psychology for disability and rehabilitation psychology: Recent advances. In D. S. Dunn (Ed.), *Positive psychology: Established and emerging issues* (pp. 236–250). Philadelphia, PA: Taylor & Francis.

Dunn, D. S., & Burcaw, S. (2013). Disability identity: Exploring narrative accounts of disability. *Rehabilitation Psychology, 58,* 148–157. doi: 10.1037/a0031691

Dunn, D. S., & Dougherty, S. B. (2005). Prospects for a positive psychology of rehabilitation. *Rehabilitation Psychology, 50,* 305–311. doi: 10.1037/0090-5550.50.3.305.

Elliott, T. R., & Kennedy, P. (2004). Treatment of depression following spinal cord injury: An evidence-based review. *Rehabilitation Psychology, 49,* 134–139. doi: 10.1037/0090-5550.49.2.134.

Individuals with Disabilities Education Act of 1990, Pub. L. No. 101-476, 104 Stat, 1142 (1991).

Isen, A. M. (2002). A role for neuropsychology in understanding the facilitating influence of positive affect on social behavior and cognitive processes. In C. R. Snyder & S. J. Lopez (Eds.), *Handbook of positive psychology* (pp. 528–540). Oxford University Press.

Keyes, C. L. M. (2009). Toward a science of mental health. In S. J. Lopez & C. R. Snyder (Eds.), *Oxford handbook of positive psychology* (2nd ed., pp. 89–95). Oxford University Press.

Keyes, C. L. M. (2013). Promotion and protection of positive mental health: Towards complete mental health in human development. In S. A. David, I. Boniwell, & A. Conley Ayers (Eds.), *The Oxford handbook of happiness.* (pp. 915–925). Oxford University Press.

Keyes, C. L. M., & Simoes, E. J. (2012). To flourish or not: Positive mental health and all-cause mortality. *American Journal of Public Health, 102*(11), 2164–2172. doi: 10.2105/AJPH.2012.300918

Langer, E. J., & Ngnoumen, C. T. (2018). Mindfulness. In D. S. Dunn (Ed.), *Positive psychology: Established and emerging issues* (pp. 97–111). Routledge.

Livneh, H., & Martz, E. (2016). Psychosocial adaptation to disability within the context of positive psychology: Philosophical aspects and historical roots. *Journal of Occupational Rehabilitation, 26,* 13–19. doi: 10.1007/s10926-015-9601-6

Lucas, R. (2007a). Adaptation and the set-point model of subjective well-being: Does happiness change after major life events? *Current Directions in Psychological Science, 16,* 75–79. doi: 10.1111/j.1467-8721.2007.00479.x.

Lucas, R. (2007b). Long-term disability is associated with lasting changes in subjective well-being: Evidence from two nationally representative longitudinal studies. *Journal of Personality and Social Psychology, 92,* 717–730. doi: 10.1037/0022-3514.92.4.717

Lund, E. M., & Ayers, K. B. (2020). Raising awareness of disabled lives and health care rationing during the COVID-19 pandemic. *Psychological Trauma: Theory, Research, Practice, and Policy, 12* (S1), S210–S211. doi: 10.1037/tra0000673

Lyubomirsky, S., King, L., & Diener, E. (2005). The benefits of frequent positive affect: Does happiness lead to success? *Psychological Bulletin, 131,* 803–855.

Marz, E., & Livneh, H. (2016). Psychosocial adaptation to disability within the context of positive psychology: Findings from the literature. *Journal of Occupational Rehabilitation, 26,* 4–12. doi: 10.1007/s10926-015-9598-x

National Institute on Consumer-Directed Long-Term Services. (1996). *Principles of consumer-directed home and community-based services.* Author.

Niemiec, R. M., Shogren, K. A., & Wehmeyer, M. L. (2017). Character strengths and intellectual and developmental disability: A strengths-based approach from positive psychology. *Education and Training in Autism and Developmental Disabilities, 52,* 13–25.

Olkin, R. (1999). *What psychotherapists should know about disability.* Guilford.

Olkin, R., & Pledger, C. (2003). Can disability studies and psychology join hands? *American Psychologist, 58,* 296–304.

Pelka, F. (1997). *The ABC-CLIO companion to the disability rights movement.* ABC-CLIO.

Peterson, C. (2006). *A primer in positive psychology.* Oxford University Press.

Peterson, C., & Seligman, M. P. (2004). *Character strengths and virtues: A handbook and classification.* American Psychological Association.

Ryff, C. D., & Springer, B. (2003). Flourishing under fire: Resilience as a prototype of challenges thriving. In C. L. M. Keyes & J. Haidt (Eds.), *Flourishing: Positive psychology and the life well-lived* (pp. 15–36). American Psychological Association.

Schalock, R. L., & Keith, K. D. (2016). *Cross-cultural quality of life: Enhancing the lives of persons with intellectual disability* (2nd ed.). Washington, DC: American Association on Intellectual and Developmental Disabilities.

Seligman, M. E. P. (1999). The president's address. *American Psychologist, 54,* 559–562.

Seligman, M. E. P. (2002). *Authentic happiness: Using the new positive psychology to realize your potential for lasting fulfilment.* Free Press.

Shogren, K. A. (2013). Positive psychology and disability: A historical analysis. In M. Wehmeyer (Ed.) *Oxford handbook of positive psychology and disability* (pp. 19–33). Oxford, UK: Oxford University Press.

Shogren, K. A., Wehmeyer, M. L., Schalock, R. L., & Thompson, J. R. (2017). Reframing educational supports for students with intellectual disability through strengths-based approaches. In M. L. Wehmeyer & K. A. Shogren (Eds.), *Handbook of research-based practices for educating students with intellectual disability* (17–30). New York: Routledge.

Shogren, K. A., Wehmeyer, M. L., & Singh, N. (2017). *Handbook of positive psychology in intellectual and developmental disabilities: Translating research into practice.* New York: Springer.

Smirnova, M., & Parks, A. C. (2018). Positive psychology interventions: Clinical applications. In D. S. Dunn (Ed.), *Positive psychology: Established and emerging issues* (pp. 276–297). Routledge.

Tugade, M. M., Shiota, M. N., & Kirby, L. D. (Eds.). (2014). *Handbook of positive emotions.* Guilford.

Wehmeyer, M. L. (2013). *Oxford handbook of positive psychology and disability.* Oxford, UK: Oxford University Press.

World Health Organization (2001). *The International Classification of Functioning, Disability and Health (ICF).* Geneva, WHO.

Wright, B. A. (1972). Value-laden beliefs and principles for rehabilitation psychology. *Rehabilitation Psychology, 19,* 38–45. doi: 10.1037/h0090837

Wright, B. A. (1983). *Physical disability: A psychosocial approach.* Harper & Row.

Chapter 3

Disability Culture, Identity, and Language

Erin E. Andrews and Anjali J. Forber-Pratt

Galvin (2003) observed that "[i]t is thus within language and discourse that the potential to unshackle the disabled identity lies" (p. 177). Disability advocates have long promoted recognition of disability as a legitimate minority group and to have disability acknowledged as a form of diversity alongside other variables such as gender identity, race and ethnicity, and sexual orientation. However, disability is often neglected and excluded from the multicultural dialogue in psychology (Mona et al., 2017). Despite training in diversity and multiculturalism, and even specialized training in disability and rehabilitation topics, most psychologists are unfamiliar with disability culture. Emerging research suggests, however, that disability culture and language and the related concept of disability identity may be important personal factors that are related to the well-being of people with disabilities and converge with the tenets of positive psychology. Disability culture can contribute to one's sense of authenticity and is inherently resilient, while the process of disability identity development embodies growth and self-actualization. The diversity model of disability postulates that disability is on the continuum of normal human experience and resists the pathologizing approach of the medical model (Andrews, 2019). The diversity model builds upon the early work of Wright (1983), who emphasized the presence of assets among disabled persons. Consistent with a biopsychosocial or social-ecological model of disability, the diversity model goes beyond those frameworks to identify aspects of disability that are positive and even worthy of celebration (Andrews, 2019; Shogren, 2013).

DISABILITY CULTURE

Disability culture is not a new phenomenon; however, it historically has not received the same degree of attention as other cultures in the United States and elsewhere around the World. Disability culture received increased attention with the emergence of the field of disability studies (Longmore, 2003). However, disability is largely still considered a medical experience rather than a cultural one (Brown, 1996; Gill, 1995). Disability culture, simply put, is the expression of disability pride through a celebration and reappropriation of an identity that has been historically viewed by society as wholly negative (Andrews, 2019). Disability culture shares some elements of other cultures in terms of parallel struggles faced by other diverse groups (Mona et al., 2017). At the same time, disability is unique in that any member of society could ostensibly join the group at any given time following injury or disease. Brown (1996) described disability culture as the promotion of connection, camaraderie, and shared purpose among the diverse range of people with disabilities. Gill (1995) emphasized that disability culture underlies the motivation to address the civil, social, political, and economic needs of the disability community positively and constructively.

Gill's (1997) model of disability culture is the predominant and most well-developed such theory. She postulated that there are four functions of disability culture, including fortification, unification, communication, and recruitment. Gill argued that identification with disability culture allows people with disabilities a sense of belongingness and the opportunity to express shared beliefs and heritage. Gill was careful to note that identification with disability culture is not based solely on the shared experience of oppression but also on a shared expression of pride. Among the core values of disability culture, Gill identified the use of disability humor, a flexible and adaptive approach to tasks, skill in managing multiple problems in systems, and appreciation of human diversity. There is creativity and resilience inherent in disability culture (Martz & Livneh, 2016).

An important core value of disability culture is interdependence. Western societies, including the United States, tend to heavily emphasize independence. In contrast, disability culture accepts interdependence and instead emphasizes autonomy. Autonomy differs from independence in that it is more important to be able to make decisions and have control about one's life then to be able to execute those tasks on one's own. For example, in disability culture, it is not important or valued to be able to complete all of one's own self-care daily activities, but rather to be able to have choices about who is assisting or completing those tasks and how such tasks are executed. This is a core feature that has been corroborated empirically (Forber-Pratt, 2018). In this way, disability culture emphasizes individual self-determination and empowerment, rather than freedom.

In addition to shared values, there are other aspects to disability culture, including shared language and terminology. Often this includes slang terms used by insiders in the disability community, such as the word "crip," a reappropriation of the word cripple. Disability culture is also marked by evolving symbols and disability art, which emphasize the positive psychology concept of authenticity. In disability culture, there is both acknowledgment of difficulties as well as recognition of strengths (Andrews, 2019). Identification of ways in which disability has helped a person make meaning of life and offered unique benefits are part of the disability cultural experience (Martz & Livneh, 2016). Disability culture in many ways is the ultimate insider experience and represents the perspective of the lived experience, which is consistently more positive than the perceptions of outsiders (Dunn et al., 2013).

Disability culture is often associated with a distinct sociopolitical worldview. This finding is corroborated by Forber-Pratt's (2018) empirical study that found elements of social justice were a core characteristic of disability culture. It is marked by a stance against physician-assisted suicide and eugenic abortion along with promotion of deinstitutionalization and emancipation from nursing homes. This is not to say that all people aligned with disability culture share all of these views, but those involved in disability rights groups such as ADAPT and Not Dead Yet are often vocal proponents of these issues. These stances are highly congruent with the positive psychology concept of life worth living.

Although disability is numerically the largest minority group in the United States, far fewer disabled people align themselves with disability culture compared with other cultural identities. There are several potential reasons for this. It is very difficult to claim disability culture because of its dissonance with many aspects of Western individualization and associated sex and gender stereotypes (Mona et al., 2017). Although some people may grow up in families of other disabled individuals, such as families with hereditary disabilities, most disabled people are the minority in their families. In these instances, disabled people are not exposed to disability culture, particularly in early life. Disability culture is not portrayed frequently or equitably in the media, which instead relies on stereotypical portrayals of disability (Ellis & Goggin, 2015). Finally, people with disabilities vary in the degree to which they identify themselves as disabled at all, much less align themselves with disability culture. This may be related to the concept of disability identity development.

DISABILITY IDENTITY DEVELOPMENT

Hahn (1985) asked, "How can one develop a sense of identity with an attribute that one has been taught to overcome?" (p. 310). The concept of disability identity development has only recently received empirical attention in the scientific literature. Instead, significant focus in the rehabilitation psychology literature has addressed adjustment to disability or adaptation to disability (Bogart, 2014). Adjustment to disability is an individual phenomenon having to do with one's personal satisfaction and well-being. Often, research examines an individual's response to disability following disability onset. Psychological adjustment primarily refers to how one thinks and feels about disability and behaves in response to it. Olkin (2017) argued that the term of adjustment is inherently pathological—implying something is wrong and that a disabled person must successfully negotiate or transition through a series of stages to finally accept their situations (p. 45). Yet, adjustment to disability is one of the foundational principles of rehabilitation psychology (Bhattarai et al., 2020). Dunn and colleagues explained that adjustment to disability is a constantly changing process that includes both adaptation and acceptance by the individual (Dunn et al., 2016). Further, it should be noted that the majority of the literature on adjustment or adaptation to disability and chronic illness has focused on people with acquired disabilities or chronic illnesses. An important tangential thread to this conversation, primarily led by disabled researchers (i.e., Andrews, Bogart, Forber-Pratt, Gill, Lund, Mona), is that of disability identity development. Rather than subscribing to a non-disabled norm being imposed *on* the disabled person, this thinking recognizes the value in finding pride and identity from within and from the community *because* of one's disability.

Disability identity, in contrast, is related to a sense of collective group identity. In other words, disability identity has to do with how an individual may or may not feel connected to a part of the larger disability community. Disability identity formation is a collective concept that "connects the social and the personal and involves the individual putting themselves in a collective context" (Shakespeare, 1996, p. 99). The extent to which one adapts (or "adjusts") to an acquired disability is related to, but not the same as, the extent to which one integrates disability as part of one's identity (Forber-Pratt et al., 2017; Putnam 2005).

Understandably, disabled people tend to internalize the predominantly negative views of disability espoused by society. Depending on the messages received by disabled people they may develop negative or incongruent perceptions of disability. Disabled people may recognize their bodies or minds as being different or abnormal or having to rely on tools such as mobility devices that others do not. Because of this socialization, it is understandable that many if not most people with disabilities reject disability as part of their identity and instead try to separate themselves from their disability. Analogous to other models of identity development, including Helms's racial identity model and LGBT identity development models (Cass, 1979;

D'Augelli, 1994), theoretical models of disability identity development began to emerge. Attitudes toward one's own disability range widely from feelings of shame and embarrassment to experiences of disability pride. Some scholars have argued that younger individuals who have been influenced by the disability rights movement may be more likely to view disability as an aspect of diversity (Andrews, 2019; Forber-Pratt et al., 2017; Putnam, 2005).

As such, disability identity has been described in prior literature as "a sense of self that includes one's disability and feelings of connection to, or solidarity with, the disability community" (Dunn & Burcaw, 2013, p. 148). As noted earlier, disability identity formation is impeded by numerous barriers. One is inaccessibility, which was a much larger barrier prior to the emergence of the Internet and social media, both of which have allowed for greater connection among the disability community. Another barrier is segregation, which occurs in many contexts, including stores and other public environments. Stigma is a significant barrier in that if people have internalized ableist rhetoric, they are unlikely to desire to affiliate with others who also have the stigmatized identity. Finally, poverty plays a role in reducing opportunities for individuals with disabilities to connect to their own community (Palmer, 2011). Like other groups, disabled people must make decisions about how much assimilation they wish to make into the dominant (i.e., nondisabled) culture. While some people have visible disabilities, other people have non-apparent disabilities and can pass as nondisabled unless they elect to disclose. As with any marginalized identity, there are inherent risks in celebrating such differences as valuable (Gill, 1997)

Scholars of disability identity development believe that self-identification is an aspect of disability identity and maybe a prerequisite for the formation of a positive disability identity (Bogart & Nario-Redmond, 2019). A strong disability identity results in particular kinds of outcomes: positive impacts on mental health (e.g., Bogart, 2015); attitudes toward cure (Hahn & Belt, 2004), and political activism and participation (Schur, 1998). For example, Bogart (2015) found that a stronger disability identity is associated with lower depression and anxiety in participants with multiple sclerosis. There are many factors associated with whether someone identifies as disabled, including the level of supports needed and visibility of their disability and their perception of stigma. Nario-Redmond and colleagues found that between 7% and 18% of disabled people identify as able-bodied or as nondisabled even though they report the presence of an impairment. Other studies have shown that despite objective impairments, functional limitations, and difficulties with activities of daily living, many people do not identify themselves as disabled (Bogart et al., 2017; Nario-Redmond et al., 2013).

There are only a few models of disability identity development, including Carol Gill's model, which may be the most well-known. Many of these models are based on Erik Erikson's (1968) psychosocial identity development process. These models share some aspect of reframing disability, becoming aware of disability identity politics, beginning to think collectively and develop a critical consciousness, constructing their own personal identity while moving toward a more open, public identification with the devalued group, and finally expressing a need to be valued and accepted as a diverse human form (McLean & Syed, 2014). Gill's (1997) disability identity development model is stage based. The first stage, called *coming to belong*, involves the disabled individual integrating into society. In this stage, the individual develops comfortable identities and social roles despite their membership in the socially marginalized disability group. It is also at this stage that the individual asserts their right to inclusion in society. *Coming home* is the second stage in Gill's model and this is where the individual integrates with the disability community. During this stage, the disabled person rejects internalized ableism and develops peer relationships with other disabled people. They value the shared experience from disability of disability and separate and individuate themselves from the dominant culture. The third stage is called *coming together*, and this is where the individual internally integrates how they are both similar and different from other disabled people. In this stage, individuals affirm disability as an important and positive feature of their identity, simultaneously asserting the right to embrace their humanity. The fourth and final stage in Gill's model is *coming out*. This is where the individual integrates how they feel with how they present themselves. At this point, people identify without hesitation as disabled and come out to the world. Gill stated that "such persons have forsaken normality in a quiet healthy defiance" (p. 45).

Weeber (2004) developed what she calls a position model. This model of disability identity development involves six positions in which the disabled person may find themselves. The first of these positions is a shame. In this position, the person will make efforts to pass as nondisabled to the extent possible and experiences internalized ableism. The second position is intellectualism, where the person may find themselves in crisis as they are forced to face disability identity. The third position is a sense of belonging, where the individual develops an allegiance to those with similar disabilities and may exhibit self-righteous anger. In Weeber's fourth position, the individual broadens their self-view. In this position, they are able to honor a full range of disability experiences. The fifth position involves the development of a social justice lens and solidarity with other diverse groups. Weeber's sixth and final position is transformational wisdom where the disabled person serves as a mentor to others with disabilities and can integrate disability into the totality of their identities.

Darling and Heckert (2010) developed a typology of orientations toward disability, which appears to be related to but broader than the concept of disability identity. Darling and Heckert's model identified three constructs on which individuals with disabilities are stratified. The first of these is the *social model*, wherein a disabled person considers disability to be more a social issue than a personal or medical one. The second construct is *identity*, which is stratified between disability pride and shame. The final construct is that of *role*, which ranges from passivity to activism. Across these three dimensions, people who identify disability as more social exhibit disability pride and tend to see their role as an activist align most closely with other models of a strong and positive disability identity (Darling, 2003; Darling & Heckert, 2010).

Forber-Pratt and Zape's model of social and psychosocial disability identity development (2017), which was informed by empirical interviews with disabled adults, proposed four developmental statuses: acceptance, relationship, adoption, and engagement. The concept of *acceptance* highlights one's ability to accept themselves as being a person with a disability and includes both internal and external components. There is a facet of internalizing about one's disability that includes anger or frustration. Frustration could be seen as a facet of acceptance; however, acceptance has a positive connotation and frustration carries a negative connotation, with both internal and external processing components. This is about one's internal frustration and wrestling with the negative aspects of one's disability. Not all people with disabilities exhibit positive acceptance of or embodiment of one's disability identity at all times. This frustration and anger may occur as a result of individual factors (i.e., pain, fatigue) or external/societal factors (i.e., inaccessible environments, discriminatory attitudes, lack of support, lack of solidarity). Acceptance is heavily impacted by the environment surrounding the individual. A person's *relationship* status relates to the social network that one builds with other disabled individuals (particularly others with similar disabilities). *Adoption* is one's desire to adopt the values and culture that lie within the disabled community. This developmental status is the midpoint between simply having relationships with other disabled individuals and engaging within the disabled community. Finally, one's feelings of obligation to this community are what defines the status of *engagement.*

The developmental processes of disability identity formation embody the positive psychology principles of growth, authenticity, and self-actualization (Dunn et al., 2013; Shogren, 2013). This parallels the concept of posttraumatic growth, wherein positive changes occur in the aftermath of a difficult or traumatic situation or personal crisis (Martz & Livneh, 2016). While disability identity is understood as fundamentally important in this body of literature, overall, the concept of disability identity development remains vastly understudied, both theoretically and empirically, and must be continued to be explored across cultures as well.

LANGUAGE

Most psychologists accept a modified version of the Sapir-Whorf hypothesis, that language to some degree affects cognition and vice versa (Kay & Kempton, 1984). This linguistic relativity hypothesis postulates that language used by people plays a role in their thoughts and perceptions of reality (Hussein, 2012). Cognitive scientists continue to explore the role of the evolution of both language and culture, because cultural evolution is primarily facilitated by language, but the extent to which language may facilitate cultural evolution is not yet clear (Perlovsky, 2009). Disability language is an area that has evolved considerably over the past century, and which remains controversial (Dunn & Andrews, 2015). Language evolves over time, particularly in multicultural societies, and people with disabilities have varied preferences about the language used to describe them. Thus, concrete guidelines about correct or appropriate terms and rules that generalize across situations are not suitable for disability language (Andrews, 2019). For example, Gernsbacher and colleagues (2016) found that some terms previously used to describe disabled people, such as the word handicapped, have almost completely fallen out of favor in contemporary times, while the phrase "people with disabilities" was almost never used prior to the 1970s and is most commonly used now. A similar analysis of Google books Ngram data revealed that the term "Hispanic" reached the height of its popularity in the 1990s, while the term "Latinx" has only been widely used within the past five years. This illustrates that disability, like Latinx communities, evolves in both identity and language.

Early disability language was characterized in large part by objectification. Terms to describe disability were often used as slurs and insults, clearly offensive toward people with disabilities. For example, the use of the "R word" was commonly used as an insult in everyday language in the United States (Albert et al., 2016). Efforts to combat the use of the "R word" resulted in the passage of legislation, including Rosa's law, which prohibits the use of the term "mental retardation" in federal documentation (Friedman, 2016). Language from the medical model of disability was also objectifying and dehumanizing. These terms reduced individuals to labels and diagnoses and emphasized categorization of disabled people. For example, people with a certain type of disability might be referred to collectively as "the epileptic" or "the cerebral palsied." Similarly, individuals with disabilities may be referred to by their diagnosis, a depersonalizing approach which was identified by Beatrice Wright as particularly problematic (Dunn, 2014; Dunn & Andrews, 2015; McCarthy, 2011).

Rehabilitation psychologists have long criticized the use of dehumanizing medical model language (Caplan, 1995; Caplan & Shechter, 1993). Beatrice

Wright proposed the use of person first language in order to reduce stigma against disability (McCarthy, 2011; Wright, 1983). History has shown that this advance was an important step in the evolution of disability language and that Wright promoted sensitivity to disabling language and "advocated the use of 'people first' language in the 1960s—long before the expression 'people first' was even used" (McCarthy, 2011, p. 71). Wright argued that the person should literally be placed ahead of the disability, emphasizing their humanity. As a result, the phrase "people with disabilities" became widely used and "person first language" was adopted in many language guides and disability guidelines, including the APA style manual. This language was also implemented in the 1990 Americans with Disabilities Act (Haller et al., 2006).

In recent years, the use of person first language has been reexamined by disability scholars. Although it is clear, the development of person first language was well-intentioned and may have effectively reduced the common use of objectifying language (Feldman et al., 2002), some disabled people wondered if person first language may have overcorrected to the point of further stigmatizing disability (Andrews et al., 2013). These advocates argued that person first language may reinforce the notion that disability is bad and drive a wedge between the person seen as good and the disability seen as bad. Gernsbacher and colleagues found evidence that person first language may not or may no longer be effectual as it was intended. They found that person first language is used most frequently to refer to children with the most highly stigmatized disabilities: developmental disabilities such as intellectual disability and autism (Gernsbacher, 2017; Gomes, 2018; Jernigan, 2009; La Forge, 1991; Vaughan, 2009)

Many contemporary disability rights advocates have elected to use identity first language. Identity first language emphasizes disability as a central facet of the person's identity. This approach is grounded in a disability rights, equality, and diversity framework. Some disability groups have always taken the identity first approach, in particular, deaf culture has consistently exerted the importance of owning and claiming the term "deaf" and dismissed efforts to be described as persons with deafness or individuals with hearing loss. This is because deaf culture is such an important part of their identity. By owning and claiming disability, disabled people reject the notion of being defective, undesirable, or broken. The choice to adopt identity first language makes sense in the context of the information that identifying as disabled is associated with improved well-being, self-esteem, and quality of life across a wide range of disabilities (Brueggemann, 2013; Dunn & Andrews, 2015; Gernsbacher, 2017; Nario-Redmond et al., 2013). In addition to adopting identity first language, disabled people have also sought to reclaim language that was previously used harmfully, such as adopting the word cripple (often "crip") as a militant source of pride (Haller, 2006). The reclaiming of the term "cripple" went mainstream with the release of the acclaimed Netflix documentary Crip Camp in 2019.

In some instances, alternative terms for disability have been created in order to purportedly be less offensive. These terms are often created by nondisabled people, often parents of disabled children, as a way of softening the term "disability" or trying to emphasize the positives of disability. Examples of these euphemisms are *differently abled, physically challenged, special needs*, and *handicapable*. The disability community has largely rejected these euphemisms as superficial and ineffective at advocating for real change (Hojati, 2012; Marks, 1999). The term *special needs* in particular is frequently used in the special education field and among parents of disabled children. The term *special needs* has been criticized as a vague euphemism that does not adequately identify people with disabilities. Gernsbacher et al. (2016) found that people were viewed more negatively when being described as having special needs than when they are described as having a disability or having a certain disability. Critics argue that the term *special needs* connotes segregation and implies that disabled people are asking for special rights rather than human rights. A prominent disability rights advocate stated, "A need isn't special if it's something everyone else takes for granted" (Carter-Long, 2017). Disability advocates have argued that attempts to avoid the word *disability* are problematic and harmful to the disability community, resulting in the social media viral hashtag #saytheword. This campaign was meant to take back ownership of the word disability and refuse to accept that disability is a wholly undesirable state.

Although the use of disability terms as "insults," such as the "R word," are less prevalent in everyday use, ableist language persists (Albert et al., 2016). Many words are used as insults, including *blind, deaf, lame*, and *crazy*. Common in everyday conversation, the use of these words as insults demonstrates the diminished status and value of disabled people in the society (Andrews, 2019). Even if referring to acts or ideas and not to people at all—their use perpetuates the stigma associated with disability. Phrases such as "the blind leading the blind," "turn a blind eye," or "turn a deaf ear" and "tone deaf" all constitute disability microaggressions which subtly insult disabled people (Albert et al., 2016; Andrews, 2019; Friedman, 2016; Whyte et al., 2013).

The choice between person first and identity first language is contentious. Individual decisions about language are ultimately personal and appear to differ based on factors such as disability acquisition and permanency, disability type, disability identity development, and previous experiences with negative terminology. For example, advocates in the intellectual disability community continue to widely use person first language, while people who identify as autistic and with the neurodiversity movement have largely opted to adopt identity first language (Brown, 2001). The most recent edition of the APA style manual, the seventh edition, discarded the previous recommendation to universally use person first language when writing about disability. This edition stated that both person first and identity first approaches are designed to respect disabled persons and that either choice is fine. The style manual explicitly guides writers to avoid euphemisms that are condescending and names special needs as one of the euphemisms that should be avoided.

The evolution of disability language demonstrates many aspects of positive psychology. Disabled people have faced adversity with resilience, literally by taking the words used against them and turning them into empowerment. Claiming disability allows people to live with authenticity and without shame and is a personal choice to embrace one's true self.

CONCLUSION

Kerkhoff and Hanson (2015) suggested that ethical practice and cultural competence must include disability culture in order to effectively serve disabled persons and their families. We agree and further postulate that providers have an ethical obligation to understand the personal factors that affect those people we support. In the case of disabled people, these personal factors must include an awareness of the degree to which the individual aligns with disability culture, the extent to which they have developed a disability identity, and their preferences for disability language.

Beyond that, these personal factors are important demonstrations of the ways that disabled people have thrived despite numerous environmental, systemic, political, and cultural barriers. Disabled people have come together to form a cultural identity against the odds, providing an environment in which they can be themselves and celebrate their lives in spite of the daily oppressive challenges they face. Many disabled people go through an arduous process of identity development to come to know and appreciate their true selves. The disability community shows resilience and creativity in all the ways in which they have adapted to a world that was not built with them in mind. Ultimately, the experience of disability culture and identity makes the case that no matter the adversity, life is indeed worth living.

REFERENCES

American Psychological Association. (2012). Guidelines for assessment of and intervention with persons with disabilities. *American Psychologist, 67*, 43–62. doi: 10.1037/a0025892

Andrews, E. E., Forber-Pratt, A. J., Mona, L. R., Lund, E. M., Pilarski, C. R., & Balter, R. (2019). #SaytheWord: A disability culture commentary on the erasure of "disability." *Rehabilitation Psychology, 64*(2), 111–118. doi: 10.1037/rep0000258

Bogart, K. R. (2014). The role of disability self-concept in adaptation to congenital or acquired disability. *Rehabilitation Psychology, 59*(1), 107–115. doi: 10.1037/a0035800

Bogart, K. R. (2015). Disability identity predicts lower anxiety and depression in multiple sclerosis, *Rehabilitation psychology, 60*(1), 105–109. doi: 10.1037/rep0000029

Bogart, K. R., & Nario-Redmond, M. R. (2019). An exploration of disability self-categorization, identity, and pride. In D. S. Dunn (Ed.), *Understanding the experience of disability: Perspectives from social and rehabilitation psychology* (pp. 252–267). Oxford University Press.

Bogart, K. R., Rottenstein, A., Lund, E. M., & Bouchard, L. (2017). Who self-identifies as disabled? An examination of impairment and contextual predictors. *Rehabilitation Psychology, 62*(4), 553–562. doi: 10.1037/rep0000132

Brown, L. X. Z. (2011). *The significance of semantics: Person-first language: Why it matters.* www.autisticadvocacy.org/home/about-asan/identity-first-language.

Cass, V. C. (1979). Homosexual identity formation: A theoretical model. *Journal of Homosexuality, 4*, 219–235. doi: 10.1300/ J082v04n03_01

D'Augelli, A. R. (1994). Identity development and sexual orientation: Toward a model of lesbian, gay, and bisexual development. In E. J. Trickett, R. J. Watts, & D. Birman (Eds.), *The Jossey-Bass social and behavioral science series. Human diversity: Perspectives on people in context* (pp. 312–333). Jossey-Bass/Wiley.

Darling, R. B., & Heckert, D. A. (2010). Orientations toward disability: Differences over the lifecourse. *International Journal of Disability, Development and Education, 57*(2), 131–143.

Dunn, D. (2014). *The social psychology of disability.* Oxford University Press.

Dunn, D. S. & Andrews, E. E. (2015). Person-first and identity-first language: Developing psychologists' cultural competence using disability language. *American Psychologist, 70*(3), 255–263. doi: 10.1037/a0038636.

Dunn, D. S., & Burcaw, S. (2013). Disability identity: Exploring narrative accounts of disability. *Rehabilitation Psychology, 58*(2), 148157. doi: 10.1037/a0031691

Dunn, D. S., Ehde, D. M., & Wegener, S. T. (2016). The foundational principles as psychological lodestars: Theoretical inspiration and empirical direction in rehabilitation psychology. *Rehabilitation Psychology, 61*(1), 1–6. doi: 10.1037/rep0000082

Dunn, D. S., Uswatte, G., Elliott, T. R., Lastres, A., & Beard, B. (2013). A positive psychology of physical disability: Principles and progress. In M. Wehmeyer (Ed.), *The Oxford handbook of positive psychology and disability* (pp. 427–441). Oxford University Press.

Ellis, K., & Goggin, G. (2015). *Disability and the Media.* New York: Palgrave Macmillan. doi: 10.1007/978-1-137-50171-4_2

Erikson, E. H. (1968). *Identity, youth and crisis.* W.W. Norton.

Forber-Pratt, A.J., Lyew, D.A., Mueller, C., & Samples, L.B. (2017). Disability identity development: A systematic review of the literature. *Rehabilitation Psychology, 62*(2), 198–210. doi: 10.1037/rep0000134

Forber-Pratt, A. J., & Zape, M. P. (2017). Disability identity development model: Voices from the ADA-generation. *Disability and Health Journal, 10*(2), 350–355. doi: 10.1016/j.dhjo.2016.12.013

Forber-Pratt, A. J., Mueller, C. O., & Andrews, E. E. (2019). Disability identity and allyship in rehabilitation psychology: Sit, stand, sign, and show up. *Rehabilitation Psychology, 64*(2), 119–129. doi: 10.1037/rep0000256

Forber-Pratt, A. J., & Zape, M. P. (2017). Disability identity development model: Voices from the ADA-generation. *Disability and Health Journal, 10*(2), 350–355. doi: 10.1016/j.dhjo.2016.12.013

Friedman, C. (2016). Outdated language: Use of "mental retardation" in Medicaid HCBS waivers post-Rosa's Law. *Intellectual and Developmental Disabilities, 54*(5), 342–353. doi: 10.1352/1934-9556-54.5.342

Galvin, R. (2003). The making of the disabled identity: A linguistic analysis of marginalisation. *Disability Studies Quarterly, 23*(2), 149–178. doi: 10.18061/dsq.v23i2.421

Gernsbacher, M. A. (2017). Editorial perspective: The use of person-first language in scholarly writing may accentuate stigma. *Journal of Child Psychology and Psychiatry, 58*(7), 859–861. doi: 10.1111/jcpp.12706

Gernsbacher, M. A., Raimond, A. R., Balinghasay, M. T., & Boston, J. S. (2016). "Special needs" is an ineffective euphemism. *Cognitive Research: Principles and Implications, 1*(1), 29–42. doi: 10.1186/s41235-016-0025-4

Gill, C. J. (1997). Four types of integration in disability identity development. *Journal of Vocational Rehabilitation, 9*(1), 39–46.

Hahn, H. D., & Belt, T. L. (2004). Disability identity and attitudes toward cure in a sample of disabled activists. *Journal of Health and Social Behavior, 45*, 453–464. doi: 10.1177/002214650404500407

Haller, B., Dorries, B., & Rahn, J. (2006). Media labeling versus the US disability community identity: a study of shifting cultural language. *Disability & Society, 21*(1), 61–75.

Hojati, A. (2012). A study of euphemisms in the context of English-speaking media. International *Journal of Linguistics, 4*(4), 552–562. doi:10.5296/ijl.v4i4.2933

Hunt, E., & Agnoli, F. (1991). The Whorfian hypothesis: A cognitive psychology perspective. *Psychological Review, 98*(3), 377–389. doi: 10.1037/0033-295x.98.3.377

Hussein, B. A. S. (2012). The Sapir Whorf hypothesis today. *Theory and Practice in Language Studies, 2*(3), 642–646. doi: 10.4304/tpls.2.3.642-646

Jaarsma, P., & Welin, S. (2012). Autism as a natural human variation: Reflections on the claims of the neurodiversity movement. *Health Care Analysis, 20*(1), 20–30. doi: 10.1007/s10728-011-0169-9

Jernigan, K. (2009). The pitfalls of political correctness: Euphemisms excoriated. *Braille Monitor, 52.* http://www.nfb.org/images/nfb/Publications/bm/bm09/bm0903/bm090308.htm

Kay, P., & Kempton, W. (1984). What is the Sapir-Whorf hypothesis? *American Anthropologist, 86*(1), 65–79. doi: 10.1525/aa.1984.86.1.02a00050

Kerkhoff, T. R., & Hanson, S. L. (2015). Disability culture: An ethics perspective. In J. M. Uomoto & T. M. Wong (Eds.), *Multicultural neurorehabilitation: Clinical principles for rehabilitation professionals* (pp. 169–202). New York: Springer.

La Forge, J. (1991). Preferred language practice in professional rehabilitation journals. *Journal of Rehabilitation, 57*, 49–51.

Martz, E., & Livneh, H. (2016). Psychosocial adaptation to disability within the context of positive psychology: findings from the literature. *Journal of Occupational Rehabilitation, 26*(1), 4–12. doi: 10.1007/s10926-015-9598-x

McCarthy, H. (2011). A modest festschrift and insider perspective on Beatrice Wright's contributions to rehabilitation theory and practice. *Rehabilitation Counseling Bulletin, 54*(2), 67–81. doi: 10.1177/0034355210386971

Mona, L. R., Cameron, R. P., & Clemency Cordes, C. (2017). Disability culturally competent sexual healthcare. *American Psychologist, 72*(9), 1000–1010. doi: 10.1037/amp0000283

Nario-Redmond, M. R., Noel, J. G., & Fern, E. (2013). Redefining disability, reimagining the self: Disability identification predicts self-esteem and strategic responses to stigma. *Self and Identity, 12*, 468–488. doi: 10.1080/15298868.2012.681118

Nario-Redmond, M. R., & Oleson, K. C. (2016). Disability group identification and disability-rights advocacy: Contingencies among emerging and other adults. *Emerging Adulthood, 4*(3), 207–218. doi: 10.1177/2167696815579830

Olkin, R. (2017). *Disability-affirmative therapy.* New York: Oxford University Press.

Palmer, M. (2011). Disability and poverty: A conceptual review. *Journal of Disability Policy Studies, 21*(4), 210–218.

Perlovsky, L. (2009). Language and emotions: Emotional Sapir–Whorf hypothesis. *Neural Networks, 22*(5–6), 518–526. doi: 10.1016/j.neunet.2009.06.034

Schur, L. A. (1998). Disability and the psychology of political participation. *Journal of Disability Policy Studies, 9*(2), 3–31. doi: 10.1177/104420739800900202

Shogren, K. A. (2013). Positive psychology and disability: A historical analysis. In M. Wehmeyer (Ed.), *The Oxford handbook of positive psychology and disability* (pp. 19–33). Oxford University Press.

Vaughan, E. C. (2009). People-first language: An unholy crusade. *Braille Monitor 52*(3). https://nfb.org/images/nfb/publications/bm/bm09/bm0903/bm090309.htm

Weeber, Joy E. (2004). Disability Community Leaders' Disability Identity Development: *A Journey of Integration and Expansion.* An unpublished doctoral dissertation. Retrieved from http://repository.lib.ncsu.edu/ir/bitstream/1840.16/5952/1/etd.pdf.

Whyte, A., Aubrecht, A., McCullough, C., Lewis, J., & Thompson-Ochoa, D. (2013). Understanding Deaf people in counseling contexts. *Counseling Today, 56*(4), 38–45.

Wright, B. (1983). *Physical disability: A psychosocial approach* (2nd ed.). New York: Harper & Row.

Chapter 4

Moving toward Well-Being

Positively Coping with and Adjusting to Chronic Illness and Disability

Susan Miller Smedema, Yunzhen Huang,
Hannah Fry, and Alexandra M. Kriofske Mainella

People who experience the onset of a chronic illness or disability (CID) will inevitably go through a process of integrating their new circumstances into their lives. The individual, as well as their families and support systems, will react to the changes that a CID brings, and if all goes well, over time they will reach a level of positive adjustment in which they are able not only to fully participate but also to flourish in all aspects of daily life. A person who has successfully adjusted to a CID will persist in working toward meaningful social, vocational, and personal goals, and will achieve a high level of overall subjective well-being (Livneh & Antonak, 1997).

Coping with and adjusting to a CID in the pursuit of successful adjustment is a complex and dynamic process that has been the focus of research for many decades. While some early conceptualizations of adaptation to disability emphasized the requirement of depression and mourning for the loss of function brought about by a CID (e.g., Thomas & Siller, 1999), the field of rehabilitation is now more often characterized by a strength-based understanding of the process by which a CID is accepted and successfully integrated into an individual's self-concept. This shift toward positive psychology in adaptation research and practice (Dunn & Dougherty, 2005) highlights positive aspects of an individual's adaptation process, such as their strengths, resilience (see chapter 8, this volume), and coping resources, supports individuals through any negative reactions that they might experience, and does not assume that all people grieve as a result of acquiring a CID.

The field of rehabilitation takes a holistic approach to the understanding of adjustment of people with CID (Dunn & Elliott, 2008), whereby it is only possible to understand how people will respond to the onset of a CID by considering the context of their environments and other personal factors (e.g., coping responses, personality, value systems; Wright, 1960, 1983). This idea is compatible with research in positive psychology which characterizes well-being as a profile of multiple factors, rather than with a single well-being indicator (Forgeard et al., 2011; Seligman, 2011). Multidimensional well-being theories, such the PERMA model (Seligman, 2011), can serve as a foundation on which to design interventions to help individuals with CID achieve optimal adjustment outcomes. According to Seligman, well-being consists of five core elements—Positive emotion, Engagement, Relationships, Meaning, and Accomplishment—which together comprise the PERMA model of well-being. PERMA reconciles various perspectives regarding the measurement and theory surrounding well-being in that it includes both eudemonic (i.e., living a life full of purpose) and hedonic (i.e., living a life full of pleasure) components. People with CID and the practitioners that support them can use PERMA to increase their adjustment and well-being by focusing on feeling good, living meaningfully, establishing good relationships, accomplishing goals, and being fully engaged with life (Jones et al., 2014).

Within the International Classification of Functioning, Disability, and Health (ICF) model (WHO, 2001), coping and adaptation can be considered as not only outcomes that are dependent upon other personal factors, such as the components that comprise PERMA, but also as personal factors that affect overall well-being outcomes themselves. Therefore, if service providers such as rehabilitation counselors can help a person develop strengths to cope with and adjust to a CID in a positive and adaptive way, their overall sense of well-being and quality of life (QOL) will improve. The goal of this chapter, therefore, is to present and discuss fundamental theories of coping and adaptation from both evidence-based and practical perspectives. This will provide researchers and practitioners a foundation on which to develop and implement services to promote the adaptation process for people who experience a CID, so as to help them to thrive.

COPING

Coping is defined as "the thoughts and behaviors used to manage the internal and external demands of situations that are appraised as stressful" (Folkman & Moskowitz, 2004, p. 745). As one of the personal factors in the ICF model (WHO, 2001), coping has been linked to various positive psychology constructs and psychosocial outcomes among individuals with CID (e.g., Livneh et al., 2004; Moskowitz et al., 2009). Understanding coping within the context of CID adaptation can help inform evidence-based practice to facilitate psychosocial adjustment and promote positive outcomes in individuals with CID.

This section will introduce two classical coping theories (Wright's coping versus succumbing framework and Lazarus and Folkman's transactional model of coping), common classifications of coping strategies, research on coping and positive psychology, and frequently used measures of coping. In addition, the clinical implications of coping in relation to positive psychology and adjustment to CID will be discussed.

Wright's Coping versus Succumbing Framework

One of the first classical theories related to coping in the context of CID was developed by Beatrice Wright. Wright (1983) proposed the coping versus succumbing framework, which described two responses to CID. In the coping response, one takes an active role in one's own life and focuses on what they can do despite the presence of CID. The person views CID as a manageable challenge and attempts to reduce its impact through environmental accommodations, medical procedures, assistive devices, and learning new skills. On the other hand, in the succumbing response, one takes a more passive role in their life, regarding oneself as a victim of CID, and is preoccupied with what they cannot do. The person exaggerates the negative impact of their condition and believes that only prevention and cure can resolve the "problem" of disability. As a result, CID is considered a barrier to a meaningful and satisfactory life, and people with CID are devalued by themselves and others who adopt the succumbing framework.

Furthermore, Wright (1983) discussed the association between coping and disability acceptance (i.e., incorporating disability into one's self-concept without devaluation), which is considered an essential outcome of psychosocial adjustment to CID. According to Wright (1983), coping can lead to four major changes in one's value system that indicate their acceptance of CID: (a) enlargement of the scope of values, that is, endorsing values other than CID-related values; (b) subordination of the physique, that is, focusing less on physical appearance and abilities; (c) containing the effects of disability, that is, limiting the impact of the CID to the impact of the actual impairment without exaggeration or overgeneralization to other aspects of oneself; and (d) transformation from comparative to asset values, that is, focusing on one's own personal assets, instead of comparing to the social norms or people without CID. Adjustment to CID maybe possible through the use of coping strategies to modify one's value system (for a review, see Keany & Glueckauf, 1993).

Lazarus–Folkman's Transactional Model of Coping

Lazarus and Folkman's (1984) transactional model of coping is one of the most influential theories in the field of stress and coping research (Biggs et al., 2017). It describes the dynamic and interactive relationship among stress, cognition, coping, and emotion. According to the model (Folkman & Lazarus, 1990; Lazarus & Folkman, 1984), people constantly evaluate the stimuli or events in their environment through primary and secondary appraisals. Primary appraisal involves determining the relevance of an event (i.e., threat or not) to the individual, and secondary appraisal involves evaluating coping options. If the event is appraised as harmful, threatening, or challenging, the person will experience stress. Coping strategies are then employed to reduce the stress, either by reducing their own negative emotions (i.e., *emotion-focused coping*) or by directly addressing the stressful event itself (i.e., *problem-focused coping*). The coping process produces an outcome, which is then reappraised by the person as favorable or unfavorable. Favorable outcomes generate positive emotions, while unfavorable outcomes generate distress and lead to further attempts to cope with the stress.

More recently, Folkman (2008) revised the transactional model and introduced *meaning-focused coping* to the model. Meaning-focused coping involves drawing on one's own beliefs, values, and existential goals to motivate and sustain coping in stressful events (Folkman, 2008). Examples include realigning priorities (i.e., reordering the priorities in life), adaptive goal processes (i.e., evaluating and changing goals if necessary), benefit finding (i.e., finding benefit in stressful experiences), benefit reminding (i.e., reminding oneself of the possible benefits stemming from the stressful experience), and infusing ordinary events with meaning (i.e., interpreting ordinary events to be personally meaningful; Folkman & Moskowitz, 2007). In the revised model (Folkman, 2008), unfavorable outcomes can trigger meaning-focused coping, which in turn generate positive emotions and their underlying appraisals. These positive emotions and appraisals influence the stress process by restoring coping resources, providing motivation needed in order to sustain problem-focused coping over the long run, and provide relief from distress.

Types of Coping Strategies

Approach versus Avoidance Coping

Coping, depending on the model or theory, has been conceptualized as a personality trait that consistently emerges during stressful events (i.e., dispositional), and/or a response pattern that varies across situations (i.e., situational; Livneh & Martz, 2007a). When viewed as a personality trait, coping is usually characterized by approach (i.e., the psychological orientation toward threat) or avoidance (i.e., the psychological orientation away from threat; Roth & Cohen, 1986). Approach coping as a personality trait can be seen as taking an active response to stressors, while avoidance coping can be seen as a passive response.

Shontz's (1975) model of coping with physical disabilities and severe illnesses is an example of the approach-avoidance conceptualization. According to Shontz (1975), the initial reactions to disability involve intense periods of encounter (approach, for example, shock, emotional flooding, despair) and retreat (avoidance, for example, a reaction against the consequences of encounter). The ideal resolution of this pattern is acknowledgment (i.e., safely incorporating the stress associated with CID into an integrated self-structure). If acknowledgment occurs, the person will gradually reach a stable equilibrium. Otherwise, the self can either be overwhelmed by the stress, or the person may split the disability from his/her self-structure. Research related to approach versus avoidance coping will be covered in a subsequent section.

Problem-Focused versus Emotion-Focused Coping

When viewed as situational factors, coping strategies are most commonly categorized into problem-focused and emotion-focused coping (Chronister & Chan, 2007). Problem-focused coping, such as making an action plan or concentrating on the next step, is task-oriented (Endler & Parker, 1990) and involves addressing the problem that is causing distress (Folkman & Lazarus, 1980, 1985). On the other hand, emotion-focused coping, such as distraction, acceptance, using alcohol or drugs, or seeking emotional support, is person-oriented (Endler & Parker, 1990) and involves reducing the negative emotions associated with the problem (Folkman & Lazarus, 1990; Lazarus & Folkman, 1984).

However, many studies suggested that there might be other dimensions of coping (Folkman & Moskowitz, 2004). Besides meaning-focused coping as proposed in the revised transactional model of coping (Folkman, 2008), avoidance coping has also been proposed as an additional dimension. According to Endler and Parker (1990), avoidance coping can include problem-focused and/or emotion-focused coping strategies. For example, an individual may avoid stressful situations by putting off the task at hand and engaging in another task (problem-focused), and/or seeking support from others (emotion-focused). Although avoidance coping is generally related to poorer outcomes (e.g., higher depression and state anxiety; Endler & Parker, 1990), the following section summarizing several meta-analyses (Suls & Fletcher, 1985; Mullen & Suls, 1982; Zeidner & Saklofske, 1996) reveal that this is not always the case.

Research on Coping and Disability

Approach versus Avoidance Coping

To date, many studies have investigated the efficacy of approach and avoidance coping, but meta-analytic studies suggest there is no conclusive evidence that one strategy is better than the other (Suls & Fletcher, 1985; Zeidner & Saklofske, 1996). For example, Suls and Fletcher (1985) conducted a meta-analytic review examining the efficacy of avoidant and non-avoidant coping and found a small effect size, suggesting that neither of the coping orientations was superior to the other. However, they also found that the efficacy of approach and avoidant coping differed depending on the context. Approach coping was more efficacious than avoidant coping when the former involved a focus on body sensations (e.g., objective feelings of the coldness of the water and numbness of the hand in a cold pressor test) rather than emotional processing (e.g., subjective feelings of the cold and emoting about the experience in a cold pressor test). In terms of long-term outcomes, they found that avoidant coping was associated with better outcomes initially, but with time, approach coping was associated with more positive outcomes. This finding was supported by another meta-analytic study conducted by Mullen and Suls (1982), which showed that avoidant coping was more effective in the short term, while approach coping was more effective in the long term. However, these studies are outdated, and efforts are needed to synthesize findings from more recent literature.

Problem-Focused versus Emotion-Focused Coping

Meta-analytic studies have provided some evidence regarding the efficacy of different coping dimensions. For example, in a meta-analysis testing a stress process model of health (Yu et al., 2007), problem-focused coping was negatively associated with health, while emotion-focused coping was positively related to health, although both effect sizes were small. Additionally, Penley et al. (2002) conducted a meta-analytic study to examine the relationship between coping strategies and physical and psychological health outcomes. In contrast to the findings of Yu et al. (2007), Penley and colleagues found negative associations between emotion-focused coping strategies and health outcomes, with wishful thinking and avoidance having the strongest negative association with health. In addition, the relationship between problem-focused coping strategies and health outcomes was inconsistent, with confrontive coping having the strongest negative association with health and Vitaliano's problem-focused coping (i.e., problem-focused coping subscale score from the Vitaliano revision of the Ways of Coping Checklist; Vitaliano et al., 1985) having the strongest positive association with health.

In summary, findings from meta-analytic studies on the effects of emotion-focused and problem-focused coping on health have been inconsistent (Penley et al., 2002; Yu et al., 2007). These findings suggest that coping is situation-specific, and the effectiveness of coping might be influenced by personal and contextual factors.

Factors Influencing Coping

Studies have linked certain coping dimensions and strategies to demographic factors. For instance, in a sample of adults with multiple sclerosis (MS), Holland et al. (2019) found that older age was associated with more adaptive coping (e.g., acceptance, planning, positive reinterpretation, growth, active coping), while younger age was associated with more frequent substance use. They also found that men were more likely to engage in maladaptive coping such as substance use, whereas women were more likely to engage in emotion-focused coping. In addition, avoidance methods were related to higher unemployment. In terms of racial differences, a meta-analysis of pain coping strategies showed that Black individuals use pain coping strategies more frequently, especially praying and catastrophizing, while White individuals focused more on task persistence (Meints et al., 2016).

Disability-related variables may also influence coping. In a study by Holland et al., (2019), greater impairment was associated with greater use of avoidance among adults with MS. In addition, Baastrup et al. (2016) compared the pattern of pain coping strategies used by adults with fibromyalgia (FM) or chronic neuropathic pain (NP), and pain-free controls. Results showed that adults with FM or NP did not cope differently with pain, but both groups used more adaptive and maladaptive coping strategies compared to the pain-free controls, indicating that the presence of CID may be stressful, which requires more coping to manage.

Relationship with Positive Psychosocial Outcomes

To date, many studies have explored the association between coping and psychosocial adjustment and health outcomes among people with CID. In a study among people with various disabilities, Livneh et al. (2004) found that problem-focused coping was the most powerful indicator of adjustment to disability, whereas avoidance-focused coping predicted poor psychosocial adjustment. In another study among people with psychiatric disabilities, coping skills such as medication management, symptom management, sleep management, relaxation, and basic hygiene were positively associated with QOL (Corrigan et al., 2005).

Meta-analysis may further demonstrate the relationship between coping and psychosocial outcomes. In a meta-analytic review on the relationship between coping strategies and well-being in adults with HIV, Moskowitz et al. (2009) found that direct action and positive reappraisal were consistently associated with better outcomes in people coping with HIV across affective, health behavior, and physical health domains. On the other hand, avoidance, such as behavioral disengagement and alcohol or drug use, was consistently associated with worse outcomes. In addition, coping effectiveness was dependent on contextual factors, such as time since diagnosis and participation in HIV treatment. Similarly, Duangdao and Roesch (2008) conducted a meta-analysis on the relationship between coping dimensions and adjustment in people with diabetes. They found that use of approach and problem-focused coping was associated with better overall adjustment with small to medium effect sizes, while avoidance and emotion-focused coping were not significantly related to overall adjustment. These findings suggest that approach coping and problem-focused coping might be associated with better psychosocial adjustment in various CID subgroups.

Clinical Implications

Recently, increased attention has been paid to the clinical application of empirical findings, particularly through coping skills interventions that target people with CID. A few studies using randomized controlled trials (RCT) have supported the efficacy of coping skills interventions for people with different types of CID. For example, Edgar et al. (2001) examined the efficacy of coping skills psychoeducational training program in people with breast and colon cancer. In this study, participants were randomly assigned to four groups: individual intervention, group intervention, self-support group, and no-intervention control. For the first two groups, participants completed the psychoeducational training program in either individual or group format. The program consisted of five 90-minute weekly sessions that taught coping skills such as problem-solving techniques, goal-setting, cognitive reappraisal, relaxation training, use of social support, and use of resources. Results showed that the individual intervention group demonstrated significantly greater improvement in well-being, indicating that the coping skills psychoeducational program, especially delivered in the individual format, is effective for people with breast and colon cancer.

Similarly, Sherwood et al. (2017) conducted an RCT on the efficacy of coping skills training in an outpatient setting of patients with heart failure. Participants were randomly assigned to a coping skills training group or a heart failure education group. The coping skills training included 16

30-minute weekly sessions, including four sessions of health behavior psychoeducation and 12 sessions of coping skills practice (e.g., relaxation training, cognitive restructuring, problem-solving, activity planning). The coping skills training group showed significantly greater improvement in QOL at posttreatment and had lower hospitalization and death rates during the three-year follow-up period.

Furthermore, White et al. (2018) proposed the THRIVE model, a framework that summarizes the external and internal facilitators of coping with chronic illness. The acronym stands for Therapeutic interventions, Habit and routine, Relational-social, Individual differences, Values and beliefs, and Emotional factors, which are all important predictors of coping with CID and should be considered in the development of coping interventions. The shift of focus from descriptive, phenomenological studies to interventional studies and clinically applicable frameworks suggests a growing interest in the application of research findings. It would indeed be beneficial to develop targeted coping skills interventions to promote healthy coping with and successful adjustment to CID in individuals with various types and severities of CID from diverse cultural backgrounds.

Measurement

Two common measures of coping include the Ways of Coping Questionnaire (WCQ; Folkman & Lazarus, 1988) and the Cope Orientations to Problems Experienced (COPE; Carver et al., 1989). The WCQ (Folkman & Lazarus, 1988) measures individual responses to a general range of stressors (i.e., situational coping). It has 66 items rated on a four-point Likert scale, although only 50 items are calculated in the 8 subscales (confrontation coping, distancing, self-controlling, seeking social support, accepting responsibility, escape-avoidance, planful problem-solving, and positive reappraisal). A higher score indicates more use of corresponding coping responses and it displays acceptable internal consistency across its subscales (Cronbach's alpha = .61–.79; Folkman & Lazarus, 1988).

The COPE (Carver et al., 1989) can measure an individual's dispositional or situational coping, depending on how the question is phrased. It has 53 items rated on a four-point Likert scale, with a higher score indicating more frequent use of certain coping strategies. The COPE has 14 factors, including adaptive coping, planning, suppression of competing activities, restraint coping, seeking instrumental social support, and so forth. It has acceptable to excellent internal consistency (Cronbach's alpha = .62–.92) and good test-retest reliability (six-week interval r = .42–.89, eight-week interval r = .46–.86) across its subscales (Carver et al., 1989).

ADAPTATION TO DISABILITY

The onset of CID can be a stressful experience of loss or threat to life that has a significant influence on an individual's life narrative. Adaptation is a "dynamic process that a person with CID experiences in order to achieve the final state of maximal person-environment congruence known as adjustment" (Livneh & Antonak, 1997, cited in Smedema et al., 2009, p. 51). It is the journey on which the person embarks to address or cope with changes brought about by CID, and is one of the most important topics in rehabilitation (Bishop, 2012).

The rehabilitation field's understanding of adaptation has matured over the years as research has continued to clarify how the many components of adaptation interact to affect the lives of people with CID. One of the first attempts at this understanding was the somatopsychology model, which is the study of the psychological effects of disability (Livneh et al., 2014). Models delineating the stages one navigates in the adaptation process subsequently emerged, followed by ecological models that promote the importance of environmental as well as contextual factors in the adaptation process. These later models coincide with the perspective of the ICF model (WHO, 2001) which highlights contextual factors in understanding the experience of CID. The introduction of these models accompanied the emergence of the field of positive psychology (Martz & Livneh, 2015) and with it the perspective of practitioners highlighting and promoting the strengths of clients and positive outcomes of adaptation to CID. In fact, the historical roots of both adaptation and positive psychology are linked and currently, they continue to inform the other given the "substantial philosophical and conceptual overlap" (p. 13). Models on adaptation provide theoretical bases for research as well as support rehabilitation professionals in efforts to promote healthy adaptation to CID in their clients.

This section will focus on the models falling under the somatopsychology, stage, and ecological umbrellas. Alongside these discussions will be current application of the models in clinical and research settings, and the primary measurements used to assess outcomes.

Somatopsychology

Somatopsychology originated from Lewin's (1935, 1936) field theory, which posits that human behavior (B) is a function of interaction of the person (P) and the environment (E). Central to somatopsychology, as well, is the Person × Situation interaction, which emphasizes the impact of the social views and personal meaning of disability on the person's adjustment to CID, including one's self-concept, body image, and acceptance of disability (Smedema et al., 2009).

Based on somatopsychological principles (Barker et al., 1953; Dembo et al., 1956), Wright (1983) developed the disability acceptance model to describe the adaptation process and outcome. Disability acceptance is considered to be the ultimate outcome of psychosocial adaptation in this model and is influenced by three major concepts: (a) value-laden beliefs and principles, (b) the coping framework, and (c) the succumbing framework. Value-laden beliefs and principles are the sociopolitical and personal assumptions that influence perceptions and responses to CID. Guided by these beliefs, individuals adopt either a coping or a succumbing framework to live a life with CID. People who adopt a coping framework take an active role in their lives and focus on what they can do with the presence of CID. As mentioned earlier, adopting a coping framework can lead to four major value changes that indicate disability acceptance: (a) enlargement of the scope of values, (b) subordination of the physique, (c) containing the effects of disability, and (d) transformation from comparative to asset values. On the other hand, people who adopt a succumbing framework take a more passive role in their life and are preoccupied with what they cannot do under the influence of their disability.

Rehabilitation Research

Empirical studies have supported the association between disability acceptance and adjustment to CID. Among people with chronic pain, acceptance of pain is a robust predictor of psychosocial adjustment, including lower levels of depression and higher levels of participation in physical activity (Baranoff et al. 2013; Kratz et al., 2017). In addition, in a sample of 1,266 adults with disabilities, Li and Moore (1998) found that disability acceptance was significantly positively associated with self-esteem. This includes the acceptance of loss that comes with CID and the values that must change for an individual to come to this acceptance.

Consistent with Wright's (1983) theory, studies have shown that coping is related to disability acceptance. In a sample of people with disabilities, Groomes and Leahy (2002) found that participants with a problem-focused coping disposition reported significantly higher levels of acceptance of disability, while participants with emotion-focused and avoidance-focused coping dispositions reported medium levels of acceptance. In another study among people with insulin-dependent diabetes, higher coping capability was related to higher degree of disability acceptance (Richardson et al., 2008).

Clinical Implications

Somatopsychology theories, particularly Wright's (1983) disability acceptance model, can be used to inform the development of disability adaptation interventions. According to Wright (1983), interventions should focus on cultivating a coping framework, with emphases on (a) what the client can do, (b) the life areas in which the client can participate, (c) the active role the client takes in shaping their life, and (d) the idea that an individual with a disability can live a meaningful and productive life.

In addition, interventions should focus on facilitating positive value changes that enhance disability acceptance. At the early stage of intervention, practitioners may prevent clients from overgeneralizing CID-related limitations to other non-affected areas of their life (Wright, 1983). Later, practitioners may help clients identify and explore personal values, replace physique-based values (e.g., physical beauty) with social and spiritual values, and focus on their current personal achievements rather than comparing with people without CID or with accomplishments before the onset of CID (Wright, 1983). Specific techniques include role-playing common situations, observing successful role models, and practicing real-life situations in various community-based settings (Livneh & Sherwood, 1991).

Measurement

Based on Wright's (1983) description of value changes, the Acceptance of Disability Scale (ADS; Linkowski, 1971) was developed to measure an individual's level of disability acceptance. The ADS has 50 items rated on a six-point Likert scale. It is a unidimensional measure, meaning that only one summative score is produced, which limits its use in practice (Smedema et al., 2009). Groomes and Linkowski (2007) revised the ADS to contain 32 items rated on a four-point Likert scale, yielding a four-factor structure that parallels the four value changes proposed by Wright (1983). The revised scale also shows excellent internal consistency, with Cronbach's alphas ranging from .71 to .88 for the subscales and .93 for the full scale (Groomes & Linkowski, 2007).

More recently, Ferrin et al. (2011) developed the Multidimensional Acceptance of Loss Scale (MALS), also based on value changes. The MALS has 42 items rated on a four-point Likert scale and shows a four-factor structure that parallels the four value changes. Cronbach's alphas range from .80 to .88 for the subscales, indicating excellent internal consistency (Ferrin et al., 2011). The scale also shows strong concurrent validity, as higher MALS scores are associated with higher QOL and self-esteem (Ferrin et al., 2011).

Stage Models

Early understanding of the onset of disability was one of the misfortune and loss, which had an impact on the understanding of adjustment to that loss. An early model of adaptation was Kubler-Ross's (1969) stages of grief. While her five-stage model was originally designed with people adapting to terminal illnesses in mind, this model has since been applied to other areas of loss such as marital separation (Maciejewski et al., 2007) and the onset of disabilities and illnesses such as AIDS (Kubler-Ross, 1987).

However, CID is no longer considered a "death sentence" (Livneh & Martz, 2007a) and understanding of the adaptation process has grown with that change in perspective. The most influential stage model of adaptation was a compilation of more than 40-stage models that were developed over two articles by Livneh (1986a, 1986b). According to this model consolidation, five stages of adaptation to CID exist: (a) initial impact (shock and anxiety), (b) defense mobilization (bargaining and denial), (c) initial realization (depression and internalized anger), (d) retaliation (externalized hostility), and (e) reintegration, (acknowledgment of the change, adjustment, and adaptation). Each stage is distinguished by the associated defense mechanisms typically utilized, the orientation a person's energy is directed toward (i.e., internal or external), and affective, cognitive, and behavioral factors. Outcomes of the psychosocial process of adaptation manifest along a continuum from maladaptive functioning to successful adaptation. This model and the stage models that it was built upon have a number of underlying assumptions, such as (a) the onset of CID has an extensive impact on the person's life and functioning, (b) adaptation is a dynamic process, (c) changes in the physical body lead to psychological imbalance, (d) there is a temporal sequence to adjustment, and (e) that while the stages are universal each person is unique and may experience adaptation differently.

Rehabilitation Research

The stage model of adaptation (Livneh, 1986a, 1986b) has been used as a basis of empirical study since its inception. Recently, research has focused on factors that influence the entrance into and exit from the stages of a number of CIDs. Sposato et al. (2018) used Livneh's stage model to assess psychosocial reactions to participants' experience of upper extremity limb salvage. They found five factors to be influential in the positive psychosocial adaptation: (a) education level, (b) age, (c) pain level, (d) time since injury, and (e) hand dominance. Psarra and Kleftaras (2013) investigated the role of meaning of life and depressive symptomatology in the adaptation process of Greek people with physical disabilities. They found that meaning of life had a positive association with healthy adjustment while depression and positive adaptation were negatively associated.

Research has also been carried out investigating specific stages and components within each stage. For example, Rodriguez and colleagues (2013) explored the influence spirituality and religion have on the adjustment process, incorporating prayer as a type of bargaining tool that may facilitate adaptation to acquired disabilities. Meyer and Kashubeck-West (2013) concentrated on how coping styles influence psychological well-being as well as acknowledgment of and adjustment to late deafness (i.e., hearing loss occurring after age 12), finding a complex relationship in which people presenting with higher levels of adaptation also endorse lower psychological well-being and more emotion-focused (compared to problem-focused) coping. The authors suggested that their sample (as compared to previous studies) reported lower levels of psychological well-being and greater perceived severity of disability. Overall, it appears that there is "a general trend toward adaptation to CID over time" (Smedema et al., 2009, p. 61), though "not everyone adapts to given conditions" (Meyer & Kashubeck-West, 2013, p. 133).

The endorsement of this model may be limited due to concerns about the linear, sequential nature of the model, its applicability to a diverse client base, and the assumption of final adjustment (Smedema et al., 2009). The universality (or lack thereof) of the stage model to explain all clients' responses to CID is recognized as an assumption shared by all stage models, as exemplified by Livneh's (1986a) emphasis that "although *most* people experience *most* of the stages, not *all* people will exhibit *all* of these stages" (p. 6; emphasis in original). Due to the reservations about these assumptions, there is limited empirical evidence to support the universality of the model. Rodriguez et al. (2013) plainly suggested the limited ability of the stage models is because they "do not provide rehabilitation professionals with enough insight as to how healthy adjustment is reached much beyond labeling stages" (p. 225), and can therefore be more descriptive in nature, rather than prescriptive.

Clinical Implications

Livneh (1986b) has devoted his research to determining processes and components of psychosocial adaptation to CID as well as practical interventions to promote adaption. In fact, the second article in his two-part series regarding stage model consolidation (1986b) consisted primarily of suggested strategies to employ at each stage of adaptation. Livneh reminded rehabilitation professionals to exercise flexibility and creativity when considering specific approaches by taking into account the individual client's personal, disability-specific, and environmental contexts. Examples of strategies at the initial impact stage include psychoeducation on CID, disease/disability progression, treatment options, trauma-informed psychotherapy, and anxiety-management techniques. During the defense-mobilization stage, one might employ gentle confrontation to work through denial, present-focused interventions to ground the client in reality, and self-awareness interventions. Any number of self-regulation and anger management strategies that are common in psychotherapy would be appropriate during the initial realization phase in which one experiences periods of depression and mourning and/or internalized anger. Approaches focused on anger management, including appropriate expression of anger and stress-reduction techniques, are most appropriate during the retaliation stage. Finally, the reintegration stage is characterized by interventions promoting personal, social, independent living, and vocational goals. Overall, it is recommended that professionals supporting clients' adaptation to CID practice strategies that promote insight into one's affect while later stages actualize approaches in the cognitive-behavioral realm (Livneh, 1986b).

Measurements

Fundamental to rehabilitation interventions from the stage-based model is determining which stage the client is in at the time of intervention. Therefore, appropriate measurement of the stages is necessary. One of the most common measurement tools for these stages is the Reaction to Impairment and Disability Inventory (RIDI; Livneh & Antonak, 1990). The RIDI is a 60-item tool on a four-point Likert scale that consists of 8 self-report subscales: shock (8 items), anxiety (11 items), denial (10 items), depression (14 items), internalized anger (8 items), externalized hostility (12 items), acknowledgment (12 items), and adjustment (15 items). Internal reliability coefficients were found to be acceptable (.69–.85; Livneh & Antonak, 1997). This measure has also been used in modified forms, such as a 53-question version of the RIDI from Sposato and colleagues (2018) who shortened it and modified the language to include population-specific content. While the RIDI was designed to measure the various processes experienced at each of the stages of adaptation based on Livneh's stage model (1986a, 1986b), the acknowledgment and adjustment subscales have been used in other models of adaptation (e.g., ecological models; Livneh & Martz, 2007; Martz et al., 2005).

Ecological Models

The understanding of one's journey toward adjustment has grown to be characterized by a holistic portrayal of the person and their adaptation to CID. These models recognize that individual differences and life situations influence reactions to even the same condition or disability, and not everyone will come to the optimal stage of adjustment (Smedema et al., 2009). Furthermore, these models take into account the positive elements important in the adaptation process rather than simply considering the impairment or functional limitations. This section will introduce two influential ecologic models: Livneh and Antonak's (1997; Livneh, 2001) adaptation to CID model and Bishop's (2005) disability centrality (DC) model.

Livneh and Antonak's Adaptation Model

Livneh and Antonak (1997; Livneh, 2001) conceptualized adaptation in terms of three unique components: (a) antecedents, (b) the process of psychosocial adaptation, and (c) outcomes. Antecedents include background and triggering events, such as medical aspects of CID and contextual variables. These are the biological (e.g., health status, type of CID), psychosocial (e.g., personal and social identities, developmental phase), and environmental characteristics (e.g., societal attitudes, economy) surrounding the individual to influence the onset and subsequent impact of CID.

The next component involves the dynamic process of psychosocial adaptation. Psychosocial reactions to CID are divided into early or short-term reactions of anxiety and shock; intermediate reactions of mourning, depression, hostility, and aggression; and late or long-term reactions of acceptance, environmental mastery, behavioral adaptation, affective equilibrium, and so on. Contextual variables within the process of psychosocial adaptation can mediate, moderate, or interact with the experience and nature of the reaction to CID. These include (a) variables associated with CID (e.g., the type of CID, the body parts that are affected, the course of the condition, pain, duration, visibility, side effects of medications, treatment); (b) variables that are associated with one's identities and the intersectionality of sociodemographic characteristics; (c) variables related to one's personality or internal psychological processes (e.g., self-esteem, ego strength, self-efficacy); and (d) the external environment (e.g., social/attitudinal barriers/facilitators, financial resources).

Ultimately, the outcomes of this model are a complex set of indicators that focus primarily on QOL. The outcomes for this model can be looked at through a variety of lenses, including the functional domain assessed (e.g., intrapersonal, interpersonal, extrapersonal, community level), content area (e.g., affective, cognitive, or behavioral), manner through which the outcome is measured (e.g., self-report, professional observation, report from a person close to the individual), time in which outcome is measured (e.g., one hour of diagnosis of onset versus three years after onset), and level of assessment (e.g., global versus disability-specific). The ultimate rehabilitation goal, as described by Livneh (2001) is QOL, a multidimensional construct that is measured both subjectively and objectively, thereby proving to be a broad enough outcome to apply to a wide array of individuals with CID.

Bishop's Disability Centrality Model

Bishop's DC model (2005a, 2005b) is a QOL model building on Devins's illness intrusiveness model (Devins, 1994; Devins et al., 1983), and a synthesis of other prominent models and commonly accepted components of adaptation. The ideal outcome within this model is increased or restored QOL. Like Livneh and Antonak's adaptation to CID model, the DC model also emphasizes the complex, multidimensionality of the adaptation process. The model has four domains that all influence overall QOL: (a) domain impact, or the extent to which a domain in life has been affected by the onset of CID; (b) domain satisfaction, or the extent to which one experiences satisfaction from a given domain; (c) domain importance, or the centrality to one's life of a given domain; and (d) domain control, or the perceived ability to navigate a given domain. Specifically, the relationship between impact of CID and one's overall QOL is mediated by the control which one perceives to have in a given domain and the satisfaction one receives from that domain. The importance of a given domain moderates the relationship between domain satisfaction and overall QOL, meaning that "overall QOL is disproportionately influenced by the degree of perceived satisfaction within those domains that are more important" (Bishop, 2005, p. 223).

Value change and adaptation is an important concept in this model. A change in overall QOL does not inherently signify or lead to diminished QOL. Rather, one needs to adapt to these changes. To do so, one must engage in either (a) importance change (i.e., shifting or altering the importance of domains so that previously important but highly affected domains become less central, and less affected domains become more central) or (b) control change (i.e., engaging in processes to increase perceived control, such as self-management or environmental accommodation, so that the important domains are less affected and remain important). If neither of the above situations occurs, the person will continue to experience reduced overall QOL.

Rehabilitation Research

The adaptation to CID model by Livneh and Antonak (1997; Livneh, 2001) has received attention from researchers since its introduction. Martz et al. (2005) used the three components of this model to develop a specific psychosocial adaptation process of people with spinal cord injury. In their proposed model of adaptation to spinal cord injury, Martz and colleagues expanded on the premises of Livneh and Antonak by delineating hypothesized paths between the broad components (a) negative affectivity, (b) disability severity/impact, (c) disengagement coping, and (d) psychosocial adaptation. They found that the first three negatively correlated with psychosocial adaptation or, in other words, positive psychosocial outcomes were associated with lower levels of negative affectivity, disability severity/impact, and disengagement coping. More specifically, negative affectivity and disability severity/impact were stronger predictors as they demonstrated a medium effect compared to disengagement coping.

The DC model (Bishop, 2005) similarly has been adopted by rehabilitation researchers since its introduction. Bishop and colleagues (2007) applied the model to people with MS and consistent with the model's hypotheses, one's overall QOL was influenced by one's perception of the impact of MS, and this relationship was mediated by the control of and satisfaction with a given domain. Additionally, domain importance moderated the relationship between domain satisfaction and overall QOL, meaning that the relationship between satisfaction of a certain domain and QOL is dependent on the importance of a given domain. Similar relationships have also been found in individuals with traumatic brain injury (Mackenzie et al., 2015).

Clinical Implications

The holistic approach and shift in outcomes of the ecological models open new avenues for assessment and intervention. Evidence suggests that measuring and addressing adaptation is important, but few rehabilitation counselors do so (Bishop, 2001). As stated previously, the ultimate rehabilitation goal is improved QOL (Livneh, 2001). Therefore, a holistic assessment of the intrapersonal, interpersonal, and extrapersonal domains within QOL is necessary. While not all components within these domains will apply to each client, it is important to assess them to determine how best to develop a treatment plan. Given the focus of clinical work on the individual and their life context, this model lends itself to assessing a consumer's needs based on their cultural identities. Once assessed and documented in the treatment plan, interventions can target those areas. Furthermore, as a theory-free framework, this model can be adapted by practitioners to cognitive-behavioral, psychodynamic, and existential approaches in the clinical setting. While not unique to this model, an important consideration is that not all variables associated with the adaptation process are able to be manipulated (e.g., gender, age, disability type), thereby limiting clinicians in their capacity for direct intervention.

The DC Model compels users to include a comprehensive assessment of QOL by assessing the four components of this model: satisfaction, perceived control, impact of CID and its treatment, and extent of domain importance to the individual to help prioritize interventions. It may be challenging to address all domains at once, so one must prioritize the most important domains for each person. For example, if spiritual expression is most important to a client, the practitioner could work with them to develop skills and manage how to engage with their spirituality, such as reading or watching videos, becoming involved in one's place of worship, setting up a physically accessible prayer corner, arranging phone calls with spiritual leaders in the community, and so on. Another implication of this model is the importance of working with individuals to find value in more peripheral domains. As previously stated, values are integrally important in the domain satisfaction portion of the DC model and will be vitally important to assess. Values are deeply tied to culture. This model allows for each consumer to take the lead in identifying their perception of satisfaction in a given domain that is important to them based on cultural values and beliefs. As proposed by Bishop (2005), the process of rehabilitation counselors supporting consumers in exploring new domains and activities related to those domains suggests that one's willingness and motivation to take on new experiences could be important in the discovery of domain importance shifts. Upon completing a comprehensive assessment, interventions can then be considered, such as self-management and skill development. Psychoeducation could be implemented to enhance perceived control by working with the consumer to understand their CID and its nature, course, possible interventions, and so on. Environmental accommodations would be important to consider and could be implemented with the assistance of independent living centers.

Measurements

The last two subscales of the RIDI (acknowledgment and adjustment) have been used to measure positive psychosocial adaptation in the context of Livneh and Antonak's ecological model (1997; Livneh, 2001). Martz et al. (2005) administered these two subscales to determine the applicability of a modified model for people with spinal cord injury by building on Livneh and Antonak's model. The internal consistency of these two subscales is good to very good (e.g., acknowledgment = .77, adjustment = .85; Livneh & Antonak, 1997).

The DC Model (Bishop, 2005) has the associated Disability Centrality Scale (DCS; Bishop, 2005) to assess QOL. It is divided into 10 life domains: physical health, mental health, work/studies, leisure activities, financial situation, spousal relationship, family relationships, social relations, autonomy/ independence, and religious/spiritual. This scale has been found to have acceptable internal consistency with a Cronbach's alpha at .74 (Bishop et al., 2007). Individual subscales vary from very good (e.g., satisfaction Cronbach's alpha = .88, control Cronbach's alpha = .84, and impact Cronbach's alpha = .89) to acceptable (e.g., importance Cronbach's alpha = .64).

CONCLUSION

People who experience the onset of a CID go through a process of incorporating their new circumstances into their lives so that they feel worthy and valuable and are able to live with a sense of purpose. This movement toward adjustment calls upon the many characteristics and resources of the individual and their environment, facilitated by thoughtful rehabilitation and psychosocial interventions. Researchers and practitioners can help individuals cope most effectively with the changes brought about by a CID and promote their adaptation process by using a positive psychology approach and by intentionally building upon their strengths. By understanding the coping and adaptation theories, such as those discussed in this chapter, in the context of a positive psychology framework such as PERMA, people with CID can be supported to achieve positive emotions, engage fully with life activities, build strong and healthy relationships, live lives full of meaning, and accomplish their goals. All of these positive outcomes will ultimately result in an optimal level of adjustment to CID, which will allow people with CID to thrive.

REFERENCES

Baastrup, S., Schultz, R., Brødsgaard, I., Moore, R., Jensen, T. S., Vase Toft, L., Bach, F. W., Rosenberg, R., & Gormsen, L. (2016). A comparison of coping strategies in patients with fibromyalgia, chronic neuropathic pain, and pain-free controls. *Scandinavian Journal of Psychology, 57*(6), 516–522.

Baranoff, J., Hanrahan, S. J., Kapur, D., & Connor, J. P. (2013). Acceptance as a process variable in relation to catastrophizing in multidisciplinary pain treatment. *European Journal of Pain, 17*(1), 101–110.

Barker, R. G., Wright, B.A., Meyerson, L., & Gonick, M. R. (1953). *Adjustment to physical handicap and illness: A survey of the social psychology of physique and disability* (2nd ed.). Social Science Research Council.

Biggs, A., Brough, P., & Drummond, S. (2017). Lazarus and Folkman's psychological stress and coping theory. In C. L. Cooper & J. C. Quick (Eds.), *The handbook of stress and health: A guide to research and practice* (pp. 351–364). John Wiley & Sons.

Bishop, M. (2005a). Quality of life and psychosocial adaptation to chronic illness and acquired disability: A conceptual and theoretical synthesis. *Journal of Rehabilitation, 71*(2), 5–13.

Bishop, M. L. (2005b). Quality of life and psychosocial adaptation to chronic illness and disability: Preliminary analysis of a conceptual and theoretical synthesis. *Rehabilitation Counseling Bulletin, 48*(4), 219–231.

Bishop, M. L. (2012). Psychosocial Adaptation to Chronic Illness and Disability: Current Status and Considerations for New Directions. In P. J. Toriello, M. L. Bishop, & P. D. Rumrill (Authors), *New directions in rehabilitation counseling: Creative responses to professional, clinical, and educational challenges* (pp. 25–53). Better World Books.

Bishop, M. L., Shepard, L., & Stenhoff, D. M. (2007). Psychosocial adaptation and quality of life in multiple sclerosis: Assessment of the Disability Centrality Model. *Journal of Rehabilitation, 73*(1), 3–12.

Carver, C. S., Scheier, M. F., & Weintraub, J. K. (1989). Assessing coping strategies: A theoretically based approach. *Journal of Personality and Social Psychology, 56*(2), 267–283.

Chronister, J., & Chan, F. (2007). Hierarchical coping: A conceptual framework for understanding coping within the context of chronic illness and disability. In E. Martz & H. Livneh (Eds.), *Coping with chronic illness and disability* (pp. 49–71). Springer.

Corrigan, P., Rao, D., & Lam, C. S. (2005). Psychiatric rehabilitation. In F. Chan, M. J. Leahy, & J. L. Saunders, (Eds.), *Case management for rehabilitation health professionals* (Vol. 2, pp. 132–163). Aspen Professional Services.

Dembo, T., Leviton, G. L., & Wright, B. A. (1956). Adjustment to misfortune: A problem of social-psychological rehabilitation. *Artificial Limbs, 3*, 4–62.

Duangdao, K. M., & Roesch, S. C. (2008). Coping with diabetes in adulthood: A meta-analysis. *Journal of Behavioral Medicine, 31*(4), 291–300.

Dunn, D. S., & Dougherty, S. B. (2005). Prospects for a positive psychology of rehabilitation. *Rehabilitation Psychology, 50*(3), 305.

Dunn, D. & Elliott, T.R. (2008). The place and promise of theory in rehabilitation psychology research. *Rehabilitation Psychology*, *53*(3), 254–267.

Edgar, L., Rosberger, Z., & Collet, J. P. (2001). Lessons learned: Outcomes and methodology of a coping skills intervention trial comparing individual and group formats for patients with cancer. *The International Journal of Psychiatry in Medicine, 31*(3), 289–304.

Endler, N. S., & Parker, J. D. (1990). Multidimensional assessment of coping: A critical evaluation. *Journal of Personality and Social Psychology, 58*(5), 844–854.

Ferrin, J. M., Chan, F., Chronister, J., & Chiu, C. Y. (2011). Psychometric validation of the multidimensional acceptance of loss scale. *Clinical Rehabilitation, 25*(2), 166–174.

Folkman, S. (2008). The case for positive emotions in the stress process. *Anxiety, Stress, and Coping, 21*(1), 3–14.

Folkman, S., & Lazarus, R. S. (1988). *Manual for the ways of coping questionnaire.* Consulting Psychologist Press.

Folkman, S., & Lazarus, R. S. (1990). Coping and emotion. In N. L. Stein, B. Leventhal, & T. Trabasso (Eds.), *Psychological and biological approaches to emotion* (pp. 313–332). Lawrence Erlbaum Associates.

Folkman, S., & Moskowitz, J. T. (2004). Coping: Pitfalls and promise. *Annual Review of Psychology, 55*, 745–774.

Folkman, S., & Moskowitz, J. T. (2007). Positive affect and meaning-focused coping during significant psychological stress. In M. Hewstone, H. A. W. Schut, J. B. F. de Wit, K. van den Bos, & M. S. Stroebe (Eds.), *The scope of social psychology: Theory and applications* (pp. 193–208). Psychology Press.

Forgeard, M. J. C., Jayawickreme, E., Kern, M. L., & Seligman, M. E. P. (2011). Doing the right thing: Measuring well-being for public policy. *International Journal of Wellbeing, 1*, 79–106.

Groomes, D. A., & Leahy, M. J. (2002). The relationships among the stress appraisal process, coping disposition, and level of acceptance of disability. *Rehabilitation Counseling Bulletin, 46*(1), 14–23.

Groomes, D. A., & Linkowski, D. C. (2007). Examining the structure of the revised acceptance disability scale. *Journal of Rehabilitation, 73*(3), 3–9.

Holland, D. P., Schlüter, D. K., Young, C. A., Mills, R. J., Rog, D. J., Ford, H. L., Orchard, K., & TONiC study group. (2019). Use of coping strategies in multiple sclerosis: Association with demographic and disease-related characteristics. *Multiple Sclerosis and Related Disorders, 27*, 214–222.

Jones, C., Scholes, L., Johnson, D., Katsikitis, M., &Carras, M. C.(2014). Gaming well: links between videogames and flourishing mental health. *Frontiers in Psychology, 5*, 1–8.

Keany, K. C., & Glueckauf, R. L. (1993). Disability and value change: An overview and reanalysis of acceptance of loss theory. *Rehabilitation Psychology, 38*(3), 199–210.

Kratz, A. L., Ehde, D. M., Bombardier, C. H., Kalpakjian, C. Z., & Hanks, R. A. (2017). Pain acceptance decouples the momentary associations between pain, pain interference, and physical activity in the daily lives of people with chronic pain and spinal cord injury. *The Journal of Pain, 18*(3), 319–331.

Kubler-Ross, E. (1969). *On death and dying*. Macmillan.

Kubler-Ross, E. (1987). *AIDS: The ultimate challenge*. Macmillan.

Lazarus, R. S., & Folkman, S. (1984). *Stress, appraisal, and coping*. Springer.

Lewin, K. (1935). *A dynamic theory of personality*. McGraw-Hill.

Lewin, K. (1936). *Principles of topological psychology*. McGraw-Hill.

Li, L., & Moore, D. (1998). Acceptance of disability and its correlates. *The Journal of Social Psychology, 138*(1), 13–25.

Linkowski, D. C. (1971). A scale to measure acceptance of disability. *Rehabilitation Counseling Bulletin, 14*, 236–244.

Livneh, H. (1986a). A unified approach to existing models of adaptation to disability: Part I: A model of adaptation. *Journal of Applied Rehabilitation Counseling, 17*(1), 5–16.

Livneh, H. (1986b). A unified approach to existing models of adaptation to disability: Part II: Intervention strategies. *Journal of Applied Rehabilitation Counseling, 17*(2), 6–10.

Livneh, H. (2001). Psychosocial adaptation to chronic illness and disability: A conceptual framework. *Rehabilitation Counseling Bulletin, 44*(3), 151–160.

Livneh, H., & Antonak, R. F. (1990). Reactions to disability: An empirical investigation of their nature and structure. *Journal of Applied Rehabilitation Counseling, 21*(4), 13–21.

Livneh, H., & Antonak, R. F. (1991). Temporal structure of adaptation to disability. *Rehabilitation Counseling Bulletin, 34*(4), 298–320.

Livneh, H., & Antonak, R. F. (1997). *Psychosocial adaptation to chronic illness and disability* (1st ed.). Aspen Publishers.

Livneh, H., Bishop, M., & Anctil, T. M. (2014). Modern models of psychosocial adaptation to chronic illness and disability as viewed through the prism of Lewin's

Field Theory: A comparative review. *Rehabilitation Research, Policy, and Education, 28*(3), 126–142.

Livneh, H., Lott, S., & Antonak, R. (2004). Patterns of psychosocial adaptation to chronic illness and disability: A cluster analytic approach. *Psychology, Health & Medicine, 9*(4), 411–430.

Livneh, H., & Martz, E. (2007a). An introduction to coping theory and research. In E. Martz & H. Livneh (Eds.), *Coping with chronic illness and disability* (pp. 3–27). Springer.

Livneh, H., & Martz, E. (2007b). Reactions to diabetes and their relationship to time orientation. *International Journal of Rehabilitation Research, 30*(2), 127–136.

Livneh, H., & Martz, E. (2015). Psychosocial adaptation to disability within the context of positive psychology: Philosophical aspects and historical roots. *Journal of Occupational Rehabilitation, 26*(1), 13–19.

Livneh, H., & Sherwood, A. (1991). Application of personality theories and counseling strategies to clients with physical disabilities. *Journal of Counseling and Development 69*, 525–538.

Maciejewski, P. K., Zhang, B., Block, S. D., & Prigerson, H. G. (2007). An empirical examination of the stage theory of grief. *Journal of the American Medical Association, 297*, 716–723.

Martz, E., & Livneh, H. (2015). Psychosocial adaptation to disability within the context of positive psychology: Findings from the literature. *Journal of Occupational Rehabilitation, 26*(1), 4–12.

Martz, E., Livneh, H., Priebe, M., Wuermser, L. A., & Ottomanelli, L. (2005). Predictors of psychosocial adaptation among people with spinal cord injury or disorder. *Archives of Physical Medicine and Rehabilitation, 86*(6), 1182–1192.

Meints, S. M., Miller, M. M., & Hirsh, A. T. (2016). Differences in pain coping between black and white Americans: A meta-analysis. *The Journal of Pain, 17*(6), 642–653.

Meyer, J. M., & Kashubeck-West, S. (2013). Well-being of individuals with late-deafness. *Rehabilitation Psychology, 58*(2), 124–136.

Moskowitz, J. T., Hult, J. R., Bussolari, C., & Acree, M. (2009). What works in coping with HIV? A meta-analysis with implications for coping with serious illness. *Psychological Bulletin, 135*(1), 121–141.

Mullen, B., & Suls, J. (1982). The effectiveness of attention and rejection as coping styles: A meta-analysis of temporal differences. *Journal of Psychosomatic Research, 26*(1), 43–49.

Penley, J. A., Tomaka, J., & Wiebe, J. S. (2002). The association of coping to physical and psychological health outcomes: A meta-analytic review. *Journal of Behavioral Medicine, 25*(6), 551–603.

Psarra, E., & Kleftaras, G. (2013). Adaptation to physical disabilities: The role of meaning of life and depression. *The European Journal of Counseling Psychology, 2*(1), 79–99.

Richardson, A., Adner, N., & Nordström, G. (2001). Persons with insulin-dependent diabetes mellitus: Acceptance and coping ability. *Journal of Advanced Nursing, 33*(6), 758–763.

Rodriguez, V. J., Glover-Graf, N. M., & Blanco, E. L. (2013). Conversations with god: Prayer and bargaining in adjustment to disability. *Rehabilitation Counseling Bulletin, 56*(4), 215–228.

Roth, S., & Cohen, L. J. (1986). Approach, avoidance, and coping with stress. *American Psychologist, 41*(7), 813–819.

Seligman, M. E. P. (2002). *Authentic happiness.* New York: Free Press.

Seligman, M. E. P. (2011). *Flourish: A visionary new understanding of happiness and well-being.* New York: Free Press.

Sherwood, A., Blumenthal, J. A., Koch, G. G., Hoffman, B. M., Watkins, L. L., Smith, P. J., O'Connor, C. M., Adams, K. F., Rogers, J. G., Sueta, C., Chang, P. P., Johnson, K. S., Schwartz, J., & Hinderliter, A. L. (2017). Effects of coping skills training on quality of life, disease biomarkers, and clinical outcomes in patients with heart failure: A randomized clinical trial. *Circulation: Heart Failure, 10*(1), e003410.

Shontz, F. C. (1975). *The psychological aspects of physical illness and disability.* Macmillan.

Smedema, S. M., Bakken-Gillen, S. K., & Dalton, J. (2009). Psychosocial adaptation to chronic illness and disability: Models and measurement. In C. Fong, E. Da Silva Cardoso, & J. A. Chronister (Eds.), *Understanding psychosocial adjustment to chronic illness and disability: A handbook for evidence-based practitioners in rehabilitation* (pp. 51–74). Springer.

Sposato, L., Yancosek, K., Lospinoso, J., & Cancio, J. (2018). Psychosocial reactions to upper extremity limb salvage: A cross-sectional study. *Journal of Hand Therapy, 31*(4), 494–501.

Suls, J., & Fletcher, B. (1985). The relative efficacy of avoidant and nonavoidant coping strategies: A meta-analysis. *Health Psychology, 4*(3), 249–288.

Thomas, K. R., & Siller, J. (1999). Object loss, mourning, and adjustment to disability. *Psychoanalytic Psychology*, 16(2), 179–197.

Vitaliano, P. P., Russo, J., Carr, J. E., Maiuro, R. D., & Becker, J. (1985). The ways of coping checklist: Revision and psychometric properties. *Multivariate Behavioral Research, 20*(1), 3–26.

White, K. Isaac, M., Kamoun, C., Leygues, J., & S. Cohn (2018). The THRIVE model: A framework and review of internal and external predictors of coping. *Health Psychology Open, 5*(2), 2055102918793552.

World Health Organization. (2001). *The International Classification of Functioning, Disability and Health (ICF).* WHO.

Wright, B.A. (1960). *Physical disability: A psychological approach.* New York: Harper & Row.

Wright, B. A. (1983). *Physical disability: A psychosocial approach* (2nd ed.). Harper and Row.

Yu, L., Chiu, C. H., Lin, Y. S., Wang, H. H., & Chen, J. W. (2007). Testing a model of stress and health using meta-analytic path analysis. *Journal of Nursing Research, 15*(3), 202–214.

Zeidner, M., & Saklofske, D. (1996). Adaptive and maladaptive coping. In M. Zeidner, N.S. Endler (Eds.), *Handbook of coping: Theory, research, and applications* (pp. 505–531). Wiley.

Chapter 5

Optimism

A Personal Factor for Promoting Functioning and Reducing Disability

Kevin L. Rand and Mackenzie L. Shanahan

INTRODUCTION

Optimists tend to focus on the positive aspects of life. In lay terms, they see the glass as "half full." At times, this positivity can be taken to unrealistic extremes. For example, the philosopher Leibniz expressed the belief that we live in the "best of all possible worlds," a view that was satirized in Voltaire's (1759) *Candide*. Unrealistic optimism is associated with unhealthy behaviors and diminished emotional well-being (Shepperd et al., 2015). In its more moderate forms, however, optimism is typically considered as a virtue. In Western culture, optimism is a personal factor thought to lead to happier and healthier lives. Over the past several decades, behavioral scientists have studied the links between optimism and life outcomes. To date, the evidence suggests that greater optimism is associated with healthy reactions to adversity, adaptive coping, effective goal-directed striving, and physical and psychological well-being (Carver & Scheier, 2002; Scheier & Carver, 1992). Although the bulk of the extant evidence comes from populations without disability, the science of optimism offers important implications for the well-being of people with disabilities and their families and the extent to which they experience disability in their efforts to be active participants in their lives.

For this chapter, we will focus on Scheier and Carver's (1985) conceptualization of optimism as a *generalized expectancy*. That is, optimism is the expectation that good things, as opposed to bad things, will happen. This definition of optimism is explicitly anchored in the future. This anticipatory belief is hypothesized to influence how people pursue important life goals and cope with disruptions to those goal pursuits. In turn, these efforts at pursuing goals influence physical and psychological well-being. To understand the potential impact of this future-oriented belief on the lives of people with disabilities, it is important to summarize a broader theory of human functioning, known as *self-regulation theory* (Carver & Scheier, 1998).

Human Functioning: Disability from the Self-Regulation Theory Perspective

As detailed in chapter 1, according to the World Health Organization (2001), disability is not a characteristic of the person, but a function of the discrepancy between their functional capacities and the demands of their environment. Hence, successful functioning involves the ability to fully engage in life's activities, including learning, working, and playing. Impairments result in disability only to the extent that they interfere with full functioning. In contrast, personal strengths, such as optimism, can mitigate the impact of such impairments.

We can begin to understand how optimism may positively influence human functioning and mitigate the impact of impairment through the lens of *self-regulation theory* (Carver & Scheier, 1998). According to this theory, all human behaviors are motivated by the pursuit of goals. In fact, goals are how people give meaning and structure to their lives. Goals are defined as desired future states or conditions, and they can be chosen intentionally (e.g., "I want to be a doctor") or activated automatically (e.g., the survival instinct).

People strive to control their thoughts, feelings, and behaviors to increase the likelihood that their goals will be achieved. In other words, people *self-regulate* to bring about desired future states. Differences in how well people regulate themselves may explain many of the differences in physical and psychological well-being. When people achieve their goals, they experience positive emotions and satisfaction; when their goals are blocked, they experience psychological distress. Indeed, prolonged experience of failure to achieve one's goals is hypothesized to give rise to clinical depression (Abramson et al., 1989).

According to self-regulation theory, two types of personal factors are important in motivating people to engage in behaviors: *expectancies* and *values* (see expectancy-value theories of motivation; Feather, 1982). The importance of a goal to the individual determines its value. The more important the goal, the more motivated a person is to pursue it. They will persist longer in the pursuit of more important goals and give up less important goals more readily.

Expectancy is the perceived likelihood that one can achieve a goal. In other words, it is a sense of confidence that a particular goal pursuit will be successful (Carver & Scheier, 2002). People are more motivated to pursue goals when they believe they will be successful. This sense of confidence about successful goal pursuits is the essence of the optimism construct (Carver & Scheier, 2002). Although people form specific expectancies for particular goals, they also have broader expectancies for outcomes across many life situations. In the context of self-regulation theory, optimism is the *generalized expectancy* that good as opposed to bad things will happen in the future. In other words, optimists not only have positive expectations about a particular endeavor (e.g., "I believe I will get an A in my organic chemistry class"), they also have positive expectations about life in general (e.g., "I believe good things will happen in the future").

Measuring Optimism

To date, there have been two instruments created to measure Carver and Scheier's (1985) optimism construct. The original measure, the Life Orientation Test (LOT; Scheier & Carver, 1985), consisted of eight statements (plus four filler items) to which respondents indicated their agreement using a 5-point scale (0 = strongly disagree through 4 = strongly agree). Four statements were positively worded, and four statements were negatively worded.

The LOT was revised to create a scale with three positively and three negatively worded items, as well as four filler items (LOT-R; Scheier, Carver, & Bridges, 1994). The LOT and the LOT-R are highly correlated (r = .95; Scheier et al., 1994), suggesting results from both scales are comparable. The LOT-R has been shown to be internally consistent and stable over time (Scheier et al., 1994). Although there is some debate as to whether optimism and pessimism represent opposite ends of a continuum or completely separate constructs (see Chang et al., 1994), we will treat optimism as a unidimensional construct. We will refer to individuals with high scores on the LOT or LOT-R as "optimists" and those with low scores as "pessimists."

Optimism's Impact on Functioning

As a generalized expectancy, optimism influences human functioning in several important ways. First, it affects people's psychological reactions to adversity, including appraisals and emotional responses. Second, it influences how people cope with stressors. Third, it affects people's goal-directed strivings, which determines their success or failure in goal pursuits. Finally, as a result of influencing these aspects of functioning, optimism influences overall well-being, including physical and psychological health.

Optimism and Psychological Reactions to Adversity

Optimists expect things to turn out well. Consequently, they experience more positive and fewer negative emotions than pessimists, especially when encountering barriers or setbacks (Carver & Scheier, 2002). Positive emotions stem from appraisals that one can successfully overcome challenges. In contrast, negative emotions are the result of believing that stressors will prevent one from reaching important life goals (Carver & Scheier, 1998).

Research has consistently shown that optimists tend to have more positive emotional experiences than pessimists, even in the face of extreme stressors. For example, greater optimism predicted better quality of life (QOL) and less psychological distress over the course of a year among women diagnosed with breast cancer (Carver et al., 1994). For men undergoing coronary artery bypass surgery, greater optimism predicted a more positive mood immediately after surgery and higher QOL six months later (Scheier et al., 1989).

The link between optimism and healthy reactions to adversity has been found in a variety of stressors, including starting graduate school (Rand et al., 2011), failed attempts at in vitro fertilization (Litt et al., 1992), being at risk for AIDS (Taylor et al., 1992), exposure to combat (Thomas et al., 2011), surviving natural disasters (Van der Velden et al., 2007), living through sociopolitical unrest (Ayyash-Abdo, 2010), and aging among elderly men (Giltay et al., 2006).

Optimism and Coping with Stressors

Because optimists perceive stressors as surmountable, they are more likely to use coping strategies that acknowledge and deal directly with stressors they experience. Because pessimists perceive problems as being more difficult or impossible to solve, they are more likely to deny the existence of stressors and use coping strategies that avoid facing their problems. For example, optimistic college students have been shown to use more active, problem-focused coping strategies; whereas their pessimistic peers were more likely to engage in denial and attempt to distance themselves from their problems (Aspinwall & Taylor, 1992).

When facing threats to one's health, optimists engage directly with the stressors, seeking more information, making plans for recovery, and attempting to notice the positive aspects of the situation (Taylor et al., 1992). Pessimists are more likely to avoid dealing directly with health-related stressors, which results in great psychological distress. For example, optimistic men undergoing coronary artery bypass surgery sought more information from their physicians and made plans for their recovery (Scheier et al., 1989). In addition, optimists were less likely to focus on their negative emotions or find avoidance coping strategies helpful (Scheier et al., 1989). Among couples who experienced failed attempts at in vitro fertilization, greater optimism predicted less reliance on escape as a coping strategy and greater use of benefit finding (Litt et al., 1992). Across several studies, optimism has been consistently linked with greater use of coping efforts that reduce, eliminate, or manage stressors and negative emotions and less use of efforts to ignore, avoid, or withdraw from stressors (Nes & Segerstrom, 2006).

It should be noted that optimists appear to be flexible in their coping strategies, depending on the stressors they encounter. When stressors are perceived to be controllable, optimism is associated with greater use of problem-focused coping; however, when stressors are perceived as being uncontrollable, optimism is associated with greater use of emotion-focused coping (Nes & Segerstrom, 2006). In other words, although optimists prefer to engage in problem-focused coping efforts when appropriate, they are not likely to waste efforts attempting to solve an unsolvable problem. Instead, they are more likely to accept the reality of the situation and cope with their emotional reactions to the situation when that is the more adaptive course of action. In sum, optimists are more likely to face reality and cope with it; pessimists are more likely to avoid or escape stressors they encounter (Nes & Segerstrom, 2006).

Optimism and Goal-Directed Striving

Optimists expect success. As a result, they are willing to persist longer in goal-directed efforts, even when encountering obstacles. This persistence, in turn, increases the likelihood that goals will be achieved. In other words, optimism can create a self-fulfilling prophecy where people believe they will succeed, so they work harder on their goals (Carver & Scheier, 1998).

Research has shown that optimists can indeed persist longer at tasks than pessimists (Nes et al., 2011). Moreover, optimistic undergraduates showed greater persistence in terms of staying in college (Nes et al., 2009). As expected, greater optimism is also associated with better success. For example, greater optimism is associated with better academic performance (Rand, 2009). In addition, more optimistic students have better faculty ratings of academic performance (Chemers et al., 2001) and leadership potential (Chemers et al., 2000).

A fundamental tenet of self-regulation theory is that people's well-being is determined by the extent to which they are able to achieve their life goals. It follows, then, that if optimism facilitates accomplishing one's goal-directed strivings, then optimists should show improved well-being compared to pessimists. The extant research supports this, showing that optimists evince better well-being, including more active participation in life, better relationships with others, and better mental and physical health. For example, optimism appears to promote better mental well-being during times of transition, uncertainty, and stress. Among college freshmen, higher levels of initial optimism predicted lower levels of psychological distress at the end of the semester (Aspinwall & Taylor, 1992). Optimism's effect on well-being continues in graduate studies. Greater optimism at the start of the semester predicted more life satisfaction among first-year law students during their final exams at the end of the semester (Rand et al., 2011).

Optimism also predicts healthier connections to others. People with higher levels of optimism have larger and more diverse social networks (Andersson, 2012). Optimists have more satisfying relationships and feel more supported (Assad, 2007). Additionally, optimistic adolescent girls are more likely to be accepted by their peers (Oberle, Schonert-Reichl, & Thomson, 2010), and optimistic mothers evince a more nurturing parenting style than their pessimistic counterparts (Taylor et al., 2012).

There is also evidence that optimism promotes physical well-being, including faster recovery from illness and injury (Ebrecht et al., 2004). For example, higher levels of optimism predicted lower rehospitalization rates among patients recovering from coronary bypass surgery (Tindle et al., 2012). Epidemiological research has shown that optimists evince lower mortality rates than pessimists (Engberg et al., 2013), including reduced risk of subsequent stroke (Kim et al., 2011) and death by cardiovascular disease (Giltay et al., 2006).

Optimism's Association with Functioning among Individuals with Disabilities

Given the evidence that optimism is associated with better psychological reactions to adversity, healthier coping, more successful goal-directed strivings, and better well-being, an important question worth asking is: How might optimism mitigate the impact of a person's impairment and reduce the likelihood of experiencing disability? In other words, how might optimism increase the ability of people with impairments to more fully engage in life activities?

Recall that the World Health Organization (2001) defined disability as a functional mismatch between a person's capabilities and the situation in which they function. This is consistent with self-regulation theory in that the impact of an impairment is determined by the extent to which it interferes with an individual's ability to pursue meaningful life goals. As we articulated previously, optimism may have important implications for people with disabilities in several ways, including psychological responses to adversity, coping, and goal-directed striving.

Optimism and Psychological Reactions to Impairment

As noted previously, optimists generally experience more positive emotions when encountering stressors. Within the framework of self-regulation theory, a stressor is a perceived interference with a goal pursuit (Lazarus, 1984). Optimists experience more positive emotions in the face of stressors because they are more likely to see the barrier as surmountable. Consistent with this, research has shown that greater optimism is associated with better psychological well-being, even during times of stress (Rand et al., 2011). Studies have typically focused on temporary stressors. People with disabilities, however, experience chronic stressors that may interfere with goals in several life domains. In this context, optimism may not be as beneficial.

Research on optimism among individuals who experience impairments is consistent with the general literature. Optimists are more likely to perceive health conditions and impairments as manageable. That is, they accept the reality of their impairment while maintaining a sense of efficacy and control over their lives. Among people who experienced an acute injury, greater optimism was associated with greater acceptance of the resulting impairment (Goertz et al., 2017; Mazur et al., 2019) while still perceiving that one can achieve important life goals, including perceiving less threat to their well-being and less discrepancy between their past selves and their current selves (Beadle et al., 2020).

Optimism also appears to be beneficial for chronic health conditions. For example, among people with hemophilia, greater optimism was associated with feeling less encumbered by their health condition (Triemstra et al., 1998). Similarly, among adolescents with impaired vision, greater optimism was associated with less worry specific to their impairment (Pinquart & Pfeiffer, 2014). Similarly, optimism in older adults with osteoarthritis was associated with perceiving fewer constraints related to their physical impairment (Sherman & Cotter, 2013).

Among people with autoimmune disorders (e.g., arthritis, lupus, multiple sclerosis [MS]), greater optimism was associated with more positive beliefs in their ability to manage their illness and control their lives (Karademas et al., 2017). One autoimmune disorder, MS, results in severe impairment. MS involves deterioration of the nerves in the central nervous system, resulting in impaired motor movement and vision. Among people with MS, greater optimism was associated with greater self-efficacy for managing this health condition, greater perceived control, and less hopelessness (Calandri et al., 2018; Wilski et al., 2020).

Among people with health conditions, optimism's benefits are not limited to appraisals of their specific impairment. Optimism also allows people to make healthier appraisals of stressors more generally. For example, greater optimism among individuals diagnosed with schizophrenia was associated with less overall perceived stress (Seo & Lim, 2019).

Optimism and Coping among Individuals with Impairments

After the initial psychological reactions to adversity, people initiate behaviors to cope with the stressor. Although there are many coping strategies, people who focus on actively navigating around the goal blockage tend to be more adaptive than people who avoid the stressor. Research among people with disabilities suggests that optimism is associated with greater use of more adaptive forms of coping and less use of avoidant coping. For example, for people with traumatic brain injuries, greater optimism was associated with greater use of adaptive coping strategies, such as positive reinterpretation, growth, and humor (Tomberg et al., 2007). Similarly, among people with impaired vision, optimism was associated with greater use of active coping, including problem-focused coping (Goertz et al., 2017).

Among people with MS, greater optimism was associated with more engagement in self-management behaviors (Wilski et al., 2020). Optimism has also been associated with greater use of problem-focused coping among people with rheumatoid arthritis, ultimately leading to better psychological adjustment (Brenner et al., 1994). Among people with multiple chemical sensitivities, greater optimism was associated with greater use of positive reinterpretation coping and less use of behavioral disengagement, a form of avoidance (Davis et al., 1998).

Enlisting the support of others is also an adaptive coping strategy for managing psychological distress and overcoming obstacles (Cohen & Wills, 1985). Optimism is linked to increased use of social support among people with impairments. For example, optimists with osteoarthritis experienced more social support and less social strain than their pessimistic peers (Luger, Cotter, & Sherman, 2009). Similarly, among people with Crohn's disease and ulcerative colitis, optimists were more likely to cope by enlisting the support of others and less likely to be emotionally preoccupied with their health condition (Flett et al., 2011). Among people with psychiatric disorders, optimism has been shown to predict greater use of positive religious coping and less use of negative religious coping (Warren et al., 2015).

Optimism and Goal-Directed Strivings

Due to their positive psychological reactions to stressors and adaptive coping strategies, optimists should experience more successful goal-directed strivings than pessimists. That is, optimists should show improved functioning compared to pessimists. Research supports the positive link between optimism and functioning in the context of experiences of impairment. For example, among people with Crohn's disease and ulcerative colitis, greater optimism was associated with better physical functioning in the context of disease (Flett et al., 2011). In patients with a spinal cord injury, optimists showed greater independence in performing activities of daily living (Hodel et al., 2020). Among people with MS, greater optimism was associated with less pain-related interference with daily functioning (Tree,

2010). Greater optimism was associated with greater physical functioning six months later in people with Type 1 Diabetes (de Ridder, Fournier, & Bensing, 2004). In adults with traumatic brain injuries (TBIs), greater optimism was associated with greater post-TBI cognitive functioning (Lee et al., 2019). Finally, in patients with inflammatory bowel disease, greater optimism was associated with less impairment and greater general functioning (Costa et al., 2019).

One important life goal for many people is to work. Among people with cystic fibrosis, greater optimism predicted the ability to work more hours (Burker et al., 2004). For people with impaired vision, greater optimism has been associated with greater functional ability (Ben-Zur & Debi, 2005) and increased likelihood of being employed (Goertz et al., 2017). A prospective study of over 38,000 workers in Finland found that optimists were less likely to experience disability related to depression over a four-year period (Kronström et al., 2011).

Optimism and Well-being

Ultimately, the result of optimism's positive influence on the self-regulation process should be better overall well-being. Research among people with impairments suggests that greater optimism is associated with better well-being, including better psychological adjustment and better relationships with others. For example, greater optimism among people with chronic impairments is associated with greater psychological well-being, including fewer negative emotions among people with hemophilia (Triemstra et al., 1998). Among people with vision impairment, greater optimism was associated with more positive emotional experiences, greater life satisfaction, and better mental health (Goertz et al., 2017; Kurtovic & Ivancic, 2019).

Among people with Parkinson's disease, greater optimism was associated with a greater sense of well-being and less psychological distress (Gison et al., 2014, 2015). Similarly, among people with MS, optimists experienced a greater sense of self-efficacy and coherence and less psychological distress (Brown et al., 2009; Calandri et al., 2018). In people with arthritic conditions, optimism is associated with better psychological adjustment, including greater life satisfaction, better self-esteem, and fewer depressive symptoms (Luger et al., 2009; Sherman & Cotter, 2013). The association between optimism and well-being has been found in a wide range of people with disability or serious health conditions, including people with Crohn's disease and ulcerative colitis (Munson et al., 2009), patients with muscular dystrophy (Graham et al., 2014), patients with systemic lupus erythematosus (Azizoddin et al., 2017), and individuals with pulmonary hypertension (Aguirre-Camacho & Moreno-Jiménez, 2018).

Given that Scheier and Carver's (1985) model of optimism is cognitive in nature, it is natural to wonder if impairments in mental functioning might also reduce optimism's salubrious effects. However, research among people with cognitive and emotional disabilities suggests that optimism continues to confer benefits. For example, among adolescents with cognitive impairments (i.e., learning disability or intellectual disability), greater optimism predicted greater life satisfaction, even when accounting for other variables thought to be associated with psychological well-being, such as hope and self-determination (Shogren et al., 2006). In a study of people with psychiatric conditions, namely psychotic disorders, greater optimism was associated with less psychological distress and greater life satisfaction (Warren et al., 2015). For people with schizophrenia, greater optimism was associated with greater life satisfaction and less perceived stress (Seo & Lim, 2019). Indeed, a large meta-analysis examining the relationships between optimism and various psychiatric symptoms found that optimism was negatively associated with depressive symptoms, anxiety symptoms, obsessive-compulsive symptoms, and symptoms of posttraumatic stress disorder (Alarcon et al., 2013)

Optimism is also related to better psychological functioning in the aftermath of body-altering surgery or traumatic injury. In a study of Norwegian patients who had recently suffered spinal cord injuries or severe traumas, those with greater optimism at admission were less likely to experience psychological distress during their hospital stay (Quale & Schanke, 2010). Similarly, among people with full paralysis of their lower limbs due to a traffic accident, greater optimism was associated with fewer depressive symptoms (Mazur et al., 2019). Among people who had lost limb function (i.e., paraplegia or quadriplegia), greater optimism was associated with higher perceptions of one's physical well-being and mental health (Rostowska & Kossak, 2011). Similarly, optimists who had limb amputations experienced fewer depressive symptoms, greater perceived control, and higher self-esteem than their pessimistic peers (Dunn, 1996).

Even when the brain itself is injured, optimistic cognitions are associated with better psychological well-being. For people who experienced TBIs, those with greater optimism experienced less psychological distress, including less irritability and fewer depressive symptoms (Peleg et al., 2009; Ramanathan et al., 2011). In addition, optimistic people with TBI had better current self-concepts and perceived less discrepancy in well-being between their former and current selves (Beadle et al., 2020).

There is emerging evidence that optimism is associated with better interpersonal relationships among people with impairments. For example, optimistic people with vision impairments perceived greater support from family, friends, and coworkers than their pessimistic peers (Kurtović &

Ivančić, 2019). Similarly, greater optimism was associated with less loneliness among college students with learning disorders (Feldman et al., 2016). Finally, among older adults with osteoarthritis, greater optimism was related to greater perceived social support (Luger et al., 2009).

Optimism and Caregivers of People with Impairments

Thus far we have reviewed the evidence that optimism is associated with benefits for individuals with impairments, reducing the likelihood and extent of experiencing disability. It is also worth wondering if optimism confers benefits to caregivers of people with disabilities. This is important because research shows that caregivers experience chronic stress and negative outcomes related to their caregiving activities. For example, two meta-analyses found that caregivers are at greater risk for physical health problems compared to non-caregivers and are more likely to experience psychological distress (Pinquart & Sörensen, 2007; Vitaliano, Zhang, & Scanlan, 2003).

Parenting children is an inherently stressful experience, especially when the children have or are at risk for disability (Lach et al., 2009). Personal factors of the parents, such as optimism, may mitigate the stress of caring for their child. For example, children with obstetrical brachial plexus injuries have damage to the nerves that control their arms resulting in partial or complete paralysis of the arm. Optimistic mothers of children with obstetrical brachial plexus injuries had better psychological adjustment (McLean et al., 2004).

Optimism has been shown to be an important predictor of well-being, positive parental feelings, and marital adjustment among parents of children with developmental delays and intellectual disability (Baker, Blacher, & Olsson, 2005; Kurtz-Nelson & McIntyre, 2017). For example, greater optimism predicted fewer depressive symptoms among mothers of children with intellectual disability (Zeedyk & Blacher, 2017). Similarly, greater optimism predicted less psychological distress and better overall psychological well-being among parents of children with autism spectrum disorders (Blacher & Baker, 2019; Tam, 2017).

Specifically, optimism appears to buffer the deleterious effects of the stress of caring for children with disability. For example, maternal optimism moderated the relationship between child behavioral problems and maternal psychological well-being (Baker et al., 2005). For optimistic mothers, more child behavioral problems were not related to greater distress or marital adjustment. Pessimistic mothers, in contrast, experienced increases in distress and decreases in marital adjustment as their child's behavioral problems increased (Baker et al., 2005).

A possible explanation for this finding is that parental optimism may engender more positive expectations for family interactions, leading to greater use of adaptive coping and positive parenting strategies. In support of this, Ekas and colleagues (Ekas et al., 2016) found that among mothers of children with autism, greater optimism predicted greater perception of family closeness and involvement, which predicted less maternal depression. Similarly, in a study of Hispanic parents of children with ASD, greater parental optimism predicted greater use of positive coping and less avoidance, which in turn predicted less depression (Willis et al., 2016). Among parents of children with developmental disabilities, including ASD, greater parental optimism was associated with greater perceived social support and more adaptive coping (Ekas et al., 2015; Slattery et al., 2017). These more adaptive coping approaches appear to be linked with more positive parenting. In a longitudinal study of 232 families of children with risk factors, including developmental delay, initial levels of maternal optimism predicted positive parenting three years later (Ellingsen et al., 2014).

The beneficial associations of parental optimism appear to persist even as children with disabilities become adults. For example, among parents of individuals with autism spectrum disorders transitioning into young adulthood, greater parental optimism was associated with less caregiver burnout, better caregiver health, and better-perceived transition experiences (Wong, McGrew, & Ruble, 2020). In contrast, lower parental optimism was associated with less use of positive coping, leading to less adaptive family outcomes. Similarly, among mothers of adult children with Down syndrome, schizophrenia, or autism, optimism was associated with better mental and physical health for the mother (Greenberg et al., 2004).

Caregiver optimism appears to benefit the individuals receiving support. For example, among caregivers of patients with rheumatoid arthritis, greater caregiver optimism was associated with greater self-efficacy and less perceived disability among patients (Beckham et al., 1995). Among children with Fragile X Syndrome, a genetic disorder that results in intellectual impairment, lower levels of maternal optimism were associated with increased negative affect in the children (Tonnsen et al., 2014).

The benefits of caregiver optimism are not limited to parents. Research also suggests that optimism protects spouses who care for individuals with impairments. For example, Lyons and colleagues (Lyons et al., 2009) conducted a decade-long study examining the link between optimism and role strain in spouses of people with Parkinson's disease. They found that initially optimistic caregiving spouses were less likely to experience worry, tension, and role strain 10 years later. Even in the mid of chronic and increasing stressors, optimism appears to proffer protection for caregivers.

Future Directions

Extant research suggests that optimism mitigates the impact of impairment on people's reactions to adversity, coping behaviors, goal-directed strivings, and well-being. This allows people with impairments to be more active in their lives and reduces the risk of disability. However, several questions merit asking. First, can optimism of people with cognitive impairments be measured validly through self-report? Initial evidence suggests that it can. For example, use of the LOT-R in adolescents with and without cognitive impairment yielded comparable results (Shogren et al., 2006). However, the internal consistency was lower among participants with cognitive impairment. More work is needed to establish the reliability and validity of optimism measures among people experiencing cognitive impairments.

Second, are optimism and pessimism separate constructs? Some have argued they are (e.g., Chang et al., 1994) and that when assessed separately, they predict different outcomes (e.g., Treharne et al., 2007). More research is needed clarifying the underlying structure of optimism and pessimism among people with impairments.

Third, are the benefits of optimism unique? Positive psychology is a relatively new area of inquiry. Several personal strength constructs, such as optimism, hope, and self-efficacy, share overlapping concepts and have similar patterns of associations with important outcomes (see Rand, 2018). Hence, it is important to determine the unique roles that optimism plays in reactions to adversity, coping, goal-related performance, and overall well-being.

Fourth, is optimism an unalloyed good? There may be instances where greater optimism is maladaptive. Under certain circumstances optimism has predicted poorer goal-directed performance (e.g., Hmieleski & Baron, 2009). Being unrealistically optimistic may be as maladaptive as being pessimistic. For example, among adolescent girls at risk for HIV infection, greater optimism was associated with reduced likelihood of getting tested for HIV (Goodman, Chesney, & Tipton, 1995). More research is needed examining the potential deleterious consequences of optimism, especially among people with impairments.

Finally, can optimism be changed? Research suggests that optimism is strongly influenced by genetics and early childhood experiences (Carver & Scheier, 2002; Plomin et al., 1992). However, initial research suggests that optimism can be increased. For example, a group cognitive-behavioral intervention increased optimism among people recently diagnosed with MS (Calandri et al., 2017). In addition, a brief intervention among first-year college students with learning disabilities temporarily increased their optimism (Rosenstreich et al., 2015). These studies are consistent with research on psychotherapy showing that people's attitudes change in response to interventions, such as cognitive-behavioral therapy (Cuijpers et al., 2010).

CONCLUSION

Optimism appears to be an important determinant of reactions to adversity, coping, goal-directed strivings, and overall well-being. Given the stressors associated with impairments, optimism is likely an important determinant how fully people with impairments can participate in their lives. Although more work is needed, initial findings suggest the beneficial influences of optimism appear to apply to individuals with impairments and their caregivers, reducing the likelihood of experiencing disability.

REFERENCES

Abramson, L. Y., Metalsky, G. I., & Alloy, L. B. (1989). Hopelessness depression: A theory-based subtype of depression. *Psychological Review, 96*(2), 358–372. doi: 10.1037/0033-295x.96.2.358

Aguirre-Camacho, A., & Moreno-Jiménez, B. (2018). Depression and anxiety in patients with pulmonary hypertension: The role of life satisfaction and optimism. *Psychosomatics, 59*(6), 575–583. doi: 10.1016/j.psym.2018.04.002

Alarcon, G. M., Bowling, N. A., & Khazon, S. (2013). Great expectations: A meta-analytic examination of optimism and hope. *Personality and Individual Differences, 54*(7), 821–827. doi: 10.1016/j.paid.2012.12.004

Andersson, M. A. (2012). Dispositional optimism and the emergence of social network diversity. *The Sociological Quarterly, 53*(1), 92–115. doi: 10.1111/j.1533-8525.2011.01227.x

Aspinwall, L. G., & Taylor, S. E. (1992). Modeling cognitive adaptation: A longitudinal investigation of the impact of individual differences and coping on college adjustment and performance. *Journal of Personality and Social Psychology, 63*(6), 989–1003. doi: 10.1037/0022-3514.63.6.989

Assad, K. K., Donnellan, M. B., & Conger, R. D. (2007). Optimism: An enduring resource for romantic relationships. *Journal of Personality and Social Psychology, 93*(2), 285. doi: 10.1037/0022-3514.93.2.285

Ayyash-Abdo, H. (2010). Subjective well-being during political violence and uncertainty: A study of college youth in lebanon. *Applied Psychology: Health and Well-Being, 2*(3), 340–361. doi: 10.1111/j.1758-0854.2010.01038.x

Azizoddin, D. R., Zamora-Racaza, G., Ormseth, S. R., Sumner, L. A., Cost, C., Ayeroff, J. R., . . . Nicassio, P. M. (2017). Psychological factors that link socioeconomic status to depression/anxiety in patients with systemic lupus erythematosus. *Journal of Clinical Psychology in Medical Settings, 24*(3–4), 302–315. doi: 10.1007/s10880-017-9505-z

Baker, B. L., Blacher, J., & Olsson, M. B. (2005). Preschool children with and without developmental delay: Behaviour problems, parents' optimism and well-being. *Journal of Intellectual Disability Research, 49*(8), 575–590. doi: 10.1111/j.1365-2788.2005.00691.x

Beadle, E. J., Ownsworth, T., Fleming, J., & Shum, D. H. K. (2020). Personality characteristics and cognitive appraisals associated with self-discrepancy after severe traumatic brain injury. *Neuropsychological Rehabilitation, 30*(3), 393–411. doi: 10.1080/09602011.2018.1469416

Beckham, J. C., Burker, E. J., Rice, J. R., & Talton, S. L. (1995). Patient predictors of caregiver burden, optimism, and pessimism in rheumatoid arthritis. *Behavioral Medicine, 20*(4), 171–178. doi: 10.1080/08964289.1995.9933734

Blacher, J., & Baker, B. L. (2019). Collateral effects of youth disruptive behavior disorders on mothers' psychological distress: Adolescents with Autism Spectrum Disorder, intellectual disability, or typical development. *Journal of Autism and Developmental Disorders, 49*(7), 2810–2821. doi: 10.1007/s10803-017-3347-2

Brown, R. F., Valpiani, E. M., Tennant, C. C., Dunn, S. M., Sharrock, M., Hodgkinson, S., & Pollard, J. D. (2009). Longitudinal assessment of anxiety, depression, and fatigue in people with multiple sclerosis. *Psychology and Psychotherapy: Theory, Research and Practice, 82*(1), 41–56. doi: 10.1348/147608308X345614

Burker, E. J., Sedway, J., & Carone, S. (2004). Psychological and educational factors: Better predictors of work status than FEV1 in adults with cystic fibrosis. *Pediatric Pulmonology, 38*(5), 413–418. doi: 10.1002/ppul.20090

Calandri, E., Graziano, F., Borghi, M., & Bonino, S. (2017). Improving the quality of life and psychological well-being of recently diagnosed multiple sclerosis patients: Preliminary evaluation of a group-based cognitive behavioral intervention. *Disability and Rehabilitation: An International, Multidisciplinary Journal, 39*(15), 1474–1481. doi: 10.1080/09638288.2016.1198430

Calandri, E., Graziano, F., Borghi, M., & Bonino, S. (2018). Depression, positive and negative affect, optimism and health-related quality of life in recently diagnosed multiple sclerosis patients: The role of identity, sense of coherence, and self-efficacy. *Journal of Happiness Studies: An Interdisciplinary Forum on Subjective Well-Being, 19*(1), 277–295. doi: 10.1007/s10902-016-9818-x

Carver, C. S., Pozo-Kaderman, C., Harris, S. D., Noriega, V., Scheier, M. F., Robinson, D. S., . . . Clark, K. C. (1994). Optimism versus pessimism predicts the quality of women's adjustment to early stage breast cancer. *Cancer, 73*(4), 1213–1220. doi: 10.1002/1097-0142(19940215)73:4<1213::aid-cncr2820730415>3.0.co;2-q.

Carver, C. S., & Scheier, M. F. (1998). *On the self-regulation of behavior.* New York: Cambridge University Press.

Carver, C. S., & Scheier, M. F. (2002). Optimism. In C. R. Snyder & S. J. Lopez (Eds.), *Handbook of positive psychology.* (pp. 231–243). New York: Oxford University Press.

Chang, E. C., D'Zurilla, T. J., & Maydeu-Olivares, A. (1994). Assessing the dimensionality of optimism and pessimism using a multimeasure approach. *Cognitive Therapy and Research, 18*(2), 143–160. doi: 10.1007/bf02357221

Chemers, M. M., Hu, L.-t., & Garcia, B. F. (2001). Academic self-efficacy and first year college student performance and adjustment. *Journal of Educational Psychology, 93*(1), 55–64. doi: 10.1037/0022-0663.93.1.55

Chemers, M. M., Watson, C. B., & May, S. T. (2000). Dispositional affect and leadership effectiveness: A comparison of self-esteem, optimism, and efficacy. *Personality and Social Psychology Bulletin, 26*(3), 267–277. doi: 10.1177/0146167200265001

Cohen, S., & Wills, T. A. (1985). Stress, social support, and the buffering hypothesis. *Psychological Bulletin, 98*(2), 310–357. doi: 10.1037/0033-2909.98.2.310

Costa, J. M., Matos, D., Arroja, B., Gonçalves, R., & Soares, J. B. (2019). The main determinants of disability in IBD and its relationship to optimism. *Revista Espanola de Enfermedades Digestivas 111*(8), 579–585. doi: 10.17235/reed.2019.6033/2018

Cuijpers, P., van Straten, A., Schuurmans, J., van Oppen, P., Hollon, S. D., & Andersson, G. (2010). Psychotherapy for chronic major depression and dysthymia: A meta-analysis. *Clinical Psychology Review, 30*(1), 51–62. doi: 10.1016/j.cpr.2009.09.003

Davis, T. H., Jason, L. A., & Banghart, M. A. (1998). The effect of housing on individuals with multiple chemical sensitivities. *The Journal of Primary Prevention, 19*(1), 31–42. doi: 10.1023/a:1022613324456

Dunn, D. S. (1996). Well-being following amputation: Salutary effects of positive meaning, optimism, and control. *Rehabilitation Psychology, 41*(4), 285–302. doi: 10.1037/0090-5550.41.4.285

Ebrecht, M., Hextall, J., Kirtley, L.-G., Taylor, A., Dyson, M., & Weinman, J. (2004). Perceived stress and cortisol levels predict speed of wound healing in healthy male adults. *Psychoneuroendocrinology, 29*(6), 798–809. doi: 10.1016/S0306-4530(03)00144-6

Ekas, N. V., Ghilain, C., Pruitt, M., Celimli, S., Gutierrez, A., & Alessandri, M. (2016). The role of family cohesion in the psychological adjustment of non-Hispanic White and Hispanic mothers of children with autism spectrum disorder. *Research in Autism Spectrum Disorders, 21*, 10–24. doi: 10.1016/j.rasd.2015.09.002

Ekas, N. V., Timmons, L., Pruitt, M., Ghilain, C., & Alessandri, M. (2015). The power of positivity: Predictors of relationship satisfaction for parents of children with autism spectrum disorder. *Journal of Autism and Developmental Disorders, 45*(7), 1997–2007. doi: 10.1007/s10803-015-2362-4

Ellingsen, R., Baker, B. L., Blacher, J., & Crnic, K. (2014). Resilient parenting of children at developmental risk across middle childhood. *Research in Developmental Disabilities, 35*(6), 1364–1374. doi: 10.1016/j.ridd.2014.03.016

Engberg, H., Jeune, B., Andersen-Ranberg, K., Martinussen, T., Vaupel, J. W., & Christensen, K. (2013). Optimism and survival: does an optimistic outlook predict better survival at advanced ages? A twelve-year follow-up of Danish nonagenarians. *Aging Clinical and Experimental Research, 25*(5), 517–525. doi: 10.1007/s40520-013-0122-x

Feather, N. T. (1982). *Expectations and actions: Expectancy-value models in psychology* (N. T. Feather Ed.). Hillsdale, NJ: Erlbaum.

Feldman, D. B., Davidson, O. B., Ben-Naim, S., Maza, E., & Margalit, M. (2016). Hope as a mediator of loneliness and academic self-efficacy among students with and without learning disabilities during the transition to college. *Learning Disabilities Research & Practice, 31*(2), 63–74. doi: 10.1111/ldrp.12094

Flett, G. L., Baricza, C., Gupta, A., Hewitt, P. L., & Endler, N. S. (2011). Perfectionism, psychosocial impact and coping with irritable bowel disease: A study of patients with crohn's disease and ulcerative colitis. *Journal of Health Psychology, 16*(4), 561–571. doi: 10.1177/1359105310383601

Giltay, E. J., Zitman, F. G., & Kromhout, D. (2006). Dispositional optimism and the risk of depressive symptoms during 15 years of follow-up: the Zutphen Elderly Study. *Journal of Affective Disorders, 91*(1), 45–52. doi: 10.1016/j.jad.2005.12.027

Gison, A., Dall'Armi, V., Donati, V., Rizza, F., & Giaquinto, S. (2014). Dispositional optimism, depression, disability and quality of life in Parkinson's disease. *Functional Neurology, 29*(2), 113–119. doi: 10.11138/fneur/2015.30.2.105

Gison, A., Rizza, F., Bonassi, S., Donati, V., & Giaquinto, S. (2015). Effects of dispositional optimism on quality of life, emotional distress and disability in Parkinson's disease outpatients under rehabilitation. *Functional Neurology, 30*(2), 105–111. doi: 10.11138/fneur/2015.30.2.105

Goertz, Y. H. H., Houkes, I., Nijhuis, F. J. N., & Bosma, H. (2017). Factors associated with participation on the competitive labour market of people with visual impairments in The Netherlands. *Work: Journal of Prevention, Assessment & Rehabilitation, 58*(3), 251–261. doi: 10.3233/WOR-172629

Goodman, E., Chesney, M. A., & Tipton, A. C. (1995). Relationship of optimism, knowledge, attitudes, and beliefs to use of HIV antibody testing by at-risk female adolescents. *Psychosomatic Medicine, 57*(6), 541–546. doi: 10.1097/00006842-199511000-00006

Graham, C. D., Weinman, J., Sadjadi, R., Chalder, T., Petty, R., Hanna, M. G., . . . Rose, M. R. (2014). A multicentre postal survey investigating the contribution of illness perceptions, coping and optimism to quality of life and mood in adults with muscle disease. *Clinical Rehabilitation, 28*(5), 508–519. doi: 10.1177/0269215513511340

Greenberg, J. S., Seltzer, M. M., Krauss, M. W., Chou, R. J.-A., & Hong, J. (2004). The effect of quality of the relationship between mothers and adult children with schizophrenia, autism, or down syndrome on maternal well-being: The mediating role of optimism. *American Journal of Orthopsychiatry, 74*(1), 14–25. doi: 10.1037/0002-9432.74.1.14

Hmieleski, K. M., & Baron, R. A. (2009). Entrepreneurs' optimism and new venture performance: A social cognitive perspective. *Academy of Management Journal, 52*(3), 473–488. doi: 10.5465/AMJ.2009.41330755

Hodel, J., Ehrmann, C., Stucki, G., Bickenbach, J. E., & Prodinger, B. (2020). Examining the complexity of functioning in persons with spinal cord injury attending first rehabilitation in Switzerland using structural equation modelling. *Spinal Cord, 58*(5), 570–580. doi: 10.1038/s41393-020-0428-4

Karademas, E. C., Ktistaki, G., Dimitraki, G., Papastefanakis, E., Mastorodemos, V., Repa, A., . . . Simos, P. (2017). Patient and partner dispositional optimism as a long-term predictor of illness representations in autoimmune diseases. *Journal of Health Psychology, 22*(13), 1691–1700. doi: 10.1177/1359105316633287

Kim, E. S., Park, N., & Peterson, C. (2011). Dispositional optimism protects older adults from stroke: The health and retirement study. *Stroke, 42*(10), 2855–2859. doi: 10.1161/STROKEAHA.111.613448

Kronström, K., Karlsson, H., Nabi, H., Oksanen, T., Salo, P., Sjösten, N., . . . Vahtera, J. (2011). Optimism and pessimism as predictors of work disability with a diagnosis of depression: A prospective cohort study of onset and recovery. *Journal of Affective Disorders, 130*(1–2), 294–299. doi: 10.1016/j.jad.2010.10.003

Kurtović, A., & Ivančić, H. (2019). Predictors of depression and life satisfaction in visually impaired people. *Disability and Rehabilitation, 41*(9), 1012–1023. doi: 10.1080/09638288.2017.1417497

Kurtz-Nelson, E., & McIntyre, L. L. (2017). Optimism and positive and negative feelings in parents of young children with developmental delay. *Journal of Intellectual Disability Research, 61*(7), 719–725. doi: 10.1111/jir.12378

Lach, L. M., Kohen, D. E., Garner, R. E., Brehaut, J. C., Miller, A. R., Klassen, A. F., & Rosenbaum, P. L. (2009). The health and psychosocial functioning of caregivers of children with neurodevelopmental disorders. *Disability and Rehabilitation: An International, Multidisciplinary Journal, 31*(9), 741–752. doi: 10.1080/08916930802354948

Lazarus, R. S., & Folkman, Susan. (1984). *Stress, appraisal, and coping.* New York: Springer.

Lee, E., Jayasinghe, N., Swenson, C., & Dams-O'Connor, K. (2019). Dispositional optimism and cognitive functioning following traumatic brain injury. *Brain Injury, 33*(8), 985–990. doi: 10.1080/02699052.2019.1606448

Litt, M. D., Tennen, H., Affleck, G., & Klock, S. (1992). Coping and cognitive factors in adaptation to in vitro fertilization failure. *Journal of Behavioral Medicine, 15*(2), 171–187. doi: 10.1007/BF00848324

Luger, T., Cotter, K. A., & Sherman, A. M. (2009). It's all in how you view it: Pessimism, social relations, and life satisfaction in older adults with osteoarthritis. *Aging & Mental Health, 13*(5), 635–647. doi: 10.1080/13607860802534633

Lyons, K. S., Stewart, B. J., Archbold, P. G., & Carter, J. H. (2009). Optimism, pessimism, mutuality, and gender: Predicting 10-year role strain in Parkinson's disease spouses. *The Gerontologist, 49*(3), 378–387. doi: 10.1093/geront/gnp046

Mazur, A., Sojka, A., Stachyra-Sokulska, A., & Łukasiewicz, J. (2019). The role of individual predispositions in coping with the sudden loss of mobility caused by a traffic accident. *Acta Neuropsychologica, 17*(2), 151–165.

McLean, L. A., Harvey, D. H. P., Pallant, J. F., Bartlett, J. R., & Mutimer, K. L. A. (2004). Adjustment of mothers of children with obstetrical brachial plexus injuries: Testing a risk and resistance model. *Rehabilitation Psychology, 49*(3), 233–240. doi: 10.1037/0090-5550.49.3.233

Munson, G. W., Wallston, K. A., Dittus, R. S., Speroff, T., & Roumie, C. L. (2009). Activation and perceived expectancies: Correlations with health outcomes among veterans with inflammatory bowel disease. *Journal of General Internal Medicine, 24*(7), 809–815. doi: 10.1007/s11606-009-1002-0

Nes, L. S., Carlson, C. R., Crofford, L. J., de Leeuw, R., & Segerstrom, S. C. (2011). Individual differences and self-regulatory fatigue: Optimism, conscientiousness, and self-consciousness. *Personality and Individual Differences, 50(4),* 475–480. doi: 10.1016/j.paid.2010.11.011

Nes, L. S., Evans, D. R., & Segerstrom, S. C. (2009). Optimism and college retention: Mediation by motivation, performance, and adjustment. *Journal of Applied Social Psychology, 39*(8), 1887–1912. doi: 10.1111/j.1559-1816.2009.00508.x

Nes, L. S., & Segerstrom, S. C. (2006). Dispositional optimism and coping: A meta-analytic review. *Personality and Social Psychology Review, 10*(3), 235–251. doi: 10.1207/s15327957pspr1003_3

Oberle, E., Schonert-Reichl, K. A., & Thomson, K. C. (2010). Understanding the link between social and emotional well-being and peer relations in early adolescence: Gender-specific predictors of peer acceptance. *Journal of Youth and Adolescence, 39*(11), 1330–1342. doi: 10.1007/s10964-009-9486-9

Peleg, G., Barak, O., Harel, Y., Rochberg, J., & Hoofien, D. (2009). Hope, dispositional optimism and severity of depression following traumatic brain injury. *Brain Injury, 23*(10), 800–808. doi: 10.1080/02699050903196696

Pinquart, M., & Pfeiffer, J. P. (2014). Worry in adolescents with visual impairment. *British Journal of Visual Impairment, 32*(2), 94–107. doi: 10.1177/0264619613511617

Pinquart, M., & Sörensen, S. (2007). Correlates of physical health of informal caregivers: A meta-analysis. *The Journals of Gerontology: Series B: Psychological Sciences and Social Sciences, 62B*(2), P126–P137. doi: 10.1093/geronb/62.2.p126

Plomin, R., Scheier, M. F., Bergeman, C. S., & Pedersen, N. L. (1992). Optimism, pessimism and mental health: A twin/adoption analysis. *Personality and Individual Differences, 13*(8), 921–930. doi: 10.1016/0191-8869(92)90009-e

Quale, A. J., & Schanke, A.-K. (2010). Resilience in the face of coping with a severe physical injury: A study of trajectories of adjustment in a rehabilitation setting. *Rehabilitation Psychology, 55*(1), 12–22. doi: 10.1037/a0018415

Ramanathan, D. M., Wardecker, B. M., Slocomb, J. E., & Hillary, F. G. (2011). Dispositional optimism and outcome following traumatic brain injury. *Brain Injury, 25*(4), 328–337. doi: 10.3109/02699052.2011.554336

Rand, K. L. (2009). Hope and optimism: Latent structures and influences on grade expectancy and academic performance. *Journal of Personality, 77*(1), 231–260. doi: 10.1111/j.1467-6494.2008.00544.x

Rand, K. L. (2018). Hope, self-efficacy, and optimism: Conceptual and empirical differences. In M. W. Gallagher & S. J. Lopez (Eds.), *The Oxford handbook of hope* (pp. 45–58). New York: Oxford University Press.

Rand, K. L., Martin, Allison, D., & Shea, Amanda M. (2011). Hope, but not optimism, predicts academic performance of law students beyond previous academic achievement. *Journal of Research in Personality, 45*(6), 683–686. doi: 10.1016/j.jrp.2011.08.004

Rosenstreich, E., Feldman, D. B., Davidson, O. B., Maza, E., & Margalit, M. (2015). Hope, optimism and loneliness among first-year college students with learning disabilities: A brief longitudinal study. *European Journal of Special Needs Education, 30*(3), 338–350. doi: 10.1080/08856257.2015.1023001

Rostowska, T., & Kossak, D. (2011). Strategies for coping with stress in patients with tetraplegia and paraplegia. *Acta Neuropsychologica, 9*(1), 31–48.

Scheier, M. F., & Carver, C. S. (1985). Optimism, coping, and health: Assessment and implications of generalized outcome expectancies. *Health Psychology: Official Journal of The Division of Health Psychology, American Psychological Association, 4*(3), 219–247. doi: 10.1037//0278-6133.4.3.219

Scheier, M. F., & Carver, C. S. (1992). Effects of optimism on psychological and physical well-being: Theoretical overview and empirical update. *Cognitive Therapy and Research, 16*(2), 201–228. doi: 10.1007/bf01173489

Scheier, M. F., Carver, C. S., & Bridges, M. W. (1994). Distinguishing optimism from neuroticism (and trait anxiety, self-mastery, and self-esteem): A reevaluation of the life orientation test. *Journal of Personality and Social Psychology, 67*(6), 1063–1078. doi: 10.1037/0022-3514.67.6.1063

Scheier, M. F., Matthews, K. A., Owens, J. F., Magovern, G. J., Sr., Lefebvre, R. C., Abbott, R. A., & Carver, C. S. (1989). Dispositional optimism and recovery from coronary artery bypass surgery: The beneficial effects on physical and psychological well-being. *Journal of Personality and Social Psychology, 57*(6), 1024–1040. doi: 10.1037//0022-3514.57.6.1024

Seo, M.-A., & Lim, Y.-J. (2019). Optimism and life satisfaction in persons with schizophrenia living in the community. *International Journal of Social Psychiatry, 65*(7–8), 615–620. doi: 10.1177/0020764019868256

Shepperd, J. A., Waters, E., Weinstein, N. D., & Klein, W. M. (2015). A primer on unrealistic optimism. *Current Directions in Psychological Science, 24,* 232–237.

Sherman, A. M., & Cotter, K. A. (2013). Well-being among older adults with OA: Direct and mediated patterns of control beliefs, optimism and pessimism. *Aging & Mental Health, 17*(5), 595–608. doi: 10.1080/13607863.2013.765831

Shogren, K. A., Lopez, S. J., Wehmeyer, M. L., Little, T. D., & Pressgrove, C. L. (2006). The role of positive psychology constructs in predicting life satisfaction in adolescents with and without cognitive disabilities: An exploratory study. *The Journal of Positive Psychology, 1*(1), 37–52. doi: 10.1080/17439760500373174

Slattery, É., McMahon, J., & Gallagher, S. (2017). Optimism and benefit finding in parents of children with developmental disabilities: The role of positive reappraisal and social support. *Research in Developmental Disabilities, 65,* 12–22. doi: 10.1016/j.ridd.2017.04.006

Tam, G. W. B. (2017). *Examining the relationships among optimism, resilience, and parenting stress of parents of children with autism spectrum disorder* [Doctoral dissertation, Northcentral University]. ProQuest Information & Learning.

Taylor, S. E., Kemeny, M. E., Aspinwall, L. G., Schneider, S. G., Rodriguez, R., & Herbert, M. (1992). Optimism, coping, psychological distress, and high-risk sexual behavior among men at risk for acquired immunodeficiency syndrome (AIDS). *Journal of Personality and Social Psychology, 63*(3), 460–473. doi: 10.1037/0022-3514.63.3.460

Taylor, Z. E., Widaman, K. F., Robins, R. W., Jochem, R., Early, D. R., & Conger, R. D. (2012). Dispositional optimism: A psychological resource for Mexican-origin mothers experiencing economic stress. *Journal of Family Psychology, 26*(1), 133. doi: 10.1037/a0026755

Thomas, J. L., Britt, T. W., Odle-Dusseau, H., & Bliese, P. D. (2011). Dispositional optimism buffers combat veterans from the negative effects of warzone stress on mental health symptoms and work impairment. *Journal of Clinical Psychology, 67*(9), 866–880. doi: 10.1002/jclp.20809

Tindle, H., Belnap, B. H., Houck, P. R., Mazumdar, S., Scheier, M. F., Matthews, K. A., . . . Rollman, B. L. (2012). Optimism, response to treatment of depression, and rehospitalization after coronary artery bypass graft surgery. *Psychosomatic Medicine, 74*(2), 200. doi: 10.1097/PSY.0b013e318244903f

Tonnsen, B. L., Cornish, K. M., Wheeler, A. C., & Roberts, J. E. (2014). Maternal predictors of anxiety risk in young males with Fragile X. *American Journal of Medical Genetics Part B: Neuropsychiatric Genetics, 165*(5), 399–409. doi: 10.1002/ajmg.b.32244

Tree, H. A. (2010). *Multiple sclerosis severity, pain intensity, and psychosocial factors: Associations with perceived social support, hope, optimism, depression, and fatigue.* [Doctoral dissertation, University of Kansas]. ProQuest Information & Learning.

Triemstra, A. H. M., Van der Ploeg, H. M., Smit, C., Briët, E., Adèr, H. J., & Rosendaal, F. R. (1998). Well-being of haemophilia patients: A model for direct and indirect effects of medical parameters on the physical and psychosocial functioning. *Social Science & Medicine, 47*(5), 581–593. doi: 10.1016/s0277-9536(98)00117-8

Van der Velden, P. G., Kleber, R. J., Fournier, M., Grievink, L., Drogendijk, A., & Gersons, B. P. (2007). The association between dispositional optimism and mental health problems among disaster victims and a comparison group: A prospective study. *Journal of Affective Disorders, 102*(1–3), 35–45. doi: 10.1016/j.jad.2006.12.004

Vitaliano, P. P., Zhang, J., & Scanlan, J. M. (2003). Is caregiving hazardous to one's physical health? A meta-analysis. *Psychological Bulletin, 129*(6), 946–972. doi: 10.1037/0033-2909.129.6.946

Warren, P., Van Eck, K., Townley, G., & Kloos, B. (2015). Relationships among religious coping, optimism, and outcomes for persons with psychiatric disabilities. *Psychology of Religion and Spirituality, 7*(2), 91–99. doi: 10.1037/a0038346

Willis, K., Timmons, L., Pruitt, M., Schneider, H. L., Alessandri, M., & Ekas, N. V. (2016). The relationship between optimism, coping, and depressive symptoms in Hispanic mothers and fathers of children with autism spectrum disorder. *Journal of Autism and Developmental Disorders, 46*(7), 2427–2440. doi: 10.1007/s10803-016-2776-7

Wilski, M., Kocur, P., Brola, W., & Tasiemski, T. (2020). Psychological factors associated with self-management in multiple sclerosis. *Acta Neurologica Scandinavica, 142*(1), 50–57. doi: 10.1111/ane.13236

Wong, V., McGrew, J., & Ruble, L. (2020). Predicting the outcomes of parents of transition-age youth or young adults with ASD. *Journal of Autism and Developmental Disorders, 50*(8), 2723–2739. doi: 10.1007/s10803-020-04362-1

World Health Organization. (2001). *International Classification of Functioning, Disability, and Health.* Geneva: WHO.

Zeedyk, S. M., & Blacher, J. (2017). Longitudinal correlates of maternal depression among mothers of children with or without intellectual disability. *American Journal on Intellectual and Developmental Disabilities, 122*(5), 374–391. doi: 10.1352/1944-7558-122.5.374.

Chapter 6

Self-Determination as a Personal Factor

Michael L. Wehmeyer

Self-determination is a foundational construct in positive psychology (Ryan & Deci, 2000) and one of the most extensively applied positive psychological constructs in the disability context (Stancliffe et al., 2020; Wehmeyer et al., 2017a). The construct's origins date back to John Locke and philosophical arguments in the Enlightenment era of the late seventeenth and early eighteenth centuries about determinism and free will (Wehmeyer et al., 2017b). The construct has been applied not only to motivational and positive psychology but to the fields of social welfare, education, and politics, among others (Biestek & Gehring, 1978; McDermott, 1975; Wehmeyer et al., 1998). The construct's alignment with the concept of autonomy facilitates its utility across these diverse fields as well as creates the situation in which different disciplines understand the construct in different ways. In social welfare, it is a principle that drives treatment practices; in motivational psychology, it is aligned with basic psychological needs; in politics, it refers to basic rights to self-governance; and in education, it has been construed as dispositional characteristic that can be taught to young people.

The intent of this chapter is to discuss issues of self-determination as a positive psychological personal factor. It is helpful to begin with conceptualizing the construct drawing from many of the aforementioned disciplines, and then identifying how it manifests as a personal factor that can promote greater well-being and life satisfaction among people with disabilities.

FOUNDATIONS FOR UNDERSTANDING SELF-DETERMINATION

As noted, self-determination was first used in reference to John Locke's proposition that human action was a function of mind, will, and/or volition.

At the heart of the meaning of the term as used by Locke was the philosophical doctrine of *determinism*, which proposes that all events, including human behavior and actions, are in some way caused. Self-determination, or self-determinism, refers to self- (versus other-) caused action. The earliest application of the construct to psychology was by Angyal (1941), who proposed that an essential feature of a psychology of personality was the fact that although we live "in a world in which things happen according to laws which are heteronomous (e.g., governed from outside)," we can "oppose self-determination to external determination" (p. 33). That is, according to Angyal, a major focus of study in personality psychology should be on autonomous-determinism, or how and why people act in self- versus other- (e.g., heteronomous-determined) ways. As conceptualized by Angyal, autonomous (as in autonomous-determinism) referred to self-governed action.

Motivational psychologists Edward Deci and Richard Ryan took the ideas formulated by Angyal into account when developing what is now known as Self-Determination Theory (SDT; Ryan & Deci, 2018). Ryan and Deci described SDT as

> centrally concerned with the social conditions that facilitate or hinder human flourishing. The theory examines how biological, social, and cultural conditions either enhance or undermine the inherent human capacities for psychological growth, engagement, and wellness. (p. 3)

Research in SDT, accordingly, "inquires into factors, both intrinsic to individual development and within social contexts, that facilitate vitality, motivation, social integration and wellbeing" (Ryan & Deci, 2018, p. 3). Within SDT, autonomy is one of the three basic psychological needs, along with competency and relatedness. The basic psychological need for autonomy "is satisfied when an individual experiences choice and volition in their action and perceives themselves to be the origin of their actions" (Wehmeyer et al., 2017b, p. 4). SDT emphasizes the importance of autonomy-as-volition versus autonomy-as-independence; autonomous actions are those that are not only or even primarily self-governed but are self-endorsed and congruent with one's values and interests (Soenens et al., 2017).

UNDERSTANDING SELF-DETERMINATION AS A PERSONAL FACTOR

As Ryan and Deci (2018) noted, SDT is principally concerned with elucidating the social conditions that facilitate or hinder human flourishing. SDT is a theory of motivation and, to that end, seeks to identify biological, social, and cultural conditions that enhance or undermine fulfillment of basic psychological needs (Ryan & Deci, 2018, p. 3). But there are applications of SDT to applied contexts, particularly education, that serve to identify how self-determination can be construed as a positive psychological personal factor. As was noted in chapter 1, the ICF defined personal factors as referring to

> the particular background of an individual's life and living and comprise features of the individual that are not part of a health condition or health states. These factors may include gender, race, age, other health conditions, fitness, lifestyle, habits, upbringing, coping styles, social background, education, profession, past and current experience (past life events and concurrent events), overall behaviour pattern and character style, individual psychological assets and other characteristics, all or any of which may play a role in disability at any level. (WHO 2001, p. 213)

SDT has a robust literature base that addresses many of these factors. However, the degree to which the construct has been applied to the disability context is much more limited, and primarily conducted in the sphere of education for students with disabilities. In the early 1990s, policy and practice in special education recognized the importance of self-determination for young people with disabilities to achieve more positive school and adult outcomes. As a result, there is a robust literature and knowledge base pertaining to the application of the self-determination construct to the education of youth and young adults with disabilities. This is, by its nature, applied, but shares common understandings of the self-determination construct with SDT and has a developmental focus that has been driven by work in SDT. The latest iteration of this work has resulted in Causal Agency Theory (Shogren, Wehmeyer, Palmer, Forber-Pratt et al., 2015), which will be discussed next, followed by a synthesis of the literature pertaining to self-determination in the disability context.

CAUSAL AGENCY THEORY

As noted, the application of the self-determination construct to the disability construct occurred first in efforts to improve educational and adult outcomes for youth with disabilities. Wehmeyer (1992a) drew from an early definition of self-determination forwarded by Deci and Ryan (1985) as "the capacity to choose and to have those choices be the determinants of one's actions" (p. 38) to examine implications of self-determination for special education. The question addressed by this work, and in the field of special education more broadly, was not as much "what is self-determination?" as "what can educators teaching students with disabilities do to promote self-determined behavior?" To that end, Wehmeyer proposed that self-determination could be considered a dispositional characteristic and self-determined behavior involved "attitudes and abilities required to act as the primary causal agent in one's life" (p. 305).

Before discussing these issues further, it is important to note that the term "self-determination" had been applied to the disability rights movement in a rights-based context. That is, the few applications of self-determination in the disability context prior to the early 1990s were in reference to the demands of people with disability for equal rights, including the "right" to self-determination (Nirje, 1972). Williams (1989) typified this, stating that

> but, without being afforded the right and opportunity to make choices in our lives, we will never obtain full, first class American citizenship. So we do not have to be told what self-determination means. We already know that it is just another word for freedom. We already know that self-determination is just another word for describing a life filled with rising expectations, dignity, responsibility, and opportunity. That it is just another word for having the chance to live the American Dream. (p. 16)

Even in the disability rights context, however, self-determination was understood as volitional action as making choices and functioning more autonomously. This empowerment focus from disability rights advocates shaped how the construct was applied in the disability context and special education.

In 2015, Shogren and colleagues proposed refinements to the theoretical and definitional framework introduced by Wehmeyer in 1992 and updated periodically over the intervening years. The result was Causal Agency Theory (Shogren, Wehmeyer, Palmer, Forber-Pratt et al., 2015), which was intended to incorporate work in positive psychology and SDT and to provide a life span model of the development of self-determination (Wehmeyer et al., 2017a). Causal Agency Theory defined self-determination as a

> dispositional characteristic manifested as acting as the causal agent in one's life. Self-determined *people* (i.e., causal agents) act in service to freely chosen goals. Self-determined *actions* function to enable a person to be the causal agent is his or her life. (Shogren, Wehmeyer, Palmer, Forber-Pratt et al., 2015, p. 258)

There are obvious influences in this definition from earlier definitions in special education, primarily the idea that self-determination is a dispositional characteristic manifested by people acting as causal agents in their lives. Shogren, Wehmeyer, Palmer, Forber-Pratt et al. defined a dispositional characteristic as "an enduring tendency used to characterize and describe differences between people; it refers to a tendency to act or think in a particular way, but presumes contextual variance (i.e., socio-contextual supports and opportunities and threats and impediments)" (p. 258). It is the application of self-determination as a dispositional characteristic in this context that most strongly highlights self-determination as a positive psychological personal factor. Young people can acquire knowledge and skills and have experiences that, in turn, enable them to become more self-determined. I will explore this in more depth in discussing the development of self-determination momentarily, but before doing so, it is important to understand the idea of *causal agency*.

One influence on the development of SDT was Richard de Charms' theory of personal causation. De Charms was an educational psychologist and thus interested in improving outcomes for students. His theory of personal causation suggested that people are *origins*—someone who perceives themselves as acting based upon their own choices—or they are *pawns*—someone who perceives that their actions are determined by external forces (de Charms, 1968). De Charms stated that "man strives to be a causal agent . . . to be the primary locus of causation for, or the origin of, his behavior; he strives for personal causation" (de Charms, 1968, p. 269).

It is easy to see linkages between Angyal's ideas of autonomous- versus heteronomous determinism in de Charms idea of origins versus pawns, and it is equally evident why de Charms' work influenced Deci and Ryan and the development of SDT. Wehmeyer (1992a) incorporated de Charms "causal agent" construct into his applied theoretical framework in special education (Wehmeyer, 1992a), and it has remained a central element of the construct's understanding in that field since. In Causal Agency Theory, Shogren et al. (2015) noted that *causal agency* implies that "it is the individual who makes or causes things to happen in his or her life." "It implies that the individual acts with an eye toward *causing* an effect to *accomplish* a *specific end* or to *cause* or *create change*" (p. 258). The use of causal agency in Causal Agency Theory reflects the important idea that not only is self-determined action a result of personal choice or volition, but it is aligned with autonomy-as-volition and not autonomy-as-independence (Soenens et al., 2017). People who are self-determined act based upon their own volition so as to make or cause things to happen in their own lives.

THE DEVELOPMENT OF SELF-DETERMINATION

One intersection between SDT and Causal Agency Theory involves the development of self-determination. Causal Agency Theory was constructed to align knowledge from SDT and positive psychology with research and practice in special education and to provide the framework for a life span approach to promoting the self-determination of people with and without disabilities (Wehmeyer et al., 2017a). Young people do not just become self-determined overnight; they become self-determined as they acquire knowledge, skills, and beliefs and engage in actions that enable them to respond to contextual and environmental challenges (i.e., opportunities or threats) that energize basic psychological needs and autonomous motivation. This, in turn, triggers a causal action sequence in which volitional and agentic actions, mediated by action-control beliefs, result in experiences of causal agency and, over time, enhanced self-determination (Palmer et al. 2017).

As noted previously, both SDT and Causal Agency Theory adopt an organismic approach to human development. That is, both frameworks share the meta-theoretical assumption that organismic aspirations drive human behavior (Little et al., 2006). This was, fundamentally, Angyal and de Charms' points: people strive to be active contributors to, or *agents* of, their own behavior; to be the origin of their own actions (Little et al., 2002). SDT and Causal Agency Theory begin with the assumption that actions are volitional and that people strive to be causal agents who use self-regulated and goal-directed agentic actions to navigate opportunities and challenges in their life.

The development of self-determination begins with the person's strivings for the fulfillment of the basic psychological needs of autonomy, competence, and relatedness. Within SDT, to be autonomous means to behave with a sense of volition, willingness, and congruence; it means to fully endorse and concur with the behavior in which one is engaged (Deci & Ryan, 2012). The basic psychological need for *autonomy* is, thus, satisfied when a person experiences choice and volition. Autonomous actions are self-endorsed and congruent with one's values and interests (Vansteenkiste et al., 2010).

The second basic psychological need in SDT is the need for *competence*, which refers not to some objective level of skill or achievement but instead to a person's need to be and feel effective within environments and to one's perceptions of competence and mastery in one's environment or the experience of perceiving increased mastery and effectiveness (Deci et al., 2013; Sheldon et al., 1996). The third basic psychological need is for *relatedness*, which refers to the need for people to feel a sense of social belonging and connectedness. The basic psychological need for relatedness refers not to physical relationships but to the need for people to feel that they belong, are cared for, and are connected to others (Hofer & Busch, 2011).

SDT proposes that people are motivated to act to meet these three basic psychological needs, which in turn energizes the development of autonomous motivation, consisting of intrinsic motivation (doing an activity because it is enjoyable) and/or internalized extrinsic motivation (doing an activity because it leads to a valued consequence separate from the activity itself) (Deci & Ryan, 2012, p. 88). There are everyday challenges and opportunities for basic psychological needs fulfillment or frustration. Those challenges or opportunities present chances to act to maintain or enhance intrinsic motivation and to fulfill or thwart the frustration of the basic psychological needs. That initiates a causal sequence in which the person engages in actions to address the opportunity or challenge.

Causal Agency Theory provides a theoretical framework within which to understand how people act to address these opportunities and challenges to fulfill or thwart the frustration of these basic psychological needs, to maintain and enhance autonomous motivation, and ultimately, to become casual agents in their lives and become more self-determined. Causal Agency Theory proposes three *essential characteristics* of self-determined action: volitional action, agentic action, and action-control beliefs (Shogren et al., 2015). *Volitional action* refers to action that is based on conscious choices that reflect one's preferences. That is, volitional actions are self-initiated and function to enable a person to act autonomously (i.e., engage in self-governed action). Importantly, volitional actions involve the *initiation* and *activation* of causal capabilities—the capacity to cause something to happen—in one's life. Such causal capabilities include choice- and decision-making skills, goal-setting and problem-solving skills, and planning skills. The initiation of volitional actions leads to the need for agentic action.

Agentic action refers to actions that are self-directed and implemented to achieve a goal. Causal Agency Theory incorporates the idea of pathways thinking from Hope Theory (Snyder et al., 2002), which suggests that people identify pathways, or engage in pathways thinking, that lead to a specific end or cause or that creates desired change. Agentic actions involve the initiation and activation of agentic capabilities, including self-management, goal-attainment, problem-solving, and self-advocacy skills. Agentic actions sustain actions initiated through the volitional action process and enable people to work toward and achieve goals they have set.

Action-control beliefs refer to three general beliefs derived from Action-Control Theory (Little et al., 2002) that are associated with the causal action sequence:

> Control expectancy [beliefs], which refers to the relation between agent and ends, meaning that individual's expectancy about their capability to achieve a given goal or end; means-ends beliefs, which represent the relation between means and ends; and agency beliefs, [which] refer to an individual's beliefs of

what means they are capable of utilizing when the self acts as an agent. (Chang et al., 2017, p. 285)

These beliefs mediate and, in turn, are strengthened by the causal action sequence involving volitional and agentic actions (Mumbardó-Adam et al., 2018).

As young children develop, they acquire skills and have experiences that enable them to respond to opportunities and threats and to become a causal agent in their lives. As they more effectively respond, motivated by basic psychological needs for autonomy, competence, and relatedness and as they implement the causal action sequence to fulfill or thwart the frustration of these needs and act as causal agents, they become more self-determined.

SELF-DETERMINATION AS A PERSONAL FACTOR AND DISABILITY

The theoretical and developmental frameworks described up to this point have driven research and intervention efforts in the disability context. This is particularly the case in activities to promote the self-determination and self-determined learning of youth and young adults with disabilities. This chapter, in particular, is interested in identifying research that links self-determination as a positive psychological personal factor with more positive life outcomes and life satisfaction. Moreover, of interest is research and practice that emphasizes personal strengths and capacities and provides evidence that people with disabilities can become more self-determined. The remainder of this chapter describes our work in promoting and enhancing the self-determination of youth and adults with disabilities as an example of how the construct serves as a personal factor.

In so doing, it is important to begin with the understanding and acknowledgment that the onus is not on people with disability to change to accommodate to environments and contexts that limit their full expression of self-determination but on society to create contexts in which people with disability have an equal opportunity to live self-determined lives. To that end, it is worth revisiting some of the points raised in chapter 1. First, within the the International Classification of Functioning, Disability, and Health or ICF (WHO, 2001) human functioning and disability are understood "as umbrella terms denoting the positive and negative aspects of functioning from a biological, individual and social perspective" (WHO, 2013, p. 5). Disability, in essence, is a function of the interaction among health conditions, environmental factors, and personal factors and their impact on activities and full participation. As we noted in chapter 1, in a concrete sense, disability within the ICF exists only when participation is impacted. Further, as noted, we defined participation as a function of a person's *self-determined involvement* in a pattern of life.

Research in the disability context has established beyond a doubt that the environments in which people with disability live, learn, work, and play limit opportunities to make choices, express preferences, and act volitionally and that these environmental and attitudinal barriers limit the opportunity of disabled people to fully participate and live self-determined lives (Stancliffe et al., 2020). Much of this research has been conducted involving people with intellectual and developmental disabilities, and findings from this body of research provide examples of the impact of environmental barriers to self-determination for disabled people as a whole. In research on choice and self-determination and people with disability, choice opportunity has been found to be the single most powerful predictor of self-determination and restrictiveness of living/working environments the most powerful predictor of limited choice (Wehmeyer & Bolding, 2001). The characteristics of far too many work and living environments available to people with disability are that they are segregated, congregate in nature, or isolating, all of which serve to limit choice opportunities. In a secondary analysis of the National Consumer Survey, Wehmeyer and Metzler (1995) found that for the majority of people with intellectual disability surveyed, someone else (other than the person with disability) chose where they lived, who their roommate was, who provided personal supports, and where they worked. Stancliffe et al. (2011) conducted an analysis of another large national dataset, the National Core Indicators, and found, similarly, that people with intellectual disability did not have the opportunity to make basic choices, including where or with whom to live.

There is clear evidence that more restrictive living and work settings limit choice opportunities for people with intellectual disability (Emerson et al., 2000). Stancliffe and Wehmeyer (1995) found that people with intellectual disability who lived in a home or apartment in their community experienced significantly more choices on a daily basis than did people with intellectual disability who lived in congregate settings (group home, institution). Wehmeyer and Bolding (1999) matched adults with intellectual disability by level of intelligence, age, and gender and examined opportunities for choice-making, autonomy, self-determination, and life satisfaction as a function of type of residence or work environment (community-based, community-based congregate, non-community-based congregate). Respondents living or working in community-based settings had significantly higher levels of choice opportunities than participants in the other more restrictive settings, higher levels of self-determination and autonomy, and more positive life satisfaction.

Heller et al. (2002) found that people with intellectual disability who had moved from a nursing home to a community setting had higher levels of adaptive behavior, community integration, and choice opportunities than people in the same sample who remained in the nursing home. Stancliffe et al. (2011) found that people living in their own home or apartment (with or without supports) were significantly more likely to have chosen whether and with whom to live than people who lived in nursing homes, institutions, or group homes. Finally, Ticha and colleagues (2012) found, among a large sample (almost 9,000 people with intellectual disability) and controlling for types of impairments, age, types of supports, communication modality, and geographic area, that people with intellectual disability who lived in congregate (16 residents or more) settings had significantly fewer opportunities to make choices than people in smaller settings, and that people had the most control over everyday choices when living in their own homes or with three or fewer residents.

More restrictive (congregate) living and work settings restrict choice opportunities and self-determination because of multiple factors, from staff density and high staff turnover to high levels of bureaucracy and excessive regulations, all of which serve to limit autonomy and choice (Duvdevany et al., 2002; Stancliffe et al., 2000). The point to make is that these are all environmental factors for which disabled people are not solely or even primarily responsible for changing. These are decisions that service systems have made in virtually every country in the world.

Acknowledging, then, that much of the work that needs to be done to promote and enhance self-determination relate to environmental factors, societal attitudes, and cultural and political actions, there are personal factors that enable people with disabilities, and indeed all people, to become more self-determined. First, research shows that participation in life events predicts enhanced self-determination and, in turn, promotes even greater participation. A common finding in the literature is that higher levels of adaptive behavior predict enhanced self-determination and more positive quality of life (QOL) and life satisfaction (Nota et al., 2007; Shogren et al., 2006). Scales of adaptive behavior fundamentally measure the degree to which a person engages in routine daily activities across multiple domains. In the education sphere, Williams-Diehm et al. (2008) showed that student participation in educational planning meetings resulted in enhanced self-determination and that higher levels of self-determination predicted greater involvement in educational planning meetings. Again, the relationship between self-determination and participation is reciprocal, with each enhancing the other.

The research shows that enhanced self-determination itself improves employment and community inclusion outcomes (Powers et al., 2012; Shogren et al., 2015) and predicts more positive QOL and life satisfaction

(Shogren et al., 2006; Wehmeyer & Schwartz, 1998). As such, it is not surprising that the development and acquisition of skills and abilities that foster volitional and agentic action promote self-determination (Shogren, Wehmeyer, & Singh, 2017). Teaching young people the skills related to problem-solving, decision-making, goal-setting, self-advocacy, and self-regulation (and providing them opportunities to practice these skills) has been shown to enhance self-determination and promote more positive school and adult outcomes (Wehmeyer & Zhao, 2020). The positive psychology movement has led to a focus on positive education (Kern & Wehmeyer, 2021) that provides a rich array of instructional and experiential strategies related to promoting well-being and flourishing, coping, character strengths, positive emotions, creativity, and self-determination.

Again, in many cases the benefits of such efforts are reciprocal; enhanced levels of and performance of volitional and agentic action enhance self-determination and enhanced self-determination, in turn, improves skills and capacities in causal action. For example, self-determination has been linked to greater success in goal-setting (DiMaggio et al., 2020)

Strengths-Based Approaches

The changing ways of understanding disability discussed in chapter 1 and illustrated by the WHO ICF have led to strengths-based approaches to disability. Strengths-based approaches "take, as a starting point, the assumptions of the social model of disability and then translate them into approaches to support, educate, or enable people with disabilities to function successfully in typical contexts" (Wehmeyer, 2021, p. 27). In our own work in the education context, we have focused on promoting self-determined learning (Wehmeyer & Zhao, 2020). Self-determined learning emphasizes full student participation in all aspects of learning, from the determination of what to learn to self-direction of learning and evaluation activities. The primary means of promoting self-determined learning in our work has been the *Self-Determined Learning Model of Instruction* (SDLMI) (Mithaug et al., 1998; Wehmeyer et al., 2000).

Mithaug and colleagues (2003, 2007) proposed a frame to guide the development of efforts to promote self-determined learning in which students act to pursue personally valued learning outcomes with expectations that they have the capacity to act as a causal agent and that if they do act, they can be successful (action-control beliefs); self-regulate a problem-solving sequence to examine priorities based upon preferences, interests, and values and prioritize action needed to reduce the discrepancy between what is known and what needs to be known and to set a goal to address that discrepancy (volitional action); create an action plan to address the goal, design a self-monitoring process; and implement the action plan, using information gathered through self-monitoring to evaluate progress toward the goal and adjusting the action plan or goal as necessary to achieve the goal (agentic action) (Wehmeyer & Zhao, 2020, p. 42).

Mithaug et al. (1998) and Wehmeyer et al. (2000) developed and evaluated a model of teaching based upon these principles called the SDLMI. The purpose of the SDLMI is to provide teachers with a model of teaching that enables them to teach and support students to self-determine learning. The model is applicable for use with students with and without disabilities (Wehmeyer & Zhao, 2020).[1] The SDLMI has a three-phase instructional process. Each phase presents a problem the student must solve (What is my Goal? What is my Plan? and What have I Learned?) by answering a series of four *Student Questions*. These questions vary in each phase to, in essence, have the student go through the same four-step problem-solving sequence:

1. Identify the problem.
2. Identify potential solutions to the problem.
3. Identify barriers to solving the problem.
4. Identify consequences of each solution.

Through the process of answering the questions in each phase, students learn a self-regulated problem-solving process. Each student question is linked to *Teacher Objectives* that provides guidance for teachers to support students to answer the questions. Finally, each teacher's objective is linked to *Educational Supports* that teachers can implement to teach or support students to answer the questions and, thus, self-regulate problem-solving to set and attain goals.

The SDLMI is constructed so that the student is the causal agent for actions in learning, from solving the problem of what to learn to setting goals to creating action plans to monitoring progress to evaluating progress and revising the action plan or goal as needed. The first time a teacher implements the model with a student, the student can reword the questions so that they have a set of questions that are their own. Although teachers are encouraged to support students to use self-regulation and self-directed learning strategies, even when an instruction to achieve a goal is teacher-directed, the student has had a meaningful voice in deciding to learn in that manner.

The SDLMI has strong evidence for its efficacy. Multiple randomized trial (RCT) studies have established a causal relationship between implementation of the SDLMI and more positive student self-determination, school, and adult outcomes. Wehmeyer, Palmer et al. (2012) conducted an RCT study of interventions to promote self-determination on the self-determination of high school students with disabilities. Students in the treatment group (*n* = 235) received instruction using the SDLMI along with other efforts to promote autonomy-supportive classrooms, while students in the control group (*n* = 132) did not. Self-determination was measured using two instruments that had been developed and validated through initiatives in the 1990s to promote the self-determination of youth with disabilities, *The Arc's Self-Determination Scale* (Wehmeyer, 1996) and the *AIR Self-Determination Scale* (Wolman et al., 1994). Measurement occurred at baseline and after two and three years of intervention. Data were analyzed using latent growth curve analysis. Findings indicated that students with disabilities who participated in interventions to promote self-determination over the three-year period showed significantly more positive gains in their overall self-determination scores than did students not exposed to interventions to promote self-determination, although most of those gains were between years 2 and 3, suggesting that promoting self-determination requires sustained effort. Shogren et al. (2020) found the same pattern when evaluating the efficacy of the SDLMI combined with a second intervention to promote student involvement in educational planning. In this RCT, students with intellectual disability showed significant gains in self-determination measured by the *Self-Determination Inventory-Student Report* (Shogren & Wehmeyer, 2016) for the second year, but not the first.

To examine outcomes related to enhanced self-determination, Shogren, Wehmeyer, Palmer, Rifenbark et al. (2015) conducted a follow-up study of the youth in the Wehmeyer, Palmer et al. (2012) study, tracking student post-school outcomes. Students in the treatment group, which had shown significant, positive gains in self-determination as a result of instruction with the SDLMI and other interventions to promote self-determination, achieved more positive post-school employment and community inclusion outcomes than did students in the control group.

In an RCT of the efficacy of the SDLMI with secondary students with disabilities, students in the treatment group who received the SDLMI became more self-determined than peers in the control group who did not (Wehmeyer et al., 2012). Students in the treatment group in this study also had more positive educational goal-attainment outcomes and were more positively engaged in classroom activities (Shogren et al., 2012). Shogren et al. (2019) conducted an RCT with youth with cognitive disabilities who set goals using the SDLMI, determining that students attained educational and transition goals at higher rates after receiving instruction with the SDLMI. Lee et al. (2015) conducted a meta-analysis of single-case design students of the SDLMI, determining that the intervention had benefits for students in academic and job training settings.

Finally, several studies of the SDLMI in South Korea provide evidence of its efficacy. Seo et al. (2014) demonstrated that students who received instruction with the SDLMI had higher levels of academic goal-attainment than students who did not, while Lee and Wehmeyer (2008) conducted a meta-analysis of research in Korean journals on the SDLMI and found positive educational benefits in goal-attainment to students from teachers using the SDLMI.

Role of Technology

Before leaving the topic of self-determination and disability, it is clear that technology has and will play an important role in enhancing adaptive functioning, self-determination, and participation for people with disabilities. There are myriad ways in which technology can support people to function successfully in typical environments and, in turn, to be able to act in a self-determined manner. Technology becomes, in a sense, as a means to support the fulfillment of basic psychological needs and to promote the causal action sequence leading to enhanced self-determination. Wehmeyer et al. (2021) described the supports that technology can provide to disabled people, from the use of GPS-enabled devices to navigate one's community, to smart homes and remote supports to enable a person to live more independently, to computer-animated work tasks using avatars to teach vocational-related skills. Technology is one way to address the barriers introduced by environments or societal contexts discussed previously, and to enable people with disabilities to live more self-determined lives.

CONCLUSIONS

As a construct, self-determination has been applied to multiple fields and disciplines and used in slightly different ways. All of the ways in which the construct has been used, however, emphasize volitional action. Within a disability context, the construct has been applied as a dispositional characteristic associated with acting as the causal agent in one's life, that is, in making or causing things to happen in one's life. In this usage, the construct takes on the features of a positive psychological personal factor. Research has linked self-determination, as such, to more positive school and post-school outcomes, QOL, and life satisfaction for disabled people.

NOTE

1. A teacher's guide to the SDLMI and instructions on implementation is available at https://selfdetermination.ku.edu/homepage/intervention/#sdlmi.

REFERENCES

Angyal, A. (1941). *Foundations for a science of personality*. Cambridge, MA: Harvard University Press.

Biestek, F.P., & Gehrig, C.C. (1978). *Client self-determination in social work: A fifty-year history*. Chicago: Loyola University Press.

Chang, R., Adams, N., & Little, T.D. (2017). Action-control beliefs and agentic actions. In M.L. Wehmeyer, K.A. Shogren, T.D. Little, & S.J. Lopez (Eds.), *Development of self-determination through the life-course* (pp. 285–295). New York: Springer.

De Charms, R. (1968). *Personal causation: The internal affective determinants of behavior*. New York: Academic Press.

Deci, E. L., & Ryan, R. M. (2012). Motivation, personality, and development within embedded social contexts: An overview of self-determination theory. In R. M. Ryan (Ed.), *The Oxford handbook of human motivation* (pp. 85–110). Oxford: Oxford University Press.

Deci, E. L., Ryan, R. M., & Guay, F. (2013). Self-determination theory and actualization of human potentials. In D. M. McInerney, H. W. Marsh, R. G. Craven, F. Guay, D. M. McInerney (Eds.), *Theory driving research: New wave perspectives on self-processes and human development* (pp. 109–133). Charlotte, NC: Information Age Publishing.

Di Maggio, I., Shogren, K.A., Wehmeyer, M.L., & Nota, L. (2020). Self-determination and future goals in a sample of adults with intellectual disability. *Journal of Intellectual Disability Research, 64*(1), 27–37.

Duvdevany, I., Ben-Zur, H., & Ambar, A. (2002). Self-determination and mental retardation: Is there an association with living arrangements and lifestyle satisfaction? *Mental Retardation, 40*, 379–389.

Emerson, E., Robertson, J., Gregory, N., Hatton, C. Kessissoglou, S., Hallam, A. … Netten, A. (2000). Quality and costs of community-based residential supports, village communities, and residential campuses in the United Kingdom. *American Journal on Mental Retardation, 105*, 81–102.

Heller, T., Miller, A.B., & Hsieh, K. (2002). Eight-year follow-up of the impact of environmental characteristics on well-being of adults with developmental disabilities. *Mental Retardation, 40*, 366–378.

Hofer, J., & Busch, H. (2011). Satisfying one's needs for competence and relatedness: Consequent domain-specific well-being depends on strength of implicit motives. *Personality and Social Psychology Bulletin, 37*(9), 147–158.

Kern, M. & Wehmeyer, M.L. (2021). *The Palgrave handbook of positive education.* New York: Palgrave Macmillan.

Lee, S.H., Wehmeyer, M.L., & Shogren, K.A. (2015). The effect of instruction with the self-determined learning model of instruction on students with disabilities: A meta-analysis. *Education and Training in Autism and Developmental Disabilities, 50*(2), 237–247.

Lee, Y., & Wehmeyer, M.L. (2008). Effects of interventions to enhance the self-determination of students with disabilities in South Korea. *Journal of International Special Needs Education, 11*, 39–49.

Little, T. D., Hawley, P. H., Henrich, C. C., & Marsland, K. (2002). Three views of the agentic self: A developmental synthesis. In E. L. Deci & R. M. Ryan (Eds.), *Handbook of self-determination research* (pp. 389–404). Rochester, NY: University of Rochester Press.

Little, T. D., Snyder, C. R., & Wehmeyer, M. L. (2006). The agentic self: On the nature and origins of personal agency across the lifespan. In D. Mroczek & T. D. Little (Eds.), *The handbook of personality development* (pp. 61–79). Mahwah, NJ: Lawrence Erlbaum and Associates.

McDermott, F.E. (1975). *Self-determination in social work.* London, UK: Routledge and Kegan Paul Ltd.

Mithaug, D.E., Mithaug, D.K., Agran, M., Martin, J.E., & Wehmeyer, M.L. (2003). *Self-determined learning theory: Construction, verification, and evaluation.* Mahwah, NJ: Lawrence Erlbaum Associates.

Mithaug, D.E., Mithaug, D.K., Agran, M., Martin, J.E., & Wehmeyer, M. L. (2007). Self-instruction pedagogy: *How to teach self-determined learning.* Springfield, IL: Charles C Thomas Publisher, LTD.

Mithaug, D., Wehmeyer, M. L., Agran, M., Martin, J., & Palmer, S., (1998). The self-determined learning model of instruction: Engaging students to solve their learning problems. In M. L. Wehmeyer & D. J. Sands (Eds.), *Making it happen: Student involvement in educational planning, decision-making and instruction* (pp. 299–328). Baltimore, MD: Paul H. Brookes.

Mumbardó-Adam, C., Guàrdia-Olmos, J., & Giné, C. (2018). Assessing self-determination in youth with and without disabilities: The Spanish version of the AIR self-determination scale. *Psicothema, 30*(2), 238–243.

Nirje, B. (1972). The right to self-determination. In W. Wolfensberger (Ed.), *Normalization* (pp. 176–193). Toronto: National Institute on Mental Retardation.

Nota, L., Ferrari, L., Soresi, S., & Wehmeyer, M.L. (2007). Self-determination, social abilities, and the quality of life of people with intellectual disabilities. *Journal of Intellectual Disability Research, 51*, 850–865.

Palmer, S.B., Wehmeyer, M.L., & Shogren, K.A. (2017). The development of self-determination in childhood. In M.L. Wehmeyer, K.A. Shogren, T.D. Little, & S. Lopez (Eds.), *Development of self-determination through the life-course* (pp. 71–88). New York: Springer.

Powers, L.E., Geenen, S., Powers, J., Pommier-Satya, S., Turner, A., Dalton, L.D., Drummond, D., & Swank, P. (2012). My life: Effects of a longitudinal, randomized study of self-determination enhancement on the transition outcomes of youth in foster care and special education. *Children and Youth Services Review, 34*(11), 2179–2187.

Ryan, R.M., & Deci, E.L. (2018). *Self-determination theory: Basic psychological needs in motivation, development, and wellness.* New York: Guilford Press.

Seo, H., Wehmeyer, M., & Palmer, S. (2014). The effects of the self-determined learning model of instruction on academic performance of students with high-incidence disabilities. *The Journal of Special Education: Theory and Practice, 15*(1), 305–330.

Sheldon, K. M., Ryan, R. M., & Reis, H. T. (1996). What makes for a good day? Competence and autonomy in the day and in the person. *Personality and Social Psychology Bulletin, 22,* 1270–1279.

Shogren, K.A., Hicks, T.A., Burke, K.M., Antosh, A., LaPlante, T., & Anderson, M.H. (2020). Examining the impact of the SDLMI and whose future is it? Over a two-year period with students with intellectual disability. *American Journal on Intellectual and Developmental Disabilities, 125*(3), 217–229.

Shogren, K.A., Lopez, S.J., Wehmeyer, M.L., Little, T.D., & Pressgrove, C.L. (2006). The role of positive psychology constructs in predicting life satisfaction in adolescents with and without cognitive disabilities: An exploratory study. *Journal of Positive Psychology, 1,* 37–52.

Shogren, K., Palmer, S., Wehmeyer, M.L., Williams-Diehm, K., & Little, T. (2012). Effect of intervention with the self-determined learning model of instruction on access and goal attainment. *Remedial and Special Education, 33*(5), 320–330.

Shogren, K.A., Raley, S.K., Wehmeyer, M.L., Grandfield, E., Jones, J., & Shaw, L.A. (2019). Exploring the relationships among basic psychological needs satisfaction and frustration, agentic engagement, motivation, and self-determination in adolescents with disabilities. *Advances in Neurodevelopmental Disorders, 3,* 119–128.

Shogren, K.A., & Wehmeyer, M.L. (2016). *Self-determination inventory: Student report.* Lawrence, KS: Kansas University Center on Developmental Disabilities.

Shogren, K.A., Wehmeyer, M.L., Palmer, S.B., Forber-Pratt, A., Little, T., & Lopez, S. (2015). Causal agency theory: Reconceptualizing a functional model of self-determination. *Education and Training in Autism and Developmental Disabilities, 50*(3), 251–263.

Shogren, K.A., Wehmeyer, M.L., Palmer, S.B., Rifenbark, G. & Little, T. (2015). Relationships between self-determination and postschool outcomes for youth with disabilities. *Journal of Special Education, 48*(4), 256–267.

Shogren, K.A., Wehmeyer, M.L., & Singh, N. (2017). *Handbook of positive psychology in intellectual and developmental disabilities: Translating research into practice.* New York: Springer

Snyder, C.R., Rand, K.L., & Sigmon, D.R. (2002). Hope theory: A member of the positive psychology family. In C.R. Snyder & S.J. Lopez (Eds.), *Handbook of positive psychology* (pp. 257–276). Oxford, UK: Oxford University Press.

Soenens, B., Vansteenkiste, M., & Van Petegem, S. (2017). *Autonomy in adolescent development: Towards conceptual clarity.* London: Routledge.

Stancliffe, R.J., Abery, B.H., & Smith, J. (2000). Personal control and the ecology of community living settings: Beyond living-unit size and type. *American Journal on Mental Retardation, 105*, 431–454.

Stancliffe, R.J., Lakin, K.C., Larson, S., Engler, J., Taub, S., & Fortune, J. (2011). Choice of living arrangements. *Journal of Intellectual Disability Research, 55*, 746–762.

Stancliffe, R.J. & Wehmeyer, M.L. (1995). Variability in the availability of choice to adults with mental retardation. *Journal of Vocational Rehabilitation, 5*, 319–328.

Stancliffe, R., Wehmeyer, M.L., Shogren, K.A., & Abery, B., (2020). *Choice, preference, and disability: Promoting self-determination across the life span.* New York; Springer.

Ticha, R., Lakin, C., Larson, S.A., Stancliffe, R.J., Taub, S., Engler, J. ... Mosely, C. (2012). Correlates of everyday choice and support-related choice for 8,892 randomly sampled adults with intellectual and developmental disabilities in 19 states. *Intellectual and Developmental Disabilities, 50*, 486–504.

Vansteenkiste, M., Niemiec, C., & Soenens, B. (2010). The development of the five mini-theories of self-determination theory: An historical overview, emerging trends, and future directions. In T. Urdan & S. Karabenick (Eds.). *Advances in motivation and achievement, vol. 16: The decade ahead.* London, UK: Emerald Publishing.

Wehmeyer, M. L. (1992a). Self-determination and the education of students with mental retardation. *Education and Training in Mental Retardation, 27*, 302–314.

Wehmeyer, M. L. (1996b). A self-report measure of self-determination for adolescents with cognitive disabilities. *Education and Training in Mental Retardation and Developmental Disabilities, 31*, 282–293.

Wehmeyer, M.L. (2021). Positive psychology and strengths-based approaches to neurodiversity. In L.K. Fung (Ed.), *Neurodiversity: From phenomenology to neurobiology and enhancing technologies* (pp. 19–38). Washington, DC: American Psychiatric Association.

Wehmeyer, M. L., Agran, M., & Hughes, C. (1998). *Teaching self-determination to students with disabilities: Basic skills for successful transition.* Baltimore, MD: Paul H. Brookes.

Wehmeyer, M. L., & Bolding, N. (1999). Self-determination across living and working environments: A matched-samples study of adults with mental retardation. *Mental Retardation, 37*, 353–363.

Wehmeyer, M. L., & Bolding, N. (2001). Enhanced self-determination of adults with mental retardation as an outcome of moving to community-based work or living environments. *Journal of Intellectual Disability Research, 45*, 371–383.

Wehmeyer, M. L., & Metzler, C. (1995). How self-determined are people with mental retardation? The national consumer survey. *Mental Retardation, 33*, 111–119.

Wehmeyer, M. L., Palmer, S., Agran, M., Mithaug, D., & Martin, J. (2000). Promoting causal agency: The self-determined learning model of instruction. *Exceptional Children, 66*, 439–453.

Wehmeyer, M.L., Palmer, S., Shogren, K., Williams-Diehm, K., & Soukup, J. (2012). Establishing a causal relationship between interventions to promote self-determination and enhanced student self-determination. *Journal of Special Education, 46*(4), 195–210.

Wehmeyer, M. L. & Schwartz, M. (1998). The relationship between self-determination, quality of life, and life satisfaction for adults with mental retardation. *Education and Training in Mental Retardation and Developmental Disabilities, 33*, 3–12.

Wehmeyer, M.L., Shogren, K.A., Little, T.D., & Lopez, S.J. (2017a). *Development of self-determination through the life-course*. New York: Springer.

Wehmeyer, M.L., Shogren, K.A., Little, T.D., & Lopez, S.J. (2017b). Introduction to the self-determination construct. In M.L. Wehmeyer, K.A. Shogren, T.D. Little, & S.J. Lopez (Eds.), *Development of self-determination through the life-course* (pp. 30–16). New York: Springer.

Wehmeyer, M.L., Shogren, K., Palmer, S., Williams-Diehm, K., Little, T., & Boulton, A. (2012). The impact of the self-determined learning model of instruction on student self-determination. *Exceptional Children, 78*(2), 135–153.

Wehmeyer, M.L., Tanis, S., Davies, S.K., & Stock, S.E. (2021). The role of applied cognitive technology and assistive technology in supporting the adaptive behavior of people with intellectual disability. In P. Sturmey & R. Lang (Eds.), *Handbook of adaptive behavior* (pp. 201–218). New York: Springer.

Wehmeyer, M.L., & Zhao, Y. (2020). *Teaching students to become self-determined learners*. Alexandria, VA: ASCD.

Williams, R.R. (1989). Creating a new world of opportunity: Expanding choice and self-determination in lives of Americans with severe disability by 1992 and beyond. In R. Perske (Ed.), *Proceedings from the National Conference on Self-Determination* (pp. 16–17). Minneapolis, MN: Institute on Community Integration.

Williams-Diehm, K., Wehmeyer, M.L., Palmer, S., Soukup, J.H., & Garner, N. (2008). Self-determination and student involvement in transition planning: A multivariate analysis. *Journal on Developmental Disabilities, 14*, 25–36.

Wolman, J. M., Campeau, P. L., DuBois, P. A., Mithaug, D. E., & Stolarski, V. S. (1994). *AIR self-determination scale and user guide*. Palo Alto, CA: American Institutes for Research.

World Health Organization (2001). *The International Classification of Functioning, Disability and Health (ICF)*. Geneva: WHO.

Chapter 7

Individual and Interpersonal Aspects of Hope and People with Developmental Disabilities

Malka Margalit, Tomer
Schmidt-Barad, and Michal Einav

INTRODUCTION

People living with a disability are confronted with many barriers that require that they cope with challenges to promote their well-being. As such, the cognitive and emotional impact of their disability and related negative experiences may affect their current identity development and future expectations. Much of the history of psychology has been dominated by considering the past of individuals as a major source of influence on their current lives (Seligman et al., 2013). Hope theory enables people, even people who have experienced a challenging past or during demanding existing situations, to plan goals for a positive future. Accordingly, although disabilities have been predominantly conceptualized within deficit-focused models (Gray et al., 2016; see chapter 1), the applicability of resilience factors and strength-based perspectives to people experiencing disability is an emerging area of interest in recent literature (Dvorsky & Langberg, 2016), emphasizing the critical role of personal strengths characteristics to optimal functioning. Hope theory extends the theoretical move from deficit conceptualizations of disability to an individual differences model, demonstrating the beneficial impacts of hope and future thinking (Shipp & Aeon, 2019).

Certainly, being hopeful, in terms of setting goals and effectively working toward achieving them, may be an essential element for the well-being of every person, but it has a unique importance for people with disabilities (Buchanan & Lopez, 2013). The goals of this chapter are to present Hope Theory, to discuss research that demonstrates the beneficial impacts of hope, and to consider factors that promote hope in terms of personal and interpersonal resources. Second, research on the hope of individuals with developmental disabilities will be addressed, as well as hope within caregivers and families of people with disability. Finally, the chapter's conclusions will emphasize prevention and intervention opportunities, while considering the impact of disabilities as an interaction between individuals' strengths and challenges.

The Hope Construct

In lay terms, hope implies a wish for achieving positive future goals. Within positive psychology, however, hope has been conceptualized as an important personal resource. Snyder's Hope Theory is based on the assumption that human actions are inherently goal-directed, and hope is the ability to successfully plan and achieve one's goals by maintaining motivation and overcoming obstacles (Snyder, 2002). Hope Theory, according to Snyder's model (Shorey et al., 2007), consists of two interacting components: agency thinking and pathways thinking about goals. *Agency thinking* refers to the individual's ability to define goals and their feeling of competence ("will") to initiate and sustain their performance until the goal is reached. This is the motivational component of hope, reflecting a person's determination to initiate and sustain goal-directed effort. It is often manifested in positive statements such as "I can do this." The goals may be short- or long-term targets (Rand & Cheavens, 2009). *Pathways thinking* refers to the cognitive component of Hope Theory, reflecting a person's perceived ability to produce plans to reach their goals, to consider possible obstacles that might prevent goal attainment, and to propose alternative ways to overcome them. Each of the components has a unique contribution to the hope construct, yet the interaction between them provides the full meaning of hopefulness.

Developmental Perspectives

From a developmental viewpoint, the goals of young people and expectations about their future are powerful forces in shaping their life paths. Erik Erikson (1997) proposed that hope is the first of the "psychosocial strengths" that emerges from resolving conflicts of early developmental stages. Accordingly, the impact of the family environment and parenting styles were examined in the development of children and adolescents' hopeful thinking (Heaven & Ciarrochi, 2008). From early stages, children develop a sense of self, together with the expectation that their future will meet their personal needs and goals. This "hopeful thinking" becomes more refined as children grow up and mature (Marques & Lopez, 2018). Parents are the first important agents who have a significant impact on children's hope development. They model hope by the way they communicate about present and future times and by setting goals, focusing effort on goal attainment, and solving problems. Children's self-perceptions about their competencies to achieve academic and social goals and to adaptively cope with different tasks predict their hope beliefs. Teachers and peers can play important roles in the development of hope. Positive hopeful experiences in childhood tend to predict and shape the emergence of hope in adulthood. In Hope Theory, hope is identified as activating action to produce or identify multiple goals, to plan various pathways, and to promote motivation to achieve desired outcomes and invest the effort to stay engaged to reach the desired goals.

Higher hope levels in typically developing children and adolescents have been linked with higher rates of personal strengths, such as self-esteem, optimism, global life satisfaction, and academic achievement, as well as lower levels of loneliness and behavior difficulties (Marques & Lopez, 2018). For adults, high levels of hope have predicted well-being and reduced distress, even during challenging times, including during the Covid-19 pandemic (Gallagher et al., 2021). Research on hope and people with disabilities has emphasized the critical role of hope in an individual's quality of life (QOL) and life satisfaction (Buchanan & Lopez, 2013). Research on hope and people with high prevalence disabilities such as specific learning disorders (SLD) and attention deficit disorders (ADHD) illuminates the beneficial impact of the construct on coping disability, revealing individual abilities and personal resources (Al-Yagon & Margalit, 2018).

Individual Differences among People with Disabilities

Generally, the experience of disability may have differential impact on individuals' identity development, focusing attention on the importance of personal resources, environmental supportive characteristics, and disability acceptance as factors in successful functioning. Thus, the impact of the experience of disability on well-being and life satisfaction is dependent on a person's strength, interpersonal resources, and the different challenges they face in their life, such as academic and employment demands.

Many studies of people with disabilities focus attention on their past and present difficulties and challenging experiences, while Hope Theory presents the mechanisms to anticipate and stay engaged with positive future goals. Since perception of the future has consistently been related to well-being, motivation, and behaviors across a range of domains (Kooij et al., 2018), it is not surprising that hope has been conceptualized as an individual protective factor associated with multiple psychological resources, including an increased sense of coherence (SOC), self-efficacy, life satisfaction, and subjective well-being, as well as reduced anxiety and loneliness and fewer depressive symptoms (Moss-Pech et al., 2021; Muyan-Yılık & Demir, 2020; Santilli et al., 2021; Satici, 2020; Satici et al., 2020; Wong & Yang, 2021). Research on the relationship between these personal resources and hope among individuals with disabilities will be presented in the next sections.

People with SLD and ADHD face many developmental challenges. These highly prevalent neurodevelopmental disorders affect a person's academic, social, emotional, and occupational domains throughout life (American Psychiatric Association, 2013; Crisci et al., 2021). People with these conditions are often easily distracted and forgetful, face academic difficulties, and may experience emotional and social struggles (Al-Yagon & Margalit, 2018; Bishop et al., 2019; Lee et al., 2016). Considering these ongoing challenges, it is not surprising that children and adolescents with SLD reported lower levels of hope in studies that compared them to their typically developing peers in various age groups, from elementary school children to college students (Mana et al., 2021). These lower levels of hope are predicted by the person's personal resources, such as their SOC and academic self-efficacy (Al-Yagon & Margalit, 2018). Nevertheless, individuals with SLD who reported higher levels of hope also reported higher levels of academic competence and well-being (Levi et al., 2013).

Similarly, among people with intellectual disability, the significance of hope has also been demonstrated. People with intellectual disability experience many challenges during their transition from school to community life and work. In a study of 120 adults with intellectual disability, Santilli et al. (2021) found that participants' levels of hope predicted their life satisfaction. A five-year longitudinal study that involved young adults with intellectual disability during their transition from school to post-school life showed the predictive role of social support from family, friends, and teachers with regard to young adults' increased levels of hope and increased life satisfaction (Al-Yagon et al., 2020). In this study, developmental changes were observed. In the first year of the study, the contribution of family support was identified as a major predictor of the youngsters' levels of hope. Yet, four years after, the support of friends became more pronounced in predicting levels of hope. These results reflect typical developmental changes in the lives of young adults with and without disabilities, whose well-being shifts from reliance on their families' support to the development of meaningful social relationships with their peers. However, levels of hope continued to function as an important source of well-being (Al-Yagon et al., 2020). These outcomes emphasized the importance of hope for individuals with different disabilities and also call for examining the relationships among hope and additional intra- and interpersonal sources of strengths and resilience.

Sense of Coherence (SOC) and Hope

SOC is considered

a global orientation that expresses the extent to which one has a pervasive, enduring, though dynamic, feeling of confidence that one's internal and external environments are predictable and that there is a high probability that things will work out as well as can reasonably be expected. (Antonovsky, 1979, p. 123)

The construct reflects the individuals' experience during current situations and their relationship with their past history. SOC is considered a personal resource that enables individuals to cope effectively with various stress situations (Pérez-Wilson et al., 2021). SOC includes three interacting main components: *comprehensibility*, *manageability*, and *meaningfulness* (Antonovsky, 1987). *Comprehensibility* is the cognitive component of SOC that manifests the person's understanding of themselves and their surroundings. *Manageability* refers to a person's belief that they have the resources to cope with challenges effectively. *Meaningfulness* represents the motivational component of SOC. Individuals with a strong SOC are more likely to believe that the sources of stress are explicable. They have confidence in their coping abilities and the motivation to overcome the distress (Antonovsky, 1996).

The relationship between SOC and hope has been widely demonstrated in previous studies (Mittelmark et al., 2017). Research in different cultures has demonstrated that SOC and hope are complementary but independent resources for coping with stress situations (Braun-Lewensohn et al., 2017). In addition, when their relationship was examined, it was determined in several studies that higher SOC was a predictor of higher levels of hope in different age groups, including adolescents (Braun-Lewensohn, 2016) and older adults (Lin et al., 2021).

Research on SOC among children, adolescents, and young adults with SLD reported consistently lower SOC and lower hope levels than for their nondisabled peers (Lackaye & Margalit, 2006; Sharabi et al., 2012, 2016). Still, individual differences were clearly noticed, and college students with SLD who reported higher SOC did not differ in hope levels from their peers. In addition, hope and SOC mediated the relationship between disability impacts and academic self-efficacy (Ben-Naim et al., 2017). Thus, research has demonstrated the important role of hope and SOC in effectively coping with distress. During the Covid-19 pandemic, research showed that higher hope and higher SOC predicted lower symptoms of distress across cultures (Braun-Lewensohn et al., 2021). Because the foundations of the development of hope and SOC can be established in the early stages of child development, research has focused attention on the attachment processes of children with disabilities.

Attachment and Hope

Attachment Theory extends the understanding of the sources of social difficulties experienced by people with disabilities and their relationship with hope (Al-Yagon, 2018; Bowlby, 1988). According to Attachment Theory, infants develop a specific and enduring relationship with their primary caretaker, typically their mother, during early developmental stages. Attachment Theory posits that infants internalize the quality of these interactions into "internal working models of attachment," which are mental representations of the relationships among significant others and the child. During development, these mental representations (i.e., secure, avoidant, anxious, or disorganized) lead to interpretive filters that continue to guide the child's beliefs and expectations about the social world through development, manifesting in later years in interpersonal relationships as well as intrapersonal formation (Mikulincer & Shaver, 2019). The process of developing a secure base from which one may venture forth, explore, and develop hope begins in infancy and continues throughout the developmental years. Thus, parental behaviors aimed at providing support to the child are vital for instilling the foundations for the emergence of hope (Shorey et al., 2018). Consequently, secure attachment has an impact on the development of a hopeful disposition that will be carried forward into adolescence and adulthood and support positive mental health outcomes (Snyder, 2002).

Research with children with ADHD and/or SLD revealed higher levels of insecure attachment and lower levels of hope when compared to their non-disabled peers. These children's basic executive function difficulties (Crisci et al., 2021) affected the establishment of early attachment interrelations. Thus, they perceived themselves as having lower pathway thinking (i.e., strategies for attaining goals), reduced agency thinking (i.e., capacity to initiate and sustain movement along the chosen pathways), and lower investment of effort (as indicated by intensity in and persistence with engagement in task accomplishment). Even when levels of scholastic grades were controlled so that the lower hope could not be attributed to difficulties in academic achievements, these children's lower hope levels remained throughout development (Al-Yagon, 2007, 2012; Lackaye & Margalit, 2006). Research has shown, however, the protective quality of social relations, and specifically social support from different sources (e.g., family, teachers, and friends), in minimizing negative developmental outcomes (Schei et al., 2018). For example, a recent study of hope and social support among Chinese children with ADHD (Ma et al., 2020) demonstrated that social support from families, teachers, and friends predicted higher hope levels. These results focused attention on the significance of social support for the development of hopeful beliefs.

Social Support and Hope

Social support consists of social relationships that can provide material and interpersonal resources of value to the recipient. Social support includes three categories: (1) social connectedness or social embeddedness; (2) actual or enacted social support; and (3) perceived social support (Lopez & Cooper, 2011). The concept of social connectedness refers to the quantity and quality of interpersonal connections that an individual has with others, including both formal and informal social relationships such as family members, friends, and teachers. Studies of social supports have examined several structural aspects of support, including the number of sources of support and the qualitative nature of the various relationships within an individual's social network, such as one's satisfaction with supportive social relationships.

The third category, perceived social support, refers to the individual's cognitive appraisal of the social support requested to promote effective coping and reduce the negative effects of stress on outcomes. Despite some methodological concerns about potential self-reporting biases of respondents, measures of perceived social support typically have the strongest relationship from among the three categories of social support with measures of hope and reduced stress, as well as with measures of improved well-being (Melrose et al., 2015). Research has consistently reported that perceived social support predicts hopeful thinking, positive experiences, and feelings of self-worth (Bryson & Bogart, 2020). Bryson and Bogart proposed a model hypothesizing that social supports facilitate a recipient's coping, which then reduces the negative effects of stress on that individual's well-being. Even in the absence of actual support being provided, a person's perceived availability of social support has been shown to reduce the negative impact of stress on their well-being and influenced positive outcomes, such as hope, health, and well-being (Bryson & Bogart, 2020).

The importance of social support has been emphasized in disability research and studies have demonstrated its buffering role in and its capacity to predict effective coping (Carawan et al., 2016; Chwalisz & Vaux, 2000; Nalavany & Carawan, 2012). Social support has been identified as a major protective factor in preventing mental health problems and as a major contributor to a more positive QOL for people with various disabilities and their families (Lippold & Burns, 2009). In a study of children at risk for disability, children with low levels of hope had more externalizing and internalizing behavior problems. In addition, children who reported less perceived social support had also more externalizing behavior problems (Hagen et al., 2005).

The results of this study illustrated the combined value of social support and hope. Indeed, hope and social support had higher positive correlations. In addition, children who experienced more social support and hope had fewer externalizing and internalizing behavior problems (Hagen et al., 2005). It is not clear if being hopeful enabled these children to benefit more from the social support or if the experience of social support enhanced their hope.

Hope and Academic Achievements

The reciprocal relations between hope and academic achievement have been widely studied and students with high hope often obtain higher grades (Marques et al., 2017). Research has found that hope served an important protective role during stressful periods due to challenging academic tasks or frustrating social situations. Students with high levels of hope reported successful progress in their academic goal attainment regardless of the intensity of their emotional distress and difficulties (Moss-Pech et al., 2021). Indeed, academic tasks present significant challenges to students with development disabilities, but social support and hope predicted their more positive academic competence and achievements (Bryce et al., 2020). For example, a recent longitudinal study examined the reciprocal relationship between hope and academic achievement in a sample of Chinese elementary school students (Chen et al., 2020). Results showed the interrelations between hope and academic achievements across three semesters among 949 elementary school students. Similarly, in a different culture, a longitudinal study of adolescents' hopes and academic achievements found that hope predicted not only academic achievement and school engagement but also the students' well-being and reduced anxiety levels (Bryce et al., 2020).

The transition periods in education are especially challenging for students with disabilities. Transition to college has often elicited excitement as well as elevated stress, especially for students with SLD and ADHD who may encounter renewed social and academic difficulties. Feldman et al. (2016) studied students with and without SLD during the first month of college, exploring the links between SLD status and two outcomes: loneliness/social isolation and academic self-efficacy. The results indicated that, as expected, SLD status predicted lower levels of academic self-efficacy and increased loneliness and social alienation, while emphasizing the important role of hope. Accordingly, students with SLD who reported higher levels of hope conveyed more confidence in their academic opportunities as well as reduced social distress and loneliness (Feldman et al., 2016). In addition, higher hope levels enabled individuals to benefit more from support provisions in college. Also, students with disabilities who reported higher levels of hope were more open and ready to take advantages of available assistive technology, and this type of support further contributed to their well-being (Heiman & Shemesh, 2012).

To successfully meet the academic demands of universities and colleges, students with SLD and ADHD often benefit from learning and testing accommodations. These accommodations are external resources that are offered to students with disabilities to help them overcome the barriers and difficulties they face due to their disabilities and to enable them to demonstrate their knowledge (Margalit, 2018). Universities and colleges around the world provide support in addition to academic and testing accommodations, such as academic and emotional assistance from university-based support centers and disability services. In a study of 2,113 college students in various universities and colleges in Israel, 668 students with SLD, and 703 students with ADHD were compared with their nondisabled peers. These two subgroups of students with disabilities had lower hope levels and lower academic competency (Mana et al., 2021). Indeed, although the academic supports provided were expected to support these students, many of them with low hope felt that these supports did not provide any meaningful help. At the same time, high levels of hope seemed to enhance student benefit from social and institutional support, and to reach higher levels of academic achievement (Mana et al., 2021). This meaningful advantage of being hopeful is not limited to individuals with disabilities but also has been found in research on families.

Families of Individuals with Disabilities and Hope

The importance of the hope construct for understanding coping of caretakers of children with disabilities has been a focus of research. Raising a child with a disability can be a life-changing experience that affects the parents' well-being, future expectations, and life satisfaction. Hopeful thinking may positively impact parents' beliefs and values about their child's disability and alter their life priorities. Research has established that hopeful parents modify their world views concerning living with a disability as well as changing future expectations for the child and the family. Thus, for example, parents of children with Down syndrome highlighted the significance of hope in their well-being. They portrayed the enabling impact of hopeful beliefs that resulted in increased awareness to varied positive possibilities for the future development of their children (Benderix et al., 2006; King et al., 2006).

Parental realization that their child has exceptional support needs is often considered emotionally challenging. Participation in an early intervention program for infants with developmental delays and intellectual disability (0–2 years) may be construed as an emotionally demanding situation for mothers and fathers who have only just realized that their infant has a disability. In a study that followed 111 Israeli mothers who participated in an early intervention program, the mothers' hopeful thinking was predicted by their personal strength in terms of their SOC, as well as by the social support from their families and from the agency that provided the program. Accordingly, mothers with higher levels of SOC were better able to cope with the extended day-to-day demands of caregiving and reported higher levels of hope for the future (Einav et al., 2012).

Many times, mothers of children with developmental disabilities have reported decreased life satisfaction and lower levels of well-being (Schmidt et al., 2017). Their increased needs for counseling, support, and help were related to their sense of entitlement (George-Levi & Laslo-Roth, 2021). This belief involves their expectation that others, including friends and public institutions, should fulfill and support their needs and the needs of their children. A recent study emphasized the importance of hope in relation to a sense of entitlement. Mothers who reported higher entitlement levels experienced decreased life satisfaction when their hope was low. Yet, entitlement was positively related to life satisfaction when mothers' hope was high. Therefore, entitlement can act either as a resource or as a risk factor for life satisfaction, depending on hope levels (George-Levi & Laslo-Roth, 2021).

To further clarify the comparisons between levels of hope experienced by mothers of children with different disabilities, levels of hope of a group of 199 mothers of children with autism were compared with those of a group of 60 mothers of children with Down syndrome. The group of mothers of children with autism reported lower levels of hope than mothers of children with Down syndrome. However, within the group of mothers of children with autism, the subgroup of mothers of children with more capacity reported higher levels of hope and lower levels of worry (Ogston et al., 2011). In a study of parents of children with and without intellectual disability, lower levels of hope were related to lower resilience levels (Sarıçam et al., 2020). Thus, higher support needs of children and higher caregiving needs impacted parents' well-being and their hope levels. Individual differences in levels of hope were related to the combined impact of parental demands and parental strengths, as well as to emotional attitudes and distress.

Differences were also noticed when hope levels of fathers and mothers were compared. Lower levels of maternal hope together with elevated child behavior problems predicted increased maternal depression. For fathers, on the other hand, anxiety and depression were predicted only by low hope agency, not by hope pathways (Lloyd & Hastings, 2009). It seems that since fathers were less involved in the day-to-day caregiving of the child, their distress was expressed in the motivational aspect of hope.

According to Snyder (2002), hope is a learned skill that is taught through the socialization in families during childhood. Hope, as an individual difference, develops over time as we learn the links between our goals, actions, and successes. Thus, the personal history of goal pursuit during growth leads to a stable sense of hope (Cheavens & Guter, 2018). However, since hope is considered an acquired skill, and as its significance has been demonstrated in many studies, it is not surprising that numerous researchers focused effort on the development of hope therapy and intervention programs.

Intervention Directions

Based upon the recognition of the beneficial value of hope, several intervention programs have been developed. These hope interventions are predicated on the belief that helping people to increase their hope will result in the acquisition of goal-setting, pathway, and agency skills that can be advantageous when coping with stressors or during challenging periods across life domains. Different populations have been the target of these interventions, including college students, community members, women in labor, and elderly and sick people (Bernardo, 2020; Cheavens & Guter, 2018; Duggleby et al., 2007; Feldman et al., 2015; Feldman & Dreher, 2012; Herth, 2000; Samavi et al., 2019). The results from these studies provide evidence that when afforded hope interventions, individuals may acquire increased levels of hope.

Hope interventions have been shown to provide participants with pathways skills (Cheavens & Guter, 2018). Participants learn to generate multiple workable routes to achieving a goal, anticipating and planning to get around obstacles, and evaluating pathways in terms of likelihood of success, costs to enact, and progress over the course of the goal pursuit. To promote agency skills, participants have been trained in cognitive-behavioral strategies, targeting goal-relevant self-talk, mental contrasting and focusing on thoughts, and visual simulations as factors that may activate motivation (Sevincer et al., 2018).

Generally, hope interventions have been found to be beneficial for students in general education (Cheavens et al., 2006; Rosenstreich et al., 2015). However, only a few studies have examined the applicability of hope interventions for students with SLD. For example, in a study that compared the impact of a focused hope intervention among college students with and without SLD, both groups reported an enhanced level of hope and optimism immediately after the intervention, as well as lower loneliness distress. However, after a month, the students with SLD returned to baseline levels of hope and loneliness (Rosenstreich et al., 2015). The results of this pilot study emphasized the need to plan for maintenance procedures to support the newly learned skills. In line with research on the beneficial value of hope for individuals with disabilities and their parents, future controlled interventions are needed, adapted to the unique needs of individuals with disabilities and their caretakers, with more extended procedures, and planned maintenance procedures.

CONCLUSIONS, IMPLICATIONS, AND FUTURE DIRECTION

In conclusion, moving from a deficits model of disability to enabling models, research has demonstrated the significance of the hope construct. Its value as a predictor of well-being and success in various areas for people with and without disabilities has been demonstrated in many domains. The presence of a disability may challenge the well-being and the life satisfaction of people with disabilities and their families. However, hopeful beliefs may empower people while supporting the shift from a "deficit disability model" to the awareness of a comprehensive model of individual differences. In addition, research has shown that both personal strengths, such as SOC, and interpersonal resources, such as social support, predict higher levels of hope, leading to well-being and academic success. Also, not only a person's hope but also the hope of parents and teachers has a significant role in predicting accomplishments and life satisfaction. Future studies need to further examine the mechanisms of hope that activate competence and personal resources. Comprehensive examinations are needed to identify the processes by which hope serves a buffering role of coping with stressful situations and examining the empowering role embraced by high hope people (Kelberer et al., 2018; Yeung et al., 2015).

Since the importance of hope for individuals and families has been previously demonstrated and intervention programs have shown that hope can be learned, future studies need to target interventions planned explicitly for people with disabilities, focusing not only on the person but also on their parents and teachers (Lopez et al., 2010). Hope Theory as an intervention strategy has a unique value not only for the individuals with disabilities but also for the professional development processes—encouraging professionals to embrace hope and future perspectives thinking. This may also support the move from "disability models" to "enabling and activating models" that support the appreciation of individual differences in effectively coping with barriers. Therefore, there is a need to examine in-depth the value of implementing the language of hope in supporting developmental processes. In line with Hope Theory, a focus on identifying future goals, considering possible barriers, and planning detailed paths may introduce an additional meaningful aspect to current intervention programs. Future studies may explore these options and assess their impact.

REFERENCES

Al-Yagon, M. (2007). Socioemotional and behavioral adjustment among school-age children with learning disabilities: The moderating role of maternal personal resources. *Journal of Special Education, 40*(4), 205–218. doi: 10.1177/00224669070400040201

Al-Yagon, M. (2012). Subtypes of attachment security in school-age children with learning disabilities. *Learning Disability Quarterly, 35*(3), 170–183. doi: 10.1177/0731948712436398

Al-Yagon, M. (2018). Models of child–parent attachment in attention deficit hyperactivity disorder: Links to executive functions. *Personal Relationships, 25*(2), 280–298. doi: 10.1111/pere.12232

Al-Yagon, M., & Margalit, M. (2006). Loneliness, sense of coherence and perception of teachers as a secure base among children with reading difficulties. *European Journal of Special Needs Education, 21*(1), 21–37. doi: 10.1080/08856250500268619

Al-Yagon, M., & Margalit, M. (2018). Hope and coping in individuals with SLD. In S. Lopez & M. Gallagher (Eds.), *Oxford Handbook of hope* (pp. 243–254). Oxford University Press.

Al-Yagon, M., Rimmerman, A., & Margalit, M. (2020). *Living in the community through the eyes of young adults with intellectual disability and their families.* Research report to Shalem Foundation. Tel-Aviv University.

American Psychiatric Association. (2013). *DSM-5: Diagnostic and statistical manual of mental disorders (Fifth ed.).* American Psychiatric Publishing.

Antonovsky, A. (1979). *Health, stress and coping.* Jossey-Bass.

Antonovsky, A. (1987). *Unraveling the mystery of health.* Jossey-Bass.

Antonovsky, A. (1996). The salutogenic model as a theory to guide health promotion. *Health Promotion International, 11*(1), 11–18. doi: 10.1093/heapro/11.1.11

Ben-Naim, S., Laslo-Roth, R., Einav, M., Biran, H., & Margalit, M. (2017). Academic self-efficacy, sense of coherence, hope and tiredness among college students with learning disabilities. *European Journal of Special Needs Education, 32*(1), 18–34. doi: 10.1080/08856257.2016.1254973

Benderix, Y., Nordstrom, B., & Sivberg, B. (2006). Parents' experience of having a child with autism and learning disabilities living in a group home: A case study. *Autism, 10*(6), 629–641. doi: 10.1177/1362361307070902

Bernardo, A. B. I. (2010). Extending hope theory: Internal and external locus of trait hope. *Personality and Individual Differences, 49*(8), 944–949. doi: 10.1016/j.paid.2010.07.036

Bernardo, A. B. I. (2020). Hope interventions for students: Integrating cultural perspectives. In G. A. D. Liem & D. M. McInerney (Eds.), *Promoting motivation and learning in contexts: Sociocultural perspectives on educational interventions* (pp. 281–302). Information Age Publishing.

Bishop, C., Mulraney, M., Rinehart, N., & Sciberras, E. (2019). An examination of the association between anxiety and social functioning in youth with

ADHD: A systematic review. *Psychiatry Research, 273*, 402–421. doi: 10.1016/j.psychres.2019.01.039

Bowlby, J. (1988). *A secure base: Clinical applications of attachment theory.* Routledge.

Braun-Lewensohn, O. (2016). Sense of coherence, values, youth involvement, civic efficacy and hope: Adolescents during social protest. *Social Indicators Research, 128*(2), 661–673. doi: 10.1007/s11205-015-1049-8

Braun-Lewensohn, O., Abu-Kaf, S., & Kalagy, T. (2017). Are "sense of coherence" and "hope" related constructs? Examining these concepts in three cultural groups in Israel. *The Israel Journal of Psychiatry and Related Sciences, 54*, 17–23.

Braun-Lewensohn, O., Abu-Kaf, S., & Kalagy, T. (2021). Hope and resilience during a pandemic among three cultural groups in Israel: The second wave of Covid-19. *Frontiers in Psychology, 12:637349.* doi: 10.3389/fpsyg.2021.637349

Bryce, C. I., Alexander, B. L., Fraser, A. M., & Fabes, R. A. (2020). Dimensions of hope in adolescence: Relations to academic functioning and well-being. *Psychology in the Schools, 57*(2), 171–190. doi: 10.1002/pits.22311

Bryson, B. A., & Bogart, K. R. (2020). Social support, stress, and life satisfaction among adults with rare diseases. *Health Psychology, 39*(10), 912–920. doi: 10.1037/hea0000905

Buchanan, C. L., & Lopez, S. J. (2013). Understanding hope in individuals with disabilities. In M. L. Wehmeyer (Ed.), *The Oxford handbook of positive psychology and disability* (pp. 154–165). Oxford University Press.

Callina, K., Snow, N., & Murray, E. D. (2018). The history of philosophical and psychological perspectives on hope: Toward defining hope for the science of positive human development In M. W. Gallagher & S. J. Lopez (Eds.), *The Oxford handbook of hope* (pp. 9–25). The Oxford University Press.

Carawan, L. W., Nalavany, B. A., & Jenkins, C. (2016, 2016/03/03). Emotional experience with dyslexia and self-esteem: The protective role of perceived family support in late adulthood. *Aging & Mental Health, 20*(3), 284–294. doi: 10.1080/13607863.2015.1008984

Cheavens, J. S., Feldman, D. B., Gum, A., Michael, S. T., & Snyder, C. R. (2006). Hope therapy in a community sample: A pilot investigation *Journal Social Indicators Research, 77*(1), 61–78. doi: 10.1007/s11205-005-5553-0

Cheavens, J. S., & Guter, M. M. (2018). Hope therapy. In M. W. Gallagher & S. J. Lopez (Eds.), *The Oxford handbook of hope* (pp. 133–142). Oxford University Press.

Chen, J., Huebner, E. S., & Tian, L. (2020). Longitudinal relations between hope and academic achievement in elementary school students: Behavioral engagement as a mediator. *Learning and Individual Differences, 78*, 101824. doi: 10.1016/j.lindif.2020.101824

Chwalisz, K., & Vaux, A. (2000). Social support and adjustment to disability. In R. G. Frank & T. R. Elliott (Eds.),*Handbook of rehabilitation psychology.* (pp. 537–552). American Psychological Association.

Crisci, G., Caviola, S., Cardillo, R., & Mammarella, I. C. (2021). Executive functions in neurodevelopmental disorders: Comorbidity overlaps between attention deficit and hyperactivity disorder and specific learning disorders. *Frontiers in Human Neurosciences, 15:594234.* doi: 10.3389/fnhum.2021.594234

Duggleby, W. D., Degner, L., Williams, A., Wright, K., Cooper, D., Popkin, D., & Holtslander, L. (2007). Living with hope: Initial evaluation of a psychosocial hope intervention for older palliative home care patients. *Journal of Pain and Symptom Management, 33*(3), 247–257. doi: 10.1016/j.jpainsymman.2006.09.013

Dvorsky, M. R., & Langberg, J. M. (2016). A Review of factors that promote resilience in youth with ADHD and ADHD symptoms. *Clinical Child and Family Psychology Review, 19*(4), 368–391. doi: 10.1007/s10567-016-0216-z

Einav, M., Levi, U., & Margalit, M. (2012). Mothers' coping and hope in early intervention. *European Journal of Special Needs Education, 27*(3), 265–280. doi: 10.1080/08856257.2012.678662

Erikson, E. H. (1997). *The life cycle completed: Extended version with new chapters on the ninth stage of development by Joan M. Erikson.* Norton.

Feldman, D. B., Davidson, O. B., Ben-Naim, S., Maza, E., & Margalit, M. (2016). Hope as a mediator of loneliness and academic self-efficacy among students with and without learning disabilities during the transition to college. *Learning Disabilities Research & Practice, 31*(2), 63–74. doi: 10.1111/ldrp.12094

Feldman, D. B., Davidson, O. B., & Margalit, M. (2015). Personal resources, hope, and achievement among college students: The conservation of resources perspective *Journal of Happiness Studies, 16,* 543–560. doi: 10.1007/s10902-014-9508-5

Feldman, D. B., & Dreher, D. E. (2012). Can hope be changed in 90 minutes? Testing the efficacy of a single-session goal-pursuit intervention for college students. *Journal of Happiness Studies, 13,* 745–759. doi: 10.1007/s10902-011-9292-4

Gallagher, M. W., Smith, L. J., Richardson, A. L., D'Souza, J. M., & Long, L. J. (2021). Examining the longitudinal effects and potential mechanisms of hope on COVID-19 stress, anxiety, and well-being. *Cognitive Behaviour Therapy,* Advance online publication. doi: 10.1080/16506073.2021.1877341

George-Levi, S., & Laslo-Roth, R. (2021). Entitlement, hope, and life satisfaction among mothers of children with developmental disabilities. *Journal of Autism and Developmental Disorders, 51*(1), 3818-3828. doi: 10.1007/s10803-020-04832-6

Gray, S. A., Fettes, P., Woltering, S., Mawjee, K., & Tannock, R. (2016). Symptom manifestation and impairments in college students with ADHD. *Journal of Learning Disabilities, 49*(6), 616–630. doi: 10.1177/0022219415576523

Hagen, K. A., Myers, B. J., & Mackintosh, V. H. (2005). Hope, social support, and behavioral problems in at-risk children. *American Journal of Orthopsychiatry, 75*(2), 211–219. doi: 10.1037/0002-9432.75.2.211

Heaven, P., & Ciarrochi, J. (2008). Parental styles, gender and the development of hope and self-esteem. *European Journal of Personality, 22*(8), 707–724. doi: 10.1002/per.699

Heiman, T., & Shemesh, D. O. (2012). Students with LD in higher education: Use and contribution of assistive technology and website courses and their correlation to students' hope and well-being. *Journal of Learning Disabilities, 45*(4), 308–318. doi: 10.1177/0022219410392047

Herth, K. (2000). Enhancing hope in people with a first recurrence of cancer. *Journal of Advanced Nursing, 32*(6), 1431–1441. doi: 10.1046/j.1365-2648.2000.01619.x

Kelberer, L. J. A., Kraines, M. A., & Wells, T. T. (2018). Optimism, hope, and attention for emotional stimuli. *Personality and Individual Differences, 124*, 84–90. doi: 10.1016/j.paid.2017.12.003

King, G. A., Zwaigenbaum, L., King, S., Baxter, D., Rosenbaum, P., & Bates, A. (2006). A qualitative investigation of changes in the belief systems of families of children with autism or Down syndrome. *Child: Care, Health and Development, 32*(3), 353–369. doi: 10.1111/j.1365-2214.2006.00571.x

Kooij, D. T. A. M., Kanfer, R., Betts, M., & Rudolph, C. W. (2018). Future time perspective: A systematic review and meta-analysis. *Journal of Applied Psychology, 103*(8), 867–893. doi: 10.1037/apl0000306

Lackaye, T., & Margalit, M. (2006). Comparisons of achievement, effort and self-perceptions among students with learning disabilities and their peers from different achievement groups . *Journal of Learning Disabilities, 39*(5), 432–446. doi: 10.1177/00222194060390050501

Lee, S. S., Sibley, M. H., & Epstein, J. N. (2016). Attention-deficit/hyperactivity disorder across development: Predictors, resilience, and future directions. *Journal of Abnormal Psychology, 125*(2), 151–153. doi: 10.1037/abn0000114

Levi, U., Einav, M., Raskind, I., Ziv, O., & Margalit, M. (2013). Helping students with LD to succeed: The role of teachers' hope, sense of coherence and specific self-efficacy. *European Journal of Special Needs Education, 28*(4), 427–439. doi: 10.1080/08856257.2013.820457

Lin, Y., Zhang, B., & Xu, R. (2021). Sense of coherence can predict hope in older adults: A cross-lagged analysis. *Aging & Mental Health*, Advance online publication. doi: 10.1080/13607863.2021.1872488

Lippold, T., & Burns, J. (2009). Social support and intellectual disabilities: A comparison between social networks of adults with intellectual disability and those with physical disability. *Journal of Intellectual Disability Research, 53*(5), 463–473. doi: 10.1111/j.1365-2788.2009.01170.x

Lloyd, T., & Hastings, R. (2009). Hope as a psychological resilience factor in mothers and fathers of children with intellectual disabilities. *Journal of intellectual disability research : JIDR, 53*, 957–968. doi: 10.1111/j.1365-2788.2009.01206.x

Lopez, M. L., & Cooper, L. (2011). *Social support measures review*. Los Angeles, CA: National Center for Latino Child & Family Research. http://www.first5la.org/files/SSMS_LopezCooper_LiteratureReviewandTable_02212011.pdf

Ma, J. L.-C., Lai, K. Y. C., & Xia, L. L. L. (2020). Perceived social support, perception of competence, and hope among Chinese children with attention deficit hyperactivity disorder in a Chinese context: Children's perspective. *Child & Family Social Work, 25*(1), 74–82. doi: 10.1111/cfs.12655

Mana, A., Saka, N., Dahan, O., Ben-Simon, A., & Margalit, M. (2021). Implicit theories, social support, and hope as serial mediators for predicting academic self-efficacy among higher education students. *Learning Disability Quarterly*, Advance online publication. doi: 10.1177/0731948720918821

Margalit, M. (2018). *Accommodation policy: An international survey.* Research report, Ministry of Education, Jerusalem. http://meyda.education.gov.il/files/shefi/liikoheylemida/Skira_mediniut_hathamot.pdf

Marques, S. C., Gallagher, M. W., & Lopez, S. J. (2017). Hope - and academic-related outcomes: A meta-analysis. *School Mental Health, 9*(3), 250–262. doi: 10.1007/s12310-017-9212-9

Marques, S. C., & Lopez, S. J. (2018). Promoting hope in children. In M. W. Gallagher & S. J. Lopez (Eds.), *The Oxford handbook of hope* (pp. 117–132). Oxford University Press. doi: 10.1093/oxfordhb/9780199399314.013.10

Melrose, K. L., Brown, G. D. A., & Wood, A. M. (2015). When is received social support related to perceived support and well-being? When it is needed. *Personality and Individual Differences, 77,* 97–105. doi: 10.1016/j.paid.2014.12.047

Mikulincer, M., & Shaver, P. R. (2019). Attachment orientations and emotion regulation. *Current Opinion in Psychology, 25,* 6–10. doi: 10.1016/j.copsyc.2018.02.006

Mittelmark, M. B., Sagy, S., Eriksson, M., Bauer, G. F., Pelikan, J. M., Lindstrrom, B., & Espnes, G. A. (2017). *The Handbook of Salutogenesis.* Springer.

Moss-Pech, S. A., Southward, M. W., & Cheavens, J. S. (2021). Hope attenuates the negative impact of general psychological distress on goal progress. *Journal of Clinical Psychology.* Advance online publication, *77*(6), 1412–1427. doi: 10.1002/jclp.23087

Muyan-Yılık, M., & Demir, A. (2020). A pathway towards subjective well-being for Turkish university students: The roles of dispositional hope, cognitive flexibility, and coping strategies. *Journal of Happiness Studies, 21,* 1945–1963. doi: 10.1007/s10902-019-00162-2

Nalavany, B. A., & Carawan, L. W. (2012). Perceived family support and self-esteem: The mediational role of emotional experience in Adults with Dyslexia. *Dyslexia: An International Journal of Research and Practice, 18*(1), 58–74. doi: 10.1002/dys.1433

Ogston, P. L., Mackintosh, V. H., & Myers, B. J. (2011). Hope and worry in mothers of children with an autism spectrum disorder or Down syndrome. *Research in Autism Spectrum Disorders, 5,* 1378–1384.

Pérez-Wilson, P., Marcos-Marcos, J., Morgan, A., Eriksson, M., Lindström, B., & Álvarez-Dardet, C. (2021). 'A synergy model of health': An integration of salutogenesis and the health assets model. *Health Promotion International, 36(3),* 884–894.. doi: 10.1093/heapro/daaa084

Rand, K. L., & Cheavens, J. S. (2009). Hope theory. In S. J. Lopez & C. R. Snyder (Eds.), *Oxford handbook of positive psychology,* 2nd ed. (pp. 323–333). Oxford University Press.

Rosenstreich, E., Feldman, D. B., Davidson, O. B., Maza, E., & Margalit, M. (2015). Hope, optimism and loneliness among first-year college students with learning disabilities: A brief longitudinal study. *European Journal of Special Needs Education, 30*(3), 338–350. doi: 10.1080/08856257.2015.1023001

Samavi, S. A., Najarpourian, S., & Javdan, M. (2019). The effectiveness of group hope therapy in labor pain and mental health of pregnant women. *Psychological Reports, 122*(6), 2063–2073. doi: 10.1177/0033294118798625

Santilli, S., Nota, L., Ginevra, M. C., & Soresi, S. (2021). Career adaptability, hope and life satisfaction in workers with intellectual disability. *Journal of Vocational Behavior, 85(*1), 67–74. doi: 10.1016/j.jvb.2014.02.011

Sarıçam, H., Deveci, M., & ahmetoğlu, E. (2020). Examination of hope, intolerance of uncertainty and resilience levels in parents having disabled children. *Global Journal of Psychology Research New Trends and Issues, 10*, 118–131. doi: 10.18844/gjpr.v10i1.4398

Satici, S. A. (2020). Hope and loneliness mediate the association between stress and subjective vitality. *Journal of College Student Development, 61*, 225–239. doi: 10.1353/csd.2020.0019

Satici, S. A., Kayis, A. R., Satici, B., Griffiths, M. D., & Can, G. (2020). Resilience, hope, and subjective happiness among the turkish population: Fear of COVID-19 as a mediator. *International Journal of Mental Health and Addiction.* doi: 10.1007/ s11469-020-00443-5

Schei, J., Nøvik, T. S., Thomsen, P. H., Lydersen, S., Indredavik, M. S., & Jozefiak, T. (2018). What predicts a good adolescent to adult transition in ADHD? The role of self-reported resilience. *Journal of Attention Disorders, 22*(6), 547–560. doi: 10.1177/1087054715604362

Schmidt, J., Schmidt, M., & Brown, I. (2017). Quality of life among families of children with intellectual disabilities: A Slovene study. *Journal of Policy and Practice in Intellectual Disabilities, 14*(1), 87–102. doi: 10.1111/jppi.12188

Seligman, M. E. P., Railton, P., Baumeister, R. F., & Sripada, C. (2013). Navigating into the future or driven by the past *Perspectives on Psychological Science, 8*(2), 119–141. doi: 10.1177/1745691612474317

Sevincer, A. T., Tessmann, P., & Oettingen, G. (2018). Demand to act and use of mental contrasting. *Social Psychology, 49*(6), 344–359. doi: 10.1027/1864-9335/a000353

Sharabi, A., Levi, U., & Margalit, M. (2012). Children's loneliness, sense of coherence, family climate, and hope: Developmental risk and protective factors. *The Journal of Psychology, 146*, 61–83. doi: 10.1080/00223980.2011.568987

Sharabi, A., Sade, S., & Margalit, M. (2016). Virtual connections, personal resources, loneliness, and academic self-efficacy among college students with and without LD. *European Journal of Special Needs Education, 31*(3), 376–390. doi: 10.1080/08856257.2016.1141542

Shipp, A. J., & Aeon, B. (2019). Temporal focus: Thinking about the past, present, and future. *Current Opinion in Psychology, 26*, 37–43. doi: 10.1016/j. copsyc.2018.04.005

Shorey, H., Bisgaier, S., & Thien, S. (2018). Attachment processes and the social/ developmental bases of hope. In M. W. Gallagher & S. J. Lopez (Eds.), *The Oxford handbook of hope* (ch. 24, pp. 313–326). Oxford University Press.

Shorey, H. S., Little, T. D., Snyder, C. R., Kluck, B., & Robitschekb, C. (2007). Hope and personal growth initiative: A comparison of positive, future-oriented constructs. *Personality and Individual Differences, 43*(7), 1917–1926. doi: 10.1016/j.paid.2007.06.011

Snyder, C. R. (2002). Hope theory: Rainbows in the mind. *Psychological Inquiry, 13*(4), 249–275. doi: 10.1207/S15327965PLI1304_01

Van Ryzin, M. J. (2011). Protective factors at school: Reciprocal effects among adolescents' perceptions of the school environment, engagement in learning, and hope. *Journal of Youth and Adolescence, 40*(12), 1568–1580. doi: 10.1007/s10964-011-9637-7

Wong, J. C. S., & Yang, J. Z. (2021). Seeing is believing: Examining self-efficacy and trait hope as moderators of youths' positive risk-taking intention. *Journal of Risk Research, 24*(7), 819–832. doi: 10.1080/13669877.2020.1750463

Yeung, D. Y., Ho, S. M. Y., & Mak, C. W. Y. (2015). Attention to positive information mediates the relationship between hope and psychosocial well-being of adolescents. *Journal of Adolescence, 42*, 98–102. doi: 10.1016/j.adolescence.2015.04.004

Zapata, M. A. (2020). Disability affirmation and acceptance predict hope among adults with physical disabilities. *Rehabilitation Psychology, 65*(3), 291–298. doi: 10.1037/rep0000364

Chapter 8

Resilience, Disability, and Intrapersonal Factors Viewed through the Lens of Rehabilitation Psychology's Foundational Principles

Dana S. Dunn

In his influential *Essays*, Michel de Montaigne (2009) observed that "he who fears he shall suffer, already suffers what he fears" (p. 1950). In other words, the psychosocial toll of fear associated with pain and illness may precede any actual suffering—but the consequence may be the same. Yet we know that resilient individuals suffer less or very little compared to others, and they often emerge from their experience not only intact but stronger than before.

Still, psychosocial resilience—the ability to adapt to and spring back from adversity—remains something of a puzzle. Most people (about two-thirds) who encounter serious challenges—natural disasters, horrific accidents, personal trauma, disabling events—seem to overcome the odds while others experience dysfunction (e.g., Bonnano & Diminich, 2013; Galatzer-Levy et al., 2018). That is, unlike the imagined but fearful person in Montaigne's observation, resilient individuals display adaptive reactions to otherwise adverse situations and upsetting life events (e.g., Masten, 2007; Masten et al., 2009). In effect, most people cope with their travails and often emerge stronger afterward. However, resilient people differ from less resilient individuals in terms of how they appraise, understand, and cope with stress. When facing a stressor, they express greater acceptance and perceive less threat than their less-hardy counterparts. Similarly, their coping efforts are more active, showing greater efficacy than those with other patterns of adjustment (e.g., Quale & Shank, 2010).

Resilience is often erroneously portrayed as a personality trait, characteristic, or attribute, but evidence indicates that it is best conceived of as a dynamic process that occurs across different conceptual levels of analysis within a given individual (Bonanno, 2012). A chief problem with psychological resilience is that it means many different things in diverse contexts (Bonanno et al., 2015). As a strengths-based process and response, however, resilience is also a representative construct linked to positive psychology (e.g., Peterson & Seligman, 2004), the study of how such strengths can be leveraged to help people flourish and be successful (i.e., experiencing high levels of well-being) in their daily lives (e.g., Csikszentmihalyi & Nakamura, 2011; Lopez & Snyder, 2009; Snyder et al., 2021). Appropriate applications of resilience as a positive, strength-based approach afford investigators the opportunity to examine its beneficial influence among various subpopulations, including people with disabilities.

Disabled individuals—people with either one or more congenital or acquired disabilities and possibly some accompanying comorbidities—can respond to their particular circumstances with resilience. However, at present, there is less focused research available on resilience and its relation to disability (Terrill et al., 2019). The goal of this chapter is to explore resilient responses to disability as potential positive psychological personal factors tied to the World Health Organization's International Classification of Functioning, Disability, and Health Model (World Health Organization, 2001), a milestone effort that appeared around the same time as the new field of positive psychology gained academic traction (see chapter 1, this volume). Within this positive model, disability is not due to the presence of an impairment itself, but results from the interaction among personal and environmental factors that mediate the impact of the impairment—positively or negatively—on a person's activity and participation in everyday life. The ICF Model also suggested that resilience is an *intrapersonal factor*—a positive quality that resides in or is developed by many disabled people. However, research examining the social psychology of disability (e.g., Dunn, 2015; Wright, 1983) also posits that resilience can result, in part, from *situational factors*, as when something outside the person that interacts with or perhaps triggers an individual's personal qualities to react.

In this chapter, I briefly review the four typical trajectories of disruption in normal function usually observed following trauma, and then consider laypersons' perspectives on resilience. I then review the role and potential of rehabilitation psychology's Foundational Principles (Bentley et al., 2019; Dunn et al., 2016) for fostering resilience. These principles were drawn from the pioneering work of Beatrice A. Wright (1983) and other rehabilitation psychologists who promoted social psychologically grounded responses to disability, which served as precursors to many related ideas in today's positive psychology (e.g., Dunn & Brody, 2008; Dunn & Dougherty, 2005). These seven principles can serve as a lens for examining both intrapersonal and situational factors linked to resilience and disability, just as they can promote resilient responses to disability. I conclude the chapter by considering how both disabled and nondisabled people can use the principles to understand and promote resilient responses to disability.

We now consider the common trajectories of response to traumatic experiences, including resilience, the modal response.

TRAJECTORIES OF RESPONSE TO TRAUMA: RESILIENCE OCCURS FREQUENTLY

Research conducted by George Bonanno and colleagues (e.g., Bonanno & Diminich, 2013; Bonanno et al., 2012; Bonanno & Mancini, 2010; Morin et al., 2017) demonstrated that resilience is a relatively common response to trauma and that individuals' coping styles are not uniform—they vary considerably from one another (e.g., Galatzer-Levy & Bonanno, 2016). The study of resilience following disasters (e.g., flooding, terrorist attacks, hurricanes, war), for example, indicates these potentially traumatic events (PTEs) yield a variety of responses—from extreme distress to active and constructive coping. We may assume that many acquired disabilities rather than congenital disabilities are likely linked to PTEs, and that individual differences in response adhere to empirically observed trajectories from other contexts.

Bonanno and Gupta (2012) demonstrated that individual variability can be captured by four prototypical trajectories: chronic dysfunction, delayed reactions, resilience, and recovery (see also, Bonanno, 2004). Relatively few people who experience a PTE display chronic pathological reactions (e.g., about 5% to 10% of affected individual display posttraumatic stress disorder [PTSD]; Kessler et al., 1995). Higher levels of PTSD and other forms of psychopathology can occur when experience of the stressor is prolonged (Bonanno & Gupta). Delayed responses to traumatic events occur (in approximately 5% to 10% of cases) when symptoms begin to become more problematic across time, thereby representing subthreshold psychopathology. Recovery is also a response that is distinct from resilience, which, as already noted, tends to be the modal trajectory.

Although scientific perspectives on resilience and disability are important, we must also not overlook how resilience is construed in the popular mind. Hence, we turn to a comparison of lay perspectives on these topics.

LAY PERSPECTIVES ON RESILIENT RESPONSES TO DISABILITY

What we might call the lay or even *naïve* perspective of resilience and disability is apt to be familiar to many readers: a nondisabled individual observes a disabled person performing an everyday task, such as shopping and navigating the aisles of a grocery store. The nondisabled observer is struck by the fact that the disabled person can do her own grocery shopping. Indeed, the disabled person is then perceived by the observer to have hidden strengths of will that allow her to overcome her impairments. These strengths of will are often seen as being representative of possessing resilience, resilient qualities, or even having a resilient personality. The important part where social perception is concerned is that the perceived attributes are tied ineffably to the person; that is, they are seen as (possibly unique) personal or dispositional factors. While the witnessed behavior may denote resilience per se, the source of the resilience may be more complex than is recognized by the observer.

Put another way, resilient behavior is tied to personal factors held by the disabled individual. However, the origin of these personal qualities is not likely to have originated entirely in the person; rather, some aspects of the environment—other people, situational factors, the life circumstances of the individual, past experiences, rehabilitation regimens, and so forth—may have also shaped and prompted the resilient responses. Observers are often unaware of this reality and end up falling prey to any number of psychosocial biases tied to disability (e.g., Dunn, 2019b), such as the *fundamental attribution error* (Ross, 1977) or *confirmation bias* (e.g., Nickerson, 1998). In the former case, observers attribute the cause of the disabled person's behavior to dispositional factors (i.e., personality traits) while ignoring any situational influences. Where the latter is concerned, observers search for supporting evidence in biased ways, generally avoiding attending to information that is inconsistent with their expectations (i.e., any non-resilient behaviors are ignored; see Dunn [2019b] for more detail on either bias).

Why does this matter? Because similar to many lay people, social and rehabilitation psychologists can presume that resilient responses—or the lack thereof—are due to the person and their character or personal qualities—and not other factors, including situational ones, that influence or interact with those qualities. It is important to remember that the study of resilience has sometimes been stymied by the fact that researchers discover that some people remain resilient in the face of loss or trauma while similar others fold and fail to thrive in the same circumstance. Thus, the actual and important factors that trigger intrapersonal resilience may be missed in any resulting analysis.

Another reason lay perspectives on resilience matter is that they may be overly simplistic, so that casual observers may assume that a person facing a challenging life circumstance, such as an acquired physical disability, may be urged to develop resilient qualities. Such "encouragement" is likely another form of *ableism* or prejudiced attitudes and discriminatory beliefs that favor nondisabled persons (Bogart & Dunn, 2019; Nario-Redmond, 2020). For example, people can be told they can be resilient by "being hopeful where their future is concerned" or "keep problems in a proper perspective"—such advice is intended as helpful but may not be when the current experience is a traumatic one. The disabled person may be regaled with well-intentioned platitudes such as "winners never quit and quitters never win" or "look at your abilities, not your disabilities" (e.g., Pulrang, 2018). Motivational memes can fit here as well, where "Don't make excuses!" or the similar captions a photo or image of a disabled individual doing something unexpected, like playing wheelchair basketball or running a marathon using running blades. At times, these simplistic messages about resilience come close to serving as a form of "inspiration porn," classified as attempted portrayals of people with disabilities as inspiring or motivating by living their lives despite having a disability (e.g., Young, 2012). Being placed on a pedestal due to disability objectifies disabled people for the benefit of nondisabled individuals (see also, Grue, 2016).

To be fair, in their taxonomy of character strengths and virtues, Peterson and Seligman (2004) claimed that individuals could acquire new beneficial personal qualities—in effect, character can be *cultivated*—by learning and demonstrating them behaviorally. In other words, people could develop positive personal qualities through their own efforts, an intriguing perspective that is at odds with much of the traditional research on personality, which rarely posits the origins or development of traits (Funder, 2019). Resilience is discussed but not highlighted as a particular strength in the character strengths taxonomy, though related constructs like bravery and persistence are classified as strengths of courage (see Peterson & Seligman, 2004).

Besides appearing in response to trauma, resilience is also a response to professional rehabilitation efforts or interventions. We now highlight how rehabilitation psychology's Foundational Principles can elicit resilience among disabled persons.

THE FOUNDATIONAL PRINCIPLES, RESILIENCE, AND DISABILITY

The field of *Rehabilitation Psychology* has codified a group of Foundational Principles that are grounded in clinical and practice efforts as well as the social psychology of disability. These principles are drawn from the work of social psychologist Kurt Lewin, his student Beatrice A. Wright, and her colleagues (e.g., Roger Barker, Tamara Dembo), who founded and shaped the field of rehabilitation psychology. The Foundational Principles, which are listed and defined in table 8.1, include (a) the person-environment relation, (b) the insider-outsider distinction, (c) adjustment to disability, (d) psychological assets, (e) self-perception of bodily states, and (f) human dignity (see Bentley

Table 8.1   The Foundational Principles of Rehabilitation Psychology

Principle	Definition
Person-Environment Relation	Attributions about people with disabilities tend to focus on presumed dispositional rather than available situational characteristics. Environmental constraints usually matter more than personality factors to living with a disability.
Insider-Outsider Distinction	People with disabilities (*insiders*) know what life with a chronic condition is like (e.g., sometimes challenging but usually manageable), whereas casual observers (*outsiders*) who lack relevant experience presume that disability is defining, all encompassing, and decidedly negative.
Adjustment to Disability	Coping with a disability or chronic illness is an ongoing dynamic process, one dependent on making constructive changes to the social and physical environment.
Psychological Assets	People with disabilities possess or can acquire personal or psychological qualities that can ameliorate challenges posed by disability and also enrich daily living.
Self-Perception of Bodily States	Experience of bodily states (e.g., pain, fatigue, distress) is based on people's perceptions of the phenomena, not exclusively the actual sensations. Changing attitudes, expectations, or environmental conditions can constructively alter perceptions.
Human Dignity	Regardless of the source or severity of a disability or chronic health condition, all people deserve respect and encouragement and to be treated with dignity.
Advocacy Efforts	Advocacy efforts aimed at promoting the health and well-being of disabled individuals are important. Such efforts should be made by disabled people themselves as well as their allies (e.g., family, friends, medical and rehabilitation professionals).

Source: The first six principles are from Dunn, Ehde, and Wegener (2016, p. 2), while the seventh principle originated in the present chapter.

et al., 2019; Dunn et al., 2016, 2021b). Advocacy, including self-advocacy by people with disabilities and that conducted by allies, is also considered to be an additional and important principle (see table 8.1; Dunn et al., 2021a). These principles can help disabled persons develop a positive disability identity while also promoting or maintaining resilience when encountering obstacles and challenges linked to disability. (For their part, nondisabled people can reduce their ableist beliefs and become allies by becoming familiar with the Foundational Principles.) Each of the principles will be further defined and related research representing resilience will be discussed in this chapter.

The Person–Environment Relation

Assumptions about people with disabilities and their behavior generally focus on presumed dispositional characteristics rather than influential situational factors (e.g., Dunn, 2015, 2019a). When it comes to living with a disability, environmental constraints usually trump personality traits or related qualities. Of course, both personal and situational factors matter; however, Kurt Lewin (1935) argued that the interaction *between* the two sources is what leads to actual behavior (see also, Lewin, 1948/1997), including resilient behavior. This subtle but important point indicates the important role that the person–environment interaction plays in the daily lives of disabled persons, just as it is also relevant to the other six Foundational Principles. Resilient behavioral responses are hypothesized to result from an individual's personal qualities (e.g., prior experiences, expectations) and the influence of situation (i.e., stressful circumstance, nature of the threat, availability of social support). Rehabilitation professionals recognize that the relationship between the person and the environment can constructively shape social, psychological, and practical opportunities for people with disabilities as they navigate their daily lives (see also, Bentley et al., 2019). This principle is also inexorably tied to the next one, the insider-outsider distinction.

The Insider-Outsider Distinction

Although people with disabilities know what living with a disability is like, nondisabled observers often presume that they do, as well. Dembo (1964, 1982) referred to this as the insider-outsider distinction, where the former (*insiders*) know disability intimately and the latter (*outsiders*) imagine what disability might or even *must* be like (generally, disability is viewed negatively, as a serious disruption to daily living, and as wholly defining of the person's experience). This biased perspective ignores the fact that disability is one personal quality among many, just as its presence neither predicts nor precludes favorable levels of well-being or quality of life. Insiders know that disability only becomes a preoccupation when it is made salient by other people (usually outsiders) or situational constraints (e.g., accessibility issues), and that it also serves as a positive part of people's identities (e.g., Dunn, 2015).

Certainly, insiders recognize that any resilient responses on their part aimed at ameliorating stressors or threats are not necessarily affected by their disabilities. Just as resilient responses may emerge from disabling experiences, they may also occur independent of them and in response to other intrapersonal or even situational factors. In contrast, outsiders need to be de-biased; that is, educated about insiders' actual experiences and perspectives.

At the same time, any resilient reactions made by insiders should be presented as normative (i.e., as the work of Bonanno and colleagues has demonstrated; see, for example, Bonnano et al., 2012) rather than extraordinary. And as Bentley and colleagues (2019) suggested, rehabilitation professionals and other health-care providers are not immune from adopting outsider views; they, too, need to be reminded that intrapersonal factors that influence insiders' resilience are dynamic. As noted earlier, many naïve observers may attribute exhibited resilience in a disabled individual or its apparent absence to dispositional factors when the actual cause may be more complex. This realization is also important for appreciating any process of adjustment to disability.

Adjustment to Disability

Coping with a disability or chronic illness is an ongoing dynamic process, one dependent on making constructive changes to the social and physical environment (see chapter 4, this volume). At the same time, successfully navigating the social and physical worlds also can be accomplished by relying on some intrapersonal factors. In a review of research linking resilience and disability, Terrill et al. (2019) identified several intrapersonal factors that can promote adjustment to disability. These factors include positive emotions, styles of coping, making meaning (i.e., seeing significance in daily life, finding a sense of purpose), optimism, and the situation-specific construct, self-efficacy. We will review each factor briefly in turn.

Positive Emotions

Stress or even distress is identified as a normal emotional response tied to acquired disabilities, including spinal cord injury (SCI) and amputation. Resilience is usually marked by a mix of or a balance among negative and positive emotions. Though the former outnumber the latter, positive emotions, including happiness, joy, and enthusiasm, entail relatively intense feelings that are of short duration (though people can prolong them through particular behavioral choices, such as helping others). In the broaden-and-build model, Fredrickson (2001; Tugade & Fredrickson, 2004) theorized and demonstrated that positive emotions can broaden a person's thought-action repertoire, which leads to greater behavioral flexibility that, across time, develops personal resources and close social bonds, and promotes physical health (Garland et al., 2010). The upshot, then, is that positive emotional states can serve as one of the foundations for resilience (Terrill et al., 2019) and that they can further build resilience (Fredrickson et al., 2008; Tugade & Fredrickson, 2007).

Evidence demonstrates that favorable emotions are associated with reduced cardiovascular risks, improved functional outcomes following acute medical interventions, and better survival rates (see, for example, Chida & Steptoe, 2008). Where disability is concerned, positive emotions are found to coincide with less perceived pain, enhanced functional status, greater participation in social events, a higher quality of life, and lowered risk for acquiring new disabilities (e.g., stroke, SCI, multiple sclerosis, among other chronic health conditions linked to aging; Alschuler et al., 2016; Berges et al., 2011, 2012; Fisher et al., 2004; Ostir et al., 2004; van Leeuwen et al., 2012; Zautra et al., 2005).

Styles of Coping

How do individuals habitually handle stressors? Styles of coping are linked to resilience but serve in a more immediate capacity, as the latter develops as time unfolds. Yet, some styles of coping do represent resilient responses. *Approach-based coping*, an active coping style associated with adaptive reactions to SCI, entails people making direct efforts to address or deal with relevant problems (e.g., Pollard & Kennedy, 2007). *Pragmatic coping*, which is focused and goal-oriented, is marked by "doing whatever is necessary" to counter particular stressors (e.g., Mancini & Bonanno, 2006). *Flexible coping* is a style where individuals have the skill to match optimal coping strategies to situational demands (Cheng, Lau, & Chan, 2014). Terrill and colleagues (2019) offered a potentially important summary observation regarding these styles of coping: although these realistic forms of coping are often linked to negative qualities (such as inflexible personalities) and appearing to "cope ugly" (see Bonanno, 2009), they nonetheless account for highly favorable adjustment to loss, disability, and related traumatic events.

Making or Finding Meaning

Another form of resilience is represented as finding some positive or higher meaning associated with an otherwise negative or even traumatic event. Indeed, some individuals find meaning or see significance in adverse events, which in turn can promote adjustment and adaptation (e.g., Dunn, 1994; see also, Dunn, 1996, where people with congenital or acquired amputations who found meaning reported high levels of well-being and lower levels of depression). Meaning can manifest itself in a variety of ways, including posttraumatic growth, accepting the life changing event, and integrating the experience's meaning into one's identity (e.g., Park, 2010). Some people find meaning by seeing or redefining their purpose-in-life (e.g., pursuing goals or objectives that provide future direction; Ryff, 1989). Acquiring a purpose-in-life orientation has been linked with favorable adjustment to SCI (Thompson et al., 2003) and to increased life satisfaction and positive emotions among individuals who have multiple sclerosis (MS) (Packenham, 2007). Of course, people who experience acquired disability or other chronic health problems should not be urged or coached to find meaning or other purpose in what has happened to them; rather, they should come to such realizations or conclusions on their own (Dunn, Uswatte, & Elliott, 2021b).

Optimism

Optimism is both dispositional, that is, predicated on holding favorable future outcome expectancies (e.g., Bouchard et al., 2019), and also a habitual way of explaining the occurrence of positive and negative events (e.g., Gillham et al., 2001) (see chapter 5, this volume). The former is more of a trait and the latter a state—albeit a consistent one that can be learned (e.g., moving away from a pessimistic way of explaining bad events, that is, no longer seeing them as internal, stable, and global; Seligman, 1991; see also, Peterson & Steen, 2021). Where health and well-being are concerned, for example, optimists have been found to have a lower incidence of coronary heart disease (CHD) (Tindle et al., 2009), stroke and CHD (Kim et al., 2011; Nabi et al., 2010), and lower mortality rates in general (e.g., Engberg et al., 2013).

What may be key here is that optimism leads to resilient coping responses (Carver et al., 1989); that is, optimists rely on both cognitive and behavioral efforts to tackle and manage stressors tied to health issues (e.g., Carver & Scheier, 1998). Put another way, optimists anticipate favorable outcomes in the future, hence stressors are more likely to be construed as challenges or even opportunities for personal growth rather than threats (Terrill et al., 2019). Related research on SCI finds that individuals who appraise their impairment as a challenge instead of a threat display both higher levels of resilience and quality of life (Bonanno et al., 2012; Peter et al., 2014).

Self-Efficacy

As a construct, self-efficacy refers to whether individuals perceive they possess the capability to achieve a desired outcome; in effect, they know what needs to be done and their self-efficacy expectations point to their level of confidence in being able to rise to the behavioral occasion (e.g., Bandura, 1997). Terrill and colleagues (2014), for example, in a large scale study of individuals with long-term physical disability, found that resilience was positively correlated with self-efficacy. A study by Amtmann et al. (2012) revealed a pronounced association between self-efficacy and active social participation (e.g., peer-socializing, volunteering, enjoying leisure activities). These investigators proposed that higher levels of self-efficacy were more confident in their abilities to control symptoms tied to their impairments, thereby enabling them to pursue their social roles. They behaved resiliently in the face of obstacles linked to their physical disabilities.

Terrill et al. (2019) suggested that self-efficacy may well account for the relations among resilience, pain interference, and depression. Thus, self-efficacy may serve as an important factor in understanding favorable outcomes experienced by people with disabilities. We now turn to personal resources—psychosocial assets—that also serve as beneficial intrapersonal qualities tied to resilient behavior among some disabled individuals.

Psychosocial Assets

What array of resources—whether real or potential, even imagined, for that matter—are distinct within each disabled person? Wright (1983) argued that the severity of a disability had no effect on any psychosocial asset or assets already possessed or acquirable by affected individuals. And in any case, available assets can ameliorate many ordeals posed by disability while also enriching daily life. Assets can be tangible (e.g., a job or career, income, property), intangible (e.g., self-concept, self-esteem), personality-related (e.g., optimism, extraversion), attainable or achieved (e.g., educational degree, elected office in an organization), a strength of character (e.g., persistence, hardiness), or an interest or hobby (e.g., birdwatching, writing poetry). Assets can be retained, acquired, or relearned, and they serve as reminders to disabled persons about their accomplishments or future potential despite bodily changes or impairments. Rehabilitation professionals can ask about a person's assets as a way to assess individuating strengths and to maintain or encourage the development of a positive outlook for the future (for a detailed list of assets, see Dunn, 2015).

McGriffin et al. (2018) considered assets in a more literal sense—socioeconomic resources—and their relation to trajectories of depression and resilience following acquired disability. Participants were drawn from the Health and Retirement Study (HRS; http://hrsonline.isr.umich.edu). At the study's start, none of the participants reported any problems with performing activities of daily living (ADLs) in five areas (i.e., walking across a room, getting dressed, bathing, eating, and getting out of bed); however, across time, they reported one or more ADLs, indicating a transition from no impairment to chronic disability. The participants had also completed at least two depression assessments across four waves of the study. Latent growth mixture modeling revealed four group trajectories for depressive symptoms: resilience (56.5% showed low depression pre- and post-disability onset), emerging depression (17.2% had low pre-disability depression that rose precipitously across time), remitting depression (13.4% displayed high pre-disability depression that declined over time), and chronic depression

(12.9% evidenced high pre-disability depression that stayed elevated across the study). However, two socioeconomically related assets—prior education and financial assets at disability onset—"robustly predicted class membership in the resilient class compared to all other classes" (p. 98). Where disability onset is concerned, these particular assets provided some protection (see also, Kavanagh et al., 2015; Smith et al., 2005). According to McGriffin and colleagues, then, assets like wealth and education serve as "unique and independent predictors of disability adjustment" (p. 101) while also mitigating the negative impact of stressful circumstances. Although the protective role these related assets play is not surprising, future research should attempt to understand the association further while also exploring whether other types of assets offer similar benefits to disabled individuals.

Self-Perception of Bodily States

This Foundational Principle serves as a reminder that people's experience of bodily states, such as pain or fatigue (or, for that matter, acute or chronic stress), is based on their perceptions of the psychophysiological phenomena and not merely the actual sensations themselves. Perception is malleable, and it is affected or altered by (positive) attitude, (favorable) expectations, and factors in the environment. In other words, people with disabilities who develop and display resilience may be able to change their assessments of their bodily states and feelings just as they are known to be able to change their appraisals of stressful threats to more manageable (and often helpful) challenges.

Similarly, Dembo et al. (1956/1975; see also, McCarthy, 2011) counseled that promoting value changes in response to disability could also be beneficial. Individuals with acquired disabilities, for example, might subordinate issues of physique relative to other important and desirable values they already possess or can acquire (the previous consideration of assets is clearly relevant here, as well). Reconciling what matters in life by broadening one's range of values is also a means to advance resilience (see also, Marmé, 2017).

Human Dignity

People with disabilities often encounter ableism in daily life, as their conditions may be stigmatizing (e.g., Andrews, 2019; Dunn, 2015; Nario-Redmond, 2020). Still, no chronic health condition or a disability—no matter its origin or serious nature—reduces or eliminates the right of all individuals to receive respect and encouragement, and to be treated with dignity. This particular Foundational Principle may be the most important one, as the other principles may be construed as emanating from it.

Where resilience is concerned, disabled individuals should be accorded patient-centered care while also being consulted as effective comanagers of such care—as insiders, their opinions and experiences are an important part of their rehabilitation regimen and a source of strength. To quote Wright (1987), "An essential core-concept of human dignity is that person is not an object, not a thing" (p. 12). Culturally competent psychologists can provide the socioemotional scaffolding where client dignity can flourish and serve as a framework where resilience will grow.

Advocacy Efforts by Disabled Individuals, the Disability Community, or Disability Allies

As Kurt Lewin (1935) argued, behavior is a function of the person and the real or perceived (i.e., psychosocial) environment. Sometimes, for example, situational demands can override an extraverted person's personality so that they remain silent during a solemn religious service. Similarly, a person with a disability may feel empowered by their identity to assert their right to non-rationed medical care during a pandemic by engaging in self-advocacy efforts (Andrews et al., 2020; Lund & Ayers, 2020). Such self-advocacy is also a form of disability advocacy, which is tied to the sociopolitical model of disability and the desire for self-determination (Dirth & Nario-Redmond, 2019). Self-advocacy, disability advocacy, and related behaviors are intrapersonal as well as situational representations of resilience that can be tied to rehabilitation psychology's Foundational Principles (Bentley et al., 2019; Dunn et al., 2016). Although Wright, Dembo, and other early rehabilitation professionals routinely advocated for the rights and welfare of disabled individuals through their research, practice efforts, and writing, advocacy per se was not identified early on as one of the main principles of rehabilitation psychology. More recently, perhaps due to the rise of disability studies, disability activism, and the renewed focus on the principles, advocacy efforts are now recognized as essential therein. Thus, a seventh principle focused on advocacy was added to the original six principles (see table 8.1).

Although it is not an intrapersonal quality possessed by people with disabilities, advocacy efforts by disability allies can also contribute to helping members of the disability community develop resilience. One way is to join with disabled people in the fight to gain social, educational, economic, political, and employment parity with the nondisabled majority. The Covid-19 pandemic revealed that many government officials and policymakers felt emboldened to ration medical care, especially that available and necessary for people with disabilities (see Andrews et al., 2020). As Terrill and colleagues (2019) reminded us: "Resilience may be reinforced by the broader environment in terms of cultural values, government policy, and healthcare systems" (p. 314). Disability allies—including rehabilitation profession-als—can help by organizing with disabled people and their sociopolitical organizations in order to eradicate such medical rationing practices (e.g., Forber-Pratt et al., 2019). Such advocacy and activism benefits all of society.

CONCLUSIONS AND FUTURE DIRECTIONS

Resilience remains an essential but still somewhat elusive topic where disability is concerned. This chapter advances the idea that rehabilitation psychology's Foundational Principles represent one arena that can guide intrapersonal understanding of resilience in disabled persons. At the same time, readers must recognize the wise counsel offered by Bonanno and his colleagues, who have long argued that only comprehensive longitudinal studies will likely provide researchers and practitioners with the most helpful data; cross-sectional designs only offer a snapshot of resilience without the causal mechanisms necessarily specified.

Similarly, rehabilitation psychology's Foundational Principles can serve as guideposts for exploring positive and resilient reactions to disability. Researchers need not examine them all but, rather, should select one or two that best demonstrate resilience or a related psychosocial response to dis-ability or another chronic illness within a particular context. Renewed study of the principles can connect original insights in rehabilitation psychology to important research occurring in the present, while also promoting posi-tive well-being among disabled persons. By learning about and applying the Foundational Principles, nondisabled individuals, whether onlookers or allies, can learn to better understand and reduce any biased perspectives they may harbor toward disability.

REFERENCES

Alschuler, K. N., Kratz, A. L., & Ehde, D. M. (2016). Resilience and vulnerability in individuals with chronic pain and physical disability. *Rehabilitation Psychology, 61*(1), 7–18. doi: 10.1037/rep000055

Amtmann, D., Bamer, A. M., Cook, K. F., Askew, R. L., Noonan, V. K., & Brockway, J. A. (2012). University of Washington self-efficacy scale: A new self-efficacy scale for people with disabilities. *Archives of Physical Medicine & Rehabilitation, 93* (10), 1757–1765. doi: S0003-9993(12)00320-6

Andrews, E. E. (2019). *Disability as diversity: Developing cultural competence.* Oxford University Press.

Andrews, E. E., Ayers, K. B., Brown, K. S., Dunn, D. S., & Pilarski, C. R. (2021). No body is expendable: Medical rationing and disability justice during the COVID-19 pandemic. *American Psychologist, 76*(3), 451–461. *https://doi.org/10.1037/amp0000709*

Bandura, A. (1997). *Self-efficacy: The exercise of control.* Worth.

Bentley, J. A., Tingey, J. L., Lum, J., & Ho, S.-E. (2019). Rehabilitation psychology's foundational principles and social psychological theory. In D. S. Dunn (Ed.), *Understanding the experience of disability: Perspectives from social and rehabilitation psychology* (pp. 74–89). Oxford University Press.

Berges, I. M., Seale, G. S., & Ostir, G. V. (2011). Positive affect and pain ratings in persons with stroke. *Rehabilitation Psychology, 56*(1), 52–57. doi: 10.1037/a0022683

Berges, I. M., Seale, G. S., & Ostir, G. V. (2012). The role of positive affect on social participation following stroke. *Disability and Rehabilitation, 34*(25), 2119–2123. doi: 10.3109/09638288.2012.673684

Bogart, K., & Dunn, D. S. (2019). Ableism. *Journal of Social Issues, 75*(3), 643–984.

Bonanno, G. A. (2004). Loss, trauma, and human resilience: Have we underestimated the human capacity to thrive after extremely aversive events? *American Psychologist, 59*(1), 20–28.

Bonanno, G. A. (2009). *The other side of sadness: What the new science of bereavement tells us about life after loss.* Basic Books.

Bonanno, G. A. (2012). Uses and abuses of the resilience construct: Loss, trauma, and health-related adversities. *Social Science & Medicine, 74,* 753–756. doi: 10.1016/j.socscimed.2011.11.022

Bonnano, G. A., & Diminich, E. D. (2013). Annual research review: Positive adjustment to adversity – trajectories of minimal-impact resilience and emergent resilience. *The Journal of Child Psychology and Psychiatry, 54*(4), 378–401. doi: 10.1111/jcpp.12021

Bonanno, G. A., & Gupta, S. (2012). Resilience after disaster. In Y. Neria, S. Galea, & F. H. Norris (Eds.), *Mental health and disasters* (pp. 145–160). Cambridge University Press.

Bonanno, G. A., Kennedy, P., Galatzer-Levy, I. R., Lude, P., & Elfström, M. L. (2012). Trajectories of resilience, depression, and anxiety following spinal cord injury. *Rehabilitation Psychology, 57*(3), 236–247. doi: 10.1037/a0029256

Bonanno, G., & Mancini, A. D. (2012). Beyond resilience and PTSD: Mapping the heterogeneity of responses to potential trauma. *Psychological Trauma: Theory, Research, Practice, and Policy, 4*(1), 74–83. doi: 10.1037/a0017829

Bonanno, G. A., Romero, S. A., & Klein, S. I. (2015). The temporal elements of psychological resilience: An integrative framework for the study of individuals, families, and communities. *Psychological Inquiry, 26,* 139–169. doi: 10.1080/1047840X.2015.992677

Bouchard, L. C., Carver, C. S., Mens, M. G., & Scheier, M. F. (2019). Optimism, health, and well-being. In D. S. Dunn (Ed.), *Positive psychology: Established and emerging issues* (pp. 112–130). Routledge.

Carver, C. S., & Scheier, M. F. (1998). *On the self-regulation of behavior.* Cambridge University Press.

Carver, C. S., Scheier, M. F., & Weintraub, J. K. (1989). Assessing coping strategies: A theoretically based approach. *Journal of Personality and Social Psychology, 56*(2), 267–283. doi: 10.1037/022-3514.56.2.267

Chan, F., da Silva Cardoso, E., & Chronister, J. A. (Eds.). (2009). *Understanding psychosocial adjustment to chronic illness and disability: A handbook for evidence-based practitioners in rehabilitation.* Springer.

Cheng, C., Lau, H. P., & Chan, M. P. (2014). Coping flexibility and psychological adjustment to stressful life changes: A meta-analytic review. *Psychological Bulletin, 140*(6), 1582–1607. doi: 10.1037/a0037913

Chida, Y., & Steptoe, A. (2008). Positive psychological well-being and mortality: A quantitative review of prospective observational studies. *Psychosomatic Medicine, 70*(7), 741–756.

Csikszentmihalyi, M., & Nakamura, J. (2011). Positive psychology: Where did it come from, where is it going? In K. M. Sheldon, T. B. Kashan, & M. F. Steger (Eds.), *Designing positive psychology: Taking stock and moving forward* (pp. 3–8). Oxford University Press.

Dembo, T. (1964). Sensitivity of one person to another. *Rehabilitation Literature, 25,* 231–235.

Dembo, T. (1982). Some problems in rehabilitation as seen by a Lewinan. *Journal of Social Issues, 38,* 131–139. 10.1111/j.1540-4560.1982.tb00848.x

Dembo, T., Ladieu-Leviton, G., & Wright, B. A. (1956). Adjustment to misfortune: A problem of social psychological rehabilitation. *Artificial Limbs, 3*(2), 4–62.

de Montaigne, M. (2009). *Essays.* Edited by W. C. Hazlitt. The Floating Press. *ProQuest Ebook Central.* https://ebookcentral.proquest.com/lib/moravian-library-ebooks/detail.action?docID=445906.

Dirth, T. P., & Nario-Redmond, M. R. (2019). Disability advocacy for a new era: Leveraging social psychology and a sociopolitical approach to change. In D. S. Dunn (Ed.), *Understanding the experience of disability: Perspectives from social and rehabilitation psychology* (pp. 347–365). Oxford University Press.

Dunn, D. S. (1994). Positive meaning and illusions following disability: Reality negotiation, normative interpretation, and value change. *Journal of Social Behavior and Personality, 9,* 123–138.

Dunn, D. S. (1996). Well-being following amputation: Salutary effects of positive meaning, optimism, and control. *Rehabilitation Psychology, 41,* 285–302.

Dunn, D. S. (2015). *The social psychology of disability.* Oxford University Press.

Dunn, D. S. (2019a). Only connect: The social psychology of disability. In L. A. Brenner, S. Reid-Arndt, T.R. Elliott, R. G. Frank, & B. Caplan (Eds.), *Handbook of rehabilitation psychology* (3rd ed., pp. 143–156). Washington, DC: American Psychological Association.

Dunn, D. S. (2019b). Judging disability: Some biases identified by social psychology and rehabilitation psychology. In D. S. Dunn (Ed.), *Understanding the experience of disability: Perspectives from social and rehabilitation psychology* (pp. 24–38). Oxford University Press.

Dunn, D. S., & Brody, C. (2008). Defining the good life following acquired physical disability. *Rehabilitation Psychology, 53,* 413–425.

Dunn, D. S., Brown, K., Forber-Pratt, A., Gorgens, K., Gray, A., Rohe, D., Tackett, M. J., & Wilson, C. (2021a, February). *Foundational principles: Responding to the crises of our time.* Town hall panel discussion at Rehabilitation Psychology Conference 2021 [virtual conference].

Dunn, D. S., & Dougherty, S. B. (2005). Prospects for a positive psychology of rehabilitation. *Rehabilitation Psychology, 50,* 305–311.

Dunn, D. S., Ehde, D. M., & Wegener, S. T. (2016). The foundational principles as psychological lodestars: Theoretical inspiration and empirical direction in rehabilitation psychology. *Rehabilitation Psychology, 61,* 1–6.

Dunn, D. S., Uswatte, G., & Elliott, T. R. (2021b). Happiness and resilience following physical disability. In C. R. Snyder, S. J. Lopez, L. M. Edwards, & S. C. Marques (Eds.), *Oxford handbook of positive psychology* (3rd ed., pp. 928–942). New York: Oxford University Press.

Engberg, H., Jeune, B., Andersen-Ranberg, K., Martinussen, T., Vaupel, J. W., & Christensen, K. (2013). Optimism and survival: Does an optimistic outlook predict better survival at advanced ages? A twelve-year follow-up of Danish nonagenarians. *Aging Clinical and Experimental Research, 25*(5), 517–525. doi: 10.1007/s40520-013-0122-x

Fisher, M. N., Snih, S. A., Ostir, G. V., & Goodwin, J. S. (2004). Positive affect and disability among older Mexican Americans with arthritis. *Arthritis and Rheumatology, 51*(1), 34–39. doi: 10.1002/art.20079

Fletcher, D., & Sarkar, M. (2016). Mental fortitude training: An evidence-based approach to developing psychological resilience for sustained success. *Journal of Sport Psychology in Action, 7,* 135–157. doi: 10.1080/21520704.2016.1255496

Forber-Pratt, A. J., Mueller, C. O., & Andrews, E. E. (2019). Disability identity and allyship in rehabilitation psychology: Sit, stand, sign, and show up. *Rehabilitation Psychology, 64*(2), 119–129. doi: 10.1037/rep0000256

Fredrickson, B. L. (2001). The role of positive emotions in positive psychology: The broaden-and-build theory of positive emotions. *American Psychologist, 56* (3), 218–226.

Fredrickson, B. L., Cohn, M. A., Coffey, K. A., Pek, J., & Finkel, S. M. (2008). Open hearts build lives: Positive emotions, induced through loving-kindness meditation, build consequential personal resources. *Journal of Personality and Social Psychology, 95,* 1045–1062.

Funder, D. C. (2019). *The personality puzzle* (8th ed.). Norton.

Galatzer-Levy, I. R., & Bonanno, G. A. (2016). It's not easy to make resilience go away: Commentary on Infurna and Luthar (2016). *Perspectives on Psychological Science, 11*(2), 195–198. doi: 10.1177/1745691615621277

Galatzer-Levy, I. R., Huang, S. H., & Bonanno, G. A. (2018). Trajectories of resilience and dysfunction following potential trauma: A review and statistical evaluation. *Clinical Psychology Review, 63,* 41–55. doi: 10.1016/j.cpr.2018.05.008

Garland, E. L., Fredrickson, B., Kring, A. M., Johnson, D. P., Meyer, P. S., & Penn, D. L. (2010). Upward spirals of positive emotion counter downward spirals of negativity: Insights from the broaden-and-build theory and affective neuroscience on the treatment of emotion dysfunctions and deficits in psychopathology. *Clinical Psychology Review, 30*(7), 849–864. doi: 10.1016/j.cpr.2010.03.02

Gillham, J. E., Shatté, A. J., Reivich, K. J., & Seligman, M. E. P. (2001). *Optimism, pessimism, and explanatory style*. In E. C. Chang (Ed.), *Optimism & pessimism: Implications for theory, research, and practice* (p. 53–75). American Psychological Association.

Grue, J. (2016). The problem with inspiration porn: A tentative definition and a provisional critique. *Disability & Society, 31*, 838–849. doi: 10.1080.09687599.2016.1205473

Kavanagh, A. M., Aitken, Z., Krnjacki, L., LaMontagne, A. D., Bentley, R., & Milner, A. (2015). Mental health following acquisition of disability in adulthood—The impact of wealth. *PLoS ONE, 10*, e0139708. doi: 10.1371/journal.pone.0139708

Kim, E. S., Park, N., & Peterson, C. (2011). Dispositional optimism protects older adults from stroke: The health and retirement study. *Stroke, 42*(10), 2855–2859. doi: 10.1161/STROKEAHA.111.613448

Lewin, K. A. (1935). *A dynamic theory of personality*. McGraw-Hill.

Lewin, K. (1948/1997). *Resolving social conflicts: Field theory in social science*. American Psychological Association.

Livneh, H. (1982). On the origins of negative attitudes toward people with disabilities. *Rehabilitation Literature, 43*, 338–347.

Lopez, S. J., & Snyder, C. R. (Eds.). (2009). *Oxford handbook of positive psychology* (2nd ed.). Oxford University Press.

Lund, E. M., & Ayers, K. B. (2020). Raising awareness of disabled lives and health care rationing during the COVID-19 pandemic. *Psychological Trauma: Theory, Research, Practice, and Policy, 12*(S1), S210–S211. doi: 10.1037/tra0000673

Mancini, A. D., & Bonanno, G. A. (2006). Resilience in the face of potential trauma: Clinical practices and illustrations. *Journal of Clinical Psychology, 62*(8), 971–985. doi: 10.1002/jclp.202283

Marmé, M. (2017). *Strengths-based theory and practice: Perspectives and strategies that enhance growth, hope, and resilience for people living with chronic illness and disability* (pp. 125–148). Routledge.

Masten, A. S. (2007). Resilience in developing systems: Progress and promise as the fourth wave rises. *Development and Psychopathology, 2*, 425–444. doi: 10.1017/S0954579400005812

Masten, A. S., Cutuili, J. J., Herbers, J. E., & Reed, M.-G. J. (2009). Resilience in development. In S. J. Lopez & C. R. Snyder (Eds.), *Oxford handbook of positive psychology* (pp. 117–131). Oxford University Press.

McCarthy, H. (2011). A modest festschrift and insider perspective on Beatrice Wright's contributions to rehabilitation theory and practice. *Rehabilitation Counseling Bulletin, 54*(2), 67–81.

McGriffin, J. N., Galatzer-Levy, I. R., & Bonanno, G. A. (2018). Socioeconomic resources predict trajectories of depression and resilience following disability. *Rehabilitation Psychology, 64*(1), 98–103. doi: 10.1037.rep0000254

Morin, R. T., Galatzer-Levy, I. R., Maccallum, F., & Bonanno, G. A. (2017). Do multiple health events reduce resilience when compared with single events? *Health Psychology, 36*(8), 721–728. doi: 10.1037/hea0000481

Nabi, H., Koskenvuo, M., Singh-Manoux, A., Korkeila, J., Suominen, S., Korkeila, K., & Kivimäki, M. (2010). Low pessimism protects against stroke: The health and social support (HeSSup) prospective cohort study. *Stroke, 41*(1), 187–190. doi: 10.1161/STROKEAHA.109.565440

Nario-Redmond, M. R. (2020). *Ableism: The causes and consequences of disability prejudice.* Wiley-Blackwell.

Nickerson, R. S. (1998). Confirmation bias: A ubiquitous phenomenon in many guises. *Review of General Psychology, 2,* 175–220.

Ostir, G. V., Ottenbacher, K. J., & Markides, K. S. (2004). Onset of frailty in older adults and the protective role of positive affect. *Psychology and Aging, 19*(3), 402–408. doi: 10.1037/0882-7974.19.3.402

Packenham, K. I. (2007). Making sense of multiple sclerosis. *Rehabilitation Psychology, 52*(4), 380–389. doi:10.1037/0090-5550.52.4.380

Park, C. L. (2010). Making sense of the meaning literature: An integrative review of meaning making and its effects on adjustment to stressful life events. *Psychological Bulletin, 136*(2), 257–301. doi: 10.1037/a0018301

Peter, C., Müller, R., Post, M.W., van Leeuwen, C. M., Werner, C. S., & Geyh, S. (2014). Psychological resources, appraisals, and coping and their relationship to participation in spinal cord injury: A path analysis. *Archives of Physical Medicine and Rehabilitation, 95*(9), 1662–1671. doi: 10.1016/j.apmr.2014.04.012

Peterson, C., & Seligman, M. P. (2004). *Character strengths and virtues: A handbook and classification.* American Psychological Association.

Peterson, C., & Steen, T. A. (2021). Optimistic explanatory style. In C. R. Snyder, S. J. Lopez, L. M. Edwards, & S. C. Marques (Eds.), *Oxford handbook of positive psychology* (3rd ed., pp. 413–424). Oxford.

Pulrang, A. (2018, August 12) Disability thought of the week: Platitudes [blog entry]. *Disability thinking.* https://disabilitythinking.com/disabilitythinking/2018/8/12/disability-platitudes

Quale, A. J., & Schanke, A.-K. (2010). Resilience in the face of coping with a severe physical injury: A study of trajectories of adjustment in a rehabilitation setting. *Rehabilitation Psychology, 55,* 12–22. doi: 10.1037/a0018415

Ryff, C. D. (1989). Happiness is everything, or is it? Explorations on the meaning of psychological well-being. *Journal of Personality and Social Psychology, 57*(6), 1069–1081. doi: 10.1037/0022-3514.57.6.1069

Seligman, M. E. P. (1991). *Learned optimism.* Knopf.

Smith, D. M., Langa, K. M., Kabeto, M. U., & Ubel, P. A. (2005). Health, wealth, and happiness: Financial resources buffer subjective well-being after the onset of a disability. *Psychological Science, 16,* 663–666. doi: 10.1111/j.1467-9280.2005.01592.x

Snyder, C. R., Lopez, S. J., Edwards, L. M., & Marques, S. C. (Eds.). (2021). *Oxford handbook of positive psychology* (3rd ed.). New York: Oxford University Press.

Terrill, A. L., Mackenzie, J., Einerson, J., & Reblin, M. (2019). Resilience and disability: Intrapersonal, interpersonal, and social environment factors. In D. S. Dunn (Ed.), *Understanding the experience of disability: Perspectives from social and rehabilitation psychology* (pp. 313–327). Oxford University Press.

Terrill, A. L., Molton, I. R., Amtmann, D., & Jensen, M. P. (2014). Resilience, self-efficacy, and pain in persons aging with long-term physical disability. *Annals of Behavioral Medicine, 47*(1), s215.

Thompson, N. J., Coker, J., Krause, J. S., & Henry, E. (2003). Purpose in life as a mediator of adjustment after spinal cord injury. *Rehabilitation Psychology, 48*(2), 100–108. doi: 10.1037/0090-5550.48.2.100

Tindle, H. A., Chang, Y.-F., Kuller, L. H., Manson, J. E., Robinson, J. G., Rosal, M. C., Siegel, G. J., & Matthews, K. A. (2009). Optimism, cynical hostility, and incident coronary heart disease and mortality in the women's health initiative. *Circulation, 120*(8), 656–662. doi: 10.1161/CIRCULATIONAHA.108.827642

Tugade, M. M., & Fredrickson, B. L. (2004). Resilient individuals use positive emotions to bounce back from negative emotional experiences. *Journal of Personality and Social Psychology, 86*(2), 320–333.

Tugade, M. M., & Fredrickson, B. L. (2007). Regulation of positive emotions: Emotion regulation strategies that promote resilience. *Journal of Happiness Studies, 5,* 223–239.

van Leeuwen, C. M., Kraaijeveld, S., Lindeman, E., & Post, M. W. (2012). Associations between psychological factors and quality of life ratings in persons with spinal cord injury: A systematic review. *Spinal Cord, 49*(12), 1193–1197. doi: 10.1038/sc.2011.120

Wehmeyer, M. L., & Dunn, D. S. (2022). Introduction and Overview of ICF [Working Title]. In M. L. Wehmeyer & D. S. Dunn (Eds.), *The positive psychology of personal factors: Implications for understanding disability* (pp. xx–xx). Rowman and Littlefield.

World Health Organization (2001). *International classification of functioning, disability, and health.* Author.

Wright, B. A. (1983). *Physical disability: A psychosocial approach.* Harper & Row.

Wright, B. A. (1987). Human dignity and professional self-monitoring. *Journal of Applied Rehabilitation Counseling, 18,* 12–14.

Young, S. (2012). We're not here for your inspiration. *The Drum.* Retrieved from http://www.abc.net.au/news/2012-07-03/young-inspiration-porn/4107006

Zautra, A. J., Johnson, L. M., & Davis, M. C. (2005). Positive affect as a source of resilience for women in chronic pain. *Journal of Consulting and Clinical Psychology, 73*(2), 212–220. doi: 10.1037/0022-006X.73.2.212

Chapter 9

Personality and Disability

Timothy R. Elliott, Laurel Wade,
Sidai Dong, and Katherine Budge

Despite the high regard it receives from the many professions in the inter-disciplinary rehabilitation enterprise, the International Classification of Functioning, Disability and Health (ICF) model of disability is an awkward conundrum for academic and professional psychologists. Its sensible con-ceptualization of disability promotes a reasonable shift in focus away from a specific and co-occurring medical diagnostic condition toward a more infor-mative appreciation of functional limitations, barriers, and facilitators that better define "disability" and "disabling conditions." This shift is important for all psychologists, and it comports with the fundamental premium reha-bilitation psychologists place on the interplay between the person and the environment.

Arguably, interdisciplinary rehabilitation research pays homage to the model and routinely recognizes the importance of the core ICF concepts of participation, activity, and "personal factors." One important work tried to inform psychologists of the ways in which the ICF model could be used in evaluating and coding behavior (with particular attention to the personality disorders; Peterson, 2011).

There is no real evidence, however, that routine clinical practice of everyday psychologists—notably, in psychological assessments and clinical interventions—have substantively changed in response to the ICF model. In the mainstream psychological literature, the ICF model has not stimulated any real programmatic research into "personal factors" that could potentially guide clinical work, above and beyond existing practice.

As others have noted, the ICF model of disability is not a psychological theory (Rath & Elliott, 2012). It is a broad-based conceptualization of factors that affect adjustment (also broadly defined). Consequently, it does not stimu-late research to test specific, potentially falsifiable hypotheses to resolve some contentious debates between colleagues who have some scholarly "skin in the game." To those who adhere to the scientist-practitioner tradition in professional psychology, this kind of peer-reviewed contest is essential to identifying and refining meaningful concepts and mechanisms that are needed for best practices. In addition, critical, thought-provoking studies cannot occur with poorly defined concepts, parameters, and mechanisms. The current lack of definitions for "personal factors" certainly undermines interest among psychologists who study and assess personality characteristics.

In this chapter, we discuss the role of personality in the adjustment of persons with disabling conditions. In doing so, we follow a long lineage of other scholars who have addressed the same topic for similar reasons (e.g., Shontz, 1971). We differ from this tradition by embracing a positive psychology perspective, and the implications it may have for research and practice. We first begin with an overview of the intellectual gaps that exist between the ICF model and personality psychology. We then summarize the primary areas of personality research relevant to a positive psychology of disability, and then integrate our discussion from a theoretical model of personality that may help organize implications for research and practice.

THE POSITIVE PSYCHOLOGY OF PERSONALITY: INDIVIDUAL DIFFERENCES IN STRENGTHS AND VIRTUES

Personality is an important component of the ICF. Using the ICF web browser (https://apps.who.int/classifications/icfbrowser/) the term "personality" can be found under "b126 Temperament and Personality Factors," which includes extraversion, agreeableness, conscientiousness, emotional stability, openness to experience, optimism, confidence, and trustworthiness. This list includes the traits known as the "Big Five" (Digman, 1997), and optimism, a popular variable in the positive and health psychology literature, is also listed. However, b126 specifically excludes concepts related to energy and drive functions (see b130) and emotional functions (see b152). The former includes vigor, motivation (in b1301), and impulse control (in b1301, defined as the ability to "regulate and resist sudden intense urges to do something"); the latter is subsumed under "specific mental functions" that are related to "feeling and affective components of the processes of the mind." Further, this segment explicitly includes the appropriateness of emotion, the regulation, and range of emotions (e.g., affect, joy, happiness, love, fear, anger, and other negative emotions).

On the whole, psychologists do not think of personality in such a fragmented manner. Elegant personality theories describe personality development and define basic motivations and drives that may be manifested in a variety of behaviors (e.g., coping, aggression, empathy) and emotions (e.g., sadness, happiness) under routine and stressful conditions. This tradition encompasses the classic models of personality described in psychoanalytic thought and derived from social learning theory (e.g., self-efficacy).

Similarly, circumscribed theoretical models of specific individual differences—that typify the bulk of contemporary personality research that appears in leading personality journals (e.g., *Journal of Personality and Social Psychology, Journal of Personality, Journal of Research in Personality, Personality and Social Psychology Bulletin*)—usually address these same features and mechanisms as they pertain to the constructs of interest to the model, accompanied by testable hypotheses about the construct and instruments designed to measure it. This tradition accounts for most of the individual difference variables that appear in the positive psychology literature (e.g., hope, optimism, meaning in life). The measures of these constructs are usually domain-specific, guided by the corresponding theory, and their proper use requires a thorough understanding of that theoretical model. Usually, these measures were primarily designed for research purposes to test the hypothesized properties of the model and the corresponding variable. Typically, these measures lack any items to assess respondent bias, and often the measure is not tied to any intervention strategy (although this may develop later). In fact, the theory, the construct(s), and the measure may initially lack clinical utility, but programmatic research of the model may eventually reveal implications for practice. Johnson and Wood (2017) observed that many variables we associate with positive psychology were developed by colleagues who were not involved in clinical practice, but who were committed to studying individual differences that "predict the ways in which people will behave and respond over time" (p. 337).

There are several notable exceptions that have clear implications for clinical practice. Two of these have intellectual roots in social learning theory, as they are well-known in the cognitive-behavioral literature, and chapters on these topics appear in each of the three volumes of the *Handbook of Positive Psychology* (beginning with Snyder & Lopez, 2002), and previously in the influential *Handbook of Social and Clinical Psychology: The Health Perspective* (Snyder & Forsyth, 1991) that arguably presaged the formal positive psychology movement as we know it.

Maddux (Maddux & Kleiman, 2021) has long promoted our understanding of self-efficacy and how it facilitates adjustment. Self-efficacy can be easily assessed in general and specific domains, and both approaches yield theoretically consistent and clinically important information when used with individuals with disabilities (e.g., van Dieman et al., 2020). Of the available interventions that address self-efficacy, its essential application in the Health

Action Process Approach (HAPA; Schwarzer et al., 2011) has been most conspicuous in the disability and rehabilitation literature. Results from randomized controlled trials (RCT) demonstrate that interventions that help participants develop reasonable action plans and coping self-efficacy engage in more leisure time physical activity than those in bona fide treatment alternatives (Arbour-Nicitopoulos et al., 2009; Latimer et al., 2006). It appears that the emphasis on behavior change techniques—as stipulated in the HAPA—account for the larger effect sizes in this literature (Ma & Martin Ginis, 2018). This work is particularly valuable to the disability community, as advocates have recognized for some time the need for accessible and health-promoting physical activities and meaningful leisure pursuits.

The social problem-solving model—as conceptualized by either Heppner (Heppner et al., 2021) or D'Zurilla and Nezu (2007)—has also demonstrated clinical importance in rehabilitation. Studied as an individual difference variable among persons with disabilities, effective, self-appraised problem-solving abilities are associated with more assertiveness skills, higher life satisfaction, better community integration, and fewer secondary complications (Elliott & Hurst, 2008). Further, social problem-solving interventions (D'Zurilla & Nezu, 2007) have shown positive effects on social functioning, personal adjustment, and cognitive and emotional self-regulation among persons with disabilities (Elliott et al., 2008; Rath et al., 2003; Wade et al., 2010). The social problem-solving model has a strong emphasis on self-regulation in addition to the acquisition of specific yet generalizable cognitive-behavioral skills.

There are two other individual difference variables strongly identified with the positive psychology literature that are relevant to adjustment and that can be addressed in clinical interventions: forgiveness and gratitude. Forgiveness, in particular, has attracted the attention of scholars for almost three decades. It has been associated with psychophysiological indicators of stress and health, and a recent meta-analysis concluded that forgiving others is positively associated with self-report and objective measures of health (Lee & Enright, 2019). Unfortunately, relatively few studies have been conducted with medical patients, generally, and with persons with disabilities, specifically (Toussaint et al., 2016). Forgiveness has been associated with less distress and lower pain ratings among individuals with low back pain (Carson et al., 2005), and health behavior and life satisfaction were significantly associated with forgiving self among individuals with SCI (Webb et al., 2010). There is an impressive literature-supporting forgiveness interventions, but the work required to reduce angry and vengeful thoughts, feelings, and motives toward an offending person and the number of therapy sessions that appear necessary to obtain a moderate effect size in response to treatment (>10 hours; Wade et al., 2014) may account, in part, for the lack of forgiveness intervention studies in the rehabilitation psychology literature. A recent pilot study comparing an online forgiveness intervention with an established coping effectiveness training program found promising results with a small number of participants with disabilities (Stuntzner et al., 2019).

In their seminal paper, Emmons and McCullough (2003) defined gratitude as a "generalized tendency to recognize and respond with grateful emotion to the role of other people's benevolence" (p. 122). Gratitude is a prosocial activity that involves an attributional process to recognize the role of others in one's positive experiences, and that are not solely due to their own personal efforts. Gratitude is associated with improved sleep quality and less distress among individuals with chronic pain (Ng & Wong, 2013) and it predicts hopeful thinking and positive affect among women with breast cancer (Ruini & Vescovelli, 2013). Recent work reveals gratitude is an important predictor of quality of life (QOL) among persons with multiple sclerosis (MS), above and beyond variance attributable to cognitive functioning, depression, and fatigue, and it buffers against the negative effects of cognitive performance on QOL (Crouch et al., 2020). Sirous and Wood (2017) found gratitude was consistently associated with self-rated health, benefit-finding, thriving, and illness acceptance in a longitudinal study of participants with arthritis and inflammatory bowel disease.

Critical reviews find relatively few studies of gratitude among individuals with chronic and disabling health problems (Jans-Beken et al., 2020), and even fewer of gratitude interventions among these individuals (Davis et al., 2016). This is surprising: the influential Emmons and McCullough (2003) found a brief gratitude intervention with 65 individuals with either congenital or adult-onset neuromuscular disorders (randomly assigned to treatment and control conditions) facilitated significant increases in positive affect, subjective well-being, optimism, and sleep length and quality (see Study 3). These benefits were confirmed in observational ratings submitted by spouses and significant others. One recent study examined a gratitude intervention in combination with mindfulness (Swain et al., 2020), and found significant reductions in pain reports (e.g., interference, intensity) and fear of movement, and an increase in pain self-efficacy.

Perhaps this study illustrates some of the problems that appear in the positive psychology intervention literature, generally, with respect to individual difference variables that have a supportive research base that suggests their clinical utility. Often "positive psychology interventions" blend a variety of exercises from different literatures that concern specific individual difference variables. A brief gratitude intervention might work well in these circumstances (one meta-analysis found no time-in-treatment effects for gratitude interventions; Davis et al., 2016), but brief forgiveness interventions are not empirically supported, and may only result in weak effects (Wade et al., 2014).

This intervention research also raises some pointed and unresolved issues about these and other popular constructs in the positive psychology literature: Do these individual difference variables represent learned behaviors, or should they be conceptualized as personality traits? This is an ongoing discussion in the positive psychology (indeed, a series of papers in the first issue of the 2019 volume of the *Journal of Positive Psychology* explicitly addressed this issue). Self-efficacy and the social problem-solving model are ensconced in the social learning tradition; therefore, we know these are learned behaviors and they are responsive to cognitive-behavioral interventions. Studies that report positive results for gratitude and forgiveness interventions imply that these, too, are behaviors that can be learned. But confusing terminology has been used to describe some of the popular variables in the positive psychology literature, and it is possible that this has contributed to some of the difficulties and mixed results we have seen in the utility of these variables in professional practice.

This is especially apparent in the research concerning the variables measure by the *Values in Action* (VIA) inventories that were initiated with the version developed by Peterson and Seligman (2004). This inventory was developed to assess 24 character strengths and virtues subsumed under *wisdom and knowledge* (which included specific strengths of creativity, critical thinking, among others), *courage* (including honesty, zest, etc.), *humanity* (e.g., kindness, social intelligence), *justice* (e.g., fairness, teamwork), *temperance* (e.g., forgiveness, self-regulation), and *transcendence* (e.g., gratitude, hope). Seligman and Csikszentmihalyi (2000) repeatedly refer to these strengths and virtues as traits in their landmark essay. The study of their classification of strengths and virtues, and the use of the VIA inventories has proliferated over the years, advancing our understanding of these characteristics.

Several of these studies demonstrate the relevance of this framework to our discussion. Hanks et al. (2014) used the 72-item version of the VIA to study the correlates of these strengths among 65 individuals with moderate to severe traumatic brain injuries (TBI). Several character strengths were significantly associated with physical health (courage and several of its subscales), and most of the strengths were associated with lower disability ratings and higher satisfaction with life and positive affect. Recently, impressive studies of 624 individuals with MS (Smedema, 2020; Smedema & Bhattari, 2020) found several of the strengths were significantly associated with QOL (notably, zest, hope, and gratitude) and, in tandem, these strengths and virtues accounted for a significant degree of variance (4%) above and beyond the "Big Five" personality traits in the prediction of QOL. Surprisingly, only eight intervention studies based in the VIA classification—character strengths interventions (CSI)—were identified in a recent meta-analysis of these interventions among persons with chronic health conditions (Yan et al., 2020). Overall, there was evidence that these interventions had beneficial effects on participants, but only one study included a sample ($n = 10$) of individuals with a disability (TBI; Andrewes et al., 2014). Further, the authors found the components of the CSIs were inconsistently applied, and only two were based in a theoretical model (and one of those was specific to personality disorders).

CSI interventions that attempt to address all of the 24 strengths and virtues are problematic because we already know much about specific interventions and the accompanying literature for some of these variables (e.g., forgiveness, gratitude, emotional self-regulation). These variables, like some of the others listed in the framework (e.g., hope) have their own theoretical models that give considerable detail about the variable, its properties, and conditions under which it may be best studied and understood. Further, Johnson and Wood (2017) argued that artificially dividing clinical psychology from the positive unnecessarily confounds our use of existing interventions. Behavioral activation is a recognized modality for increasing the frequency and quality of positive emotional experiences (improving "zest," if you will), and effective problem-solving therapy promotes emotional and behavioral self-regulation. These interventions are used to help individuals acquire new skills and behaviors to improve their well-being and QOL, in addition to their utility in treating depression and anxiety.

Furthermore, factor analytic studies have repeatedly failed to support the presumed structure of the VIA inventories, and the best work to date indicates that these inventories appear to assess three factors: caring, self-control, and inquisitiveness (McGrath et al., 2018). Others have offered alternative conceptualizations that also recognize three higher-order concepts that likely subsume the variables assessed by the VIA inventories (e.g., warmth-based virtues that include love and empathy; epistemic-based virtues that include prudence and knowledge; and conscientiousness-based virtues that include justice and self-control; Worthington & Hampson, 2011). These alternative models do not negate the use of the VIA inventories, but they compel us to acknowledge the overlapping and interrelated nature of the 24 character strengths and virtues. McGrath et al. (2018) acknowledge the statistical associations found between personality traits and virtues (assessed by the VIA), and observe that virtues and strengths may be "more than a set of individual difference constructs," and they could be "basic for aspirations for change, as a product of practice" (p. 389). To further our understanding of the nature of these individual difference variables, a brief overview of personality traits and the study of these in the disability literature is warranted.

THE POSITIVE PSYCHOLOGY
OF PERSONALITY TRAITS

In practice, the personality traits and characteristics listed by the ICF are not routinely assessed. But the study of these traits—specifically, those listed in the ICF—has a long history in rehabilitation research and practice. Definitions of a personality trait vary but from Allport to the present day there is a general, shared understanding that traits reflect a relatively enduring dispositional pattern in cognition, affect, and behavior. The measurement of traits typically evolves from one of two traditional methods: the lexical approach (that examines salient personality and socially relevant characteristics used in natural language to describe people) and empirical keying (in which items are developed that presumably reflect a certain characteristic, and the item then demonstrates it successfully differentiates between those who have that characteristic from those who do not). To illustrate the former, Allport (1961) used factor analysis to derive as many as 4,000 common words from which he then studied further to determine the ones that efficiently assess the frequency, intensity, and range of responses that reflect a measurable trait. Raymond Cattell also began with as many as 4,500 descriptions and, relying on ratings and factor analysis, this pool was eventually reduced to the "source" traits that are assessed by the 16PF (Cattell & Mead, 2008). In contrast, Gough (Donnay & Elliott, 2003) relied on "folk concepts" of personality to develop items, taking more than a few items from the Minnesota Multiphasic Personality Inventory (MMPI) to develop the California Psychological Inventory (CPI). A theoretical model of temperaments guided the development and selection of items in the Multidimensional Personality Questionnaire (MPQ; Tellegen, 2003).

The lexical approach weighed heavily in the research that identified and measured the Big Five traits of Extraversion, Agreeableness, Neuroticism (also labeled as Emotional Stability in some instruments), Openness to Experience, and Conscientiousness. For McRae and Costa (1996), these traits constitute the "Five Factor Model" and they are assessed with the NEO Five Factor inventories they developed using several approaches for item selection: first mining Cattell's work, borrowing some items from other related measures, and developing their own item pool for subsequent item and factor analysis.

All of these measures have been used in the study of adjustment following disability. The 16PF and the CPI have a long history in rehabilitation research. The 16PF demonstrated independence from measures of psychopathology among individuals with chronic disabling conditions, providing a broad-based assessment of non-pathological personality traits (Bolton, 1979; Bolton & Dana, 1988). However, it has not attracted any real systematic study in relation to indicators of positive adjustment in the rehabilitation literature.

A pioneering study with the CPI foreshadowed our contemporary interest in personality with participation and activity. Kemp and Vash (1971) found persons with SCI who were rated as "more productive" (in terms of employment status, avocational and leisure pursuits, involvement in community groups) had higher scores on 17 of the 18 traits measured by the CPI than those rated as "less productive." In particular, the more productive respondents reported significantly higher levels of dominance, capacity for status, sociability, social presence, self-acceptance, tolerance, psychological mindedness, and achievement via conformity and via independence. This pattern implied that the productive individuals were more outgoing, confident, sociable, poised, and perhaps possessed more interpersonal and self-regulatory skills than those who were less productive.

Subsequent research found higher scores on CPI factors that reflected a capacity for independent thought and action and for well-being were associated with fewer physical limitations (among persons with MS; Zeldow & Pavlou, 1984), and employed individuals (in a sample of persons with a variety of disabling conditions) were significantly higher in self-acceptance, communality, capacity for status, and achievement via conformity compared to those who were not employed (Fowler et al., 1984). The cross-sectional nature of these studies undermines our sense of causality, but their findings underscore the bidirectional relationships that exist between these traits and active participation in interpersonal, social, and vocational roles following disability.

Studies of Big Five traits appear in the rehabilitation literature, albeit to a much less degree than that observed in the personality literature, generally. Many of these findings are consistent with the extant literature: higher Extraversion scores were associated with higher life satisfaction among persons with SCI, and the disposition for positive affect was a salient facet in the prediction of life satisfaction (Krause & Rohe, 1998). Krause (1997) also found that individuals with SCI who were gainfully employed were significantly higher in positive affectivity and achievement than those who were not employed. Conscientiousness was associated with employment among individuals with SCI (Krause, 1997; Krause & Rohe, 1998), and with vocational status and health-related QOL among persons with MS (Benedict et al., 2005).

In one of the most impressive prospective studies using personality data obtained pre-injury, agreeableness significantly predicted positive shifts in life satisfaction within four years following disability onset (Boyce & Wood, 2011). Importantly, this trait and the prosocial characteristics associated with it—warmth, friendliness, sociability, patience, kindness, trust, altruism, and cooperation—accounted for more variance in life satisfaction than the other four traits, and its influence was apparent among those with moderate levels of agreeableness as well as those with higher levels. The authors specu-lated that these prosocial characteristics facilitated an individual's ability to get along with others, while also creating and maintaining social and personal relationships that then contributed to higher life satisfaction.

This study is particularly impressive to careful readers of the Big Five literature, who would reasonably expect neuroticism to predict adjustment post-injury. Neuroticism is characterized by a chronic pessimism, differential exposure to stress, a bias toward negative appraisals, learned sensitivity, and difficulties in regulating negative moods (Suls & Martin, 2005). This pattern was apparent in the van Leeuwen et al. (2012) study, in which neuroticism exerted a detrimental effect on life satisfaction and QOL through its negative influence on cognitive appraisals of helplessness, acceptance, and benefits of disability. Neuroticism significantly predicts depression among persons with disabling conditions (Rovner & Casten, 2001), and it can predict functional impairment independent of the degree of impairment that would be expected from objective measures of disability severity (Rovner et al., 2014). In a longitudinal study of twins over a 30-year time period, neuroticism was a significant risk factor for disability compensation for low back pain, above and beyond the variance attributable to socioeconomic status, education, and marital status (Ropponen et al., 2012).

Taken together, results from studies of the Big Five might seem a hodge-podge of unrelated and somewhat interesting correlations with various indica-tors of adjustment, with unclear implications for clinical practice. To be sure, there is nothing compelling about a significant, inverse correlation between neuroticism and satisfaction with life. Further, Shadel (2010) argues that the Big Five traits have descriptive value in making comparisons between people, and in making predictions about outcomes at a population level but they do not inform client conceptualizations, guide therapeutic plans, or assist in monitoring client response to treatment.

These are stinging indictments for a set of well-established variables that have empirical evidence sufficient to justify their inclusion as personal fac-tors, in the ICF. None of the three handbooks on positive psychology (starting with the Snyder & Lopez, 2002) have a dedicated chapter to the Big Five, nor is there any in-depth discussion of traits assessed by the other, established instruments mentioned in this section (e.g., CPI, 16-PF; extraversion is dis-cussed in the handbooks as it pertains to positive affectivity). Measures of the Big Five appear routinely in studies published in the leading peer-reviewed journals that showcase personality research, but they received no attention in the book *Positive Psychology Assessment: A Handbook of Models and Measures* (Lopez & Snyder, 2003). Perhaps the overtly negative connota-tions of neuroticism contaminate any consideration of the Big Five as they might relate to positive psychology, artificially relegating them to "clinical" measures (rather than a "positive psychology" measure; Johnson & Wood, 2017). To be sure, any mention of the neuroticism variable in a context involving personnel and organizational decisions probably violates basic tenets of the Americans with Disabilities Act (and inverting it as "emotional stability" is an unlikely remedy). Nevertheless, the prosocial attributes of the other four traits merit our consideration, and it is likely several of them—and the positive characteristics associated with the traits assessed by the other instruments mentioned in this section—are discussed as they relate to the specific theoretical models mentioned earlier in this chapter (and addressed in several chapters throughout this book). These theoretical perspectives, as we have seen, provide specific, testable hypotheses to stimulate research, and some provide theoretical directions for clinical practice. Throughout its brief history, we know positive psychologists value a good theory.

Scholarly criticisms of the Big Five are unambiguous about the lack of a priori and comprehensive theorizing in this research. DeYoung (2010) was not convinced that dependence on factor analysis to identify the traits—used extensively in the development of all of the Big Five measures—could provide a definitive and integrative model of personality that could explicate specific psychological mechanisms that unify the traits and how they operate in a systemic manner. For many years, Block (1995, 2001, 2010) repeatedly criticized the "Five Factor Approach" (his preferred term) on several fronts, including (a) the fact that developers of the five-factor model (FFM) insisted that the traits should be identified first, and an explanatory theoretical model would then follow; (b) the reliance on the lexical approach, generally, to generate items; and (c) that the Big Five researchers relied on mathematical models—especially factor analysis—as the way to "discover" the "truth" that these traits exist. For Block, the traits were descriptive, but without a meaningful theoretical model to explain intraindividual dynamics their usefulness was questionable, and even the names given to the traits were debatable.

None of these criticisms have hampered the ongoing study of the Big Five traits in their different forms, constellations, and correlates. This research has flourished, and it has proved to be useful and informative. From a broader perspective, all of the instruments we mention in this section share some overarching properties:

> Regardless of the manner in which these measures of "normal," non-pathological traits were developed, and regardless of the many labels for the various traits used by the developers in their conceptualizations, advanced modeling techniques confirm the existence of the basic five factors, which can then be further demarcated into two meta-traits: Alpha and Beta (Hopwood et al., 2011). These measures and their constructs may be in search of a theory, but the implications of these two meta-traits bring us to a "fortuitous convergence between

the theoretical and empirical approaches" to our understanding of personality. (DeYoung, 2010, p. 29)

Block's Theory of Ego Control and Ego Resiliency

In constructing their developmental model of personality, Block and Block (1980) incorporated several important concepts from psychoanalytic perspectives (e.g., ego, secure, and insecure attachment) with Lewin's (1936) conceptualization of the dynamic systems that enable an individual to maintain a sense of self in interactions with the environment. Lewin described two particular boundary characteristics that operate in a dynamic fashion: permeability and elasticity. Permeability is the individual capacity to regulate basic needs and resolve psychological demands and internal states. It serves to regulate impulse control, to delay the gratification of emotional and motivational drives, and to maintain a stable, functioning system. Elasticity is the capacity to respond as needed to meet, alleviate, or accommodate demands, pressures, and changes in the immediate environment, and to resolve intrapersonal concerns and motivations, modulating the individual's boundaries of permeability as necessary to return to its original modal state. Elasticity reflects the capacity to explore the environment, learn, and integrate new information, and to flexibly adapt to environmental demands to maintain a sense of self.

Block and Block (1980) proposed two constructs—ego control (EC) and ego resiliency (ER)—as embodiments of Lewin's (1936) concepts of permeability and elasticity, respectively. EC is the individual's characteristic response to internal impulses, to delay gratification, and to self-regulate their behavior to achieve higher-order goals. People with low EC tend to be attentive to and act on internal impulses (Block & Block, 1980). In contrast, ER is the individual's ability to adapt to change, or to temporarily change their reactions and perceptions to meet different situational demands of life (Block & Block, 1980), and by modifying their level of ego control depending on the environmental context. Individuals with high ER are resourceful and generally quick to adapt to changes, while those with low ER tend to exhibit little adaptive flexibility when facing stressful or novel situations, and fail to adapt to new conditions or recover from stress (Block & Block, 1980). From this perspective, EC and ER work in concert for a well-adapted individual to delay the gratification of impulses and exercise restraint to achieve long-term goals (Asendorpf et al., 2001). This conceptualization also describes a U-shaped model of impulse control in which individuals at the extremes of EC and ER would experience difficulties, either being too inhibited and restrained, or by being too impulsive and unable to harness and direct their motivations.

Inventive colleagues closely studied the three personality prototypes defined by the varying levels of EC and ER: resilient (high ER, moderate EC), overcontrolled (high in EC, low in ER), and undercontrolled (low in EC and ER). They also carefully examined the way these prototypes were initially assessed (e.g., card sorting techniques, observer ratings), and how they were described (Caspi & Silva, 1995). From this work, colleagues concluded that the three prototypes reflected variations on the Big Five traits: the resilient prototype involves low Neuroticism (N), and above-average scores on Agreeableness (A), Conscientiousness (C), Openness to Experience (O) and Extraversion (E); the undercontrolled prototypes involves low C and A, moderate N, and average O and E; and the overcontrolled is associated with high N, low E, and average on the remaining domains (Chapman & Goldberg, 2011; Robins et al., 1996).

This is the approach we have used in our research to isolate the mechanisms that facilitate adjustment among those with a resilient prototype. In our first foray, we used cluster analysis to identify the three personality prototypes among persons with SCI (Berry et al., 2007). Those with a resilient prototype had a significantly greater ability to regulate their emotions when facing problems, and in their use of rational problem-solving skills, and in their disinclination to avoid problems they encounter. In a series of longitudinal studies of veterans with and without TBI incurred during warzone deployment, structural equation models revealed that resilience exerted beneficial effects through psychological flexibility, social support, and a decreased use of avoidant coping to predict fewer symptoms of depression and posttraumatic disorder, less functional impairment, and higher QOL, independent of TBI status (Elliott et al., 2015; Elliott et al., 2019). Further, resilient veterans were more likely to report adaptive health and sleep behaviors, more stress management techniques, and a greater tolerance for emotional distress than those who had non-resilient personality prototypes (Elliott et al., 2017). These specific mechanisms (psychological flexibility, social support, and ineffective, disengaged coping) and behavioral issues (distress tolerance, stress management techniques, sleep hygiene) can be addressed with empirically supported interventions to help others learn how to become resilient in routine and stressful conditions.

Block explicitly relied on Lewin's (1936) notions of permeability and elasticity in developing the theoretical concepts and mechanisms of EC and ER. The meta-traits, Alpha and Beta, evolved from a sophisticated use of factor analytic modeling of the Big Five (Digman, 1997). The parallels with Block's constructs are remarkable: Alpha is characterized by higher Conscientious and Agreeableness, and low Neuroticism; Beta is characterized by higher Extraversion and Openness to Experience. Alpha is the component that provides stability in emotional, motivational, and social functioning, and it accomplishes this, in part, by imbuing an individual with perseverance, intrinsic motivations, and self-regulatory abilities to delay gratification that facilitate socially acceptable behavior and emotional stability (Strus & Cieciuch, 2017). Beta captures the behavioral "openness" to change engagement in new experiences and explore the environment, and an adaptive reflexiveness to environmental demands; it also conveys a sense of initiative and a willingness to be innovative in personal relationships, and it may reflect a predisposition for personal growth. These meta-traits appear as empirically derived counterparts to Block's theory–driven EC and ER constructs, and by extension, to Lewin's ideas about permeability and elasticity (DeYoung, 2010; Farkas & Orosz, 2015).

To the best of our knowledge, there are no systematic studies of the two meta-traits among persons with disabilities. In a recent cross-sectional study from our group, Alpha significantly and inversely predicted psychological distress among 1,151 emerging adults with chronic health conditions, and this relationship was independent of several clinically and theoretically important mediating variables (Barron, 2019). However, the model was a poor fit for the data. Reanalyzing the data with the resilient and non-resilient prototypes resulted in an excellent fit, revealing important mediating effects: a resilient prototype predicted distress through its beneficial associations with social support, positive affect, and intentions to participate in desired activities.

This illustrates some of the differences in a "person-centered" versus a "variable-centered" approach to personality research. To be sure, variable-centered research dominates the study of personality, including the disability literature. It is a convenient and straightforward way to focus on a single variable and its possible association with another. The focus is on the variable, and not the person. Assumptions are made about an individual from the results, but the real unit of analysis is the variable (Block, 1995). This is a persistent shortcoming in extrapolating from the Big Five literature to psychological practice. We know that neuroticism inversely predicts life satisfaction (and it may account for more variance in the outcome variable than optimism in that model); similarly, a predictive model may inform us that the Alpha meta-trait is significantly and inversely predictive of distress. Unfortunately, this provides little "information on internal psychological mechanisms at the level of the individual . . . that could be the target of change via intervention or therapeutic technique" (Shadel, 2010, p. 336).

In contrast, a person-centered approach posits theoretical mechanisms that operate between the personality traits within the person, and the focus is not on a single variable, but on the organization of these constructs and the way in which they systematically operate to regulate motivations, behavior, affect, perceptions, and cognitions (Gramzow et al., 2004). From this perspective, we can examine differences between those who have a resilient personality prototype and those do not, theoretically expecting to confirm differences between the two groups not just in terms of adjustment but in the mechanisms by which this occurs, because we know a priori that these prototypes differ in their self-regulatory capacities under routine and stressful conditions. We want to know how and why these prototypes differ in adjustment. Using the resilient prototype as a reference group, and guided by a theoretical sense of how ER and EC operate to meet internal and external demands while in pursuit of higher-order goals, we can isolate specific mechanisms that facilitate their adjustment that may, in turn, inform our practice with individuals who do not have this prototype.

Convergence of the Theoretical and the Empirical

Using this integration of the theoretical and the empirical, we may now interpret findings from disparate literatures—including the social-cognitive and individual difference variables that routinely appear in positive psychology research—in a fashion that might advance our understanding of personality and disability. This requires an appreciation of variables that have transdiagnostic value across conditions, and to accomplish this, we blur the boundaries that artificially separate the "positive" from the "clinical" (Johnson & Wood, 2017).

Psychological inflexibility, for example, is a critical, transdiagnostic component of Acceptance and Commitment Therapy (ACT), in which behavior problems are believed to stem, in part, from rigid thought processes that are not helpful in the environment or the person's valued direction in life (Hayes et al., 2006). As it often used in the literature, it has a negative connotation (inflexibility) and ACT has been examined in the treatment of many clinical problems (e.g., depression, anxiety). Kashdan and Rottenberg (2010) noticed the theoretical similarity between psychological flexibility and the regulatory process described in Block's personality model (Block & Block, 1980). Just as there is an ideal level of EC to suppress urges to meet present needs, psychological flexibility involves a willingness to tolerate present discomfort to meet long-term goals (Bond et al., 2011). Psychological flexibility consistently mediated the relationship of personality prototypes to positive and negative indicators of adjustment in our studies of warzone veterans with and without TBI.

Similarly, problem-solving interventions have demonstrated efficacy in the treatment of distress across an array of clinical settings. In the D'Zurilla and Nezu (2007) conceptualization, training in the problem-orientation component is critical to self-regulation, providing the individual with skills to identify and work through problematic, negative emotions and cognitions. Theoretically, a negative orientation thwarts effective problem-solving, and the subsequent problems with self-regulation result in dysfunctional, avoidant, impulsive, and careless attempts to address personal problems. But there is a positive orientation as well, and it serves to promote a sense of self-efficacy, confidence, and facilitate positive emotional experiences. Several of these dynamics were observed in a study of 186 individuals in an SCI inpatient rehabilitation program (Elliott, 1999). A negative orientation was significantly predictive of depression, as expected, but it was also inversely associated with an established measure of disability acceptance. A positive problem orientation was significantly associated with greater disability acceptance. A negative orientation was also associated with a perceived need for more information and support for making vocational and career-related decisions. Problem-solving interventions may be used to help an individual learn self-regulating abilities, and to acquire constructive, goal-directed problem-solving skills, and be less likely to rely on avoidant, disengaged coping strategies to manage or distract from negative emotions.

Goal-directed behavior is a core element in the Block personality theory. As we discussed earlier in this chapter, several studies using omnibus trait measures (e.g., the CPI, the MPQ) found that employed, productive, and active individuals with disabilities were higher on several indicators of achievement, sociability, and in independent thought and action than those who were unemployed and who were participating less in personal, social, and vocational roles. Active goal engagement is significantly predictive of positive affect among persons with disabilities, regardless of age (Mackay et al., 2011). This pattern implies that these active, productive individuals may have possessed the resourcefulness, flexibility, social competence, and the tendency to actively engage with the environment (as stipulated in the Block model) to pursue personally meaningful goals. Goal orientation and goal stability is a central component in Kohutian self-psychology (Kohut, 1971), a model that shares Block's appreciation for pre-verbal factors in infant and child development that influence subsequent views of the self, others, and the environment. Neo-Freudian models are rarely entertained in positive psychology and the notion of "goal instability" (as an indicator of a stable sense of self as described by Kohut) certainly sounds more "clinical" than "positive." In a paper that reported some of the most comprehensive and thorough empirical studies of neo-Freudian concepts and adjustment following disability, a greater sense of goal stability was significantly predictive of lower distress (upon admission to an inpatient unit), greater disability acceptance (at discharge from the unit), of higher life satisfaction and less perceived stigma (among those in an outpatient clinic), and it prospectively predicted greater subjective well-being one year after discharge from inpatient SCI rehabilitation program (accounting for 28% of the variance in well-being; Elliott et al., 2000). Consistent with Kohutian thinking—and with

Block's model, as well—the enduring capacity to maintain, identify, and pursue personally meaningful goals was associated with several important indicators of positive adjustment, independent of the impositions, functional impairments, and other issues that may have been associated with their physical disabilities.

CONCLUSIONS

Traditionally, psychologists working with individuals with disability rely on empirically derived instruments designed to detect behavioral problems and adjustment issues that could complicate the rehabilitation enterprise, or that might require some clinical attention to enhance rehabilitation efforts and outcomes. From these assessments, personality characteristics are inferred, but as Wright and Fletcher (1982) observed some time ago, the procedure is inherently skewed toward the negative. In this chapter, we deliberately focused on individual difference and personality variables that have implications for a positive psychological approach to the study of disability and rehabilitation. It is true that most of these are not used in everyday clinical practice, but we contend these characteristics are clinically relevant, and we hope for their integration. We appreciate the inclusion of the Big Five traits in the ICF, but we hope to see a greater appreciation of the theoretical mechanisms through which these and other characteristics facilitate adjustment following disability. From our vantage point, most of the constructs we have discussed in this chapter relate in some form or fashion to the overarching, functional qualities we see in the Block model of personality: the capacity for self-regulation and goal-directed activity, a prosocial capacity for initiating, developing, and nurturing interpersonal and social relationships, and flexible adaptability that serves to maintain the individual's sense of self, goal orientation, authenticity, and personal meaning.

There are many issues we did not address. We need a greater empirical understanding of pre-disability characteristics and their possible influence on later adjustment. We know social participation is critical to QOL and societal integration; we do not really know the degree to which engagement in desired activities and participation is enhanced or complicated by the variables we discussed in this chapter, and how these matters may be best addressed. There are very few data about individuals who have a "road to Damascus experience" following traumatically acquired disability, and if and how these positive changes endure over time, and if they are associated with unique personality characteristics. We know that the instruments we use to study personality require a respondent to engage in introspection, a retrospective memory search, deliberate self-presentation, and with some devices, directed attention outward to create meaning (Bornstein, 2017). All of these activities are within the realm of explicit, controlled processing. We wonder if there are other more creative and indirect ways to assess these characteristics in a psychometrically sound and theoretically important manner. We leave these and other unresolved issues in the study of personality and disability for colleagues to consider in their future scholarly endeavors.

REFERENCES

Allport, G.W. (1961). *Pattern and growth in personality*. Holt, Rinehart &Winston.

Andrewes, H. E., Walker, V., & O'Neill, B. (2014). Exploring the use of positive psychology interventions in brain injury survivors with challenging behaviour. *Brain Injury, 28*(7), 965–971. doi: 10.3109/02699052.2014.888764

Arbour-Nicitopoulos, K. P., Martin Ginis, K. A., & Latimer, A. E. (2009). Planning, leisure-time physical activity, and coping self-efficacy in persons with spinal cord injury: A randomized controlled trial. *Archives of Physical Medicine and Rehabilitation, 90,* 2003–11.

Asendorpf, J. B., Borkenau, P., Ostendorf, F., & Van Aken, M. A. (2001). Carving personality description at its joints: Confirmation of three replicable personality prototypes for both children and adults. *European Journal of Personality, 15*(3), 169–198. doi: 10.1002/per.408

Barron, L. L. (2019). *Resilience in the general factor of personality: Understanding the role of positive affect, social support, and participation in distress related to chronic illness or disability*. Doctoral dissertation, Texas A&M University. Available electronically from https://hdl.handle.net/1969.1/186388.

Benedict, R. H. B., Wahlig, E., Bakshi, R., Munshauer, F., Weinstock-Guttman, B. (2005). Predicting quality of life in multiple sclerosis: Accounting for physical disability, fatigue, cognition, mood disorder, personality, and behavior change. *Journal of the Neurological Sciences, 231,* 29–34. doi: 10.1016/j.jns.2004.12.009

Berry, J., Elliott, T., & Rivera, P. (2007). Resilient, undercontrolled, and overcontrolled personality prototypes among persons with spinal cord injury. *Journal of Personality Assessment, 89,* 292–302. doi: 10.1080/00223890701629813

Block, J. (1995). A contrarian view of the five-factor approach to personality description. *Psychological Bulletin, 117,* 187–215.

Block, J. (2001). Millennial contrarianism: The five-factor approach to personality description 5 years later. *Journal of Research in Personality, 35,* 98–107.

Block, J. (2010). The five-factor framing of personality and beyond: Some ruminations. *Psychological Inquiry, 21,* 2–25, doi: 10.1080/10478401003596626

Block, J. H., & Block, J. (1980). The role of ego control and ego resiliency in the organization of behavior. In W. A. Collins (Ed.), *The Minnesota symposium on child psychology: Vol. 13. Development of cognition, affect, and social relations* (pp. 39–101). Erlbaum.

Bolton, B. (1979) The relationship between two personality questionnaires: The mini-mult and the 16PF-E. *Journal of Personality Assessment*, *43*(3), 289–292, doi: 10.1207/s15327752jpa4303_11

Bolton, B., & Dana, R. H. (1988). Multivariate relationships between normal personality functioning and objectively measured psychopathology. *Journal of Social and Clinical Psychology*, *6*(1), 11–19. doi: 10.1521/jscp.1988.6.1.11

Bond, F. W., Hayes, S. C., Baer, R. A., Carpenter, K. M., Guenole, N., Orcutt, H. K., Waltz, T., & Zettle, R. D. (2011). Preliminary psychometric properties of the acceptance and action Questionnaire–II: A revised measure of psychological inflexibility and experiential avoidance. *Behavior Therapy*, *42*(4), 676–688. doi: 10.1016/j.beth.2011.03.007

Bornstein, R. F. (2017). Evidence-based psychological assessment. *Journal of Personality Assessment*, *99*(4), 435–445. doi: 10.1080/00223891.2016.1236343

Boyce, C. J., & Wood, A. M. (2011). Personality prior to disability determines adaptation: Agreeable individuals recover lost life satisfaction faster and more completely. *Psychological Sciences*, *22*, 1397–1402. doi: 10.1177/0956797611421790

Carson, J. W., Keefe, F. J., Goli, V., Fras, A. M., Lynch, T. R., Thorp, S. R., & Buechler, J. (2005). Forgiveness and chronic low back pain: A preliminary study examining the relationship of forgiveness to pain, anger, and psychological distress. *The Journal of Pain*, *6*, 84–91.

Cattell, H. E. P., & Mead, A. D. (2008). The sixteen personality factor questionnaire (16pf). In G. J. Boyle, G. Matthews, & D. H. Saklofske (Eds.), *The Sage handbook of personality theory and assessment* (pp. 135–198). Sage.

Chapman, B. P., & Goldberg, L. R. (2011). Replicability and 40-year predictive power of childhood ARC types. *Journal of Personality and Social Psychology*, *101*, 593–606.

Crouch, T. A., Verdi, E. K., & Erickson, T. M. (2020). Gratitude is positively associated with quality of life in multiple sclerosis. *Rehabilitation Psychology*, *65*, 231–238. doi: 10.1037/rep0000319

D'Zurilla, T. J., & Nezu, A. M. (2007). *Problem-solving therapy: A positive approach to clinical Intervention* (3rd ed.). Springer.

Davis, D. E., Choe, E., Meyers, J., Wade, N., Varjas, K., Gifford, A., Quinn, A., Hook, J. N., Van Tongeren, D. R., Griffin, B. J., & Worthington, E. L., Jr. (2016). Thankful for the little things: A meta-analysis of gratitude interventions. *Journal of Counseling Psychology*, *63*, 20–31. doi: 10.1037/cou0000107

DeYoung, C. G. (2010). Toward a theory of the Big Five. *Psychological Inquiry*, *21*(1), 26–33.

Digman, J. M. (1997). Higher-order factors of the Big Five. *Journal of Personality and Social Psychology*, *73*, 1246–1256.

Donnay, D., & Elliott, T. (2003). California personality inventory. In L. Beutler & G. Groth-Marnat (Eds.), *Integrative assessment of adult personality* (2nd ed., pp. 227–261). Guilford Press.

Elliott, T. R. (1999). Social problem-solving abilities and adjustment to recent-onset spinal cord injury. *Rehabilitation Psychology*, *44*, 315- 332. doi: 10.1037/0090-5550.44.4.315

‌‌‌

‌‌‌‌‌‌‌‌‌‌‌‌‌‌‌‌‌‌‌‌‌‌

Elliott, T., Brossart, D., Berry, J. W. & Fine, P. R. (2008). Problem-solving training via videoconferencing for family caregivers of persons with spinal cord injuries: A randomized controlled trial. *Behaviour Research and Therapy, 46,* 1220–1229.

Elliott, T. R., Hsiao, Y., Kimbrel, N. A., DeBeer, B. B., Gulliver, S. B., Kwok, O., Morissette, S. B., & Meyer, E. C. (2019). Resilience facilitates adjustment through greater psychological flexibility among Iraq/Afghanistan war veterans with and without mild traumatic brain injury. *Rehabilitation Psychology, 64*(4), 383–397. doi: 10.1037/rep0000282

Elliott, T. R., Hsiao, Y. Y., Kimbrel, N., Meyer, E., DeBeer, B., Gulliver, S., Kwok, O. M., & Morissette, S. (2015). Resilience, traumatic brain injury, depression and posttraumatic stress among Iraq/Afghanistan war veterans. *Rehabilitation Psychology, 60,* 263–276. doi: 10.1037/rep0000050

Elliott, T., Hsiao, Y. Y., Kimbrel, N., Meyer, E., DeBeer, B., Gulliver, S. B., Kwok, O. M., & Morissette, S. B. (2017). Resilience and traumatic brain injury among Iraq/Afghanistan war veterans; Differential patterns of adjustment and quality of life. *Journal of Clinical Psychology, 73.* 1160–1178. doi: 10.1002/jclp.22414

Elliott, T., & Hurst, M. (2008). Social problem solving and health. In W. B. Walsh (Ed.), *Biennial Review of Counseling Psychology* (pp. 295–314). Lawrence Erlbaum Press.

Elliott, T., Uswatte, G., Lewis, L., & Palmatier, A. (2000). Goal instability and adjustment to physical disability. *Journal of Counseling Psychology, 47,* 251–265. doi: 10.1037/0022-0167.47.2.251

Emmons, R. A. & McCullough, M. E. (2003). Counting blessings versus burdens: An experimental investigation of gratitude and subjective well-being in daily life. *Journal of Personality and Social Psychology, 84,* 377–389.

Farkas, D., & Orosz, G. (2015). Ego-resiliency reloaded: A three-component model of general resiliency. *PLoS ONE, 10*(3), e0120883. doi: 10.1371/journal.pone.0120883

Fowler, W., Abresch, R., Koch, T., Brewer, M., Bowden, R., & Wanlass, R. (1997). Employment profiles in neuromuscular diseases. *American Journal of Physical Medicine & Rehabilitation. 76*(1), 26–37.

Gramzow, R. H., Sedikides, C., Panter, A. T., Sathy, V., Harris, J., & Insko, C. A. (2004). Patterns of self-regulation and the Big Five. *European Journal of Personality, 18*(5), 367–385

Hanks, R. A., Rapport, L. J., Waldron-Perrine, B., & Millis, S. R. (2014). Role of character strengths in outcome after mild complicated to severe traumatic brain injury: A positive psychology study. *Archives of Physical Medicine and Rehabilitation, 95*(11), 2096–2102.

Hayes, S. C., Luoma, J. B., Bond, F. W., Masuda, A., & Lillis, J. (2006). Acceptance and commitment therapy: Model, processes and outcomes. *Behaviour Research and Therapy, 44*(1), 1–25. doi: 10.1016/j.brat.2005.06.006

Heppner, P. P., Lee, D.-G., & Tian, L. (2021). The important role of problem solving appraisal in creating a positive life across cultural contexts. In C. R. Snyder, S. J. Lopez, L. M. Edwards, & S. Marques (Eds.), *The Oxford handbook of positive psychology* (pp. 453–470). Oxford.

Hopwood, C. J., Wright, A. G. C., & Donnellan, M. B. (2011). Evaluating the evidence for the general factor of personality across multiple inventories. *Journal of Research in Personality, 45*, 468–478.

Jans-Beken, L., Jacobs, N., Janssens, M., , Peeters , S., Reijnders, J., Lechner, L., & Lataster, J. (2020) Gratitude and health: An updated review. *Journal of Positive Psychology, 15*, 743–782, doi: 10.1080/17439760.2019.1651888

Johnson, J., & Wood, A. M. (2017). Integrating positive and clinical psychology: Viewing human functioning as continua from positive to negative can benefit clinical assessment, interventions and understandings of resilience. *Cognitive Therapy and Research, 41*(3), 335–349. doi: 10.1007/s10608-015-9728-y

Kashdan, T. B., & Rottenberg, J. (2010). Psychological flexibility as a fundamental aspect of health. *Clinical Psychology Review, 30*(7), 865–878. doi: 10.1016/j. cpr.2010.03.001

Kemp, B., & Vash, C. (1971). Productivity after injury in a sample of spinal cord injured persons: A pilot study. *Journal of Chronic Disease, 24*, 259–275.

Kohut, H. (1971). *The analysis of the self.* International Universities Press.

Krause, J. S. (1997). Personality and traumatic spinal cord injury: Relationship to participation in productive activities. *Journal of Applied Rehabilitation Counseling, 40*, 202–214.

Krause, J. S., & Rohe, D. E. (1998). Personality and life adjustment after spinal cord injury: An exploratory study. *Rehabilitation Psychology, 43*(2), 118–130. doi: 10.1037/0090-5550.43.2.118

Latimer, A. E., Ginis, K. A. M., & Arbour, K. P. (2006). The efficacy of an implementation intention intervention for promoting physical activity among individuals with spinal cord injury: A randomized controlled trial. *Rehabilitation Psychology, 51*(4), 273–280. doi: 10.1037/0090-5550.51.4.273

Lee, Y.-R., & Enright, R. D. (2019). A meta-analysis of the association between forgiveness of others and physical health. *Psychology & Health, 34*(5), 626–643. doi: 10.1080/08870446.2018.1554185

Lewin, K. (1936). *Principles of topological psychology.* McGraw-Hill.

Lopez, S., & Snyder, C. (2003). *Positive psychological assessment: A handbook of models and measures.* American Psychological Association. doi: 10.1037/10612-000

Ma, J. K., Cheifetz, O., Todd, K., Chebaro, C., Phang, S. H….Martin Ginis, K. A. (2020). Co-development of a physiotherapist-delivered physical activity intervention for adults with spinal cord injury. *Spinal Cord, 58*, 778–786.

Mackay, J., Charles, S., Kemp, B., & Heckhausen, J. (2011). Goal striving and maladaptive coping in adults living with spinal cord injury: Associations with affective well-being. *Journal of Aging and Health, 23*, 158–176.

Maddux, J. E., & Kleiman, E. M. (2021). Self-efficacy: The power of believing you can. In C. R. Snyder, S. J. Lopez, L. M. Edwards, & S. Marques (Eds.), *The Oxford handbook of positive psychology* (pp. 443–452). Oxford.

McCrae, R. R., & Costa, P. T., Jr. (1996). Toward a new generation of personality theories: Theoretical contexts for the five-factor model. In J. S. Wiggins (Ed.), *The five-factor model of personality: Theoretical perspectives* (pp. 51–87). Guilford Press.

McGrath, R. E., Greenberg, M. J., & Hall-Simmonds, A. (2018). Scarecrow, tin woodsman, and cowardly lion: The three-factor model of virtue. *Journal of Positive Psychology, 13*(4), 373–392. doi: 10.1080/17439760.2017.1326518

Ng, M.-Y., & Wong, W.-S. (2013). The differential effects of gratitude and sleep on psychological distress in patients with chronic pain. *Journal of Health Psychology, 18*, 263–271.

Peterson, C., & Seligman, M.E.P. (2004). *Character strengths and virtues: A classification and handbook.* American Psychological Association; Oxford University Press.

Peterson, D. B. (2011). *Psychological aspects of functioning, disability, and health.* Springer Publishing Co.

Rath, J. F., & Elliott, T. R. (2012). Psychological models in rehabilitation psychology. In P. Kennedy (Ed.), *The Oxford handbook of rehabilitation psychology* (pp. 32–46). Oxford University Press.

Rath, J. F., Simon, D., Langenbahn, D. M., Sherr, R. L., & Diller, L. (2003). Group treatment of problem-solving deficits in outpatients with traumatic brain injury: A randomized outcome study. *Neuropsychological Rehabilitation, 13*, 461–488.

Robins, R. W., John, O. P., Caspi, A., Moffitt, T. E., & Stouthamer-Loeber, M. (1996). Resilient, overcontrolled, and undercontrolled boys: Three replicable personality types. *Journal of Personality and Social Psychology, 70*, 157–171. doi: 10.1037/0022-3514.70.1.157

Ropponen, A., Svedberg, P., Huunan-Seppala, A., Koskenvuo, K., Koskenvuo, M., Kaprio, J. (2012). Personality traits and life dissatisfaction as risk factors for disability pensions due to low back diagnoses: A 30-year longitudinal cohort study of Finnish twins. *Journal of Psychosomatic Research, 73*, 289–294. doi: 10.1016/j.jpsychores.2012.07.003

Rovner, B. W., & Casten, R. J. (2001). Neuroticism predicts depression and disability in age-related macular degeneration. *Journal of the American Geriatrics Society, 49*, 1097–1100.

Rovner, B. W., Casten, R. J., Hegel, M. T., Massof, R. W., Leiby, B. E., Tasman, W. S. (2014). Personality and functional vision in older adults with age-related macular degeneration. *Journal of Visual Impairment & Blindness, 108*(3), 187–199.

Ruini, C., & Vescovelli, F. (2013). The role of gratitude in breast cancer: Its relationships with post-traumatic growth, psychological well-being and distress. *Journal of Happiness Studies: An Interdisciplinary Forum on Subjective Well-Being, 14*, 263–274. doi: 10.1007/s10902-012-9330-x

Schwarzer, R., Lippke, S., & Luszczynska, A. (2011). Mechanisms of health behavior change in persons with chronic illness or disability: The Health Action Process Approach (HAPA). *Rehabilitation Psychology, 56*, 161–170. doi: 10.1037/a0024509

Seligman, M. E. P., & Csikszentmihalyi, M. (2000). Positive psychology: An introduction. *American Psychologist, 55*, 5–14. doi: 10.1037/0003-066X.55.1.5

Shadel, W. G. (2010). Clinical assessment of personality: Perspectives from contemporary personality science. In J. E. Maddux & J. P. Tangney (Eds.), *Social foundations of clinical psychology* (pp. 329–348). Guilford Press.

Shontz, F. C. (1971). Physical disability and personality. In W. S. Neff (Ed.), *Rehabilitation psychology* (pp. 33–73). American Psychological Association Press.

Sirois, F. M., & Wood, A. M. (2017). Gratitude uniquely predicts lower depression in chronic illness populations: A longitudinal study of inflammatory bowel disease and arthritis. *Health Psychology, 36*, 122–132. doi: 10.1037/hea0000436

Smedema, S. M. (2020). An analysis of the relationship of character strengths and quality of life in persons with multiple sclerosis. *Quality of Life Research, 29*, 1259–1270.

Smedema, S. M., & Bhattarai, M. (2020). The unique contribution of character strengths to quality of life in persons with multiple sclerosis. *Rehabilitation Psychology, 66*(1), 76–86. doi: 10.1037/rep0000363

Snyder, C. R., & Forsyth, D. R. (1991). *Handbook of social and clinical psychology: The health perspective.* Pergamon Press.

Snyder, C. R., & Lopez, S. J. (2001). *Handbook of positive psychology.* Oxford University Press.

Strus, W., & Cieciuch, J. (2017). Towards a synthesis of personality, temperament, motivation, emotion and mental health models within the circumplex of personality metatraits. *Journal of Research in Personality, 66,* 70–95.

Stuntzner, S., Lynch, R., Enright, R., Hartley, M., & MacDonald, A. (2019). Forgiveness and psychosocial reactions to disability: A pilot study to examine change in persons with spinal cord injury. *International Physical Medicine & Rehabilitation Journal, 4.* doi: 10.15406/ipmrj.2019.04.00194

Swain, N. B. Thompson, B. L., Gallagher, S., Paddison, J., & Mercer, S. (2020). Gratitude enhanced mindfulness (GEM): A pilot study of an internet-delivered programme for self-management of pain and disability in people with arthritis. *Journal of Positive Psychology, 15*, 420–426. doi: 10.1080/17439760.2019.1627397

Tellegen, A. (2003). *Multidimensional personality questionnaire.* Minneapolis, MN: University of Minnesota Press.

Toussaint, L. L., Worthington, E. L., Williams, D. R., & Webb, J. R. (2019). Forgiveness and physical health. In E. L. Worthington & N. G. Wade (Eds.), *Handbook of forgiveness* (2nd ed., pp. 178–187). Routledge.

van Diemen, T., Craig, A., van Nes, I. J. W., Stolwijk-Swuste, J. M., Geertzen, J. H. B., Middleton, J., & Post, M.W.M. (2020). Enhancing our conceptual understanding of state and trait self-efficacy by correlational analysis of four self-efficacy scales in people with spinal cord injury. *BMC Psychology, 8.* doi: 10.1186/s40359-020-00474-6

van Leeuwen, C.M., Post, M.W., Westers, P., van der Woude L.H., de Groot S., Sluis, T., Slootman, H., & Lindeman, E. (2012). Relationships between activities, participation, personal factors, mental health, and life satisfaction in persons with spinal cord injury. *Archives of Physical Medicine and Rehabilitation, 93*(1), 82–89.

Wade, N. G., Hoyt, W. T., Kidwell, J. E. M., Worthington Jr., E. L. (2014). Efficacy of psychotherapeutic interventions to promote forgiveness: A meta-analysis. *Journal of Consulting and Clinical Psychology, 82*, 154–170.

Wade, S. L., Walz, N.C., Carey, J., Williams, K.M., Cass, J., Herren, L., Mark. E., Yeates, K.O. (2010). A randomized trial of teen online problem solving for improving executive function deficits following pediatric traumatic brain injury. *Journal of Head Trauma Rehabilitation, 25*(6), 409–415. doi: 10.1097/HTR.0b013e3181fb900d.

Webb, J. R., Toussaint, L., Kalpakjian, C. Z., & Tate, D. G. (2010) Forgiveness and health-related outcomes among people with spinal cord injury, *Disability and Rehabilitation, 32*, 360–366. doi: 10.3109/09638280903166360

Worthington, E. L., Jr., & Hampson, P. J. (2011). Forgiveness, reconciliation, and the hard march to peace. In J. H. Ellens (Ed.), *Explaining evil, Vol 3: Approaches, responses, solutions* (pp. 109–124). ABC-CLIO.

Wright, B. A., & Fletcher, B. L. (1982). Uncovering hidden resources: A challenge in assessment. *Professional Psychology, 13*(2), 229–235. doi: 10.1037/0735-7028.13.2.229

Yan, T., Chan, C. W. H., Chow, K. M., Zheng, W., & Sun, M. (2020). A systematic review of the effects of character strengths-based intervention on the psychological well-being of patients suffering from chronic illnesses. *Journal of Advanced Nursing, 76*, 1567–1580.

Zeldow P. B., & Pavlou, M. (1984). Physical disability, life stress, and psychosocial adjustment in multiple sclerosis. *The Journal of Nervous and Mental Disease, 172*(2), 80–84. doi: 10.1097/00005053-198402000-00003

Chapter 10

The Experience of Meaning in Life in the Context of Pain-Related Disability

Devin Guthrie[1], Brandon L. Boring, Joseph Maffly-Kipp, Vani A. Mathur, and Joshua A. Hicks

INTRODUCTION

Pain is a leading cause of disability worldwide (Vos et al., 2017) and frequently accompanies chronic and debilitating conditions. Chronic pain can present as a symptom of a disease or condition (e.g., rheumatoid arthritis), as sequelae following injury, tissue damage, or medical procedures (e.g., spinal cord injury, burns, or knee replacement surgery), or may have no known underlying cause (e.g., fibromyalgia, lower back pain). Chronic pain affects up to 20% of Americans (Dahlhamer et al., 2018), and is more prevalent than cancer and heart disease combined (Vos et al., 2017). However, pain is a highly subjective experience, and the personal factors that contribute to secondary aspects of pain such as pain disability are not fully understood. The goal of this chapter is to review how one important personal factor, the experience of meaning in life (MIL), is associated with aspects of pain-related disabilities.

The World Health Organization (2011, p. 4) defines disability as "the umbrella term for impairments, activity limitations, and participation restrictions, referring to the negative aspects of the interaction between an individual (with a health condition) and that individual's contextual factors (environmental and personal factors)." Disability is a biopsychosocial process that can involve a spectrum of physical and mental conditions that prevent people from fully engaging in their lives. Within the realm of pain-related disabilities, this is frequently measured using two separate but similar constructs that assess the effects of pain on activity and daily living: pain disability and pain interference. While these two terms are sometimes used interchangeably, they have slight differences in connotation and are assessed using different measures. Pain disability refers to the extent to which pain prevents someone from performing baseline tasks (e.g., getting dressed) and is assessed using measures such as the Pain Disability Index (Pollard, 1984) and the Pain Disability Questionnaire (Anagnostis et al., 2004). Pain interference is the degree of disruption and discomfort the pain causes not only in daily living but in psychological domains such as mood and enjoyment of life and is assessed using measures such as the Brief Pain Inventory (Cleeland & Ryan, 1994). Pain interference has been shown to be distinct from physical functioning and disability due to physical impairment, reflecting that the experience of pain itself can impede daily living and well-being (Cruz-Almeida et al., 2009; Karayannis et al., 2017).

MIL and its related constructs have been studied in relation to both pain disability and interference. MIL has been defined as "the sense made of, and significance felt regarding, the nature of one's being and existence" (Steger et al., 2006, p. 81). A large body of research shows that having MIL is correlated with good physical health whereas the experience of meaninglessness is correlated with poorer physical health (e.g., King & Hicks, 2021; Leontiev, 2013). In this chapter, we will review the current literature connecting pain-related disabilities to MIL and its subcomponents and provide suggestions for future research.

The Meaning of Meaning

Since existential meaning first entered the realm of psychological inquiry with Victor Frankl's influential proposal that finding meaning is a central human drive (Frankl, 2000), meaning has been defined in a number of different ways. For example, King and colleagues (2006, p. 180) stated, "Lives may be experienced as meaningful when they are felt to have significance beyond the trivial or momentary, to have purpose, or to have a coherence that transcends chaos," while Steger (2012, p. 165) defined MIL as "the web of connections, understandings, and interpretations that help us comprehend our experience and formulate plans directing our energies to the achievement of our desired future." Because of the difficulty researchers have agreeing on a definition of this abstract construct, MIL is often measured by assessing people's subjective beliefs about whether their lives feel meaningful (Hicks & King, 2009; Leontiev, 2013). In the last 20 years, MIL has gained a place of importance in the field of positive psychology (Leontiev, 2013), and research has converged to demonstrate that subjective experiences of MIL are associated with important outcomes, including psychological and physical health (e.g., King & Hicks, 2021). Recently, there has been a call to better understand MIL by directly measuring its theorized facets or subcomponents. These facets include coherence, purpose, and significance.

Martela and Steger (2016) defined *coherence* as "the feeling that one's experiences or life itself makes sense" (p. 533), *purpose* as one's "future-oriented aims and goals that give direction to life . . . and lend significance to one's present actions" (p. 534), and *significance* as "a value-laden evaluation of one's life as a whole regarding how important, worthwhile, and inherently valuable it feels" (p. 535). Significance can be broken down further into two subcomponents. The first labeled *existential mattering* assesses how significant you judge your life to be in a context larger than yourself (e.g., interpersonal relationships, society, the universe) (George & Park, 2016; Guthrie et al., 2021b). The second *experiential appreciation* (EA) represents how inherently significant you feel your lived experience is to yourself (Kim et al., 2021).

We should note that researchers have only recently developed scales to assess each of these constructs as facets of MIL (e.g., Costin & Vignoles, 2020; George & Park, 2016). As such, many of the studies we use to support the relationships between specific facets of MIL and pain-related outcomes use measures that do not perfectly correspond to the definitions of the facets we have provided (e.g., the Sense of Coherence (SOC) scale measures more than just coherence; Antonovsky, 1993). We discuss the limitations of drawing conclusions based on these studies throughout the chapter.

The Search for Meaning

The onset of a disabling illness or injury can disrupt people's ability to experience MIL in any of the facets we have discussed. Disability can make people feel like life no longer makes sense by challenging the coherence of their worldviews (e.g., belief in a just world). It can make people feel like they do not matter (e.g., due to the discrimination disabled people face). It can interfere with people's ability to appreciate experience (e.g., because they are focused on the experience of pain to the exclusion of all else). Or, it can block people's pathways to purpose. When people's ability to make meaning is disrupted in these ways, it typically initiates a search for meaning[2] to attempt to reestablish their ability to experience MIL.

Early research suggested that disability leads people to search for meaning to understand and accept their new life circumstances and that those who succeed experience better health outcomes (Dunn, 1994, 1996). More recent research with people with chronic illnesses demonstrated that the best physical and mental health outcomes were predicted by the combination of a high presence of MIL and a low search for meaning, and the worst by low presence and high search (Camacho et al., 2014; Davis & Morgan, 2008; Davis

& Novoa, 2013; Dezutter, Luyckx, & Wachholtz, 2015), though it must be noted that these studies all examined only purpose and coherence and not significance or global MIL. These studies support the idea that coming to a successful conclusion to the process of searching for meaning leads to better adjustment to disability but also indicate that adjustment may become worse during the process of searching than before it has begun. However, since these studies did not check to see if all of the individuals involved engaged in a process of searching for meaning, it is also possible that people who experienced high MIL before the onset of chronic illness simply maintained their MIL and experienced its associated benefits.

This alternative explanation highlights the importance of being able to determine the extent to which disability has disrupted people's ability to make meaning. If two people who derive much of their MIL from their work—a carpenter and a business manager—both develop arthritis with the same severity, the carpenter's purpose pathways may be significantly more disrupted due to the more physically involved nature of carpentry. In this example, the carpenter may need to engage in the stressful and uncertain process of searching for new pathways to purpose while the business manager may be able to maintain more or less the same pathways as before they developed arthritis. For the carpenter, the difficulty of living with a painful illness is compounded by the fact that their illness is also preventing them from meeting their basic need for MIL as derived from their creations, so it would not be surprising if the carpenter experienced worse health outcomes until they are able to find new pathways to purpose. However, even within this example it is imperative that all individual experiences of disability (pain-related or not) are validated and supported regardless of perceived hardship, functional disruption, or biases against how others' livelihoods are made (Kool et al., 2009). Circumstances of pain-related disability do not discriminate and can alter one's life in profound ways in both physical and psychological domains.

We suggest that developing a thorough understanding of how disability and pain disrupt people's ability to make meaning may be key to both helping improve the lives of people with chronic pain and disabilities and the pain associated therein, potentially limiting their impact on daily living. We also posit that it is critical to understand the ways disability and pain can disrupt each facet of MIL—coherence, purpose, mattering, and EA—and how each of these facets of MIL can improve the well-being of people with disability and chronic pain. In the sections that follow, careful attention will be paid to the bidirectional relationships between pain-related disability and each facet of MIL, understanding that with an eye to the research still needed to understand both the complex nature of these relationships and how to best apply our understanding.

Coherence

Having a coherent understanding of one's past, present, and predicted future is theorized to contribute to favorable outcomes in relation to disability (George & Park, 2016). Being able to make sense of their situation and accept disability as a part of life may help people move past unproductive rumination on the physically and psychologically painful aspects of their experiences and begin to adjust by focusing on the parts of their lives they can control and improve (Park, 2010). In this way, coherence could help those with pain-related disabilities come to terms with their personal experiences in relation to the grand scheme of life. Conversely, for people with lower levels of coherence, chronic pain may manifest dissonance between their reality and their expectations and foster frustration about why they must endure these hardships (e.g., "Why me?"), stymying growth and engagement with life. Even among people high in coherence, acquiring pain-related disabilities can undermine worldviews, sowing doubt about what they once thought they knew about their life and the world (George & Park, 2016; Park, 2010). This doubt could lead to distress, negatively affect mental health, and may worsen disability and pain interference in a negative feedback loop.

Research in this area aligns with theory as higher coherence is associated with making healthier lifestyle choices that may benefit people living with chronic pain (Wainwright et al., 2007). For instance, in one study of people with Ehlers-Danlos syndrome, those with a greater sense of coherence tended to be more accepting of their disability and had better functional health (Berglund et al., 2003). Similarly, in a longitudinal study of people with lower back pain following surgery, people with a higher sense of coherence[3] had less total disability as measured by the Oswestry Disability Index (Baker, Pynsent, & Fairbank, 1989; Santavirta et al., 1996). This effect was strongest for participants who were over the age of 50, and for women relative to men. Another longitudinal study assessed people 3, 6, and 12 months after experiencing a severe hand injury (Cederlund et al., 2010). People with a greater SOC had fewer disabilities of the arm, shoulder, and hand (DASH; Hudak et al., 1996), less pain, and improved sleep, as well as greater satisfaction with aspects of everyday life including work, leisure, and self-care as assessed by the Satisfaction with Daily Occupations Scale (Eklund, 2004).

It is necessary to note that not all studies have found a benefit of SOC in relation to pain-related disabilities. For instance, one study followed workers who went on leave due to nonspecific musculoskeletal pain and underwent a 57-week rehabilitation (Lillefjell et al., 2007). While SOC improved during this time, SOC did not significantly predict reentry into the workplace. However, for those who had not returned to work in any capacity following the rehabilitation program, SOC was associated with lower levels of anxiety and depression, suggesting some benefits for those most highly impacted by their pain.

The first study to directly assess the relationship between coherence as a facet of MIL and pain-related outcomes demonstrated that higher coherence was associated longitudinally with decreased odds of developing chronic pain, and with less frequent and severe instances of pain cross-sectionally (Boring et al., 2021). This effect persisted even after other facets of MIL (purpose and mattering), mental health (depression, anxiety, and self-rated health), and physical health (BMI, number of other chronic conditions) were accounted for, suggesting that coherence might have a robust relationship with the experience and development of pain. As such, we believe clinically assessing coherence could identify people who may be at risk for unfavorable outcomes in relation to their disabilities and that they should be monitored longitudinally to detect whether coherence declines over time. Ultimately, coherence may provide an important framework through which people with disabilities can navigate through life.

Purpose

Having purpose in life may help people living with pain-related disabilities persevere through their difficult circumstances and continue to pursue and attain goals that are important to them (McKnight & Kashdan, 2009). The magnitude of these goals can range from accomplishing milestones in one's career to something as seemingly mundane as getting out of bed; however, striving to achieve even small goals and celebrating when one successfully meets them can create personal empowerment and motivation to not give in to life's hardships. However, pain-related disabilities can also disrupt your goal pursuits and, in turn, your overall purpose, leading to increased distress or depression that may contribute to a vicious cycle of impaired goal actualization, hopelessness, reduced life purpose, and worsened disability (Pinquart et al., 2009). Therefore, helping reestablish or recreate purpose among people affected by pain-related disabilities may improve their functioning and well-being.

For people like our imaginary carpenter, whose major goals in life have been blocked by disability, the idea of reestablishing purpose may be daunting. It is therefore important to recall two things: The first is that goals are oriented around purpose, not the other way around; the second is that purpose exists in many domains of life (Dahl, 2010). Even if disability forces the carpenter from completing any more woodwork, working wood may have only been one way of moving toward a broader value or purpose. If their purpose was creative expression, for example, there are many other avenues for them to pursue that goal. Additionally, most people have a multitude of purposes in many domains (e.g., interpersonal relationships, personal growth, family, spirituality, work, etc.). When disability interferes with people's pursuit of purpose in one domain, they may be able to reestablish purpose by focusing on a different valued domain.

In pain-related disability research, higher purpose is almost uniformly linked to positive outcomes (McKnight & Kashdan, 2009). For example, Thompson et al. (2003) found that among patients with a spinal cord injury, purpose was associated with better adjustment to their disability. Delving further into purpose's positive relationship with adjustment, purpose mediated the relationship between aspects of personality such as aggression and sociability and adjustment, as well as one's internal locus of control over health and adjustment, suggesting that having greater purpose may promote more favorable outcomes in response to disability regardless of other personal characteristics.

Trompetter et al. (2013) found that higher scores on the Engaged Living Scale[4] (ELS) were related to both less pain interference and pain disability among chronic pain patients over and above other constructs such as psychological inflexibility and mindfulness. Nsamenang and colleagues (2016) found that among those with multiple sclerosis (MS), having greater meaning[5] was associated with less pain interference. A separate study assessed purpose in relation to interference due to fatigue among women with rheumatoid arthritis, and both disability of physical functioning and interference due to fatigue among women with fibromyalgia (FM) (Schleicher et al., 2005). Having greater purpose was associated with less disability for those with FM, and less interference for both groups.

Additionally, Yeung et al. (2019) found that having purpose was associated with a higher quality of life (QOL) and with a greater capability of achieving personal standards of living (e.g., social connection and activity restrictions) among disabled older adults. Purpose remained associated with greater QOL when controlling for other factors such as depression, loneliness, and self-rated physical health.

Finally, purpose predicts longitudinal outcomes of pain disabilities. Smith and Zautra (2004) followed people with knee osteoarthritis who underwent total knee replacement surgery. Two weeks before the surgery, participants completed baseline surveys assessing purpose, personality characteristics such as optimism and emotionality, mental health indicators like anxiety, depression, and affect, and physical health measures including functional disability, pain, and stiffness. Six months after the surgery, the participants completed the assessments again. While purpose was not associated with disability or stiffness at baseline, it predicted less disability and stiffness following surgery, as well as less anxiety, depression, and negative affect, and greater positive affect. After controlling for other personal characteristics (optimism, pessimism, and emotionality), purpose still predicted favorable mental health outcomes, although it was no longer predictive of disability.

Similar to other facets of MIL, purpose can both be unsettled by pain-related disability or promote perseverance and resiliency through difficult circumstances. Clinically assessing purpose and understanding the unique goals of each patient may contribute to favorable outcomes and identify those who may need support in continuing or generating new purpose in life.

Significance

A third component of MIL is the feeling of significance. Martela and Steger (2016) argued that significance is "a sense of life's inherent value and having a life worth living" (p. 532). In the MIL literature, most research has examined a component of significance-related feeling that one's actions and life in general matter to others. This perception is generally referred to as existential mattering (George & Park, 2016, 2017). Recently, scholars have argued that EA represents another component of the feeling of significance (Kim et al., 2021). Specifically, EA represents that significance one feels in their life experiences. Below, we discuss how each of the components of significance relate to pain and pain-related disabilities.

Existential Mattering

The subjective perception that one's life matters in contexts larger than oneself has important theoretical implications for the ways in which people cope with pain-related disabilities. While no published research has focused on the role of mattering in these contexts, investigations of related constructs can help provide insight. For example, pain can lead to subjective feelings of helplessness, which predicts future functional disability in individuals with chronic pain (Samwel et al., 2007). Disability can likewise lead individuals to feel powerless or worthless based on the norms of the society that they inhabit (Strandmark, 2004). This sort of helplessness and powerlessness based on the broader context of one's existence is deeply related to mattering. For example, if a person experiencing pain-related disabilities feels helpless/powerless because they are unable to meaningfully contribute to their family, workplace, or community, their mental health (and experience of pain) may worsen. Conversely, retaining a sense that one's life does ultimately matter, despite pain-related disability, could theoretically buffer these negative outcomes. Interestingly, the only known investigation to examine the relationship between chronic pain mattering in a cosmic context (i.e., in the "grand scheme of the universe") found a positive relationship between existential mattering and pain severity (Boring et al., 2021), which is difficult to interpret. Overall, much more research is needed to fully elucidate the relationship between the mattering facet of MIL and pain.

Social mattering, a construct that has traditionally been studied independently of MIL but which is now being integrated into the existential mattering literature (Guthrie et al., 2021b), has been studied slightly more in the context of pain-related disabilities. Social or interpersonal mattering is generally defined as the subjective feeling that one adds value, and is valued, in relation to their community, culture, and social groups (Prilleltensky et al., 2020). Flett (2018) reviewed the role of social mattering in disabled populations and ultimately suggested that these groups struggle to achieve a sense of mattering relative to normative populations. Furthermore, multiple researchers have found that social mattering is an important component of psychological well-being for older adults as they experience declining health and the loss of autonomy (Fazio, 2009; Pearlin & LeBlanc, 2001). Finally, a 2011 study by Raque-Bogdan and colleagues found that social mattering was a positive predictor of broad physical health. Together, these studies help to illustrate the idea that chronic pain and its associated disabilities and a sense that one's life matters are all interrelated. Unfortunately, no existing research sheds light onto the directionality of these relationships. Therefore, it is important to be cautious in interpreting this nascent field of inquiry, especially given the lack of research directly involving mattering with regards to MIL. Nevertheless, these related findings provide a promising starting point for future research.

Experiential Appreciation

Although many scholars have stressed how one's experiences can directly influence the experience of MIL (Csikszentmihalyi, 2008; Frankl, 1986), only recently have these ideas been empirically tested (Kim et al., 2021). Among all the facets of MIL we have outlined, EA currently has the most well-established connection to pain. EA is believed to include at least three components: mindfulness, awareness of beauty, and appreciation of experience (Guthrie et al., 2021a). These components can also be thought of as steps. Mindfulness is present moment awareness, a state of engagement with one's experience of the world from which the other steps flow. Awareness of beauty is the act of noticing the things in one's present environment that inherently evoke positive emotions, often things like art, aspects of nature, or other people. Appreciation is the act of feeling the positive emotions evoked by one's mindful awareness of beauty ("experiential savoring," a common term in pain research, is a form of appreciation). It is in the act of appreciation that it is possible to make meaning (Wong, 2014), which is believed to directly influence the degree that one feels their existence is significant.

EA is likely undermined and opposed by a maladaptive response style common in people with chronic pain called "experiential avoidance" (Esteve et al., 2012; Kashdan et al., 2009; Zettle et al., 2005). Experiential avoidance is the attempt, either subconsciously or deliberately, to dissociate from aspects of in-the-moment-experience. Because pain is a highly unpleasant experience, it is natural to try to avoid it. However, in the case of chronic pain, which either cannot be completely avoided or can only be avoided by significantly limiting one's activities, the attempt to avoid pain tends to lead to more pain and pain interference over time (Gutierrez et al., 2004). Experiential avoidance also interferes with people's lives by cutting them off from experiences they would enjoy, adding to the burden of disability (Hayes et al., 1999).

Although no studies have directly examined the relationship between EA as a facet of MIL and pain-related outcomes, a multitude of studies show that lower experiential avoidance is associated with decreased pain severity, pain interference, and pain disability in people with chronic pain (Kashdan et al., 2009; Costa & Pinto-Gouveia, 2011; Costa & Pinto-Gouveia, 2013; Karademas et al., 2017). Moreover, treatments targeted at reducing experiential avoidance have seen significant success at decreasing pain interference and improving the physical and psychological well-being of people with chronic pain (Wetherell et al., 2011; Dahl, 2010).

Treatments targeting the mindfulness component of EA have demonstrated remarkable results in a variety of chronic pain populations. Early randomized controlled trials (RCTs) showed significant improvement in pain symptoms and mental health outcomes for patients who took part in a 10-week mindfulness meditation Stress Reduction and Relaxation Program (Kabat-Zinn, 1982; Kabat-Zinn et al., 1985). More recent and streamlined RCTs with eight-week Mindfulness Based Stress Reduction (MBSR) training improved pain and mental health outcomes for people with chronic back pain (Cherkin et al., 2016; Morone et al., 2016) and irritable bowel syndrome (Garland et al., 2011; Zernicke et al., 2012). One of the newest mindfulness-based programs to show promise in treating chronic pain, called Mindfulness-Oriented Recovery Enhancement, closely resembles the steps EA we outlined, teaching patients to first use mindfulness to expand their awareness of positive experiences in the moment and then apply cognitive reappraisal and savoring techniques to better appreciate those positive experiences (Garland, 2021).

Though not as expansive as the literature on mindfulness, research on gratitude, a construct related to appreciation, is also worth noting. Generally, there is a positive association between gratitude and physical health (Lavelock et al., 2016). Among chronic pain patients specifically, higher levels of gratitude are associated with better mental health outcomes (Ng & Wong, 2012). Because a variety of methods already exist to teach people both how to increase EA directly (e.g., by increasing either the mindfulness facet with MBSR or increasing the appreciation facet with experiential savoring training) and how to decrease experiential avoidance, which could indirectly increase EA, we suggest that this facet of MIL is a particularly good target for psychological interventions.

CLINICAL PSYCHOLOGY APPLICATIONS

The relationship between MIL and pain-related disabilities holds important implications for clinical practice centered on pain-related disability treatment. Treatment for patients who present to therapy with chronic pain is often suboptimal, in part because many clinicians are ill-equipped to address the experience of chronic pain and disabilities resulting from it (Breivik et al., 2006; Robinson et al., 2011). In theory, a patient's ability to find meaning in their experience of pain (presumably with the help of a therapist) should improve their overall well-being and ability to cope with their pain. This idea is supported by qualitative accounts of people addressing pain with meaning-making efforts, which ultimately led to improved coping, resilience, and subjective well-being (West et al., 2012; Winger et al., 2020). Further, Park (2010) suggested that people's ability to find meaning in stressful life experiences directly affects their overall perception that life is meaningful. Following this logic, it may be useful for clinicians to encourage and facilitate meaning-making among clients who struggle with pain in an effort to improve overall MIL, resilience, and functional outcomes.

One potential way to achieve this would be to target MIL as an adjunct to existing evidence-based therapies that target chronic pain, of which there are several. A 2020 Cochrane review found evidence that both Cognitive Behavioral Therapy (CBT) and Behavior Therapy were efficacious in the treatment of chronic pain and related disabilities (Williams et al.). Additionally, Majeed and colleagues (2018) reviewed evidence that Acceptance and Commitment Therapy (ACT), CBT, and MBSR treatments all may be able to reduce the extent to which patients rely on opioids for pain management. Since many consider MIL to be an important component of psychotherapy in general (Debats, 1996; Hill et al., 2015), efforts to directly foster meaning-making could reasonably complement one of these evidence-based approaches.

Purpose may be the most straightforward (and common) facet of MIL to address in therapy. Clinicians can help clients identify ways to participate in their communities, explore purpose-driven career paths, and find value-driven means of benefiting some sort of "greater good." Working toward these values by setting (and achieving) goals within the bounds of a client's pain-related disability should theoretically lead to an increased sense of purpose. Coherence could potentially be increased by working with clients to create a more clear narrative of their life (drawing on Narrative Therapy techniques; see Vromans & Schweitzer, 2009; White, 2007), or a more cohesive and functional worldview (by encouraging the active articulation of and engagement with clients' belief systems). Social mattering could certainly be addressed by helping clients seek and create more meaningful social connections. Mattering in large contexts like the "grand scheme of the universe," on the other hand, may be difficult to address without directly challenging or altering existential schemas (e.g., religious beliefs). Due to this complication, and the fact that its relationship with pain is less clear (Boring et al., 2021), it may be smart to address more immediate forms of mattering (like social mattering) first, with the hope that this will have downstream implications for larger contexts of mattering. Finally, EA could potentially be improved in multiple ways. Positive Affect Therapy (Craske et al., 2019) is a relatively new treatment approach that encourages the savoring of positive sensory experiences. This, combined with approaches centered on mindfulness and present moment awareness (drawn from MBSR or ACT), should lead to greater EA. For all of these approaches, the direct targeting of MIL through therapy may allow patients to adopt more effective coping techniques and more adaptive cognitive orientations toward their pain, which would presumably improve pain-related outcomes. While these adjunct approaches could prove effective, they nevertheless require more research in order to be confidently recommended as a treatment for pain-related disability.

ACT is currently the only evidence-based treatment for chronic pain approved by the APA Division 12 task force that has the potential to directly facilitate meaning-making. Other therapies exist that address meaning more directly (see Wong, 2010), but they lack the evidence base of ACT. The focus on forging a values-based life in ACT is conceptually related to the development of a sense of purpose and could likely indirectly improve clients' sense of coherence and mattering. A few studies do demonstrate that ACT can increase subjective judgments of MIL (Datta et al., 2015; Moghbel et al., 2019), but the mechanisms through which it does so are currently unverified. One potential avenue for understanding these mechanisms, thus potentially informing treatment for pain-related disability, is mindfulness. A core tenant of ACT is teaching patients cognitive defusion, or the separation of thoughts and emotions from the immediate, present experiencing of reality. This mindful practice is a critical component of ACT, which has been repeatedly demonstrated to reduce distress associated with chronic pain (Hughes et al., 2017; Robinson et al., 2004). Numerous empirical investigations have verified the link between mindfulness and MIL (see Chu & Mak, 2020). Separately, Garland and Fredrickson (2019) have theorized that mindfulness leads directly to the creation of meaning, in part by fostering self-transcendence and the savoring of positive affective experiences (i.e., EA), which they assert may be helpful for chronic pain patients. Though more research is certainly needed, this suggests that MIL could be an understudied mechanism in the efficacy of ACT (as well as other mindfulness-based interventions) for pain.

LITERATURE LIMITATIONS, GAPS, AND FUTURE RESEARCH

The extant literature assessing the relationship between MIL and pain-related disabilities provides a foundation for understanding the importance of assessing existential constructs—both as factors that can promote beneficial health outcomes and as fundamental aspects of existence that can be disrupted by disability. Empirical research over the past five years has substantially expanded our understanding of the facets of MIL, paving the way for new insights into the interplay between specific facets of MIL and the experiences of people with pain-related disability. As such, it is critical that future research use the most up-to-date measures of the facets of MIL, since many older measures (which are still commonly used) combine and incorporate multiple facets of MIL without distinguishing among them, thus diluting our ability to analyze the unique contributions of these distinct concepts. For instance, though seemingly robust, the literature assessing the role of coherence in relation to pain-related disabilities is fundamentally limited by the widespread use of the SOC scale (SOC), which is discordant with our current understanding of coherence. Similarly, the FACIT-SP combines purpose and spirituality, introducing confounds that cloud interpretation of what might be clinically relevant. Using measures that accurately assess specific facets of meaning (e.g., The Multidimensional Meaning in Life Scale; Costin & Vignoles, 2020) would help clarify the differential effects of the various facets of MIL in relation to pain-related disability and aid in identifying the most important facets to target in clinical interventions.

   Many current clinical interventions aim to foster a general sense of MIL; however, using interventions designed specifically to bolster the facets associated most closely with pain-related disabilities may improve pain outcomes. While conducting clinically relevant research, it is important to recognize that there may be reciprocal relations between MIL and pain-related disabilities, and that these relations are not yet well-understood. That is, MIL can buffer negative health outcomes and can also be disrupted by negative health outcomes. For this reason, we suggest that assessing the ways in which different facets of MIL serve both as protective and risk factors for pain-related disabilities will be a fruitful area for future research.

Finally, there are far more conditions involving pain-related disability than there are studies examining meaning-making processes associated with pain, disability, and interference. For instance, findings on MIL in cancer patients may not be generalizable to FM patients due to the fundamental differences in the experiences, expected outcomes, and current treatments for each condition. In order to achieve the best treatment outcomes, it is imperative to evaluate the interaction of all facets of MIL within groups of specific pain-related disabilities.

CONCLUSION

Pain-related disabilities can be highly disruptive to a person's life, both physically and psychologically. Research has consistently shown the importance of MIL in promoting favorable physical and mental health. Although the role of MIL in relation to pain-related disabilities is not a new area of study, a recent rise in positive psychological research on MIL has altered scientific understanding of the construct, especially with regard to the components that comprise it. We believe applying this more nuanced understanding of MIL to research on pain-related disabilities will provide new opportunities to increase our understanding of how chronic pain can disrupt the experience of MIL and how MIL can help increase the well-being of people experiencing chronic pain. These emerging understandings have the potential to profoundly alter the clinical interventions used to treat pain-related disabilities.

Although current research on this subject is germinal, it is clear people are fully capable of simultaneously living with chronic pain and living with meaning, a fact with the power to transform society's understanding of disabilities and, for many disabled people, their understanding of themselves. People do not need to put their lives on hold until doctors deliver an antidote to their suffering. As Viktor Frankl wrote, "Suffering ceases to be suffering at the moment it finds a meaning" (2000, p. 113). Even in the absence of a medical cure, people with pain-related disabilities can learn to thrive. Positive psychological research, and research on MIL in particular, can pave the path for people to flourish even in the midst of pain.

NOTES

1. DG and BLB contributed equally to this work.
2. The notion of searching for MIL is most closely associated with searching for purpose and for coherence (e.g., searching to make sense of yourself, the world, and your place in it) (Steger et al., 2006). If someone wants to experience mattering, they typically search for a means through which they might matter more, which is

essentially still searching for purpose. Likewise, though you can learn to be more appreciative of your experience, experiential appreciation is not typically associated with a search process.

3. Although the Sense of Coherence Scale (SOC; Antonovsky, 1993) has been often used to assess the relationship between coherence and pain/disability-related outcomes, the SOC was developed to tap into more than coherence (e.g., manageability; Costin & Vignoles, 2020; King & Hicks, 2021). As such, our interpretations of these findings are limited because they do not accurately assess the scope of the relationship between coherence specifically and pain-related disabilities. Nevertheless, we believe studies using the SOC do, at minimum, demonstrate preliminary evidence for the connections between pain-related outcomes and coherence.

4. The ELS was developed to assess the response of people with chronic pain to Acceptance and Commitment Therapy, a form of therapy for which increasing people's sense of purpose is one major goal. The ELS consists of two subscales, one relating closely to purpose and the other relating closely to life satisfaction.

5. This study used the FACIT-SP (Petermen et al., 2002), which incorporates spirituality items related to finding peace in one's life, but also includes many items designed to specifically assess purpose.

REFERENCES

Anagnostis, C., Gatchel, R. J., & Mayer, T. G. (2004). The pain disability questionnaire: a new psychometrically sound measure for chronic musculoskeletal disorders. *Spine*, *29*(20), 2290–2302.

Antonovsky, A. (1993). The structure and properties of the coherence scale. *Social Science and Medicine*, *36*(6), 725–733.

Baker, D. J., Pynsent, P. B., Fairbank, J. C., Roland, M. O., & Jenner, J. R. (1989). The Oswestry disability revisited. *Back pain: new approaches to rehabilitation and education* (pp. 174–186). Manchester, UK: Manchester University Press.

Berglund, B., Mattiasson, A. C., & Nordström, G. (2003). Acceptance of disability and sense of coherence in individuals with Ehlers–Danlos syndrome. *Journal of Clinical Nursing*, *12*(5), 770–777.

Boring, B.L., Maffly-Kipp, J., Mathur, V.A., Hicks, J.A. (2021). *The differential effects of coherence, purpose, and mattering on pain severity, frequency, and the development of chronic pain*. Manuscript submitted for publication.

Breivik, H., Collett, B., Ventafridda, V., Cohen, R., & Gallacher, D. (2006). Survey of chronic pain in Europe: Prevalence, impact on daily life, and treatment. *European Journal of Pain*, *10*(4), 287–333.

Camacho, A. A., Garland, S. N., Martopullo, C., & Pelletier, G. (2014). Positive and negative meanings are simultaneously ascribed to colorectal cancer: relationship to quality of life and psychosocial adjustment. *Palliative Support Care, 12*(4), 277–286.

Cederlund, R. I., Ramel, E., Rosberg, H. E., & Dahlin, L. B. (2010). Outcome and clinical changes in patients 3, 6, 12 months after a severe or major hand injury - Can sense of coherence be an indicator for rehabilitation focus? *BMC Musculoskeletal Disorders, 11*(1), 286.

Cherkin, D. C., Sherman, K. J., Balderson, B. H., Cook, A. J., Anderson, M. L., Hawkes, R. J., Hansen, K. E., & Turner, J. A. (2016). Effect of mindfulness-based stress reduction vs cognitive behavioral therapy or usual care on back pain and functional limitations in adults with chronic low back pain. *JAMA, 315*(12), 1240.

Chu, S. T.-W., & Mak, W. W. S. (2020). How mindfulness enhances meaning in life: A meta-analysis of correlational studies and randomized controlled trials. *Mindfulness, 11*(1), 177–193.

Cleeland, C.S.; Ryan, K. M. (1994). Pain assessment: Global use of the brief pain inventory. *Annals, Academy of Medicine, Singapore, 23*(2), 129–138.

Costa, J., & Pinto-Gouveia, J. (2013). Experiential avoidance and self-compassion in chronic pain. *Journal of Applied Social Psychology, 43*(8), 1578–1591.

Costin, V., & Vignoles, V. L. (2020). Meaning is about mattering: Evaluating coherence, purpose, and existential mattering as precursors of meaning in life judgments. *Journal of Personality and Social Psychology, 118*(4), 864–884.

Craske, M. G., Meuret, A. E., Ritz, T., Treanor, M., Dour, H., & Rosenfield, D. (2019). Positive affect treatment for depression and anxiety: A randomized clinical trial for a core feature of anhedonia. *Journal of Consulting and Clinical Psychology, 87*(5), 457.

Cruz-Almeida, Y., Alameda, G., & Widerström-Noga, E. G. (2009). Differentiation between pain-related interference and interference caused by the functional impairments of spinal cord injury. *Spinal Cord, 47*(5), 390–396.

Csikszentmihalyi, M. (2008). *Flow: the psychology of optimal experience.* Harper Perennial.

Dahl, J. C. (2010). *Living beyond your pain: acceptance and commitment therapy to ease chronic pain.* New Harbinger.

Dahlhamer, J., Lucas, J., Zelaya, C., Nahin, R., Mackey, S., DeBar, L., Kerns, R., Von Korff, M., Porter, L., & Helmick, C. (2018). Prevalence of chronic pain and high-impact chronic pain among adults — United States, 2016. *Morbidity and Mortality Weekly Report, 67*(36), 1001–1006.

Datta, A., Aditya, C., Chakraborty, A., Das, P., & Mukhopadhyay, A. (2016). The potential utility of acceptance and commitment therapy (act) for reducing stress and improving wellbeing in cancer patients in Kolkata. *Journal of Cancer Education, 31*(4), 721–729.

Davis, C. G., Morgan, M. S. (2008). Finding meaning, perceiving growth, and acceptance of tinnitus. *Rehabilitative Psychology, 53*(2):128–38.

Davis, C. G., Novoa, D. C. (2013). Meaning-making following spinal cord injury: Individual differences and within-person change. *Rehabilitative Psychology, 58*(2): 166–77.

Debats, D. L. (1996). Meaning in life: Clinical relevance and predictive power. *British Journal of Clinical Psychology, 35*(4), 503–516.

Dezutter, J., Luyckx, K., & Wachholtz, A. (2015). Meaning in life in chronic pain patients over time: associations with pain experience and psychological well-being. *Journal of Behavioral Medicine, 38*(2), 384–396.

Dunn, D. S. (1994). Positive meaning and illusions following disability: Reality negotiation, normative interpretation, and value change. *Journal of Social Behavior and
Personality*, 9(5), 123.

Dunn, D. S. (1996). Well-being following amputation: Salutary effects of positive
meaning, optimism, and control. *Rehabilitation Psychology*, 41(4), 285.

Eklund, M. (2004). Satisfaction with daily occupations: A tool for client evaluation in
mental health care. *Scandinavian Journal of Occupational Therapy*, 11(3), 136–142.

Esteve, R., Ramírez-Maestre, C., & López-Martínez, A. E. (2012). Experiential
avoidance and anxiety sensitivity as dispositional variables and their relationship to
the adjustment to chronic pain. *European Journal of Pain*, 16(5), 718–726.

Fazio, E. M. (2010). Sense of Mattering in Late Life. In W. R. Avison, C. S.
Aneshensel, S. Schieman, & B. Wheaton (Eds.), *Advances in the conceptualization
of the stress process: essays in honor of Leonard I. Pearlin* (pp. 149–176). New
York: Springer.

Flett, G. (2018). *The psychology of mattering: Understanding the human need to be
significant*. Academic Press.

Frankl, V. E. (1986). *The doctor and the soul: From psychotherapy to logotherapy*.
New York: Vintage.

Frankl, V. E. (2000). *Man's search for meaning: An introduction to logotherapy*.
New York: Houghton, Mifflin.

Garland, E. L., Gaylord, S. A., Palsson, O., Faurot, K., Douglas Mann, J., &
Whitehead, W. E. (2011). Therapeutic mechanisms of a mindfulness-based treatment for IBS: effects on visceral sensitivity, catastrophizing, and affective processing of pain sensations. *Journal of Behavioral Medicine*, 35(6), 591–602.

Garland, E. L., & Fredrickson, B. L. (2019). Positive psychological states in the arc
from mindfulness to self-transcendence: Extensions of the mindfulness-to-meaning
theory and applications to addiction and chronic pain treatment. *Current Opinion
in Psychology*, 28, 184–191.

George, L. S., & Park, C. L. (2016). Meaning in life as comprehension, purpose,
and mattering: Toward integration and new research questions. *Review of General
Psychology*, 20(3), 205–220.

George, L. S., & Park, C. L. (2017). The multidimensional existential meaning
scale: A tripartite approach to measuring meaning in life. *The Journal of Positive
Psychology*, 12(6), 613–627.

Guthrie, D., Holte, P., & Hicks, J. A. (2021a). *Assessing experiential appreciation:
mindfulness, awareness of beauty, and appreciation of experience*. Manuscript
submitted for publication.

Guthrie, D., Martela, F., & Hicks, J. A. (2021b, in review). *What mattering means
most: Introducing interpersonal mattering to the tripartite model of meaning*.

Gutiérrez, O., Luciano, C., Rodríguez, M., & Fink, B. C. (2004). Comparison
between an acceptance-based and a cognitive-control-based protocol for coping
with pain. *Behavior Therapy*, 35(4), 767–783.

Hayes, S. C., Strosahl, K., & Wilson, K. G. (2003). *Acceptance and commitment
therapy: an experiential approach to behavior change*. Guilford Press.

Hicks, J. A., & King, L. A. (2009). Meaning in life as a subjective judgment and a lived experience. *Social and Personality Psychology Compass, 3*(4), 638–653.

Hill, C. E., Kline, K., Bauman, V., Brent, T., Breslin, C., Calderon, M., ... & Knox, S. (2015). What's it all about? A qualitative study of meaning in life for counseling psychology doctoral students. *Counselling Psychology Quarterly, 28*(1), 1–26.

Hudak, P. L., Amadio, P. C., & Bombardier, C. (1996). Development of an upper extremity outcome measure: The DASH (disabilities of the arm, shoulder, and head). *American Journal of Industrial Medicine, 29*(6), 602–608.

Hughes, L. S., Clark, J., Colclough, J. A., Dale, E., & McMillan, D. (2017). Acceptance and Commitment Therapy (ACT) for Chronic Pain. *The Clinical Journal of Pain, 33*(6), 552–568.

Kabat-Zinn, J., Lipworth, L. & Burney, R. (1985). The clinical use of mindfulness meditation for the self-regulation of chronic pain. *Journal of Behavioral Medicine, 8*, 163–190.

Kabat-Zinn, J. (1982). An outpatient program in behavioral medicine for chronic pain patients based on the practice of mindfulness meditation: Theoretical considerations and preliminary results. *General Hospital Psychiatry, 4*, 33–42.

Karademas, E. C., Karekla, M., Flouri, M., Vasiliou, V. S., Kasinopoulos, O., & Papacostas, S. S. (2017). The impact of experiential avoidance on the relations between illness representations, pain catastrophising and pain interference in chronic pain. *Psychology & Health, 32*(12), 1469–1484.

Karayannis, N. V., Sturgeon, J. A., Chih-Kao, M., Cooley, C., & Mackey, S. C. (2017). Pain interference and physical function demonstrate poor longitudinal association in people living with pain: A PROMIS investigation. *Pain, 158*(6), 1063–1068.

Kashdan, T. B., Morina, N., & Priebe, S. (2009). Post-traumatic stress disorder, social anxiety disorder, and depression in survivors of the Kosovo War: Experiential avoidance as a contributor to distress and quality of life. *Journal of Anxiety Disorders, 23*(2), 185–196.

Kim, J., Holte, P., Lee, Z., Shanahan, C., Schlegel, R. J., & Hicks, J. A. (2021). *Experiential appreciation as a pathway to meaning in life.* Manuscript submitted for publication.

King, L. A., & Hicks, J. A. (2021). The science of meaning in life. *Annual Review of Psychology, 72*(1), 1–24.

King, L. A., Hicks, J. A., Krull, J. L., & Del Gaiso, A. K. (2006). Positive affect and the experience of meaning in life. *Journal of Personality and Social Psychology, 90*(1), 179–196.

Kool, M. B., van Middendorp, H., Boeije, H. R., & Geenen, R. (2009). Understanding the lack of understanding: invalidation from the perspective of the patient with fibromyalgia. *Arthritis Care & Research, 61*(12), 1650–1656.

Lavelock, C. R., Griffin, B. J., Worthington Jr, E. L., Benotsch, E. G., Lin, Y., Greer, C. L., . . . & Hook, J. N. (2016). A qualitative review and integrative model of gratitude and physical health. *Journal of Psychology and Theology, 44*(1), 55–86.

Leontiev, D. A. (2013). Personal meaning: A challenge for psychology. *The Journal of Positive Psychology, 8*, 459–470.

Lillefjell, M., & Jakobsen, K. (2007). Sense of coherence as a predictor of work reentry following multidisciplinary rehabilitation for individuals with chronic musculoskeletal pain. *Journal of Occupational Health Psychology, 12*(3), 222–231.

Maffly-Kipp, J., Flanagan, P., Kim, J., Schlegel, R. J., Vess, M., & Hicks, J. A. (2020). The role of perceived authenticity in psychological recovery from collective trauma. *Journal of Social and Clinical Psychology, 39*(5), 419–448.

Maffly-Kipp, J., Flanagan, P., Kim, J., Rivera, G., Friedman, M. D., Vess, M., & Hicks, J. A. (2020). Meaning-making, psychological distress, and the experience of meaning in life following a natural disaster. *Social Psychological and Personality Science, 12*(5), 812–820.

Majeed, M. H., Ali, A. A., & Sudak, D. M. (2018). Mindfulness-based interventions for chronic pain: Evidence and applications. *Asian Journal of Psychiatry, 32*, 79–83.

Martela, F., & Steger, M. F. (2016). The three meanings of meaning in life: Distinguishing coherence, purpose, and significance. *The Journal of Positive Psychology, 11*(5), 531–545.

McKnight, P. E., & Kashdan, T. B. (2009). Purpose in life as a system that creates and sustains health and well-being: An integrative, testable theory. *Review of General Psychology, 13*(3), 242–251.

Moghbel Esfahani, S., & Haghayegh, S. A. (2019). The effectiveness of acceptance and commitment therapy on resilience, meaning in life, and family function in family caregivers of patients with schizophrenia. *The Horizon of Medical Sciences, 25*(4), 298–311.

Morone, N. E., Greco, C. M., Moore, C. G., Rollman, B. L., Lane, B., Morrow, L. A., ... & Weiner, D. K. (2016). A mind-body program for older adults with chronic low back pain: a randomized clinical trial. *JAMA Internal Medicine, 176*(3), 329–337.

Ng, M. Y., & Wong, W. S. (2013). The differential effects of gratitude and sleep on psychological distress in patients with chronic pain. *Journal of Health Psychology, 18*(2), 263–271.

Nsamenang, S. A., Hirsch, J. K., Topciu, R., Goodman, A. D., & Duberstein, P. R. (2016). The interrelations between spiritual well-being, pain interference and depressive symptoms in patients with multiple sclerosis. *Journal of Behavioral Medicine, 39*(2), 355–363.

Park, C. L. (2010). Making sense of the meaning literature: An integrative review of meaning making and its effects on adjustment to stressful life events. *Psychological Bulletin, 136*(2), 257–301.

Pearlin, L. I., & LeBlanc, A. J. (2001). Bereavement and the loss of mattering. In T. J. Owens, S. Stryker, & N. Goodman (Eds.), *Extending self-esteem theory and research: Sociological and psychological currents* (pp. 285–300). Cambridge University Press.

Peterman, A. H., Fitchett, G., Brady, M. J., Hernandez, L., & Cella, D. (2002). Measuring spiritual well-being in people with cancer: The functional assessment of chronic illness therapy—spiritual. *Annals of Behavioral Medicine, 24*(1), 49–58.

Pinquart, M., Silbereisen, R. K., & Fröhlich, C. (2009). Life goals and purpose in life in cancer patients. *Supportive Care in Cancer, 17*(3), 253–259.

Pollard, C. A. (1984). Preliminary validity study of the pain disability index. *Perceptual and Motor Skills*, *59*(3), 974.

Prilleltensky, I. (2020). Mattering at the intersection of psychology, philosophy, and politics. *American Journal of Community Psychology*, *65*(1–2), 16–34.

Raque-Bogdan, T. L., Ericson, S. K., Jackson, J., Martin, H. M., & Bryan, N. A. (2011). Attachment and mental and physical health: Self-compassion and mattering as mediators. *Journal of Counseling Psychology*, *58*(2), 272–278.

Robinson, K., Kennedy, N., & Harmon, D. (2011). Is occupational therapy adequately meeting the needs of people with chronic pain? *American Journal of Occupational Therapy*, *65*(1), 106–113.

Robinson, P., Wicksell, R. K., & Olsson, G. L. (2004). ACT with chronic pain patients. In A practical guide to acceptance and commitment therapy (pp. 315–345). Boston, MA: Springer.

Samwel, H. J. A., Kraaimaat, F. W., Evers, A. W. M., & Crul, B. J. P. (2007). The role of fear-avoidance and helplessness in explaining functional disability in chronic pain: A prospective study. *International Journal of Behavioral Medicine*, *14*(4), 237–241.

Santavirta, N., Björvell, H., Konttinen, Y. T., Solovieva, S., & Poussa, M. (1996). Sense of coherence and outcome of low-back surgery: 5-year follow-up of 80 patients. *European Spine Journal*, *5*(4), 229–235.

Schleicher, H., Alonso, C., Shirtcliff, E. A., Muller, D., Loevinger, B. L., & Coe, C. L. (2005). In the face of pain: The relationship between psychological well-being and disability in women with fibromyalgia. *Psychotherapy and Psychosomatics*, *74*(4), 231–239.

Smith, B. W., & Zautra, A. J. (2004). The role of purpose in life in recovery from knee surgery. *International Journal of Behavioral Medicine*, *11*(4), 197–202.

Steger, M. F. (2012). Experiencing meaning in life – Optimal functioning at the nexus of well-being, psychopathology, and spirituality. In P. T. P. Wong (Ed.), *The human quest for meaning: Theories, research, and applications* (2nd ed., pp. 165–184). New York: Routledge.

Steger, M. F., Frazier, P., Oishi, S., & Kaler, M. (2006). Meaning in life questionnaire: assessing the presence of and search for meaning in life. *Journal of Counseling Psychology*, *53*(1), 80–93.

Strandmark, K.M. (2004). Ill health is powerlessness: a phenomenological study about worthlessness, limitations, and suffering. *Scandinavian Journal of Caring Sciences*, *18*(2), 135–144.

Thompson, N. J., Coker, J., Krause, J. S., & Henry, E. (2003). Purpose in life as a mediator of adjustment after spinal cord injury. *Rehabilitation Psychology*, *48*(2), 100–108.

Trompetter, H. R., Ten Klooster, P. M., Schreurs, K. M. G., Fledderus, M., Westerhof, G. J., & Bohlmeijer, E. T. (2013). Measuring values and committed action with the engaged living scale (ELS): Psychometric evaluation in a nonclinical sample and a chronic pain sample. *Psychological Assessment*, *25*(4), 1235–1246.

Vos, T., Abajobir, A. A., Abbafati, C., Abbas, K. M., Abate, K. H., Abd-Allah, F., Abdulle, A. M., Abebo, T. A., Abera, S. F., Aboyans, V., Abu-Raddad, L. J., Ackerman, I. N., Adamu, A. A., Adetokunboh, O., Afarideh, M., Afshin, A., Agarwal, S. K., Aggarwal, R., Agrawal, A., ... Murray, C. J. L. (2017). Global, regional, and national incidence, prevalence, and years lived with disability for 328 diseases and injuries for 195 countries, 1990–2016: A systematic analysis for the Global Burden of Disease Study 2016. *The Lancet, 390*(10100), 1211–1259.

Vromans, L. P., & Schweitzer, R. D. (2011). Narrative therapy for adults with major depressive disorder: Improved symptom and interpersonal outcomes. *Psychotherapy Research, 21*(1), 4–15.

Wainwright, N. W., Surtees, P. G., Welch, A. A., Luben, R. N., Khaw, K. T., & Bingham, S. A. (2007). Healthy lifestyle choices: could sense of coherence aid health promotion?. *Journal of Epidemiology & Community Health, 61*(10), 871–876.

West, C., Stewart, L., Foster, K., & Usher, K. (2012). The meaning of resilience to persons living with chronic pain: An interpretive qualitative inquiry. *Journal of Clinical Nursing, 21*(9–10), 1284–1292.

Wetherell, J. L., Afari, N., Rutledge, T., Sorrell, J. T., Stoddard, J. A., Petkus, A. J., Solomon, B. C., Lehman, D. H., Liu, L., Lang, A. J., & Atkinson, H. J. (2011). A randomized, controlled trial of acceptance and commitment therapy and cognitive-behavioral therapy for chronic pain. *Pain, 152*(9), 2098–2107.

White, M. K. (2007). *Maps of narrative practice*. WW Norton & Company.

Williams, A. C. de C., Fisher, E., Hearn, L., & Eccleston, C. (2020). Psychological therapies for the management of chronic pain (excluding headache) in adults. *Cochrane Database of Systematic Reviews, 8.*

Winger, J. G., Ramos, K., Steinhauser, K. E., Somers, T. J., Porter, L. S., Kamal, A. H., Breitbart, W. S., & Keefe, F. J. (2020). Enhancing meaning in the face of advanced cancer and pain: Qualitative evaluation of a meaning-centered psychosocial pain management intervention. *Palliative & Supportive Care, 18*(3), 263–270.

Wong, P. T. (2010). Meaning therapy: An integrative and positive existential psychotherapy. *Journal of Contemporary Psychotherapy, 40*(2), 85–93.

Wong, P. T. (2014). Viktor Frankl's meaning-seeking model and positive psychology. In A. Batthyany & P. Russo-Netzer (Eds.), *Meaning in positive and existential psychology* (pp. 149–184). New York: Springer.

World Health Organization. (2011). *World report on disability 2011*. World Health Organization.

Yeung, P., & Breheny, M. (2021). Quality of life among older people with a disability: the role of purpose in life and capabilities. *Disability and Rehabilitation, 43*(2), 181–191.

Zernicke, K. A., Campbell, T. S., Blustein, P. K., Fung, T. S., Johnson, J. A., Bacon, S. L., & Carlson, L. E. (2012). Mindfulness-based stress reduction for the treatment of irritable bowel syndrome symptoms: A randomized wait-list controlled trial. *International Journal of Behavioral Medicine, 20*(3), 385–396.

Zettle, Hocker, Mick, Scofield. (2005). Differential strategies in coping with pain as a function of level of experiential avoidance. *Psychology Record, 55*, 511–524.

Chapter 11

Negotiating Stigma

Disability in the Workplace

Elisabeth R. Silver, Elisa S. M.
Fattoracci, Timothy Oxendahl,
Megan McSpedon, and Mikki Hebl

Conceptualizations of disability have varied over time, with important implications for how people with disabilities see themselves and are seen by others. As discussed extensively in chapter 1, three predominant models of disability have been proposed. The first, a medical model of disability, focuses on physical impairments, illness and etiology, and activities of daily living—it approaches disability from a deficit perspective, emphasizing discrepancies between people who are disabled (and therefore ill) and people who are not disabled (and therefore healthy; LoBianco & Sheppard-Jones, 2007). The medical model pathologizes disability and positions individuals with disabilities as needing to be "fixed" to function in a society centered on nondisabled people (Blanck, 2020). By contrast, the second major approach is the social model, which views disability as the result of environmental barriers to accessibility and social attitudes that restrict opportunities for those with disabilities (LoBianco & Sheppard-Jones, 2007). Finally, the third approach encompasses biopsychosocial models of disability, which integrate medical and social models, emphasizing the interaction between variation in physical ability and social appraisals of these variations.

The World Health Organization's International Classification of Functioning, Disability, and Health (ICF) was intended to formalize this third, more integrative approach to disability (ICF, 2001). This taxonomy classifies people according to their body functions and structures, capacity and performance, personal characteristics, and environments. Thousands of studies have been conducted using this classification (Cerniauskaite et al., 2011) despite lingering criticisms that disability organizations have had far too little say in developing and modifying the ICF, which has been misused by many and is not known by others (Lundälv, 2015).

As criticisms of the ICF suggest, existing research on disability has disproportionately focused on aspects related to functioning at the expense of understanding environmental, personal, and social factors. The profound impact of the latter factor is illustrated in the following quote from Corrigan (2014):

> Disease and disability strike with a double whammy: Not only do they cause pain, distress, and loss, but they also trigger a social reaction, and the prejudice and discrimination that often accompany illness can be as limiting as the condition itself. (p. 3)

Indeed, social reactions to disability too often gravely affect the lived experiences of people with disabilities. Such reactions can be referred to as *stigma*, and the consideration of disability as stigma, particularly in a workplace context, is the focus of the current chapter. Although other chapters in this book focus on various positive psychological personal factors (e.g., resilience, optimism) that may boost positive outcomes for people with disabilities, we focus our chapter on stigma, or the extent to which the very nature of how disabilities are perceived within interactions can dramatically influence outcomes. Additionally, we focus our chapter on how individuals can mitigate or disarm the negative impact of stigmas and stereotypes.

Before examining how stigma is socially constructed, it is critically important to acknowledge the potentially absurd notion that we are writing a chapter that elucidates ways that people with disabilities can manage or reduce the stigma they face. In no uncertain terms, the burden lies with allies, organizations, and society to reduce persistent discrimination against people with disabilities. Yet, we know that stigma exists within social interactions or contexts, and it often involves negotiating identity-related concerns between a perceiver and target. Given this negotiation and the fact that doing so strategically might provide benefits to people with disabilities, we focus on the actions that the targets are able to take, particularly in the workplace, to manage and reduce stigmatization. This focus does not in any way, however, remove the onus for nondisabled people to confront and challenge ableism.

The word "stigma" means to "mark" or "brand" and derives from the Ancient Greek practice of branding the body to signify that one was enslaved or owned as property. With time, such marks were also emblazoned on criminals and traitors to signify to others in society that these stigmatized individuals should be recognized and avoided. Over the last several centuries, stigma has come to be associated with a wide variety of "marks"—whether visible or invisible—that can have tremendous and often negative social consequences. In contemporary society, social labels such as being heavy, identifying with a certain religion, or using a wheelchair evoke a similar reaction to Greek marks, serving as labels that trigger stereotypes, prejudice, and discrimination. Stigma can be life-threatening, as seen in the case of leprosy. People who have leprosy, otherwise known as Hansen's disease, sometimes experience permanent damage to the skin, including the feet, hands, and eyelids. Although we now know that 95% of people are naturally immune to contracting the disease, before the turn of the century, leprosy was considered so contagious and unsightly that people with leprosy were separated from their families and communities, often living their entire lives in exile (see Senthilingam, 2015). A more modern-day example involves the stigmatizing effects of having a physiological condition that leads one to become fat. Indeed, people are so averse to becoming fat that 15% of those surveyed said that if given a choice, they would rather give up 10 years of their lives (Schwartz et al., 2006). Although there is a societal belief that labeling someone as "obese" might actually lead them to lose weight (Puhl et al., 2008), the research shows that the stigma actually leads to more negative psychological and physical consequences (Puhl et al., 2007; Puhl & King, 2013; see also Fulton & Srinivasan, 2021).

Stigma is not an individual phenomenon, but rather one that is produced and negotiated interpersonally both by the stigmatized individual and their interaction partner(s). The perspectives of individuals with disabilities and other stigmas were first given attention some 60 years ago when Erving Goffman published his seminal book *Stigma: Notes on the Management of Spoiled Identity* (Goffman, 1963). This book was important not only because it was one of the first to give voice to the rich perspectives of diversely stigmatized individuals but also because it more clearly defined the concept of stigma and the potential power of stigma in interactions. In this chapter, we focus specifically on the role that stigma can play in interactions between people who do and do not have some sort of mental/physical impairment. These interactions may be of a personal or professional nature and typically involve at least one person who has a disability (the target) and another who does not (the perceiver). The current chapter focuses on stigma that emanates from perceivers (rather than issues of internalized ableism) as well as the ways in which people with disability strategically navigate this stigma.

In this chapter, then, we begin by focusing on defining disability stigma in the workplace. This context is currently most interesting to us as all five of the authors work in the arena. We describe the incidence of disability and define the characteristics of disability stigma. Next, we articulate stereotypes about and the difficulties and barriers that people with disabilities face in the workplace. Then, we present identity management and other workplace strategies that people with disabilities might adopt to assuage the impact of stigma in workplace settings. Finally, we conclude with future directions that we hope researchers in this area will pursue.

DISABILITY IN THE WORKFORCE

An estimated 61.4 million, or one in four, American adults have a disability (CDC, 2020). In 2020, only 17.9% of people with disabilities were employed in the United States, compared to 61.8% of people without a disability (Bureau of Labor Statistics, 2021). While part of this discrepancy can be attributed to the greater incidence of disability among older adults who are no longer in the workforce, adults without disabilities across all age ranges are employed at higher rates than that of adults with disabilities, despite the legal protections of the Americans with Disability Act (ADA; Americans with Disabilities Act of 1990; Bureau of Labor Statistics, 2021).

The ADA requires employers to provide employees and applicants with disabilities *reasonable accommodations*, or accommodations that do not place *undue hardship* on an employer (EEOC, 2002). The ADA broadly defines a disability as a "physical or mental impairment that substantially limits one or more major life activities, a person who has a history or record of such an impairment, or a person who is perceived by others as having such an impairment" (Americans with Disabilities Act of 1990). Thus, both the legal definition of "what counts" as a disability and the legal requirements for accommodating employees with disabilities are subject to interpretation. The ambiguity surrounding the very nature of disability and accommodation is further complicated by the fact that, as with other protected identities such as race and gender, people with disabilities face stigma that may not be legally actionable, but is nonetheless harmful.

There are multiple barriers that restrict the rates at which people with disabilities are employed (Santuzzi & Waltz, 2016). For example, stigma-based biases impact all junctures of job hiring, evaluation, and promotion cycles (Jans et al., 2012). Additionally, people with disabilities face structural barriers (e.g., lack of public transportation, designs that are not universal, buildings without elevators) that limit their access to both personal and professional spheres (e.g., see Blanck, 2016; Gray et al., 2012). Finally, financial barriers prevent people with disabilities from accessing the workplace (e.g., see Hansen, 2019), and it remains legal to pay employees with disabilities less than the minimum wage (U.S. Department of Labor, n.d.). In short, the externally imposed impediments of stigma, discrimination, and structural barriers limit the available labor force and reduce opportunities for employees with disabilities.

Creating accessible and equitable employment opportunities and experiences for people with disabilities is both a moral and an economic imperative (see Lysaght et al., 2012). A recent systematic review of 39 studies revealed many financial benefits of hiring people with disabilities, including "improvements in profitability (e.g., profits and cost-effectiveness, turnover and retention, reliability and punctuality, employee loyalty, company image), competitive advantage (e.g., diverse customers, customer loyalty and satisfaction, innovation, productivity, work ethic, safety), inclusive work culture, and ability awareness" (Lindsay et al., 2018, pp. 1–2). Moreover, the increased quality of life (QOL) and enhanced sense of community that accompanies these tangible benefits are inestimable benefits. Further, because anyone can develop a disability over the course of their lifetime, disability research is important for individuals regardless of their current dis/ability status and for organizations.

UNDERSTANDING STIGMA

Goffman (1963) conceptualized stigma as a label that is negotiated within a single or several social interaction(s). Specifically, a perceiver observes or discovers some attribute of a target's identity and decides that it is different, lesser, or somehow incomplete compared to normative and/or highly valued social identities. The target may actively try to reject or accept this label, and hence, a negotiation of sorts occurs. This negotiation is complicated by the fact that some stigmas are not immediately discernible and/or are associated with other characteristics that make them more or less stigmatizing. Specifically, certain stigmas are visible, or discredited, and can be readily perceived by outsiders, while others are invisible, or discreditable, and may remain concealed. According to Goffman (1963), stigmas fall into one of the three categories: (a) "abominations of the body," or physical disabilities; (b) "blemishes of individual character," or mental illnesses and other conditions historically understood as within an individual's control; (c) and "tribal stigmas," or group membership such as race and religion (Goffman, 1963). Jones et al. (1984) provided a different conceptualization of stigma based on six unifying dimensions: (a) concealability, the degree to which a stigma can be hidden by the target during an interaction; (b) course, the stigma's persistence over time; (c) disruptiveness, the degree to which a stigma is perceived as influencing an interaction; (d) aesthetics, the visual appeal, or lack thereof, of an identity; (e) origin, whether the stigma was present since birth or is perceived as resulting from a target's action; and (f) peril, a perceiver's sense of endangerment from the stigma (Jones et al., 1984). Each of these six dimensions maps onto a spectrum across which a unique stigma is situated. Consequently, stigma is not inherent to an individual's personal attributes, but rather is the socially constructed product of the interactions between a person and relevant broader cultural influences.

Just as stigma is a multilevel phenomenon, the process through which it affects individuals is multifaceted. According to the social process of stigmatization, four interconnected mechanisms negatively impact targets of stigma (Major & O'Brien, 2005). First, *negative treatment and discrimination* respectively describe incivility in interpersonal interactions and institutional processes that restrict access to resources such as education, housing, or employment opportunities (Major & O'Brien, 2005). Second, *expectancy confirmation processes* occur when a nonstigmatized person behaves toward a stigmatized person in ways that compel the target to act in accordance with the perceiver's expectations (Major & O'Brien, 2005). Third, *automatic stereotype activation-behavior* unfolds when stereotypes about a target's stigmatized identity are primed (independent of a perceiver), which in turn promotes stereotype-consistent behavior from the stigmatized individual (Major & O'Brien, 2005). Finally, stigma affects targets via *social identity threat*—that is, the feeling of threat brought on by environmental cues that one's identity is devalued (Major & O'Brien, 2005; Steele et al., 2002). Thus, stigma influences not only others' perceptions of those with disabilities but also serves to restrict the behaviors of people with disabilities themselves.

Compared to other stigmatized identities that are legally protected in the workplace, disability status carries unique implications. First, selection tools such as tests of cognitive ability and personality attributes potentially contain items that could disqualify applicants on the basis of a psychiatric or neurological disability (Melson-Silimon et al., 2019). Second, workers must step forward to report and claim a disability identity to receive the legal protections and accommodations guaranteed by the ADA (Santuzzi & Waltz, 2016). The necessity of disclosure or acknowledgment of one's disability status to receive accommodations means that the benefit of receiving accommodations to which an employee is entitled comes at the potential cost of increased risk of discrimination or mistreatment (Baldridge & Veiga, 2006). Finally, an employee's own disability identity and the accommodations that they require or could benefit from differentiate it from other identities that may not have direct implications for job demands (Santuzzi & Waltz, 2016). In the next section, we expand on the unique barriers imposed on people with disabilities through stereotyping and stigmatization in the workplace.

STEREOTYPES OF AND BARRIERS FACED BY INDIVIDUALS WITH DISABILITIES

Stereotypes are generalizations that influence an observer's expectations of and reactions to the stereotyped individual (Stone and Colella, 1996). Once formed, stereotypes are activated automatically by environmental cues and act as a filter through which future encounters with stereotyped people are perceived (Hays-Thomas, 2017). Such cognitive processes can have negative effects, including prejudice and discrimination. In this section, we discuss stereotypes about people with disabilities, with a particular focus on the ambivalent nature of disability stereotypes (i.e., stereotypes that have both positive and negative characteristics; Dovidio et al., 2011; Fiske et al., 2002) and address how these stereotypes result in barriers at work for people with disabilities.

Synthesizing the empirical research, Stone and Colella (1996) proposed a model of the antecedents and consequences of disability-related stereotypes. They identified six dimensions of disability stereotypes: social skills, task competence, emotional adjustment, integrity, concern for others, and potency. Within this model, people with disabilities are stereotyped according to both positive (i.e., as caring and truthful) and negative (i.e., lacking independence/task competence, being shy, lacking emotional stability, and being submissive) qualities (Stone & Colella, 1996). Similarly, the Stereotype Content Model (SCM) developed by Fiske et al. (2002) identified two dimensions along which stereotypes are constructed: competence and warmth. These two dimensions govern social interactions and influence perceptions of one's ability to work with and trust other people. In the SCM (Fiske et al., 2002), people with disabilities are perceived to be high in warmth but low in competence. Although they are not seen as a competitive threat, they are categorized as lacking skills and proficiencies. These warmth and competence judgments engender perceptions of low social status among people with disabilities, resulting in pity and paternalistic stereotypes. This "mixed stereotype hypothesis" in which people with disabilities are stereotyped as having both positive and negative attributes is akin to ambivalent racism (e.g., Katz & Hass, 1988) and ambivalent sexism (e.g., Glick & Fiske, 1996), both of which emphasize that stereotypes are harmful even if they include some "positive" or benevolent content.

Ambivalent stereotypes are often pernicious because their positive content can make them seem more socially acceptable. Indeed, linking ambivalent stereotype content to behavior, Cuddy and colleagues (2007) proposed that perceptions of warmth elicit *active* behaviors—typically behaviors that involve either helping (facilitation) or harassing (harm). Perceptions of competence facilitate *passive* types of behaviors—typically behaviors that include either neglecting (harm) or associating with (facilitation) targets. In this paradigm, disabled people who, according to the SCM, are pitied due to their warmth and incompetence (Fiske et al., 2002) elicit helping behaviors (active facilitation) as well as neglect (passive harm). Demonstrating the real-world implications of neglect, a major issue facing people with disabilities is the failure of organizations to provide reasonable accommodations to them

(Graham et al., 2019). Failure to accommodate individuals at work is further compounded by workers' concerns about imposing on others (coworkers and supervisors), which decreases the likelihood of accommodation requests (Baldridge & Veiga, 2006).

Research suggests that stereotypes and their associated content exist at implicit and explicit levels: Rohmer and Louvet (2012) found that people rated people with disabilities high in warmth and low in competence on explicit measures (indexed via questionnaires), but low in both warmth and competence on implicit measures (indexed via response latency on a reaction time task associating people with disabilities with a series of attributes). Perceptions of low competence are clearly detrimental for people with disabilities as organizations may view them as impediments to productivity (Kwon, 2020). Likewise, Rohmer and Louvet's (2012) findings of low warmth attributions at an implicit level suggest that high explicit warmth perceptions may be a function of participants' desire to respond in nonprejudicial ways. Consequently, employees with disabilities may simultaneously (and unjustifiably) be stereotyped as impeding productivity and as unlikable colleagues, while people harboring such views justify them based on explicit attributions of warmth.

The negative stereotypes associated with people with disabilities can impact their achievement in the workplace through stereotype threat (Steele, 1997). Stereotype threat occurs when a member of a group is made aware of a negative group-related stereotype, which impedes their performance and leads to avoidance of potentially threatening situations (Steele, 1997). Studying a population of adults with visual impairment, Silverman and Cohen (2014) found that stereotype threat was positively related to stress and unemployment and negatively related to satisfaction and challenge-seeking behaviors, relationships that were mediated by decreases in self-integrity. In a second study with visually impaired students, Silverman and Cohen (2014) found that higher self-integrity was positively associated with performance.

Research suggests that the general content of disability stereotypes can interact with specific job demands to influence perceptions and experiences of employees with disabilities. For instance, Colella et al. (1998) studied how people with dyslexia were rated as potential team partners. They found that, regardless of disability-job fit—that is, the relationship between a disability and the demands of a job—people with dyslexia received lower ratings when rewards for teamwork were interdependent (e.g., the team's compensation was based on their aggregated contributions) compared to when each team member was compensated for their own contributions independently. Additionally, when there was poor disability-job fit, people with dyslexia were rated as less desirable work partners (e.g., lower perceived task and teamwork skills, less leadership potential). Likewise, Louvet (2007) found that when a job was described as having high interpersonal demands or as being stereotypically masculine, applicants with disabilities were rated more harshly than applicants without disabilities. This finding is troubling as the high-warmth stereotypes associated with disability do not appear to result in more favorable workplace outcomes even when there are high interpersonal job demands.

In addition to job type, disability type also impacts judgments of employees—a meta-analysis found that both mental and physical disabilities negatively impact hiring decisions, but that this effect is more pronounced for people with mental (versus physical) disabilities (Ren et al., 2008). Wang et al. (2010) studied how visual impairment impacts the selection process through the visual appeal of resumes. They found that applicants who perceived to be visually impaired received higher ratings of extraversion, openness to experience, agreeableness, and conscientiousness from hiring managers. However, those ratings did not translate into increased hireability, supporting the high-warmth/low-competence disability stereotype. The nature of one's disability also impacts perceptions of and responses to requests for workplace accommodations. When a disability is perceived as resulting from an employee's choices, workplace accommodation requests are viewed less favorably by managers (Florey & Harrison, 2000). These findings demonstrate that the workplace implications of negotiating disability-related stigma are multifaceted and context-dependent.

Whether positive and/or negative, stereotypes are cognitive processes that seep into interpersonal interactions. People with disabilities are most often stereotyped as being warm and cooperative, but, at the same time, lacking in competence and agency. These ambivalent stereotypes result in workplace barriers, such as difficulties in gaining employment, unfavorable coworker evaluations, and barriers to both requesting and receiving workplace accommodations. Rather than trying to suppress or deny these stereotypes, perceivers should interrogate these biases and seek out individuating information from people with disabilities to dispel generalizations based on categorical distinctions. Finally, organizations should acknowledge the institutional barriers faced by people with disabilities and make structural adjustments accordingly.

IDENTITY MANAGEMENT STRATEGIES

There are many identity management strategies that people with disabilities adopt in the workplace. Such strategies allow people with stigmatized identities to negotiate these identities and potentially reduce the negative effects of stigmatization (Blanz et al., 1998). Before reviewing research on identity management strategies, we emphasize what was stated previously: that the burden of overcoming ableism rests primarily on nondisabled supervisors, coworkers, and followers, rather than on people with disabilities. That employees with disabilities continue to face employment discrimination despite legislative protections highlight the pervasiveness of ableism and the need for employers and nondisabled coworkers to create space for employees with disabilities to define their identities on their own terms. Unfortunately, however, organizational change takes time, and in the meantime, employees with disabilities may find it beneficial to consider impression management strategies when negotiating persistent stigmatization at work.

The ICF framework recognizes that the presence of an impairment or chronic illness does not necessarily mean that one identifies as a person with a disability. Because of this distinction, understanding how disability identity is developed internally and socially has implications for how disability is negotiated in the workplace. Santuzzi and Waltz (2016) conducted a comprehensive overview of disability identity development and its role at work. They presented a four-level framework of increasingly broad influences on disability identity development. First, the *intraindividual level* describes the process in which one detects an impairment, connects it to a disability identity, and negotiates one's own (potentially negative) internalized attitudes toward disabled people. Next, the *interpersonal level* concerns how multiple factors influence self-identification decisions, including the centrality of one's disability status to one's identity, the relevance of the disability/ies to one's work context, anticipated stigma, and perceived legitimacy of the disability label. Third, at the *organizational level*, inclusive cultures, provision of accommodations and flexible work arrangements, job demands, and workplace stress and injuries impact self-identification decisions within the work context. Finally, *legal, medical, and cultural forces* dictate who is entitled to accommodations, what counts as a disability, and how disability is viewed societally. Each of these four levels can exert or alleviate pressures on individuals that, in turn, influence their likelihood of identifying as disabled. The dynamic nature of these forces suggests that employees may or may not identify as disabled at a given time, and Santuzzi and Waltz (2016) highlighted that research on disability identity disclosure often incorrectly assumes "that a worker who has a disability has a disability identity and carries the burden of stigma" (p. 1125).

In terms of who self-identifies as disabled, a recent study using a convenience sample found that out of 710 participants with at least one health condition (broadly defined to include allergies, attention deficit-hyperactivity disorder, asthma, chronic pain, migraines, etc.), a narrow majority (51%) did not identify as a person with a disability (Bogart et al., 2017). They also reported that perceived stigma, impairment severity, age, and lower income independently predicted self-identification with the disability label. In a mediation model, there were both direct effects of severity on self-identification and indirect effects through perceived stigma, suggesting that stigma partially mediates the impact of impairment severity on disability self-identification (Bogart et al., 2017). In essence, these findings highlight that not everyone who could potentially identify as a person with a disability does in fact identify as such. Rather, personal factors related to one's disability status, level of impairment, and perceived stigma play a role in disability identity development.

For employees who do identify as people with disabilities, there is yet another distinction to be made, with implications for the workplace, between *visible* and *concealable* identities. We recognize that this distinction is tenuous and flexible, as the visibility of one's disability can change over time (e.g., with varying levels of symptom severity), and not all people with the same disability identity experience the same level of visibility. Nonetheless, we make this distinction to highlight the differences in navigating interpersonal interactions that might emerge as a result. In particular, we highlight ways of navigating disability *disclosure* for people with concealable disabilities and disability *acknowledgment* for people with visible disabilities.

For people with concealable disabilities, disclosure can be a double-edged sword. On the one hand, research suggests that suppressing a concealable identity is positively associated with perceived discrimination and, in turn, poorer job satisfaction and turnover intentions (Madera et al., 2012). On the other hand, disclosure can carry risks related to discrimination and stigma (Jones & King, 2014). However, the decision to disclose is not necessarily binary. For instance, employees with concealable stigmatized identities may engage in *signaling*—that is, hinting at one's identity but falling short of openly disclosing it (Jones & King, 2014). Likewise, people with disabilities may choose to selectively disclose their identity to different individuals, such as supervisors, coworkers, followers, and/or human resources. Both organizational context and disability characteristics can influence employees' disclosure and acknowledgment decisions (Jans et al., 2012; Jones & King, 2014).

Employees' disclosures are facilitated by *personal* and *interpersonal* factors, such as needing an accommodation and/or having a supportive relationship with a supervisor (von Shrader et al., 2014). Environmental or organizational facilitating factors include awareness of conscious efforts by organizations to recruit and retain employees with disabilities, knowing other employees in the organization with disabilities, and including disability rights in diversity statements (von Shrader et al., 2014). In terms of specific types of disability disclosure and their impacts on perceptions of job applicants with disabilities, Lyons et al. (2017) compared strategies involving *integration* (focusing on the positive aspects of a disability identity), *de-categorization* (emphasizing other aspects of one's identity and down-playing disability identity), and no disclosure. They further investigated the impacts of onset controllability, or the extent to which one's disability status is perceived to be under one's personal control. They found that integration was positively associated with admiration, but there was not an interaction between integration and onset controllability. By contrast, decategorization interacted with onset controllability, such that people seen as having high onset controllability were perceived with greater pity, which, in turn, led to lower hiring intentions. In a second study reported by Lyons and colleagues (2017), both integration and decategorization were associated with lower pity reactions (and, subsequently, more favorable hiring decisions), but only when the disclosing individual's condition was deemed low in onset controllability.

Compared to research on disability disclosure, research on disability acknowledgment is relatively less common (cf. Hebl & Skorinko, 2005). In one of the few papers to study this topic, Lyons and colleagues (2018) investi-gated two different strategies of acknowledging a visible disability: *claiming* and *downplaying*. Like integration, claiming emphasizes the positive aspects of a disability identity. By contrast, like decategorization, downplaying aims to minimize negative perceptions of, or shift attention away from, one's dis-ability. Although participants with visible disabilities downplayed more often than they claimed, they reported using both strategies often. In addition to describing how people acknowledge their own disabilities, Lyons et al. exam-ined how nondisabled people perceive different acknowledgment strategies, including claiming, downplaying, and not acknowledging. Participants rated people who claimed more favorably than those who did not acknowledge, which was explained by higher perceptions of competence for those who claimed. However, downplaying was not significantly associated with more favorable ratings than not acknowledging. They also found that the level of interpersonal job demands influenced the effects of acknowledgment strat-egy: when a job had high (versus low) interpersonal demands, there was a positive effect of claiming on overall evaluations (via competence).

In a similar study, Madera and Hebl (2019) investigated how acknowledg-ing another type of visible bodily stigma, facial scars, impacted patterns of visual attention to an applicant's scar while listening to the applicant's job interview. They found that although visual attention to the applicant's scar decreased over time (as measured by 30-second intervals during an 8-minute interview), the rate of the decrease in attention to the scar was faster when the applicant explicitly acknowledged their scar. Together, these findings highlight that initially acknowledging a visible disability, perhaps especially by focusing on beneficial aspects of one's identity, can help foster positive workplace relationships.

When negotiating a disability identity at work, there are considerations regarding not only *how* one acknowledges or discloses one's identity, but also *when* disclosure or acknowledgment occurs during interactions with an organization. Jans and colleagues (2012) interviewed employees with disabilities regarding disclosure and acknowledgment timing. Based on these interviews, they proposed a three-axis taxonomy of disclosure and acknowledgment decisions during initial encounters with an organization (e.g., interviews, offer consideration). Along the first axis is the time at which an employee or applicant might require an accommodation: during the interview, during work, or never. The second and third axes concern visibility and stigmatization, respectively. When an employee requires accommodations for an interview, they are likely to disclose their disability prior to the interview, across varying levels of visibility and stigmatization. When employees need accommodations on the job, employees with visible disabilities tend to disclose their status early in their interactions with an organization. But, when a disability requiring workplace accommodations is concealable, people with stigmatized disabilities may delay disclosure until after they have received an offer or have passed their probationary period in order to avoid potential negative reactions to their disability status.

The decision to self-identify as a person with a disability is complex and dynamic, but theoretical and empirical evidence suggests that disclosing or acknowledging one's disability identity is associated with positive workplace outcomes while suppressing a concealable disability is associated with negative outcomes (Santuzzi & Waltz, 2016). For instance, suppressing a stigmatized identity at work is positively associated with perceived discrimination, and turnover intentions and negatively associated with job satisfaction (Madera et al., 2012) and lower sense of belonging in interpersonal interactions (Newheiser & Barreto, 2014). Perhaps the most obvious benefit of disability disclosure and acknowledgment is initiating conversations surrounding workplace accommodations. Requesting and receiving such accommodations can be beneficial, as doing so is positively associated with job satisfaction and performance (Dong & Guerette, 2013). The benefits of seeking and granting disability accommodations also extend to employers, as making accommodations allows them to retain qualified employees, avoid training new employees, and increase productivity (Solovieva et al., 2011).

Finally, disclosure and acknowledgment decisions can be motivated by a variety of reasons, including a need for accommodations, connection with coworkers, and/or a desire to effect change directed toward disability rights (Jain, 2020). Jain termed the latter motivation "political disclosure," or disclosure aimed at benefiting the collective, based on interviews with self-identified disabled medical students. Many of the students in this study emphasized the importance of claiming their disability identity to challenge marginalization and stigma, particularly in healthcare workplaces. Doing so allowed these students to raise awareness of systemic ableism, create space for other students with disabilities to disclose, and encourage nondisabled medical students to challenge ableist assumptions of patients and colleagues with disabilities (Jain, 2020). Although participants recognized that not all people with disabilities are in a safe space to share this aspect of their identity, their reports highlight that claiming one's disability identity can serve not only logistical purposes related to accommodations but also symbolic and political purposes related to challenging ableism (Jain, 2020).

ADDITIONAL CONSIDERATIONS: SITUATING PEOPLE WITHIN ENVIRONMENTS

Before turning to future directions, we pause briefly to highlight the importance of environmental factors within the ICF model. Identity not only stems from inner notions of the self but also from social reactions to that identity (Santuzzi & Waltz, 2016). As such, coworkers and supervisors can positively influence the experiences of people with disabilities by fostering supportive environments in which people with disabilities feel comfortable communicating their needs. Specifically, high levels of perceived organizational support, or the extent to which employees believe that their organization cares about them and their well-being, may influence their identity disclosure and accommodation requests (Eisenberger et al., 1986). In general, perceived organizational support is positively associated with job satisfaction, affective commitment, and performance, and negatively associated with withdrawal behaviors (Rhoades & Eisenberger, 2002). For employees with disabilities in particular, Kirk-Brown and colleagues (2014) found that among employees with Multiple Sclerosis (MS), organizations that responded to disclosure with inclusive decision-making and a focus on employee abilities saw reduced turnover intentions compared to companies that stigmatized or were paternalistic toward employees with MS. These findings suggest that organizations can actively shape workplace experiences for employees with disabilities.

Further, well-intentioned yet inappropriate support (i.e., excessive demonstration of care and concern) is nearly as counterproductive as discrimination (Kirk-Brown et al., 2014). For instance, a research participant with epilepsy reported that after experiencing a large seizure at work, management transferred him to a different department without notice, assuming that reducing the employee's work demands would benefit him and his colleagues (Beatty, 2012). When the employee expressed disinterest in the reassignment, he was told he would be fired if he did not assume the new position (Beatty, 2012). This experience illustrates the impact of disability on perceptions of employee ability as well as the relationship between disability and agency. Individuals tend to infantilize people with disabilities (see Robey et al., 2006, for a discussion of the Infantilization Implicit Association Test), and, as previously discussed, view people with disabilities as less competent than their nondisabled counterparts (Fiske et al., 2002; Rohmer & Louvet, 2012). Inclusive decision-making, including supporting employees with disabilities to define their identities and accommodations on their own terms, creates space to avoid these harmful stereotypes.

In addition to supportive environments, allyship behaviors are essential for including people with disabilities in the workplace. As Baldridge and Veiga (2006) detailed, many employees are reluctant to request disability accommodations despite protection under the ADA due to perceived personal costs (e.g., fear of inequity) and reactions to their requests (e.g., asking for "special treatment"). Illustrative of these concerns, an employee with epilepsy feared her illness would impede her career because her supervisor doubted her competence and viewed her illness as an "uncontrolled impairment" (Beatty, 2012, p. 99). Similarly, research suggests that employees judge the fairness of accommodations made for coworkers with disabilities based on perceived warrantedness—that is, the extent to which coworkers perceive a disability as legitimate and meriting an accommodation (Colella, 2001). These findings highlight that others' reactions to disability-related processes influence the lived experiences of employees with disabilities.

One key avenue for remediation is allyship or the practice of emphasizing inclusion and dispelling stereotypes to bring about positive change (Salter & Migliaccio, 2019). In this context, allyship refers to people without disabilities advocating for the fair treatment of people with disabilities. Given that identity is an exchange process between individuals as much as it is an internal process, allies can play an active role in the development of disability identities and positive experiences (Forber-Pratt et al., 2019). To be effective allies, coworkers and supervisors must first educate themselves on the stigma and discrimination perpetrated by nondisabled individuals. Next, allies should advocate alongside those with disabilities and confront ableist treatment and assumptions. Last but not the least, allies should support their peers (for a review of workplace allyship, see Salter & Migliaccio, 2019). In practice, allyship entails being receptive of accommodations, working to eradicate erroneous assumptions or stereotypes, and providing support without patronization or pity.

PERSONAL FACTORS

While other chapters in this volume have focused specific attention on personal factors, we have taken a somewhat different approach, electing to discuss the interpersonal nature of stigma and the systemic nature of discrimination. This perspective does not mean that personal factors are irrelevant in navigating stigma. For instance, people with disabilities may choose to negotiate stigma through strategic disclosure and acknowledgment, or by strategically timing disclosure or acknowledgment, in the workplace. Nonetheless, as we mentioned at the beginning of this chapter, focusing disproportionately on personal factors of those with disabilities, as they relate to stigma, improperly places the burden of ending ableism on people with disabilities, therefore victimizing the target twice.

Likewise, although personal factors highlighted in other contexts throughout this volume such as hope, resilience, and optimism likely shape processes and experiences of stigmatization, the notion that people with disabilities should simply overcome ableism through positive attitudes places undue burden onto them. Thus, while we acknowledge the importance of personal factors in negotiating disability-related stigma in the workplace, we also emphasize that the impact of personal factors on the lived experiences of people with disabilities is ultimately constrained by the social processes of stereotyping and stigma discussed in this chapter.

FUTURE DIRECTIONS

The dearth of organizational research on disability and disability identity is problematic: data suggest that while life expectancy has increased, younger Americans are increasingly likely to have a disability and/or chronic illness (Crimmins et al., 2016). As the workforce ages and disability rates rise, organizations will undoubtedly employ more workers with disabilities since disability onset does not necessarily signal the end of employment (Finch & Robinson, 2003). Thus, research centered around disability and related organizational processes is critical.

Many current organizational policies regarding illness assume short-lived interruptions to work (e.g., taking a sick day), so scholars need to determine which policies would best support people with disabilities and chronic illness on a long-term basis. In pursuing this line of inquiry, researchers must view their work through a stigma lens. The ADA has proven somewhat limited to this end because employees fear stigmatization as a result of how leaders and peers will perceive their requests (Baldridge & Veiga, 2006). Even after passage of the ADA, organizations still denied up to one in three accommodation requests (Harlan & Robert, 1998). Research employing a stigma paradigm is warranted to better understand how the process of stigmatization impacts all aspects of work for people with disabilities.

In response to the Covid-19 pandemic, a large percentage of the workforce experienced significant shifts in the workplace procedures and policies that complied with social distancing guidelines (Parker et al., 2020), with many organizations implementing telecommuting for all staff. Although this shift has not been as widespread for many low-wage essential workers, such as employees in retail and food service, it suggests that pre-pandemic denials of accommodation requests for telecommuting and the insistence that work must be conducted at an office were unfounded. This shift in employment practices offers insight into accommodation feasibility for individuals who will continue to need accommodations in a post-pandemic labor market.

In addition to investigating ways to systematize support for employees with disabilities, researchers need to consider the complex nature of disability identity. As reviewed, disability identity varies on intraindividual, interpersonal, organizational, legal, medical, and cultural planes (Santuzzi & Waltz, 2016). Further, "disability" is an all-encompassing term for a myriad of heterogeneous conditions, and two individuals with the same medical diagnosis may experience and manage their disability identity differently. Consequently, future research on disability must clearly identify the specific population being studied and employ nuanced operationalizations, methodological approaches, and conclusions relevant to the population of interest. To highlight one demonstrative example discussed previously in this chapter, identity management strategies for visible versus concealable illnesses are remarkably different and should be researched as such.

Particularly relevant here is the concept of "intersectionality," a term coined by Kimberlé Crenshaw (1989), which postulates that social identities such as gender, race, and disability influence and depend upon one another to form unique experiences and systems of (dis)advantage (Collins, 1990; Crenshaw, 1989; hooks, 1981). While the intersectionality framework highlights that individuals experience their realities through overlapping identities (e.g., a queer woman with depression), psychologists traditionally investigate identity-related processes by operationalizing social identities as discrete (e.g., a woman, a queer person, *or* someone with a disability; Bowleg et al., 2008; Cole, 2009). Research examining the intersection of ableism, racism, and sexism is currently sparse, though there are some exceptions (e.g., Coleman et al., 2015). The full inclusion of people with disabilities in the workplace and beyond is therefore inextricably linked to combating racism, sexism, and other types of oppression. Future research will benefit from exploring these relationships.

In this chapter, we have reviewed research defining and examining the impacts of disability-related stigma and stereotypes in the workplace. In doing so, we have highlighted that stigma is not an individual phenomenon, but rather the result of complex interactions between personal and environmental factors. Although identity management strategies represent one resource that employees with disabilities can draw from to navigate these complex processes, we emphasize that this personal factor is only useful insofar as environmental factors permit the full inclusion of people with disabilities. To this point, we encourage future research to investigate the dynamic nature of disability, the multilevel nature of stigmatization, and the intersections of ableism with other types of discrimination in organizational processes.

REFERENCES

Adams-Shollenberger, G. E., & Mitchell, T.E. (1996). A comparison of janitorial workers with mental retardation and their non-disabled peers on retention and absenteeism. *Journal of Rehabilitation, 62*(3), 56–60.

Ameri, M., Schur, L., Adya, M., Bentley, F. S., McKay, P., & Kruse, D. (2018). The disability employment puzzle: A field experiment on employer hiring behavior. *ILR Review, 71*(2), 329–364.

Americans with Disabilities Act of 1990, 42 U.S.C. § 12101 et seq. (1990). https://www.ada.gov/pubs/adastatute08.htm

Baldridge, D. C., & Veiga, J. F. (2006). The impact of anticipated social consequences on recurring disability accommodation requests. *Journal of Management, 32*(1), 158–179. doi: 10.1177/0149206305277800

Beatty, J. E. (2012). Career barriers experienced by people with chronic illness: A US study. *Employee Responsibilities and Rights Journal, 24*(2), 91–110. doi: 10.1007/s10672-011-9177-z

Blanck, P. (2016). The coming importance of universal design. *Progressive AE: Thought leadership.* https://www.progressiveae.com/importance-universal-design/

Blanck, P. (2020). Disability inclusive employment and the accommodation principle: Emerging issues in research, policy, and law. *Journal of Occupational Rehabilitation, 30*(4), 505–510. doi: 10.1007/s10926-020-09940-9

Blanz, M., Mummendey, A., Mielke, R., & Klink, A. (1998). Responding to negative social identity: A taxonomy of identity management strategies. *European Journal of Social Psychology, 28*(5), 697–729. doi: 10.1002/(SICI)1099-0992(199809/10)28:5<697::AID-EJSP889>3.0.CO;2-%23

Bogart, K. R., Rottenstein, A., Lund, E. M., & Bouchard, L. (2017). Who self-identifies as disabled? An examination of impairment and contextual predictors. *Rehabilitation Psychology, 62*(4), 553–562. doi: 10.1037/rep0000132

Bowleg, L., Craig, M. L., & Burkholder, G. (2004). Rising and surviving: A conceptual model of active coping among Black lesbians. *Cultural Diversity and Ethnic Minority Psychology, 10,* 229–240. doi: 10.1037/1099-9809.10.3.229

Bureau of Labor Statistics. (2021). *Persons with a disability: Labor force characteristics-- 2020* (USLD-21-0316; p.11).

Cerniauskaite, M., Quintas, R., Boldt, C., Raggi, A., Cieza, A., Bickenbach, J. E., & Leonardi, M. (2011). Systematic literature review on ICF from 2001 to 2009: Its use, implementation and operationalisation. *Disability Rehabilitation, 33,* 281–309. doi: 10.3109/09638288.2010.529235.

Cole, E. R. (2009). Intersectionality and research in psychology. *American Psychologist, 64,* 170–180. doi: 10.1037/a0014564

Colella, A. (2001). Coworker distributive fairness judgments of the workplace accommodation of employees with disabilities. *Academy of Management Review, 26*(1), 100–116. doi: 10.2307/259397

Colella, A., DeNisi, A. S., & Varma, A. (1998). The impact of ratee's disability on performance judgments and choice as partner: The role of disability-job fit stereotypes and interdependence of rewards. *Journal of Applied Psychology, 83*(1), 102–111. doi: 10.1037/0021-9010.83.1.102

Coleman, J. M., Brunell, A. B., & Haugen, I. M. (2015). Multiple forms of prejudice: How gender and disability stereotypes influence judgments of disabled women and men. *Current Psychology, 34*(1), 177–189. doi: 10.1007/s12144-014-9250-5

Collins, P. H. (1990). *Black feminist thought: Knowledge, consciousness, and the politics of empowerment.* New York: Routledge.

Corrigan, P. W. (Ed.). (2014). *The stigma of disease and disability: Understanding causes and overcoming injustices.* Washington, DC: American Psychological Association.

Corrigan, P. W. (2016). Lessons learned from unintended consequences about erasing the stigma of mental illness. *World Psychiatry, 15*(1), 67–73. doi: 10.1002/wps.20295

Crenshaw, K. (1989). Demarginalizing the intersection of race and sex: A black feminist critique of antidiscrimination doctrine, feminist theory and antiracist politics. University of Chicago Legal Forum, 1989, 139–167. iss1/8. Retrieved from https://chicagounbound.uchicago.edu/uclf/vol1989/

Crimmins, E. M., Zhang, Y., & Saito, Y. (2016). Trends over 4 decades in disability-free life expectancy in the United States. *American Journal of Public Health, 106*(7), 1287–1293. doi: 10.2105/AJPH.2016.303120

Cuddy, A. J. C., Fiske, S. T., & Glick, P. (2007). The BIAS map: Behaviors from intergroup affect and stereotypes. *Journal of Personality and Social Psychology, 92*(4), 631–648. doi: 10.1037/0022-3514.92.4.631

Dong, S., & Guerette, A. R. (2013). Workplace accommodations, job performance and job satisfaction among individuals with sensory disabilities. *Australian Journal of Rehabilitation Counselling, 19*(1), 1–20. doi: 10.1017/jrc.2013.1

Dovidio, J. F., Pagotto, L., & Hebl, M. R. (2011). Implicit attitudes and discrimination against people with physical disabilities. In R. L. Wiener & S. L. Willborn (Eds.), *Disability and aging discrimination* (pp. 157–183). Springer.

EEOC. (2002). *Enforcement guidance on reasonable accommodation and undue hardship under the ADA.* US Equal Employment Opportunities Commission. https://www.eeoc.gov/laws/guidance/enforcement-guidance-reasonable-accommodation-and-undue-hardship-under-ada

Eisenberger, R., Huntington, R., Hutchison, S., & Sowa, D. (1986). Perceived organizational support. *Journal of Applied Psychology, 71*(3), 500–507. doi: 10.1037/0021-9010.71.3.500

Finch, J., & Robinson, M. (2003). Aging and late-onset disability: Addressing workplace accommodation. *Journal of Rehabilitation, 69*(2), 38–42.

Fiske, S. T., Cuddy, A. J. C., Glick, P., & Xu, J. (2002). A model of (often mixed) stereotype content: Competence and warmth respectively follow from perceived status and competition. *Journal of Personality and Social Psychology, 82*(6), 878–902. doi: 10.1037/0022-3514.82.6.878

Florey, A.T., & Harrison, D.A. (2000). Responses to informal accommodation requests from employees with disabilities: Multistudy evidence on willingness to comply. *The Academy of Management Journal, 43*(2), 224–233. doi: 10.2307/1556379

Forber-Pratt, A. J., Mueller, C. O., & Andrews, E. E. (2019). Disability identity and allyship in rehabilitation psychology: Sit, stand, sign, and show up. *Rehabilitation Psychology, 64*(2), 119–129. doi: 10.1037/rep0000256

Glick, P., & Fiske, S. T. (1996). The ambivalent sexism inventory: Differentiating hostile and benevolent sexism. *Journal of Personality and Social Psychology, 70*(3), 491–512. doi: 10.1037/0022-3514.70.3.491

Goffman, E. (1963). *Stigma: Notes on the management of spoiled identity.* Prentice-Hall.

Graham, K. M., McMahon, B. T., Kim, J. H., Simpson, P., & McMahon, M. C. (2019). Patterns of workplace discrimination across broad categories of disability. *Rehabilitation Psychology, 64*(2), 194–202. doi: 10.1037/rep0000227

Gray, J. A., Zimmerman, J. L., & Rimmer, J. H. (2012). Built environment instruments for walkability, bikeability, and recreation: Disability and universal design relevant?. *Disability and Health Journal, 5*(2), 87–101. doi: 10.1016/j.dhjo.2011.12.002

Hansen, B. (2019). 10 Barriers to employment for people with disabilities. *Inroads to Opportunities.* https://www.inroadsto.org/new-blog/2019/5/29/barriers-to-employment

Harlan, S. L., & Robert, P. M. (1998). The social construction of disability in organizations: Why employers resist reasonable accommodation. *Work and Occupations, 25*(4), 397–435. doi: 10.1177/0730888498025004002

Hays-Thomas, R. (2017). *Managing workplace diversity and inclusion: A psychological perspective.* Taylor & Francis.

Hebl, M. R., & Skorinko, J. L. (2005). Acknowledging one's physical disability in the interview: Does "when" make a difference? *Journal of Applied Social Psychology, 35*(12), 2477–2492. doi: 10.1111/j.1559-1816.2005.tb02111.x

hooks, b. (1981). *Ain't I a woman? Black women and feminism.* South End Press.

International Classification of Functioning, Disability And Health (ICF; 2001). World Health Organisation; Geneva, Switzerland.

Jain, N. R. (2020). Political disclosure: Resisting ableism in medical education. *Disability & Society, 35*(3), 389–412. doi: 10.1080/09687599.2019.1647149

Jans, L. H., Kaye, H. S., & Jones, E. C. (2012). Getting hired: Successfully employed people with disabilities offer advice on disclosure, interviewing, and job search. *Journal of Occupational Rehabilitation, 22*(2), 155–165. doi: 10.1007/s10926-011-9336-y

Jones, E. E., Farina, A., Hastorf, A. H., Markus, H., Miller, D. T., & Scott, R. A. (1984). *Social stigma: The psychology of marked relationships*. Freeman.

Jones, K. P., & King, E. B. (2014). Managing concealable stigmas at work: A review and multilevel model. *Journal of Management, 40*(5), 1466–1494. doi: 10.1177/0149206313515518

Katz, I., & Hass, R. G. (1988). Racial ambivalence and American value conflict: Correlational and priming studies of dual cognitive structures. *Journal of Personality and Social Psychology, 55*(6), 893–905. doi: 10.1037/0022-3514.55.6.893

Kirk-Brown, A. K., Van Dijk, P. A., Simmons, R. D., Bourne, M. P., & Cooper, B. K. (2014). Disclosure of diagnosis of multiple sclerosis in the workplace positively affects employment status and job tenure. *Multiple Sclerosis Journal, 20*(7), 871–876. doi: 10.1177/1352458513513967

Kwon, C. (2020). Resisting ableism in deliberately developmental organizations: A discursive analysis of the identity work of employees with disabilities. *Human Resource Development Quarterly*. doi: 10.1002/hrdq.21412

Lindsay, S., Cagliostro, E., Albarico, M., N., & Karon, L. (2018). A systematic review of the benefits of hiring people with disabilities. *Journal of Occupational Rehabilitation, 28*, 634–655 . doi: 10.1007/s10926-018-9756-z

LoBianco, A. F., & Sheppard-Jones, K. (2007). Perceptions of disability as related to medical and social factors. *Journal of Applied Social Psychology, 37*(1), 1–13. doi: 10.1111/j.0021-9029.2007.00143.x

Louvet, E. (2007). Social judgment toward job applicants with disabilities: Perception of personal qualities and competences. *Rehabilitation Psychology, 52*(3), 297–303. doi: 10.1037/0090-5550.52.3.297

Lundälv, J., Törnbom, M., Larsson, P., & Sunnerhagen, K. S. (2015). Awareness and the arguments for and against the International Classification of Functioning, Disability and Health among representatives of disability organisations. *International Journal of Environmental Research and Public Health, 12*(3), 3293–3300. doi: 10.3390/ijerph120303293

Lyons, B. J., Volpone, S. D., Wessel, J. L., & Alonso, N. M. (2017). Disclosing a disability: Do strategy type and onset controllability make a difference? *Journal of Applied Psychology, 102*(9), 1375–1383. doi: 10.1037/apl0000230

Lysaght, R., Ouellette-Kuntz, H., & Lin, C. J. (2012). Untapped potential: Perspectives on the employment of people with intellectual disability. *Work, 41*(4), 409–422.

Madera, J. M., & Hebl, M. (2019). To look or not to look: Acknowledging facial stigmas in the interview to reduce discrimination. *Personnel Assessment and Decisions, 5*(2), 12–22. doi: 10.25035/pad.2019.02.003

Madera, J. M., King, E. B., & Hebl, M. R. (2012). Bringing social identity to work: The influence of manifestation and suppression on perceived discrimination, job satisfaction, and turnover intentions. *Cultural Diversity and Ethnic Minority Psychology, 18*(2), 165–170. doi: 10.1037/a0027724

Major, B., & O'Brien, L. T. (2005). The social psychology of stigma. *Annual Review of Psychology, 56*, 393–421. doi: 10.1146/annurev.psych.56.091103.070137

Melson-Silimon, A., Harris, A. M., Shoenfelt, E. L., Miller, J. D., & Carter, N. T. (2019). Personality testing and the Americans with disabilities act: Cause for concern as normal and abnormal personality models are integrated. *Industrial and Organizational Psychology: Perspectives on Science and Practice, 12*(2), 119–132. doi: 10.1017/iop.2018.156

Newheiser, A.-K., & Barreto, M. (2014). Hidden costs of hiding stigma: Ironic interpersonal consequences of concealing a stigmatized identity in social interactions. *Journal of Experimental Social Psychology, 52*, 58–70. doi: 10.1016/j.jesp.2014.01.002

Parker, K., Menasce Horowitz, J., & Minkin, R. (2020; December 9). How the coronavirus outbreak has - and hasn't - changed the way America work. *Pew Research Center*. https://www.pewresearch.org/social-trends/2020/12/09/how-the-coronavirus-outbreak-has-and-hasnt-changed-the-way-americans-work/

Poinsett, P. M. (2020). Cerebral palsy myths. *Cerebral palsy guidance*. https://www.cerebralpalsyguidance.com/cerebral-palsy/myths/

Puhl R. M., & King, K. M. (2013). Weight discrimination and bullying. *Best Practices & Research Clinical Endocrinology Metabolism, 27*(2), 117–127.

Puhl, R. M., Moss-Racusin, C. A., & Schwartz, M. B. (2007). Internalization of weight bias: Implications for binge eating and emotional well-being. *Obesity, 15(1)*, 19–23.

Puhl, R. M., Moss-Racusin, C. A., Schwartz, M. B., & Brownell, K. D. (2008). Weight stigmatization and bias reduction: perspectives of overweight and obese adults. *Health Education Resource 23*(2), 347–358. doi: 10.1093/her/cym052

Ren, L. R., Paetzold, R. L., & Colella, A. (2008). A meta-analysis of experimental studies on the effects of disability on human resource judgments. *Human Resource Management Review, 18*(3), 191–203. doi: 10.1016/j.hrmr.2008.07.001

Rhoades, L., & Eisenberger, R. (2002). Perceived organizational support: a review of the literature. *Journal of Applied Psychology, 87*(4), 698. doi: 10.1037/0021-9010.87.4.698

Robey, K. L., Beckley, L., & Kirschner, M. (2006). Implicit infantilizing attitudes about disability. *Journal of Developmental and Physical Disabilities, 18*(4), 441–453. doi: 10.1007/s10882-006-9027-3

Rohmer, O., & Louvet, E. (2012). Implicit measures of the stereotype content associated with disability. *British Journal of Social Psychology, 51*(4), 732–740. doi: 10.1111/j.2044-8309.2011.02087.x

Salter, N. P., & Migliaccio, L. (2019). Allyship as a diversity and inclusion tool in the workplace. *Diversity within Diversity Management*. (Advanced Series in Management, Vol. 22) (pp. 131-152). Bingley, UK: Emerald Publishing Ltd. doi: 10.1108/S1877-636120190000022008

Santuzzi, A. M., & Waltz, P. R. (2016). Disability in the workplace: A unique and variable Identity. *Journal of Management, 42*(5), 1111–1135. doi: 10.1177/0149206315626269

Schwartz, M. B., Vartanian, L. R., Nosek, B. A., & Brownell, K. D. (2006). The influence of one's own body weight on implicit and explicit anti-fat bias. *Obesity, 14*(3), 440–447. doi: 10.1038/oby.2006.58

Senthilingam, M. (2015). *Taken from their families: The dark history of Hawaii's leprosy colony.* https://www.cnn.com/2015/09/09/health/leprosy-kalaupapa-hawaii

Silverman, A. M., & Cohen, G. L. (2014). Stereotypes as stumbling-blocks: How coping with stereotype threat affects life outcomes for people with physical disabilities. *Personality and Social Psychology Bulletin, 40*(10), 1330–1340. doi: 10.1177/0146167214542800

Solovieva, T. I., Dowler, D. L., & Walls, R. T. (2011). Employer benefits from making workplace accommodations. *Disability and Health Journal, 4*(1), 39–45. doi: 10.1016/j.dhjo.2010.03.001

Steele, C. M. (1997). A threat in the air. How stereotypes shape intellectual identity and performance. *The American Psychologist, 52*(6), 613–629. doi: 10.1037//0003-066x.52.6.613

Steele, C. M., Spencer, S. J., & Aronson, J. (2002). Contending with group image: The psychology of stereotype and social identity threat. In M. P. Zanna (Ed.), *Advances in experimental social psychology* (Vol. 34, pp. 379–440). Elsevier.

Stone, D. L., & Colella, A. (1996). A model of factors affecting the treatment of disabled individuals in organizations. *The Academy of Management Review, 21*(2), 352–401. doi: 10.2307/258666

U.S. Department of Labor. (n.d.). *Subminimum wage.* Retrieved March 17, 2021, from https://www.dol.gov/general/topic/wages/subminimumwage

von Schrader, S., Malzer, V., & Bruyère, S. (2014). Perspectives on disability disclosure: The importance of employer practices and workplace climate. *Employee Responsibilities and Rights Journal, 26*(4), 237–255. doi: 10.1007/s10672-013-9227-9

Wang, K., Barron, L. G., & Hebl, M. R. (2010). Making those who cannot see look best: Effects of visual resume formatting on ratings of job applicants with blindness. *Rehabilitation Psychology, 55*(1), 68–73. doi: 10.1037/a0018546

Zivolich S., & Weiner-Zivolich, J. S. (1997). A national corporate employment initiative for persons with severe disabilities: A 10-year perspective. *Journal of Vocational Rehabilitation, 8*(1), 75–87. doi: 10.3233/JVR-1997-8109

Chapter 12

Social Support for Adults with Rare Disorders as a Personal and Environmental Factor

Kathleen R. Bogart and Brooke Bryson

Rare disorders or diseases (RDs) present a unique challenge to social support. In the United States, a disorder or disease is defined as rare if it affects fewer than 200,000 Americans each year (National Institutes of Health [NIH], Genetic and Rare Diseases Information Center, n.d.). Altogether, there are more than 7,000 different RDs. When considered collectively, RDs affect one in ten Americans (NIH Genetic and Rare Diseases Information Center, n.d.). Social support is an important protective factor for people with chronic health conditions; however, people with RDs report insufficient social support (Limb et al., 2010). Because there is a lack of public understanding about RDs, family members and friends of people with RDs may fail to give appropriate social support or validation (Bryson et al., 2021). RDs are isolating: their low prevalence and geographic dispersion mean that most people with RDs will never meet someone else with their condition in their everyday life, even though most strongly desire to do so (Huyard, 2009). When people with RDs do have the opportunity to meet others with RDs, many report feeling validated, normalized, and understood (Bogart et al., 2017).

According to the International Classification of Functioning, Disability, and Health (ICF; WHO, 2001), a disability is the interaction of an impairment, personal factors, and environmental factors. Most RDs are considered impairments, that is, abnormalities in bodily structures or functions. A RD is more or less disabling depending on personal factors such as resilience, appraisal, and spirituality, socioeconomic status, age, and gender, and environmental factors such as accessibility barriers and discrimination. Social support lies at the intersection of personal and environmental factors. As we will discuss further in this chapter, personal qualities such as resilience, gender, and age play a role in whether an individual perceives, receives, and sustains social support. Likewise, environmental factors such as stigma and access to social participation influence whether others provide social support to individuals with RDs. We will place special emphasis on the potential role of positive psychological personal factors, and the need for future research in this area.

TYPES OF SUPPORT

There are four types of social support generally described in psychological research: emotional, companionship, informational, and tangible (Bambina, 2007). Emotional is any information leading a person to feel they are esteemed, understood, and accepted. Informational support is any information that helps in defining, understanding, and coping with problematic events. Tangible support includes receiving assistance with activities of daily living as well as financial assistance. Lastly, companionship support refers to feeling a sense of belonging with others and engaging in leisure activities (Taylor, 2011). These types are often referred to as functional support, meaning each of these support types refer to the specific services social relationships provide to individuals with RDs.

Although RDs differ in their etiology and symptoms, individuals living with RDs face similar psychosocial challenges such as a lack of social support and unmet information needs (Bryson et al., 2021). Indeed, approximately two-thirds of individuals with RDs report their support needs as being unmet (Nutt & Limb, 2011). Of the different types of support, one large cross-sectional survey identified companionship and informational support as the top support-related challenges of living with a RD (Bryson et al., 2021). Within this study, participants who mentioned companionship support as challenging frequently discussed how isolating living with a RD was and described their desire to meet others with their same condition. Problems with informational support included unhelpful advice from friends and family that sometimes delegitimized their experience and difficulty finding doctors knowledgeable in their condition (Bryson et al., 2021). Other research has described the benefits of receiving these types of support from others. Among adults with Moebius syndrome—a rare form of facial paralysis—attendees at a support conference described how companionship support reduced feelings of isolation; how emotional support helped with anxiety, depression, self-esteem, and social skills; and how informational support made individuals feel more informed about medical, psychological, and social aspects of living with their RD (Bogart et al., 2017). Companionship support is less frequently studied in the social support literature, yet emerging research shows that it may be the most desired and beneficial type of social support for adults with RDs

(Bogart & Hemmesch, 2016; Bogart et al., 2017; Bryson et al., 2021; Bryson & Bogart, 2020). Companionship support shares some conceptual overlap with the ICF notion of participation, namely their shared focus on engaging in meaningful leisure activities connected with a shared identity or community. Thus, companionship support is especially important to study because as part of the ICF, participation is crucial in the definition of disablement.

The paucity of social support people with RDs receive may be contributing to current quality of life (QOL) disparities among people with RD. In one study that surveyed 232 unique RDs, findings indicated that these individuals experienced worse anxiety, depression, pain, and reduced participation in social roles than did the general population and people with more common chronic conditions, such as arthritis or migraines (Bogart & Irvin, 2017). Using this same population, another study found that companionship and emotional support were associated with greater life satisfaction regardless of individual levels of stress (Bryson & Bogart, 2020). Further, companionship support predicted positive life satisfaction over and above all other factors. Although the specific mechanisms regarding why companionship support provides superior benefits to overall life satisfaction remain unknown, it is likely that through spending time with others doing leisure activities, which are not always accessible to people with RDs, companionship support destigmatizes. For example, a group of friends might make their potluck more accessible to someone with a RD involving food restrictions by ensuring all dishes are labeled with ingredients and most are safe for the person with the RD to eat.

Research on specific RDs also finds benefits of social support on overall QOL. For example, across diverse blood cancers—which meet the US definition of "rare"—having fewer unmet support needs and greater satisfaction with received support has been linked to various QOL outcomes (Pereira et al., 2020; van Walsem et al., 2017). Similarly, research focused on adults with cystic fibrosis finds that greater psychosocial support predicts better psychological functioning (Anderson et al., 2001). Looking at specific support types, both companionship and emotional support were shown to be associated with reduced depression and anxiety among adults with Moebius syndrome (Bogart & Hemmesch, 2016).

PERSONAL FACTORS

Several personal factors associated with greater received or perceived social support have been identified in the broader social support literature among the general public and people with chronic conditions, including gender, age, socioeconomic status, cognitive appraisals, and resilience. Women have been previously found to perceive and receive more social support compared to men

(Kendler et al., 2005; Wohlgemuth & Betz, 1991), yet this effect may be different for people with RDs. Bryson and Bogart (2020) found that men reported more available companionship, emotional, and tangible support than women, but there were no gender differences in availability of informational support. This finding may be because women may have higher standards and expectations for social support, yet impairment and environmental factors may limit the quality and appropriateness of the support given (Bryson & Bogart, 2020). Also in this study, older adults reported more social support than younger adults, perhaps because chronic illness is more expected in later life, meaning peers are more understanding and more effective at providing social support. In addition to the tangible resources that come with higher socioeconomic status, a survey of adults with the RD Moebius syndrome found that education was positively associated with all four types of social support and higher income was associated with more companionship and emotional support (Bogart & Hemmesch, 2016).

In addition to sociodemographic personal factors, the way individuals cope with adverse health challenges may impact their overall well-being and their perceptions of support. For example, people with diverse disabilities who are resilient, or have more adaptive reactions to adverse events, often display high levels of self-esteem, self-efficacy, problem-solving skills, and generally have a positive outlook when faced with stressors (Dunn, 2015). Though limited, some research on diverse RDs suggests resilience confers mental and physical health benefits. In one survey representing a wide range of RDs, those who were more resilient reported better physical and emotional health when controlling for comorbidities and treatment status (Schwartz et al., 2017). Individuals who used cognitive appraisal processes that focused on relationships, pursuing one's dreams, having a balanced lifestyle, independence, recent challenges, spirituality, and maintaining their social roles were more resilient, which in turn was associated with better well-being. In contrast, those who focused more on their declining health were less resilient and had poorer physical and emotional health (Schwartz et al., 2017). These findings suggest that focusing on positive aspects of ones' life and maintaining social relationships are crucial to developing resilience in the face of health challenges.

ENVIRONMENTAL FACTORS

Environmental factors, such as accessibility and discrimination, seem to be more impactful than personal factors in the availability and perception of social support among adults with RDs. Many environmental and structural barriers restrict the ability of people with RDs to engage in activities of daily living and social participation. In a content analysis, Bryson et al. (2021) found that activity limitations and their environmental barriers were the second most commonly mentioned challenge among adults with RDs. Similarly, leisure activities are often disrupted by the lack of accommodations for certain symptoms of RDs. For example, one study found that friends and family not incorporating the individual's energy and dietary needs into their social events made them unable to participate in these events, further exacerbating feelings of isolation (Munro et al., 2021). As a result, some people withdrew from their networks, assuming it would be a relief to loved ones to not have to plan around their accessibility needs (Munro et al., 2021).

Stigma and discrimination also affect the availability and perception of social support for individuals with RDs. Stigma has been previously described as one of the most challenging aspects of living with a RD, with individuals reporting disease-related prejudice and discrimination, feeling judged and pitied by others, and feeling a sense of shame due to symptom-related limitations (Bogart et al., 2012; Bryson et al., 2021). Others have described how friends and family members disbelieve, minimize, invalidate, blame, and fail to make an effort to understand adults with RDs (Munro et al., 2021, in press). Having stigmatizing experiences such as these has been linked to reduced availability of all types of support, reduced disclosure of illness, and greater overall stress levels in diverse RD populations (Bogart & Hemmesch, 2016; Zhu et al., 2017). For these reasons, one of the most common requests from people with RDs is a call for greater public awareness of RDs so that others will believe and support them (Bogart et al., 2012). Likewise, environmental and social accessibility barriers such as workplace discrimination and inaccessible leisure activities must be ameliorated.

Sources of Support

Given the importance of social support to improve overall QOL for people with RD, it is crucial to identify sources of support and effective ways to provide support. Online support communities have been identified as one such source. Within RD online support communities, informational support is the most commonly given and received type of support followed by emotional support, though individuals also report receiving companionship support from these groups (Coulson et al., 2007; Lasker et al., 2005). Though online communities have been described as valuable sources of many types of support, some individuals report that online support does not compensate for the lack of tangible support in their offline relationships (MacLeod et al., 2017). Additionally, seeing others face-to-face, in person or even via videoconferencing, may be an especially powerful way to deliver support, especially for people who have visible conditions (Bogart et al., 2017).

Because people with RDs are unlikely to meet others with their RD in their local area, some RD-specific organizations hold regional or national support conferences. These support conferences offer opportunities to connect with others with their RD and learn from experts in the field. Among adults with Moebius syndrome, attending Moebius Syndrome Foundation support conferences was associated with greater companionship and emotional support (Bogart & Hemmesch, 2016). A subsequent content analysis found that companionship and informational support were most frequently mentioned as reasons for and benefits of attending the conference. One participant remarked that the conference was the "rare place I feel normal" (Bogart et al., 2017). Being surrounded by others who share one's condition offers a unique opportunity for destigmatizing companionship and emotional support, which normalizes, reduces isolation, and promotes solidarity.

Given the benefits of support conferences, it is important to consider their accessibility. Time, finances, travel, energy, time off work, and health are all noted barriers to attending conferences (Bogart et al., 2017). Indeed, support groups tend to disproportionally attract participants with higher socioeconomic status (Taylor et al., 1986). Scholarships and travel funds are sometimes offered by RD organizations to increase equity in attendance. Similarly, a variety of smaller, regional accessible events and resting rooms can help attendees manage their energy.

Social support can also come from friends and family, though some types of support are deemed less helpful from these sources than are others. For example, in one study of support needs among adults with multiple myeloma—a rare blood cancer—participants reported that information support from their family was often unhelpful or unwanted (Monterosso et al., 2018). Indeed, several studies on common chronic conditions suggested that informational support is only perceived as helpful when it comes from a health-care professional; when received from friends or family, informational support is generally considered unhelpful (Helgeson & Cohen, 1996). Emotional support from family members has also been described as unhelpful when members seem uncomfortable when providing this type of support (Monterosso et al., 2018). In some cases, however, friends and family have been described as great sources of other types of support, such as tangible and companionship. Indeed, in a study focused on adolescents with cystic fibrosis, family members were described as excellent sources of tangible support, while friends were considered important sources of companionship (Barker et al., 2012).

IMPLICATIONS AND FUTURE RESEARCH

Just as the general public is unaware of the support needs of people with RDs, even psychologists who study more familiar forms of disability often have little knowledge or training about RDs. Interested psychologists can learn more about rare disease support and advocacy from umbrella organizations like the National Organization for Rare Disorders or Global Genes. Information about specific rare diseases can be found at the NIH GARD website.

The field of RD research, and, specifically, social support for RDs, is nascent but growing. The majority of research has focused on individual RDs, which can limit sample sizes. A novel approach is to examine RDs collectively, allowing for greater power and generalizability, revealing broad commonalities in the need for social support. Longitudinal research is needed to examine the time course of social support needs from the point of symptom onset, diagnosis, and throughout the disease course, especially if the disease progresses or fluctuates over time. No randomized controlled trials (RCTs) of social support interventions for people with RDs have been conducted; there is an urgent need for evidence-based support interventions. Malleable positive personal factors such as resilience and self-efficacy are also promising points of intervention to improve social support and QOL.

As noted previously, initial research suggests RD-specific support conferences hold promise for improving support and reducing stigma (Bogart & Hemmesch, 2016; Bogart et al., 2017). That work focused on a visible RD; future work should consider invisible RDs as well. People with concealable stigma may experience more or different benefits from support meetings. People with invisible RDs may be more likely to attempt to "pass" by hiding their condition, making them less likely to seek support meetings. They may experience more psychological distress than people with visible stigma and being connected to people who are known to share their stigma reduces this distress (Frable et al., 1998).

Future work should examine the effectiveness of other types of peer support for people with RDs, including cross-RD conferences like those held by Global Genes or the National Organization for Rare Disorders, and online conferences and videoconferencing. Relatedly, there is a need to examine and bolster social support for caregivers of people with RDs, who may experience similar challenges of insufficient or inappropriate support and associative stigma.

CONCLUSION

Social support is an important, yet understudied, factor supporting the well-being and full participation of people with RDs. More funding and resources are needed to research interventions to bolster positive psychological personal factors like resilience, coping, and social support for people with RDs and to enable them to access these interventions. Broad societal-level changes are also needed to reduce the stigma and environmental barriers limiting people with RDs.

REFERENCES

Anderson, D. L., Flume, P. A., & Hardy, K. K. (2001). Psychological functioning of adults with cystic fibrosis. *Chest, 119*(4), 1079–1084. doi: 10.1378/chest.119.4.1079

Bambina, A. (2007). *Online social support: The interplay of social networks and computer-mediated communication.* Amherst, NY: Cambria press

Barker, D. H., Driscoll, K. A., Modi, A. C., Light, M. J., & Quittner, A. L. (2012). Supporting cystic fibrosis disease management during adolescence: The role of family and friends. *Child: Care, Health and Development, 38*(4), 497–504. doi: 10.1111/j.1365-2214.2011.01286.x

Bogart, K. R., Frandrup, E., Locke, T., Thompson, H., Weber, N., Yates, J., Zike, N., & Hemmesch, A. R. (2017). "Rare place where I feel normal": Perceptions of a social support conference among parents of and people with Moebius syndrome. *Research in Developmental Disabilities, 64,* 143–151. doi: 10.1016/j.ridd.2017.03.014

Bogart, K. R., & Hemmesch, A. R. (2015). Benefits of support conferences for parents of and people with Moebius syndrome. *Stigma and Health, 1*(2), 109. doi: 10.1037/sah0000018

Bogart, K. R., & Irvin, V. L. (2017). Health-related quality of life among adults with diverse rare disorders. *Orphanet Journal of Rare Diseases, 12*(1), 177. doi: 10.1186/s13023-017-0730-1

Bogart, K. R., Tickle-Degnen, L., & Joffe, M. (2012). Social interaction experiences of adults with Moebius syndrome: A focus group. *Journal of Health Psychology, 17*(8), 1212–1222. doi: 10.1177/1359105311432491

Bryson, B., Bogart, K. R., Atwood, M., Fraser, K., Locke, T., Pugh, K., & Zerrouk, M. (2021). Navigating the unknown: A content analysis of the unique challenges faced by adults with rare diseases. *Journal of Health Psychology.* 26(5), 623-635. doi: 10.1177/1359105319828150

Coulson, N. S., Buchanan, H., & Aubeeluck, A. (2007). Social support in cyberspace: A content analysis of communication within a Huntington's disease online support group. *Patient Education and Counseling, 68*(2), 173–178. doi: 10.1016/j.pec.2007.06.002

Dunn, D. (2014). *The social psychology of disability.* Oxford University Press.

Frable, D. E., Platt, L., & Hoey, S. (1998). Concealable stigmas and positive self-perceptions: feeling better around similar others. *Journal of Personality and Social Psychology, 74*(4), 909-922.

Helgeson, V. S., Cohen, S., Schulz, R., & Yasko, J. (2000). Group support interventions for women with breast cancer: who benefits from what?. *Health Psychology, 19*(2), 107.

Huyard, C. (2009). What, if anything, is specific about having a rare disorder? Patients' judgements on being ill and being rare. *Health Expectations, 12*(4), 361–370.

Kendler, K. S., Myers, J., & Prescott, C. A. (2005). Sex differences in the relationship between social support and risk for major depression: a longitudinal study of opposite-sex twin pairs. *American Journal of Psychiatry, 162*(2), 250–256.

Lasker, J. N., Sogolow, E. D., & Sharim, R. R. (2005). The role of an online community for people with a rare disease: Content analysis of messages posted on a primary biliary cirrhosis mailinglist. *Journal of Medical Internet Research, 7*(1), e10. doi: 10.2196/jmir.7.1.e10

Limb, L., Nutt, S., & Sen, A. (2010). *Experiences of rare diseases: An insight from patients and families.* Retrieved from http://www.raredisease.org.uk/documents/ RDUK-Family-Report.pdf

MacLeod, H., Bastin, G., Liu, L. S., Siek, K., & Connelly, K. (2017). "Be Grateful You Don't Have a Real Disease": Understanding rare disease relationships. *Proceedings of the 2017 CHI Conference on Human Factors in Computing Systems, 1660–1673.* doi: 10.1145/3025453.3025796

Monterosso, L., Taylor, K., Platt, V., Lobb, E., Musiello, T., Bulsara, C., Stratton, K., Joske, D., & Krishnasamy, M. (2018). Living with multiple myeloma: A focus group study of unmet needs and preferences for survivorship care. *Journal of Patient Experience, 5*(1), 6–15. doi: 10.1177/2374373517715011

Munro, M., Cook, A. M., & Bogart, K. R. (2021). An inductive qualitative content analysis of stigma experienced by people with rare diseases. *Psychology and Health.* https://doi.org/10.1080/08870446.2021.1912344

National Institutes of Health, Genetic and Rare Diseases Information Center. (n.d.). *FAQs about rare diseases.* Retrieved from https://rarediseases.info.nih.gov/diseases/pages/31/faqs-about-rare-diseases

Nutt, S., & Limb, L. (2011). Survey of patients' and families' experiences of rare diseases reinforces calls for a rare disease strategy. *Social Care and Neurodisability, 2*(4), 195–199. doi: 10.1108/20420911111188443

Pereira, M. G., Silva, I., Pereira, M., Faria, S., Silva, B., Monteiro, S., & Ferreira, G. (2020). Unmet needs and quality of life in multiple myeloma patients. *Journal of Health Psychology, 25*(10–11), 1717–1731. doi: 10.1177/1359105318772073

Schwartz, C. E., Michael, W., & Rapkin, B. D. (2017). Resilience to health challenges is related to different ways of thinking: mediators of physical and emotional quality of life in a heterogeneous rare-disease cohort. *Quality of Life Research, 26*(11), 3075–3088.

Taylor, S. E. (2011). Social support: A review. In H.S. Friedman (Ed.), *The handbook of health psychology* (pp. 189–214). New York: Oxford University Press.

van Walsem, M. R., Howe, E. I., Ruud, G. A., Frich, J. C., & Andelic, N. (2017). Health-related quality of life and unmet healthcare needs in Huntington's disease. *Health and Quality of Life Outcomes, 15*(1), 6. doi: 10.1186/s12955-016-0575-7

Wohlgemuth, E., & Betz, N. E. (1991). Gender as a moderator of the relationships of stress and social support to physical health in college students. *Journal of Counseling Psychology, 38*(3), 367.

World Health Organization (WHO). (2001). *International classification of functioning, disability and health.* Retrieved from http://www.who.int/classifications/icf/en/

Zhu, X., Smith, R. A., & Parrott, R. L. (2017). Living with a rare health condition: the influence of a support community and public stigma on communication, stress, and available support. *Journal of Applied Communication Research, 45*(2), 179–198. doi: 10.1080/00909882.2017.1288292

Chapter 13

Disability and Life Satisfaction

The Social Nature of Personal Factors

Michelle R. Nario-Redmond,
Thomas P. Dirth, and Jeffrey G. Noel

In 2003, Paul Longmore noted that

> the movement of disabled Americans has entered its second phase. The first
> phase has been a quest for civil rights, for equal access, and equal opportu-
> nity. . . . The second phase is for collective identity (p. 221).

Recent literature in the rehabilitation field incorporates the perspective
of positive psychology and presents a changing view of disability, evolving away from a biomedical approach centered on bodily impairment[1] and
toward a more social-ecological framework that takes the whole person into
account (Wehmeyer, 2013). This includes the social and physical surroundings in which disabled people live and work, and their subjective experiences
within a community of people that constitute the largest minority in the
United States (Brault, 2012). Research from a variety of theoretical perspectives supports the importance of these environmental and subjective factors
to positive outcomes for disabled and nondisabled people alike (Buntinx,
2013; Jetten et al., 2014). This chapter focuses on life satisfaction (LS), a
well-researched conceptualization of the subjective appraisal of one's life,
which is recognized as a personal factor (Müller, R., & Geyh, 2015) and as a
key component of health, longevity, and well-being (Diener & Chan, 2011;
Lyubomirsky et al., 2005).

Defined as a global evaluation of the quality of one's life as a whole, LS is
described in the literature as more stable over time than temporary emotional
states like joy or contentment (Diener et al., 2002). Empirical work has found
that LS is associated with a myriad of health-promoting behaviors, college

and work success outcomes, and positive interpersonal relationships as well as efficacy and self-determination (Diener, 2009; Helliwell, 2007; Proctor et al., 2017). In this chapter, we begin with a brief summary of how LS has been defined and then review some key predictors and outcomes of LS across nondisabled and disabled populations.

As we review these various factors, however, we will demonstrate that LS as a concept holds both promise and peril for persons with disabilities. The promise is inherent in the subjectivity of LS; because it is defined in terms of the person's experience, the "authority" to define a satisfying life is shifted from the larger nondisabled society and the medical profession, in particular, toward the thoughts, emotions, and daily lived experiences of people with disabilities themselves. The peril lies in how we define the *sources* of LS and, based on that, where we place emphasis when studying its predictors. If we circumscribe the sources of LS too tightly within the realm of individual predispositions, strengths, and strategies for "overcoming" limitations, then our work risks reifying the very stereotypes we seek to disrupt. For example, many people assume that people with physical or cognitive impairments are to be admired to the degree that they have the grit, courage, and self-determination to conquer or rise above personal limitations and function like the majority of nondisabled persons (Nario-Redmond et al., 2019). Moreover, sourcing LS from within an individual neglects the font of psychological resources that flow from the external to the internal when we identify and engage with the social groups that are important to us (Haslam et al., 2018). For example, positive identification with our groups predicts greater trust in others (Reicher & Haslam, 2006), feelings of greater purpose and direction in our endeavors (Hopkins et al., 2016), and greater feelings of self-efficacy and personal control over our lives (Greenaway et al., 2016).

To address both the salutary and the more restricting aspects of the literature on LS sources, we acknowledge the utility of the personal factors that predict LS as studied under the broad rubric of positive psychology: that is, positive emotion, hope, optimism, and extraversion, strength of character (Proctor et al., 2017; Shogren et al., 2006). We then lay out the criticism that by privileging the individual as the ultimate source and conduit for character strengths and coping strategies grounded in those strengths, the positive psychology perspective largely neglects the role of the collective in constructing and sustaining a person's sense of self (Becker & Merecek, 2008), even though satisfaction with the *self* is one of the most highly correlated predictors of LS and subjective well-being (SWB) as a whole (Diener, 2009). Furthermore, the tendency to assume an autonomous self depoliticizes the sources of LS, and fails to address the stigma, ableism, and structural inequalities that disable marginalized minds and bodies (Nario-Redmond, 2019; Sugarman, 2015).[2]

Following our review and critical analysis, we introduce the social identity approach (SIA) (Dirth & Branscombe, 2018; Haslam et al., 2018) which enables a shift in the locus of LS and related factors from the individual to the group. We suggest that many personal strengths and individual responses to environmental factors are embedded within one's social (or group) identities such that stronger identification with social groups (e.g., family, professional, civic, or religious groups) catalyzes and sustains many resources constitutive of LS (Haslam et al., 2018; Jetten et al., 2012). For people with disabilities, these sources of LS can extend beyond social capital and material support to include the company of others who share the experience of disability and who collectively define disability as something more than one's impairment conditions or perceived limitations. We will argue that a more holistic understanding of LS pathways for people with disabilities must account for the ways social identity processes are integral to the self. For example, the shared experience and creative redefinition of disability as a positive group membership and a central aspect of one's identity become a means of incorporating the social *into* the personal, and we will argue that this merging of the social into the self is the most empowering conduit to participation, self-direction, and LS. Moreover, connectedness to others in the group affirms the group as a source of strength and solidarity, especially when encountering the stigma and discrimination that is the uniting feature of many disability experiences. Indeed, disability social identity serves as a protective factor against the deleterious effects of discrimination on well-being outcomes like LS (Bogart et al., 2018). In the final sections of the chapter, we outline some implications of this perspective for service delivery and public policy.

LIFE SATISFACTION: DEFINITION, OUTCOMES, AND PREDICTORS

Distinguishing Life Satisfaction from Related Constructs

LS is considered a more stable construct than the SWB construct within which it is often embedded (Diener et al., 2013). SWB is broader than LS because SWB includes both emotional well-being (e.g., positive and negative emotional states) and cognitive well-being, which is comprised of the global appraisal of one's life as a whole (LS) and the appraisal of domain-specific life facets such as work, school, self, and social relationships (Diener et al., 2013). One of the reasons LS is so consistent over time is the availability of chronically accessible information (Eid & Diener, 2004); on the other hand, when people perceive important areas of their lives have changed, this perception may contrast with chronically accessible information and therefore lead to change in the appraisal of LS. Accumulating research shows that certain life events and role transitions can have more persistent effects on individuals' cognitive appraisals of LS while feelings or moods are more short-lived and used to monitor progress toward goals (Luhmann et al., 2012; Fujita & Diener, 2005). Life events are considered "time-discrete transitions that mark the beginning or the end of a specific status" (Luhmann et al., 2012, p. 594), so for some, disability can be conceptualized as a life event, especially if a disability is acquired after birth. However, others may instead view their disability status as a temporary state, as a personal characteristic, and increasingly, as a minority group membership.

Measuring Life Satisfaction and National Polls

Given its subjective nature, LS has typically been measured by self-report where people are asked to evaluate their lives on the basis of their own chosen criteria. LS can be assessed either as a unidimensional concept (Adelman et al., 1989; Diener et al., 1985; Seligson et al., 2003) or as part of a multidimensional SWB framework (Alfonso et al., 1996; Huebner, 2004) that includes satisfaction with specific life domains (e.g., work, family life, health; Loewe et al., 2014). Evidence supports that people often base their subjective evaluations of overall LS in ways that draw upon their satisfaction from important life domains and context-specific influences like work, family, and relationship status (Luhmann et al., 2012). In addition to these "bottom-up" influences, however, LS judgments can also derive from more "top-down" influences including personality factors and particular self-construals. In fact, global LS ratings correlate highly with average satisfaction ratings across multiple life domains (Diener et al., 2013).

In a 2020 nationally representative poll, Americans reported that their satisfaction with life was among the highest it had been in four decades, with 66% saying they were "very satisfied" with the way things were going in their lives overall. This was before the coronavirus pandemic. In 2021, only 51% said they were "very satisfied." Yet, the vast majority of Americans (82%) still said they were generally "satisfied" with their lives, down from a record high of 90% in 2020 (Jones, 2021; McCarthy, 2020). Similarly, in cross-national and international studies, most people report LS ratings that are in the "mostly" to "highly" satisfied range (Proctor et al., 2017). This is consistent with hedonic adaptation theories that argue that most people grow accustomed not only to life's windfalls (e.g., winning the lottery) but to a variety of challenging circumstances as well (e.g., acquired injuries; Brickman et al., 1978). Famously, Brickman and colleagues (1978) reported that a small sample of disabled people with paraplegia or quadriplegia was just as "happy" as their able-bodied counterparts as both scored well above the neutral point on a happiness scale. Based on these early adaptation studies, many argued that because of the human potential to adapt, satisfaction has a short half-life (Ryan, 1999). However, the time it takes to adapt to some major life events and the extent of adaptation depends on several factors, including individual differences in temperament and the availability of sources from which a sense of satisfaction can be drawn (Pavot & Diener, 2008). For example, according to a 2012 meta-analysis of over 180 longitudinal studies, the effects on well-being of major life events like the death of a spouse can endure for some years (Luhmann et al., 2012). Similarly, adaptation is somewhat slower for some major life events like acquired disability, bereavement, and unemployment than for other life events like marriage and childbirth where people tend to return to pre-event levels of SWB within fewer years.

In the review that follows, we focus on the factors consistently associated with global LS but also include some domain-specific findings and some results where LS is only assessed as part of broader constructs like SWB; in describing those latter findings, we therefore use the term "SWB" in keeping with the literature being described.

Predictors of Life Satisfaction across Populations

To identify the primary predictors of LS that have received the most research attention, we searched the literature for systematic reviews, meta-analyses, and nationally representative longitudinal studies conducted on the general population and people with a variety of health-related conditions (de Hond et al., 2019; Diener, 2009; Lucas, 2007; Oswald & Powdthavee, 2008; Pavot & Diener, 2008).

Demographic Factors

A 2017 review of literature on LS (Proctor et al., 2017) reported that demographic factors, including age, gender, and ethnicity, were all poor predictors of global LS across several student and adult samples (Adelman et al., 1989; Huebner et al., 2000; Stock et al., 1983). Some of these studies found that lower socioeconomic status (SES) was moderately related to lower LS (Ash & Huebner, 2001), but other studies did not (Dew & Huebner, 1994). Diener (2009) suggested that while the effects of income are small and relative to social expectations, at extreme levels of poverty income as a proxy for status and power remains an influential determinant of LS. Based on another recent review, even the association between income inequality and LS was quite weak and depended on a country's economic development (Ngamaba et al., 2018).

Education level is also not predictive of LS when other variables are controlled (Diener, 2009). While Ng et al. (2015) found that academic achievement can predict LS even when controlling for SES, a recent meta-analytic review did not confirm this, as both high and low achieving students' ratings of SWB (of which LS is a component) were quite similar (Bücker et al., 2018). In terms of relational demographics, satisfaction with one's current love life is a strong predictor of LS (Emmons & Deiner, 1985), and more generally, married persons tend to report higher SWB, particularly when assessed in terms of *satisfaction* with one's marriage and family (Campbell et al., 1976; but see DePaulo, 2017 as being single does not necessarily undermine SWB); the same cannot be said of parenthood (Glenn & Weaver, 1979) which has had negligible effects on SWB.

Employment status is more consistently associated with higher LS (Campbell et al., 1976; Hirschi, 2009). For example, Lucas et al. (2003) found that unemployment can have lasting negative effects even after new employment is secured. What is it about employment that matters? Is it the salary, the sense of contribution, or participation in a valued social role or group? Clearly, having a purpose in life is a significant predictor of LS (Bronk et al., 2009). A 2016 review of the job satisfaction literature found that both people with and without cognitive impairments reported similar factors as important; people are more satisfied with jobs that allow for social interaction, employee support, monetary, and non-monetary compensation (Kocman &Weber, 2016; see also, Erdogan et al., 2012). For example, an important predictor of LS relates to volunteering or opportunities to give back or to support others in need (Borgonovi, 2008; Piliavin & Siegl, 2007; Thoits & Hewitt, 2001).

In a meta-analytic review of 115 studies, Okun and colleagues found that social participation was directly predictive of the general SWB construct even when factors like health and SES were controlled, particularly for more formal than informal social activities (Okun et al., 1984). Furthermore, people who reported stronger social relationships also reported higher SWB (Diener & Seligman, 2002). According to Diener (2009), social contact is clearly related to SWB although the specific mechanisms and parameters of this effect remain uncertain. Okun's findings suggested that the participation opportunities afforded by social group memberships may be one mechanism linking social contact to SWB and LS.

Individual Differences

Moving from demographics to meta-analytic studies of temperament and other more stable individual differences, conscientious personalities who consistently set higher achievement goals for themselves and tend to follow the rules have higher LS while more anxious/neurotic personalities score consistently lower (DeNeve & Cooper, 1998). Looking at other Big Five personality traits, those who scored highest on agreeableness who tend to be cooperative and trusting of others, and those higher in extraversion (who also tend to be warm and seek out many friendships) also had higher LS scores; however, none of the personality traits explained more than 15% of the variance in LS. These dispositional effects on LS seem to be mediated in part by their impacts on chronic mood states (Schimmack et al., 2002), and via positive attributions that explain life events in ways that promote well-being (DeNeve & Cooper, 1998).

Several large-scale twin studies have also revealed how heritable dispositions (e.g., Stubbe et al., 2005) contribute to SWB. In a 2015 meta-analytic review of 30 twin studies, Bartels concluded that genetic factors seem to explain about 35% of the variance in SWB. This suggests that the majority of predictors of LS (and SWB) are socially or environmentally produced. The personal factors of *hope and optimism* have also consistently emerged as significant predictors of LS among adolescents with and without cognitive impairments—and to an equivalent degree (Shogren et al., 2006). These authors also found that neither locus of control nor self-determination was associated with higher LS in either group, although these may function more as mediators between negative/stressful life events and LS.

In a comparative 30-year review of Japanese and American studies conducted between 1981 and 2011, *sense of freedom* was one of the strongest predictors of LS across data collection waves, stronger than health condition, household income and marital status in both Japan and the United States. In fact, sense of freedom had a larger effect size in the prediction of LS in the American samples (Nakazato et al., 2017). In this study, *sense of freedom* was operationalized similarly to constructs like perceived control and autonomous decision-making where people can "pursue the realization of their preferences by freely choosing the way to live their lives" (p. 372). Interestingly, people attach greater importance to freedom to make choices about their lives as they attain higher levels of physical and economic security. That is, they shift their valuing of financial satisfaction to valuing more emancipative values when assessing overall LS (Diener et al., 2013).

Summary

An important lesson learned from the broader literature on LS in the general population is that similar factors across a variety of populations seem to drive evaluations of what it means to have a good life: once basic income needs are met, social relationships are critical to LS; employment and volunteer opportunities that facilitate social participation, support, and interaction with others also matter, along with dispositional tendencies like extraversion that require a steady diet of human interactions in addition to a sense of freedom, hope, and optimism about the future that most people cherish. The following section elaborates on these and other unique predictors as studied within various populations of disabled people experiencing physical, cognitive, sensory, and/or psychiatric conditions.

Predictors of Life Satisfaction among Disabled People

The empirical research on adaptation to health-related conditions, including disability, has been described as quite limited (de Hond et al., 2019; Lucas, 2007; Oswald & Powdthavee, 2008), especially in terms of methodologies considered complex enough to appropriately assess changes in LS across time and relative to pre-disability levels or prior to the onset of long-term health conditions. Many early studies used cross-sectional instead of longitudinal approaches and/or focused primarily on short-term impacts of newly acquired disabling conditions. For example, much previous research shows that when perceptions about one's life are assessed shortly following an acquired impairment or traumatic injury, people typically reported a sharp decline in self-reported LS (Boyce & Wood, 2011; Lucas, 2007; Oswald & Powdthavee, 2008). However, with the passage of time, most people (though not all) adapt to their circumstances and report satisfaction levels at or above what they experienced before disability onset (Amundson, 2010; Fellinghauer et al., 2012). For this reason, in studies examining LS across a range of impairment types, disability onset (and the duration or proportion of life lived with disability) are critical variables that must be considered when interpreting findings. This section synthesizes the often contradictory findings describing what lessons have been learned about the factors that consistently predict LS in several impairment communities, and organizes these findings according to disability-specific factors like time of onset, duration, severity, progression, and impairment type including studies that examine predictors of the extent of adaptation or return to baseline satisfaction levels, along with the key moderators and mediators of relationships.

Onset of Disability—Congenital or Acquired

Most impairments are acquired after birth, and many studies of adaptation to disability have necessarily focused on acquired conditions like spinal cord injuries (SCIs) and traumatic brain injuries (TBIs). Yet, some research has compared LS scores of people with congenital conditions (impairments people are born with) to people with conditions acquired later in life. For example, Bogart (2014) found that adults with acquired impairments tend to have lower LS scores than those born with their impairments (see also, Jamal et al., 2021), which may reflect greater self-acceptance and perceived normativity of life with disability for those who have lived their entire lives as disabled people. In fact, the earlier the onset of disability, the more strongly people accepted the identity of disability for themselves (Bat-Chava, 1994; Nario-Redmond et al., 2013; Seligman & Darling, 2009); Bogart (2014) also found that the positive effect of early onset on LS was mediated by the degree to which people self-identify as disabled.

Duration. This is consistent with studies on impairment duration. In a sample of people with long-standing, chronic conditions (e.g., upper respiratory diseases, back problems, migraines, and high blood pressure), Cubí-Mollá and colleagues found that people with chronic health conditions reported better self-perceived health the longer they had lived with their conditions (Cubí-Mollá et al., 2016). Similar results were found in a cross-impairment national sample of people with disabilities in the UK (Oswald & Powdthavee, 2008). The authors concluded that while disability may hurt LS initially, "it does so to a smaller degree the longer the individual has been disabled" (p. 1067).

Age of Onset. In terms of age of onset, higher LS is associated with people who acquired disabilities earlier in life (Alfano et al., 1993). Similarly, older adults living with SCI that occurred before they were 60 years old reported being less restricted ("handicapped") in their social participation than those who experienced late onset SCI, after age 60 (Barrett et al., 2002). Furthermore, in a very recent European and Israeli sample of over 5,000 older adults who were at least 50 years old and not disabled prior to the study, de Hond and colleagues tracked changes in LS over a 10-year period (2004–2015) using the number of functional limitations in daily living tasks (e.g., preparing hot meals, shopping, doing housework, etc.) as an indicator of permanent disability (de Hond et al., 2019). They found that while people who had developed disabilities in the last two years had lower LS scores than those without disabilities, people who had been living with disability for *more than five years* had higher LS scores than people who had become disabled in the last two years. In fact, people who had lived with disability the longest were most likely to report the highest levels of LS—even more likely than people without disabilities.

Severity and Functional Limitations of Impairment

In terms of impairment severity, several studies using a variety of methods to capture the extent of impairment have found that as individuals report more functional limitations, they also tend to report lower LS (de Hond, 2019; see also, Chase et al., 2000; Ville & Ravaud, 2001). Lucas (2007) is often cited as among the first to examine adaptation to disability using cross-impairment nationally representative samples from Germany and Britain with people who started off without disability but become disabled sometime during the longitudinal study. His research found that while people who acquired more severe disabilities had pre-disability satisfaction levels similar to those with milder disabilities, people with more severe conditions (e.g., unable to do at least one activity of daily living) experienced more decline in LS which did not rebound in the subsequent five-year time frame. By contrast, people with milder conditions were more likely to rebound to pre-disability satisfaction levels. This work, however, used the criterion of being officially registered with the government as a disabled person to indicate disability status. Moreover, baseline levels of well-being were below average even before participants were officially certified as disabled, which may have underestimated adaptation by failing to include people who did not self-certify as disabled for government benefits (Lucas, 2007). Using the same British national dataset but with a different statistical technique, Oswald and Powdthavee (2008) did not replicate Lucas (2007). Instead, they found that while LS ratings fell abruptly during the year participants became disabled, satisfaction scores rose back up after two years although did not fully return to pre-disability levels. Specifically, for moderately disabled people, the degree of adaptation was estimated to be from 50% to 100% post-disability onset but only 30–60% for people with more severe functional limitations. These results are described as partial adaptation to pre-disability levels of LS. What may be even more intriguing are the contradictory findings in some studies showing that people with *less severe* impairments have *lower* LS than people with more severe impairments (Jones et al., 2011; Roy & MacKay, 2002; Silverman & Cohen, 2012).

Prognosis of Condition

In addition to disability onset, duration, and severity, the progressive (and/or unpredictable) nature of some impairments has been linked to lower levels in some LS domains but not in others. Specifically, in a nationally representative sample of people with a variety of impairments, participants with multiple sclerosis (MS) reported lower satisfaction ratings with their health and their jobs but higher levels of satisfaction with friends and family compared to other impairment groups, which may be related to unique adaptation patterns associated with conditions that progress over time (Patten et al., 2012). Similarly, other cross-impairment studies have found that people with continual or episodic experiences of pain, fatigue, and feelings of lost control were much more likely to report poorer subjective life quality. However, higher quality of life (QOL) was reported when the "gap between individual capacity and environmental constraints was reduced through social support, use of assistive devices and reduction of barriers" (Albrecht & Devlieger,

1999, p. 985). Consistent with cross-cultural studies on the predictive power of one's sense of freedom on LS (Nakazato et al., 2017), the ability to take control over the events of one's life is considered critical to the impact these events can have (Reich & Zautra, 1981). Some research has demonstrated that a higher frequency of negative life events can lower LS (Seery et al., 2010), but this relationship is also mediated by reduced perceptions of control (Ash & Huebner, 2001). In other words, life events per se may not have a direct effect on individuals' LS to the extent that people are able to exercise autonomous control in their daily lives. Relatedly, perceptions of choice over one's life decisions consistently predict SWB in the general population as well (Diener, 2009).

Impairment Specific Studies: Physical, Cognitive, and Psychiatric Conditions

In terms of impairment-specific studies, research with people with SCIs has found that LS ratings were in the "slightly dissatisfied" range 12-month post-injury but only for those who were not currently married (Putzke et al., 2001). In addition, people with SCIs who had previous mentoring experiences reported greater LS relative to participants who did not (Sherman et al., 2004). Dijkers (1997) did a meta-analytic review of studies and reported that SWB was lower among people with SCIs compared to population norms. Furthermore, the primary predictors of lower SWB in these samples focused on participation restrictions ("handicaps") including (in the order of their predictive power): the lack of social support, the lack of social integration into formal organizations or informal networks of friends, and the lack occupation (work or school) and family role (spouse or parent). Interestingly, based on a population survey from 2009 to 2015, adults with disabilities were just as likely as people without to report informal volunteering, and accumulated the same number of hours of formal volunteering as people who do not experience disability (Shandra, 2017), even though several barriers to accessing such social roles remain.

In terms of impairments that impact cognitive functioning, several studies have focused on students with intellectual and learning disabilities. In general, findings with this population identify positive levels of overall LS across studies (see Proctor et al., 2017, for a review). Some find no differences in global or domain-specific LS between students with learning disabilities and those without (McCullough & Huebner, 2003). Nevertheless, in some studies, students with mild cognitive impairments have expressed less satisfaction with their friendships but more satisfaction with school than their typically achieving peers (Brantley et al., 2002). Other unique predictors of LS among those who experience intellectual disability include emotional competence, which refers to "one's abilities to identify, understand, use and manage one's own feelings and those of others" (Rey et al., 2013, p. 147). LS is also higher among students with intellectual disability who demonstrate adaptability in terms of career choices; however, this relationship was driven by feelings of agency and pathways that make on the job practice possible (Santilli et al., 2014). According to disability studies scholars, "being able to choose for oneself the direction of one's life is a necessary component to having any kind of life at all" (Smith & Routel, 2010, para 23). This is consistent with the extensive research on self-determination as a predictor of LS in this population (Wehmeyer & Schwartz, 1998; Nota et al., 2007; Shogren et al., 2006).

Some studies have found lower ratings of LS among people who have experienced severe TBI, especially if complicated by posttraumatic stress disorder (PTSD; Bryant et al., 2001). Yet more recent studies have documented a phenomenon known as posttraumatic growth (PTG) among people living with TBIs (Barskova & Oesterreich, 2009). Expanding the construct of resilience, which involves the capacity to rebound following a traumatic event (Seery et al., 2010), PTG is defined as the *positive impacts* that result from experiencing traumatic events. For example, in their 2012 longitudinal study, Powell et al. followed people who had been living with TBI for at least 10 years, and found several factors associated with PTG including having a sense of personal meaning (purpose and coherence), high *post-disability* LS, strong social support, high activity levels, paid work, and new stable relationships post-injury. Interestingly, LS is also higher among people who experience at least some adversity in life compared to people who report no adverse experiences and to those who report many. Described as "adversarial growth," the experience of a moderate number of adverse events allows some people to cultivate a sense of their own strength and capacity to cope in addition to engaging their social networks which can lead to improved relationships and the development of resilience (Seery et al., 2010).

Several years ago, Arrindell et al. (2001) found lower LS scores among psychiatric patients compared to controls (see also, Meyer et al., 2004). However, recent evidence does not identify the presence of psychiatric conditions (e.g., depression, PTSD, schizophrenia) as a risk factor undermining LS or SWB. That is, young people who demonstrate symptoms of "psychopathology" are just as likely to report being highly satisfied with life as those who do not (Greenspoon & Saklofske, 2001). In fact, perceptions of LS have been shown to buffer against the development of psychiatric disorders and can protect people from the negative implications of chronic stress (McKnight et al., 2002; Suldo & Huebner, 2004). That is, LS is associated with reduced risk of suicidal ideation (Chang & Sanna, 2001; Diener & Seligman, 2002; Heisel & Flett, 2004) and suicide attempts that remained reduced 20 years later (Koivumaa-Honkanen et al., 2001).

Individual Differences and Contextual
Variables for People with Disabilities

In a nationally representative, longitudinal study designed to extend the literature on disability adaptation, Boyce and Wood (2011) focused on the impact of stable individual differences among people who acquired disabilities over a four-year period. These authors found that while LS decreased after the first year of acquired disability, after two years of living with disability LS steadily improved—but only for people with agreeable personalities. Specifically, after four years of living with acquired disabilities, people with more agreeable personalities prior to disability onset adapted more quickly and more completely compared to people with more disagreeable orientations who may require more support (Boyce & Wood, 2011). Agreeable personalities tend to be cooperative, polite, and have an optimistic view of human nature. These findings are consistent with previously reported research on the general population finding that traits associated with low neuroticism, high extraversion, and agreeableness were all linked to higher degrees of LS (DeNeve & Cooper, 1998). It may be that among people with acquired disabilities, agreeableness—which is associated with following health-care advice, seeking social support, and quality relationships (Berry et al., 2000; Ingledew & Brunning, 1999)—may be particularly beneficial to people newly coping with impairment.

In addition to personality, LS also depends on how people with disabilities conceptualize their sense of self and evaluate their various identities. Jones et al. (2011) found that the largest predictor of LS after brain injury was the degree to which people positively self-identified as "survivors," followed by the number of new close relationships they formed post-injury. In fact, these two factors alone explained the counterintuitive positive relationship between more severe injury and higher LS in this sample. In another study, Silverman and colleagues (2017) found that disabled adults who reported more friends with disabilities had higher LS, and higher overall QOL than disabled adults without disabled friends (see also Silverman et al., 2017). This is consistent with a growing body of research on the many benefits of disability identity (e.g., Bogart et al., 2018; Nario-Redmond et al., 2013; Nario-Redmond & Oleson, 2016).

In studies of college students with disabilities, positive core self-evaluations are strongly associated with higher LS, which is true for the general population as well (Chang et al., 2012). Specifically, using an index of self-esteem, self-efficacy, emotional stability, and locus of control to measure core self-evaluations, Smedema and colleagues (2015) found that positive self-evaluations are linked to LS through the mediating mechanisms of social support, low perceived stress, and positive mood.

Similarly, LS is also higher among people with positive perceptions of their own bodies (Valois et al., 2003), but lower among people with negative perceptions of their physical or mental health and activity limitations (Zullig et al., 2005). This suggests the importance of body esteem regardless of objective body type, weight, shape, or form (Lindly et al., 2014). Relatedly, among people with physical or mobility impairments, Atkinson and Martin (2020) found that LS was highest among participants in team sports like wheelchair basketball, who demonstrated high resiliency in terms of their ability to adapt to trauma, stress, and adversity. Furthermore, although across impairments people with disabilities are less likely to participate in sports compared to people without disabilities, when they do participate, disabled people derive much higher levels of LS than their nondisabled counterparts (Pagan, 2018). Physical activity may affect LS through body esteem or the self-worth derived from one's own physicality (Elavsky & McAuley, 2005).

Finally, in terms of some key contextual variables, neighborhood composition and place of residence have been linked to differences in LS. Based on a nationally representative sample, Knies et al. (2016) found that while immigrants and ethnic minorities tended to report lower LS than their majority counterparts, living in neighborhoods where more members of one's own minority in-group community are prevalent is associated with higher LS. Such findings also depend on the particulars of one's living arrangement. For example, LS increases substantially among disabled people who have transitioned from institutional to community living settings (Sheth et al., 2019). Similarly, deaf/hard-of-hearing (D/HH) students educated in segregated settings reported lower LS (and lower living environment satisfaction) than their nondisabled peers while D/HH students educated in more integrated settings had similar satisfaction ratings to nondisabled peers (Gilman et al., 2004).

Sociocultural Factors—Impact of Stigma and Discrimination

The impact of stigma, marginalization, and exclusion, particularly when pervasive, can have deleterious effects on LS and well-being among people who are the targets of intergroup prejudice (Major & O'Brien, 2005; Pascoe & Smart Richman, 2009). Specifically, research has shown how perceptions of prejudice and discrimination are linked to reduced feelings of self-worth and LS (Nario-Redmond, 2019; Seaton et al., 2010). Across stigmatized groups, people who perceive more discrimination in daily life reported more physical and mental health problems (Pascoe & Smart Richman, 2009). For example, LS among people living with HIV/AIDS was lower among those who perceived they were the targets of AIDS-related discrimination; however, social support seems to protect LS (Heckman, 2003). Similarly, in a study of mental health service consumers, perceived prejudice and discrimination were associated with more severe symptoms and lower LS (Bahm & Forchuk, 2008). This is also consistent with work finding that prosocial peer interactions are protective of LS even among people victimized by peer aggression (Martin & Heubner, 2007).

What is fascinating, however, and is directly relevant to the argument we make in this chapter, is that these negative outcomes do not seem to generalize to people who strongly identify as members of a social group—a group that is not inherently defective or devalued but that has been systematically disadvantaged by society. That is, the process of recognizing and accepting disability as a minority group identity seems to facilitate a reappraisal of the negative outcomes one confronts. This creative reappraisal process can be transformative to those who have been consistently excluded once they begin to recognize that there is nothing "wrong" with them, with their appearance, impairment, or way of being in the world—but realize instead that a discriminating society is to blame for inequitable policies and the misinformed prejudice of others (Major et al., 2002, 2003).

Conclusions from the Life Satisfaction Literature

The complex literature on LS and adaptation to disability yields some consistent lessons learned along with some ongoing points of contention. Clearly, disability-specific characteristics influence the avenues available to access the sources of LS that seem to matter most in both disability and non-disability populations: social relationships and opportunities that give purpose and freedom to exercise control over one's life.

One reason we see so much variability in the trajectories of individuals' adaptation to disability is that experiences of adversity may harm satisfaction with life for some people (especially in the short-term) while these same experiences contribute to resilience and PTG for others. In general, people experiencing extremely low or extremely high levels of adversity report relatively low LS; however, when adversity is at a level where coping efforts are necessary but not perceived as impossible, people learn to cultivate the capacity for future resilience. This may be why studies find that not only do many disabled people rebound to pre-disability LS levels and why some report even higher levels of satisfaction including the revaluing of their own disability experiences.

There are some clues in the literature reviewed here as to factors that may promote or impede this kind of PTG. Several studies converge to find that LS is lower the more 'severe' one's functional limitations are (e.g., the fewer activities of daily living people report doing independently), or the more painful, unpredictable, and/or progressive one's conditions are. However, this literature is equivocal in that impairment severity is not only measured in very different ways across studies but critically depends on context or the extent to which the environment is inaccessible and therefore restrictive of citizen participation—not because of limitations that are inherent to particular body minds, but because of limitations in the structural, policy, and attitudinal environments that fail to accommodate for disability as part of human variation. Perhaps this is one reason why research on condition severity is so mixed. A similar pattern is observed in studies focusing on the number of impairments one experiences or the number of major life events confronted. The relationship between these variables and LS depends upon how people appraise what these events mean to them, what they have learned from them, and whether they perceive that they have grown more resilient not *in spite of* them, but *because* of them.

Across impairment categories, being born with one's disability, having an earlier age of onset, and living longer with disability all contribute to higher satisfaction with life, which likely reflects greater opportunity to accept one's disability as an important aspect of the self. In fact, the few studies examining time spent with disability find that it is the cultivation of a *positive disability identity* that seems to mediate the relationship between time of disability onset and LS even after controlling for duration and condition severity (Bogart, 2014). This positive identity is not something the individual must create alone; its components have been shaped through history by the collective efforts of disabled people seeking to strengthen themselves and empower one another. It is to this collective effort, and the importance of including it in the discussion and understanding of LS for people with disabilities, that this review now turns.

An Expanded View of Personal Factors: From Individual Strength to Social Connectedness

The preceding review of LS literature emphasized the subjective appraisal of LS, and linked levels of and changes in LS to contextual and personal factors. This is in keeping with the social-ecological framework that, when considering LS among people with disabilities, moves beyond stereotyped understandings of disability as a tragedy to overcome or medical condition to hide, overcome, or eliminate. Herein lies the *promise* of the LS lens on disability, by accounting for the subjective appraisal of one's own disability as an ingredient of health and well-being, and the contextual factors ranging from employment status and the availability of social support to the length of time living with disability. Notably the ultimate sources of leverage in creating LS, emerging from cross-population and disability-focused work, are personal factors such as agreeableness/extraversion or adaptability, framed as strengths located within the individual. That is, personal factors within the individual allow resilience or growth when contextual factors bring hardship.

This perspective is consistent with two of the broad themes in positive psychology related to the importance of positive personal traits/character strengths and resiliency when experiencing adversity (Seligman & Csikszentmihalyi, 2000; Shogren, 2013). Many of the individual characteristics that predict LS map onto those themes. But intensive focus on these personal factors, as positive as they may be, is what can unintentionally create the *peril* of the LS construct for disabled people, to the extent that some have difficulty accessing internal pathways to LS. Positive psychology in general has faced critiques for its emphasis on individualistic values and an intrapersonal locus of strength and fitness, at the expense of more socio-politically-centered values of interdependence, solidarity, and social connection (Becker & Merecek, 2008; Sugarman, 2015).

To better understand the pathway from belonging to LS and generate research questions and applications to policy and practices, the SIA provides a particularly well-established and generative perspective. Drawing on the motivationally focused social identity theory (SIT; Tajfel & Turner, 1979) and the cognitively focused self-categorization theory (SCT; Hogg & Abrams, 1988; Turner et al., 1987), the SIA posits that a significant part of a person's self-concept is informed by their group memberships. When people self-categorize as part of a social group, their self-concept aligns with the group, is informed by the norms, values, and goals of the group, and is motivated to maintain the view that the group is worthy (Reicher et al., 2010). Appreciating the psychological processes involved in social identification is crucial to widening the scope of the personal to include the social and affording a more comprehensive understanding of how people actively create LS.

Social Identities Supporting Well-being—A Social Cure Perspective

Social identities are significant to our physical and psychological wellness for several reasons, not least of which is because they make group-life possible. Consequently, they are the psychological conduit by which we can be supported by and enjoy the various benefits of groups. The social connectedness that groups bring, also known as social capital, is well-established as a key predictor of health and LS around the world (Bourdieu, 1983; Elgar et al., 2011). Social identities bring social capital into a psychological space, providing mechanisms by which social connectedness can benefit a person. Haslam and colleagues (2018), for example, developed the social identity approach to health—deploying theoretical propositions about intergroup behavior from both SIT (Tajfel & Turner, 1979) and SCT (Turner et al.,

1987)—to locate specific areas of psychological benefit that groups provide (for reviews see Haslam et al., 2009; Jetten et al., 2012; Jetten et al., 2017; Haslam et al., 2018).

First and most broadly, self-identification with groups provides a basis for positive attraction toward other people who share our group memberships or social identities. We are drawn to others who share our social identities because of similarities and the sense that they share key aspects of their selves with us (Turner, 1985). Likewise, that shared social identity provides us a sense of liking and trust in the other that does not even require face-to-face contact or previous familiarity. This benefit of social identity is exemplified by the fact that for a strongly identified activist, a protest march is a place of comfort and solidarity, whereas for the non-identified onlooker, it can be a place for suspicion and fear.

A second benefit of group identification is the way that it can draw us into purposeful interactions. Engagement in everything from a choir rehearsal to a wheelchair basketball game or to a fundraiser is made meaningful and imbued with more passion when there is a sense of common purpose and direction involved (Haslam et al., 2018). Likewise, this engagement is self-sustaining to the degree that working on common goals is considered integral to the norms and values of the group. Practicing your own part in the choral arrangement is therefore a worthy endeavor, because you want the *choir*, more so than your*self*, to sound good.

Third, social identities form the basis for social support, which is a critical aspect of both the instrumental and emotional benefits of groups for individual well-being. Simply put, social identification with a group allows the "other" to be seen as part of the "self," and that psychological connectedness turns a group member's welfare into a shared concern rather than an imposition (Haslam et al., 2019). Moreover, that social support can come in a variety of forms including instrumental (i.e., personal care assistance or help during an emergency; Haslam et al., 2012) or informational or emotional support (i.e., someone to talk to and get advice from; Inoue et al., 2015). In fact, SIA research generally recommends having multiple group memberships to provide a broader base of support to weather the storms of inevitable life transitions that can be stressful if not traumatic (Haslam et al., 2008; Iyer et al., 2009; Jones et al., 2011; Steffens et al., 2016). For example, one's ability to transition through identity loss and new identity formation that comes with acquiring a condition like MS is enhanced through the support of a strong stable group identity (i.e., family; Barker et al., 2014). While sources of support can be wide-ranging, support is more readily received and beneficial when it comes from other members of one's in-group (Haslam et al., 2012). For example, around the country, Centers for Independent Living (CIL) born out of the Independent Living Movement of the 1970s "offer support, advocacy, and information on empowerment in the attainment of independence from a peer viewpoint" (National Council on Independent Living, 2021). The benefits of CIL are far-reaching, but most notably include the reframing of disability from a personal and isolating tragedy to an experience infused with collective strength and resilience (Little, 2010).

Finally, social identity affects health and well-being by increasing people's sense of agency and control over their outcomes—important predictors of LS. One way in which this works is through SIT-proposed identity management strategies, where stigmatized group members can engage in collective coping strategies that revalue the comparison dimensions of the group or pursue collective action efforts to increase the actual social status of the group (Tajfel et al., 1979). In other words, increased identification with the stigmatized group can transform a profound sense of helplessness in the face of discriminatory experiences, into resistance and empowered action. For example, in Mejias et al.'s (2014) examination of a small disability empowerment group, not only did participation in the group positively affect members' self-worth, but it also increased feelings of self-confidence that they could direct toward engaging in social change. The second way in which social identity increases feelings of personal control is by expanding the self-concept once a person internalizes the group identity into their self-system. For example, evidence from Greenaway and colleagues' (2015) study using the World Values Survey shows that identification with community and nation positively predict a person's sense of personal control.

To summarize, social identity provides the psychological conduit for the individual to participate in and gain the myriad benefits from their group memberships—even stigmatizing ones. Feelings of connectedness, support, purpose, and control all manifest themselves as a person comes to accept and internalize these memberships as self-defining. Yet, in the context of extant work on positive psychological approaches to well-being and LS, the role of a person's past and present group memberships has been secondary at best. This is particularly the case given the typical conceptualization of group participation either as "purely utilitarian or in service of the more authentic individual 'self'" (Dirth & Branscombe, 2018, p. 4), or as in conflict with a person's truest aspirations. However, from the perspective of SIT/SCT, the social groups we belong to are not *apart* from the personal psyche, but rather become embedded into one's self-system such that "a strong sense of 'me' flows from a strong sense of us" (Haslam et al., 2018, p. 31).

Social Identities Buffer against Psychological Distress—A Stigma Management Perspective

It is important to recognize that social categories exist in broader sociostructural relations with one another. Within these often-hierarchical socio-structural relations come status differences that ultimately impact inter-group stereotypes, prejudices, and discriminatory behaviors. Belonging to a low-status group in society, as people with disabilities have historically been, means that they are frequently the targets of ableism (Nario-Redmond, 2019) which is not only disempowering, but can have deleterious consequences for health, well-being, and life-satisfaction (Pascoe & Smart Richman, 2011; Schmitt et al., 2014). However, it does not have to be this way: when members of stigmatized groups reconceptualize the group in positive ways, social identities can provide much-needed support and buffer against the deleterious consequences of prejudice and discrimination (Branscombe et al., 1999). Specifically, the perception that one's disability category membership is valuable and enriching mitigates the pernicious effects of stigma on self-esteem (Bogart et al., 2018).

Within the SIA, SIT (Tajfel & Turner, 1979) provides clear propositions about the nature of group versus individual-centered strategies for managing the negative effects of stigma, hypotheses about when each type of strategy is likely to be used, and the advantages and disadvantages of each approach (see Branscombe & Ellemers, 1999; Dirth & Branscombe, 2018; Nario-Redmond, 2019). Notably, the strengths of individual-centered strategies—where a person seeks to rescue the personal self by physically or symbolically distancing the personal from the collective—depend on whether group boundaries are permeable enough for a person to legitimately disavow their group membership (Ellemers et al., 1988). For example, individual strategies for a person with a physical disability might include passing as nondisabled if their condition is not too conspicuous or seeking therapy or surgery to correct the aspects of their condition that compare unfavorably with nondisabled others (e.g., limb-lengthening surgery for people with dwarfism; Branscombe et al., 2012; Fernández et al., 2012). Unfortunately, individual-centered strategies are not always feasible for people with disabilities given the diverse nature of the impairment conditions. In these cases, disabled people attempting to use individual-centered strategies can risk internalizing the stigmatizing narratives of the outgroup and experience lower self-worth (Nario-Redmond et al., 2013).

Contrary to individual-centered strategies, group-based strategies leverage stigmatized group identities to both rehabilitate the image of the stigmatized group and to agitate for change in the status of the in-group overall (Tajfel & Turner, 1979). For example, some people with disabilities have promoted reclaiming the meaning of the word "crip" from the demeaning term "cripple" as a signifier of unabashed pride (Lewis, 2015). Likewise, by redefining and revaluing the stigmatizing characteristics of their group, people with disabilities have challenged the unequal status quo more generally as disability activists engage in various protests and demonstrations (i.e., US disability rights movement; Fleischer et al., 2012; Shapiro, 1993). While group-based stigma management strategies carry risks of alienating and even engendering animosity among higher status group members, the strengths of collective strategies include greater empowerment to engage in actions for social change and greater well-being (Bogart et al., 2018; Fernández et al., 2012; Hahn & Belt, 2004; Nario-Redmond et al., 2013). This is what evidence following the rejection-identification model (RIM; Branscombe et al., 1999) shows across numerous studies (Bogart et al., 2018; Schmitt et al., 2002, 2003; Ramos et al., 2012). In the face of stigma and discrimination (rejection), there is resiliency and strength in moving toward rather than away from the group (identification).

Intervening to Facilitate Positive Social Identity

As we have argued, a significant source of psychological benefit comes from connection and belonging—identification—with meaningful social groups (Haslam et al., 2019). Unfortunately, there is a tendency for people to largely underestimate the importance of the group in fostering health and well-being outcomes (Haslam et al., 2018). Building both awareness and capacity toward the development of positive social identities is tremendously important for leveraging social identity as a catalyst for LS. In line with SIA propositions, there are several critical processes that need to be encouraged to cultivate the beneficial impacts of positive social identifications (Ball & Nario-Redmond, 2014).

Redefining the Self

First, to enhance positive social identity processes, individuals should be encouraged to redefine the self in line with collective rather than personal self-categories (Turner et al., 1987). Necessarily, one must navigate several barriers that can work against this collective self-categorization. First, contemporary society informed by capitalist ideology tends to engender an acute focus on one's personal identities and chronic self-comparisons at the interpersonal level (Baumeister, 1987; Turner, 2006; Turner & Oakes, 1986). Therefore, the default self-category that is most chronically accessible tends to be at the level of the individual. Additionally, the cognitive processes enabling self-categorization (see Turner et al., 1987) tend to respond automatically in relation to cues from one's social context. Due to this unconscious process, a person might internalize significant group identities into their self-concept and underestimate how much of the self is informed by shared group memberships. Lastly, people may not belong to many groups, thereby making it challenging to find such avenues for self-redefinition.

In light of these cultural and cognitive barriers, it is worthwhile to facilitate opportunities where people can develop self-awareness in relation to their group memberships. An example intervention known as the Groups4Health program (G4H; Haslam et al., 2018) has participants "scope" out their existing social connections or possibilities for social growth and subsequently "source" skills that can help a person connect with existing groups, reconnect with previous groups, or explore new groups. Participants are finally encouraged to reflect on the compatibility between their group memberships, how these group memberships fit with their personal values and goals, and how the groups might contribute to their overall well-being. This process of "scaffolding" one's groups helps people become more aware of the impact of groups and provides lasting change as their attention and motivation changes and the salience of group memberships are likely to increase.

While the G4H program is in its infancy and has not yet been applied to samples of people with disabilities, available evidence supporting the program has been promising. For example, a G4H intervention with a sample of undergraduate college students who were experiencing social isolation and affective disruption produced significant reductions in psychological distress variables (i.e., depression, anxiety, and stress), and elevated LS and self-esteem. These positive changes were sustained in follow-up surveys six months later (Haslam et al., 2016). Facilitating opportunities for people with disabilities to reflect on and scaffold potential group memberships can have tremendous results for fostering community belonging and building resilience in the face of ableist experiences (Daley et al., 2018).

Affirming Stigmatized Identities and Fostering Collective Action Intentions

As one takes stock of their group memberships, it is equally important to identify those that might be perceived negatively or as a threat to the self (i.e., stigmatized groups). Because stigmatized identities cause distress and sizeable decrements to LS and general well-being (Pascoe & Smart Richman, 2009; Schmitt et al., 2014), particularly for people with disabilities (Silván-Ferrero et al., 2020), it is essential to find ways to leverage positive identity processes (Ball & Nario-Redmond, 2014).

First, it is important to be aware of the feasibility and risks of individual-centered strategies to distance oneself from the stigmatized group (Dirth & Branscombe, 2018). With greater awareness, one can begin to combat internalized stigma that develops from trying to assimilate to higher status norms and instead move *toward* rather than *away from* the group (Lindly et al., 2014). In negotiating group identity with fellow group members, it is possible to transform stigmatized characteristics to signifiers of pride which can enhance well-being and establish a similar basis for others who share the group membership (Lindly et al., 2014). For instance, online disability arts and culture groups, and "hashtag" communities readily reclaim previously derogatory labels such as "gimp" or "crip" (Kafer, 2013; McRuer, 2006) and reinterpret physical and mental differences as valuable and instructive (e.g., #spoonies, #disabledandcute, #CripplePunk, #wheelchairlife) rather than abnormal and pathological.

Affirming one's social identities provides an added benefit of challenging the legitimacy of the lower status position of one's group, which can stimulate collective action intentions among many disadvantaged minorities (Tajfel & Turner, 1979). For example, as people with disabilities reinterpret disability-related restrictions as the product of an ableist society, they begin to assert the resilience of the group for navigating other-imposed oppression and promote the notion that there is no credible justification for why the group should face discriminatory treatment (Dirth & Branscombe, 2019). This strategy of confronting the dominant group to challenge unequal status relations constitutes another crucial intervention to leverage the benefits of group membership (Ball & Nario-Redmond, 2014). Collective action efforts can certainly be beneficial for agitating for social change, but in terms of psychological consequences, collective action brings group members together and allows for more affiliation, connection, and affirmation of group values in addition to cultivating trust as group members display their commitment to the group. Moreover, collective action provides a visible demonstration of the social support resources the group can provide to buffer stigma and discrimination, building a sense of collective efficacy, a shared language, and an impetus or drive to respond to injustice (Van Zomeran et al., 2008). Finally, since high social identification, feelings of collective self-efficacy, and perceptions of injustice are all central predictors of collective action intentions (Van Zomeran et al., 2008), interventions to promote collective action efforts can perpetuate a virtuous cycle whereby action begets more action.

Enhancing Life Satisfaction through Disability-Specific Group Memberships

While interventions and factors predicting LS can come in many shapes and sizes, it is our contention that positive social identification with the group serves as a central conduit for activating a plethora of salutary outcomes (e.g., sense of freedom and control, meaning and purpose, adaptability) traditionally presented as *personal* factors. Therefore, it is essential that we take the general recommendations for developing and enhancing positive social identity and locate them within extant disability community formations working to translate research into new policies and practices. This is not to discourage efforts to source positive group memberships wherever they may be found (e.g., school, workplace, family, community, etc.) as positive group membership is not picky when it comes to psychological benefits. Instead, we would like to emphasize the rich possibilities within disability communities for enhancing social identity processes. While it is not possible to make an exhaustive list, we would like to point to a couple of areas that exemplify a strong connection between social identity principles and LS outcomes.

Adaptive Sports

The adaptive sporting community, including sporting organizations, competitions, and related tourism, accounts for over 100 million dollars annually (LABS, 2021). Participants of all ages with disabilities can compete in individual and team sports at levels ranging from friendly to international competitions (i.e., Special Olympics International, Paralympic games). An abundance of evidence supports the physical and psychological benefits of adaptive sport participation for people with disabilities for general outcomes, including QOL, LS, community reintegration, mood, and employment (see Diaz et al., 2019, for a review). Through participation, people with disabilities are immersed in social networks of shared experience and common objectives that can redefine their sense of normalcy and success (Lundberg et al., 2011). Particularly important can be the redefinition of the self that comes from participating in organized competitions that provide a well-defined sense of mission and purpose. For instance, Crawford et al. (2015) found participating in sports was beneficial in general for people with intellectual disabilities, but the greatest benefits to self-esteem and QOL came from participating in the Special Olympic International games rather than participating in a sport through other programs.

Teammates and mentors who share disability group memberships support the development of individual competency and self-efficacy (crucial predictors of LS) by providing tips and support for growth and development (Lape et al., 2018). Finally, adaptive sports provide a unique opportunity for people with disabilities to "level the playing field" and make positively distinct comparisons with nondisabled people. For example, anyone who has tried wheelchair basketball or wheelchair rugby can tell you these are no easier to play for a nondisabled person than it is for someone who has paralysis. In fact, these sports undoubtedly favor someone who is more comfortable and experienced using a wheelchair.

While involvement in adaptive sports demonstrates a proven record of catalyzing sources of LS via social identity processes, too few people with disabilities are aware of or have access to adaptive sports programs (Labbé et al., 2019). Therefore, it is essential that research and practice recognize the potential for adaptive sports to support pathways to LS that stem from social identity processes. Likewise, policies that support the funding and distribution of adaptive sports programs, especially to underserved and rural areas, are crucial to ensuring greater access to these valuable opportunities.

Disability Culture—Arts and Studies

Another substantial collective identity structure for people with disabilities can be found within the various platforms of disability culture. The formations of disability culture found in artistic and intellectual production provide unique opportunities for people with disabilities to be a part of a community of generative others (Brueggemann, 2013). Importantly, the social identity processes involved in group membership represents a transformative shift from individual succumbing to impairment-related restrictions to redefining the self in collective terms, allying one's fate to the disability community at large and working alongside others, disabled people can negotiate what "we" means, independent of nondisabled outsiders. For example, Soorenian's (2005) investigation of the impact of disability arts found that the cultural identity of being disabled was significant for every participant, even while not everyone agreed completely about how that cultural identity was to be defined. Moreover, engaging in disability arts production offered participants liberatory purpose to communicate to society-at-large about what disability means to them. Participants noted their experience was distinct from an art-therapy exercise, such that they were being creative in a manner that transcended their own individual identities and competencies, toward a cultural disability identity.

Like disability arts, disability studies can provide a community structure and purpose for people with disabilities to explore and articulate their experiences through myriad disciplinary perspectives (Linton, 2005). Anecdotally, one of the authors (Dirth) credits much of his positive disability social identification to his introduction to disability studies in graduate school. Growing up with cerebral palsy, he had very few opportunities to connect to disability culture and recognized a pattern of internalized stigma where he would distance himself from disability category membership. It was not until he started independent research on disability stigma that he was introduced to the social model and the disability rights movement through the works of Adrienne Asch, Harlan Hahn, Simi Linton, and others. In discovering disability culture via disability studies, he has developed and strengthened his disability identity and the subsequent meaning that his disability carries for him. Moreover, in his professional role as a social psychologist, he recognizes the feelings of empowerment that the disability studies community provides as he unapologetically offers his perspective and experiences as a disabled person to his discipline of social psychology.

Disability-Directed Advocacy. The last community structure that is well-established and shows great potential for enhancing social identity processes for people with disabilities involves disability-directed advocacy (DDA) organizations. DDA tend to be those led by lay volunteers and professionals with disabilities that take a more sociopolitical approach to disability and practice advocacy that builds coalitions across impairment groups (Dirth & Nario-Redmond, 2019). In addition, DDA's advocacy efforts are characterized by securing more rights and greater representation of people with disabilities across a variety of domains. Examples of such organizations include CIL, the National Association of the Deaf, the Autism Self-advocacy network, Self-Advocates Becoming Empowered, and ADAPT.

Becoming a member of a DDA organization likely offers many of the same benefits of the other community structures mentioned previously. Distinctively, DDA organizations provide a setting where most of the decision-makers are people with disabilities. This means that the mission of the organization is defined and carried out by insiders (Little, 2010). In this way, DDA organizations offer critical opportunities for informational and emotional support and insider perspectives on common sociopolitical issues faced (e.g., securing health-care benefits, navigating bureaucratic agencies) and everyday experiences of microaggressions, prejudice, and discrimination. Finally, DDA organizations can serve as a foundation for participating in collective action. Collective action engagement can be enormously consequential for strengthening group identification and fostering self-efficacy (Van Zomeren et al., 2008) and collective empowerment independent of successful outcomes (Drury & Reicher, 2005). Participation also shows benefits for group cohesion and enhanced LS (Klar & Kasser, 2009). As Little's (2010) study of CILs indicated, by raising members' awareness of disability history, representations, and narratives, a DDA organization can be influential in fostering a sense of confidence and empowerment that is ultimately required for people to engage in collective action in the first place (Van Zomeren et al., 2008).

CONCLUSIONS AND IMPLICATIONS

The quote from Longmore (2003) that opened this chapter is from a discussion of disability rights and emphasizes the push for equal access and equal opportunity as well as the importance of collective identity. Our chapter topic is LS, a broad and subjective appraisal of one's life grounded in one's experience, independent of externally defined "impairment" status; the LS concept draws from social-ecological models of well-being and positive psychology and is potentially empowering and in line with Longmore's quote. But to the degree that our view of LS is focused on the external context impinging on an individual, with said individual then needing to manage that context with inner resources such as adaptability and agreeableness, we risk reinforcing stereotypes of disability as personal tragedy that admirably brave individuals strive to overcome. For those to whom a sense of internal control is not so easily discernible—people who are socially isolated, or who suddenly acquire a disability later in life—linking LS to inner strength and overcoming may create despair. Further, the individualistic perspective does not directly address external barriers ranging from lack of physical access to stigma and discrimination that *creates* disability (preventing or limiting participation) above and beyond a person's impairment.

Based on these critiques, we have argued here for inclusion of a social identity perspective on health into the study of LS and its predictors to create an enhanced emphasis on connecting disabled people to the social groups important to them, including, but not limited to, others who share their disability status and who therefore share in their lived experience. We have reviewed literature demonstrating that social identification offers sources of social and political strength and creative expression, that social identification offers a rooted and positive sense of self, and that interventions and programs exist that help disabled people tap into these empowering collective sources.

We have drawn these connections between social identity and LS by carefully and critically reviewing the literature. Going forward, new research is needed that demonstrates empirical connection between LS and variables derived from SIT. For example, personal factors known to predict LS, such as self-efficacy or even relatively stable individual differences such as agreeableness, may be influenced by the number and strength of social identifications across populations and among disabled people. The mediating or moderating role of social identity between situational predictors like employment status and LS should also be studied. In addition to building the research case linking personal factors, LS, and social identity, practical applications of this work should be continued and extended. Awareness could be raised among mental and physical health-care providers, and social connection and identity could be assessed as one indicator of health versus risk. Finally, promising programs that can be implemented at the level of institutions or agencies, such as Groups-4-Health, should be tested for their effectiveness among people with disabilities, and disseminated more widely if such effectiveness is supported. Given that interventions exist that are supported by evidence of effectiveness, policy and funding should prioritize the dissemination of programs guided by or consistent with the SIA into underserved settings where they are needed most. Applied research in implementation science—focused on the diffusion of evidence-based practices—highlights the challenges associated with translating science into policy and service. Even when a program is evidence-based, successful implementation in a given setting requires needs ongoing assessment to determine whether the program fills a gap in a given setting, along with organizational buy-in, training, and fidelity monitoring (see Rapport et al., 2017, for an overview of implementation science).

Because such efforts require funding, we encourage government and other funding sources such as foundations to consider the evidence in support of effective programs as well as the broader research literature demonstrating how social participation and identity strengthen the self and enhance health and economic, political, and creative participation in life. Based on this evidence, funders could increase support for efforts to provide what SIT describes as *social cures* to people with disabilities. Within any subpopulation and location, specific barriers to social participation and identity (including opportunities for regular and supportive social contact via formal resource centers, recreational and employment settings) should be identified; buy-in from organizations or groups who are willing to adopt and implement an evidence-based approach can then be sought and leveraged, with members of the disability community actively involved in providing and evaluating the program. Like any science-to-practice effort, translating SIT and LS evidence into funded and carefully implemented practice may be something of a heavy lift in early stages, but based on the evidence we have reviewed in this chapter, the resulting benefits for disabled people and the communities in which they live would justify the effort (e.g., see Cook & Odom, 2013).

This work deserves further study, funding, and dissemination because it meets a human need that is both universal and sharply relevant to disabled people striving to build LS in an ableist world. In a qualitative study of mental health consumers reporting on the kinds of information they most needed to increase well-being and enhance the effectiveness of their services, a key theme was the importance of learning about the experience of other people in their situation. The authors noted that participants used remarkably similar language when describing this need, for example, "It's reassuring to know you're not alone"; "It's nice to know you're not alone" (Powell & Clarke, 2006, p. 363). The SIA to health and LS begins here—ensuring that people realize they are not alone—and from that foundation help create a sense of community, a strong and positive sense of self, and a life enriched by opportunities for participation, creativity, and direct impact on social change. The collective becomes a personal factor and strengthens the individual; the individual can in turn strengthen and improve the fate of the collective. Further empirical work and application may support and clarify the case we are making here; meanwhile, the existing literature we have reviewed suggests that an SIT-informed conceptualization of the self and personal factors can open the door to a satisfying life for people with all kinds of disabilities, free of stigma and rich with belonging.

NOTES

1. Impairments are defined as problems in body function or alterations in body structure (e.g., blindness or paralysis; WHO 2011). While sometimes used interchangeably in the literature, according to the ICF, disability is an umbrella term that includes bodily impairments, activity limitations, and participation restrictions.

2. In discussing these limitations, it is important to note that our review does include LS research that accounts for the role of social support and other contextual factors ranging from employment status to neighborhood/living situation (e.g., see Diener et al., 2013 for national correlates of LS). But even here, the person is understood as an atomized individual impinged upon by events and situations in their social space.

REFERENCES

Adelman, H. S., Taylor, L., & Nelson, P. (1989). Minors' dissatisfaction with their life circumstances. *Child Psychiatry and Human Development, 20*(2), 135–147. doi: 10.1007/BF00711660

Albrecht, G. L., & Devlieger, P. J. (1999). The disability paradox: high quality of life against all odds. *Social Science & Medicine, 48*(8), 977–988. doi: 10.1016/S0277-9536(98)00411-0

Alfonso, V. C., Allison, D. B., Rader, D. E., & Gorman, B. S. (1996). The extended satisfaction with life scale: Development and psychometric properties. *Social Indicators Research, 38*(3), 275–301. doi: 10.1007/BF00292049

Amundson, R. (2010). Quality of life, disability, and hedonic psychology. *Journal for the Theory of Social Behaviour, 40*(4), 374–392. doi: 10.1111/j.1468-5914.2010.00437.x

Arrindell, W. A., van Nieuwenhuizen, C., & Luteijn, F. (2001). Chronic psychiatric status and satisfaction with life. *Personality and Individual Differences, 31*(2), 145–155. doi: 10.1016/S0191-8869(00)00125-2

Ash, C., & Huebner, E. S. (2001). Environmental events and life satisfaction reports of adolescents: A test of cognitive mediation. *School Psychology International, 22*(3), 320–336. doi: 10.1177/0143034301223008

Atkinson, F., & Martin, J. (2020). Gritty, hardy, resilient, and socially supported: A replication study. *Disability and Health Journal, 13*(1), doi: 10.1016/j.dhjo.2019.100839

Bahm, A., & Forchuk, C. (2008). Interlocking oppressions: The effect of a comorbid physical disability on perceived stigma and discrimination among mental health consumers in Canada. *Health and Social Care in the Community, 17*, 63–70. doi: 10.1111/j.1365-2524.2008.00799.x

Ball, T. C., & Nario-Redmond, M. R. (2014). Positive social identity interventions: Finding a conduit for well-being in stigmatized group memberships. In A. C. Parks & S. M. Schueller (Eds.), *The Wiley Blackwell handbook of positive psychological interventions* (pp. 327–343). Wiley Blackwell.

Barker, A. B., das Nair, R., Lincoln, N. B., & Hunt, N. (2014). Social identity in people with multiple sclerosis: a meta-synthesis of qualitative research. *Social Care & Neurodisability, 5*(4), 256–267. doi: 10.1108/SCN-05-2014-0009

Barrett, J. J., Putzke, J. D., & Richards, J. S. (2002). Early versus late onset of spinal cord injury among the elderly. *Journal of Clinical Psychology in Medical Settings, 9*(3), 219–226. doi: 10.1023/A:1016051311531

Barskova, T., & Oesterreich, R. (2009). Post-traumatic growth in people living with a serious medical condition and its relations to physical and mental health: A systematic review. *Disability and Rehabilitation, 31*(21), 1709–1733. doi: 10.1080/09638280902738441

Bartels, M. (2015). Genetics of wellbeing and its components satisfaction with life, happiness, and quality of life: A review and meta-analysis of heritability studies. *Behavior Genetics, 45*(2), 137–156. doi: 10.1007/s10519-015-9713-y

Bat-Chava, Y. (1994). Group identification and self-esteem of deaf adults. *Personality and Social Psychology Bulletin, 20*(5), 494–502. doi: 10.1177/0146167294205006

Baumeister, R. F. (1987). How the self became a problem: A psychological review of historical research. *Journal of Personality and Social Psychology, 52*(1), 163–176. doi: 10.1037/0022-3514.52.1.163

Becker, D., & Marecek, J. (2008). Dreaming the American dream: Individualism and positive psychology. *Social and Personality Psychology Compass, 2*(5), 1767–1780. doi: 10.1111/j.1751-9004.2008.00139.x

Berry, D. S., Willingham, J. K., & Thayer, C. A. (2000). Affect and personality as predictors of conflict and closeness in young adults' friendships. *Journal of Research in Personality, 34*(1), 84–107. doi: 10.1006/jrpe.1999.2271

Bogart, K. R. (2014). The role of disability self-concept in adaptation to congenital or acquired disability. *Rehabilitation Psychology, 59*(1), 107–115. doi: 10.1037/a0035800

Bogart, K. R., Lund, E. M., & Rottenstein, A. (2018). Disability pride protects self-esteem through the rejection-identification model. *Rehabilitation Psychology, 63*(1), 155–159. doi: 10.1037/rep0000166

Borgonovi, F. (2008). Doing well by doing good. The relationship between formal volunteering and self-reported health and happiness. *Social Science & Medicine, 66*(11), 2321–2334.

Bourdieu, P. (1983). The forms of capital. English version published 1986 in J. G. Richardson (Ed.), *Handbook for Theory and Research for the Sociology of Education.* (pp. 183–198). Greenwood Press.

Boyce, C. J., & Wood, A. M. (2011). Personality prior to disability determines adaptation: Agreeable individuals recover lost life satisfaction faster and more completely. *Psychological Science, 22*(11), 1397–1402. doi: 10.1177/0956797611421790

Branscombe, N. R., & Ellemers, N. (1999). Coping with group-based discrimination: Individualistic versus group-level strategies. In J. K. Swim & C. Stangor (Eds.), *Prejudice: The target's perspective* (pp. 243–266). Academic Press.

Branscombe, N. R., Fernández, S., Goméz, A., & Cronin, T. (2012). Moving toward or away from group identity: Different strategies for coping with pervasive discrimination. In J. Jetten, C. Haslam, & S. A. Haslam. (Eds.). *The social cure: Identity, health and well-being* (pp. 115–131). Psychology Press.

Branscombe, N. R., Schmitt, M. T., & Harvey, R. D. (1999). Perceiving pervasive discrimination among African Americans: Implications for group identification and well-being. *Journal of Personality and Social Psychology, 77*(1), 135–149. doi: 10.1037/0022-3514.77.1.135

Brantley, A., Huebner, E. S., & Nagle, R. J. (2002). Multi-dimensional life satisfaction reports of adolescents with mild mental disabilities. *Mental Retardation, 40,* 321–329. doi: 10.1352/0047-6765(2002)040<0321:MLSROA>2.0.CO;2

Brault, M. W. (2012). Americans with Disabilities: 2010. Current Population Reports [P70-131]. Washington, DC: US Census Bureau. https://www.census.gov/prod/2012pubs/p70-131.pdf

Brickman, P., Coates, D., & Janoff-Bulman, R. (1978). Lottery winners and accident victims: Is happiness relative? *Journal of Personality and Social Psychology, 36*(8), 917–927. doi: 10.1037/0022-3514.36.8.917

Bronk, K. C., Hill, P., Lapsley, D.K., Talib, T., & Finch, H. (2009). Purpose, hope, and life satisfaction in three age groups. *Journal of Positive Psychology, 4*(6), 500–510. doi: 10.1080/17439760903271439

Brueggemann, B. J. (2013). Disability studies/disability culture. In M. L. Wehmeyer (Ed.), *Oxford handbook of positive psychology and disability* (pp. 279–299). Oxford University Press.

Bryant, R. A., Marosszeky, J. E., Crooks, J., Baguley, I. J., & Gurka, J. A. (2001). Posttraumatic stress disorder and psychosocial functioning after severe traumatic brain injury. *The Journal of Nervous and Mental Disease, 189*(2), 109–113.

Bücker, S., Nuraydin, S., Simonsmeier, B. A., Schneider, M., & Luhmann, M. (2018). Subjective well-being and academic achievement: A meta-analysis. *Journal of Research in Personality, 74,* 83–94. doi: 10.1016/j.jrp.2018.02.007

Buntinx, W. H. (2013). Understanding disability: A strengths-based approach. In M. Wehmeyer (Ed.), *The Oxford handbook of positive psychology and disability* (pp. 7–18). Oxford University Press.

Campbell, A., Converse, P. E., & Rogers, W. L. (1976). *The quality of American life.* Russell Sage Foundation.

Chang, C. H., Ferris, D. L., Johnson, R. E., Rosen, C. C., & Tan, J. A. (2012). Core self-evaluations: A review and evaluation of the literature. *Journal of Management, 38,* 81–128. doi: 10.1177/0149206311419661

Chang, E. C., & Sanna, L. J. (2001). Optimism, pessimism, and positive and negative affectivity in middle-aged adults: A test of a cognitive-affective model of psychological adjustment. *Psychology and Aging, 16,* 524–531. doi: 10.1037/0882-7974.16.3.524

Chase, B. W., Cornille, T. A., & English, R. W. (2000). Life satisfaction among persons with spinal cord injuries. *Journal of Rehabilitation, 66*(3), 14–20.

Cook, B. G., & Odom, S. L. (2013). Evidence-based practices and implementation science in special education. *Exceptional Children, 79,* 135–144. doi: 10.1177/001440291307900201

Crawford, C., Burns, J., & Fernie, B. A. (2015). Psychosocial impact of involvement in the Special Olympics. *Research in Developmental Disabilities, 45,* 93–102. doi: 10.1016/j.ridd.2015.07.009

Cubí-Mollá, P., Jofre-Bonet, M., & Serra-Sastre, V. (2017). Adaptation to health states: Sick yet better off? *Health Economics, 26*(12), 1826–1843. doi: 10.1002/hec.3509

Daley, A., Phipps, S., & Branscombe, N. R. (2018). The social complexities of disability: discrimination, belonging and life satisfaction among Canadian youth. *SSM-population Health, 5,* 55–63. doi: 10.1016/j.ssmph.2018.05.003

de Hond, A., Bakx, P., & Versteegh, M. (2019). Can time heal all wounds? An empirical assessment of adaptation to functional limitations in an older population. *Social Science & Medicine, 222,* 180–187. doi: 10.1016/j.socscimed.2018.12.028

DeNeve, K. M., & Cooper, H. (1998). The happy personality: a meta-analysis of 137 personality traits and subjective well-being. *Psychological Bulletin, 124*(2), 197–229. doi: 10.1037/0033-2909.124.2.197

DePaulo, B. (2017). Toward a positive psychology of single life. In D. S. Dunn (Ed.), *Positive psychology: Established an emerging issues* (pp. 251–275). Routledge.

Dew, T., & Huebner, E. S. (1994). Adolescents' perceived quality of life: An exploratory investigation. *Journal of School psychology, 32*(2), 185–199. doi: 10.1016/0022-4405(94)90010-8

Diaz, R., Miller, E. K., Kraus, E., & Fredericson, M. (2019). Impact of adaptive sports participation on quality of life. *Sports Medicine and Arthroscopy Review, 27*(2), 73–82. doi: 10.1097/JSA.0000000000000242

Diener, E. (2009). Subjective well-being. In E. Diener (Ed.), *The science of well-being: The collected works of Ed Diener* (Vol. 37, pp. 11–58). Springer Science + Business Media.

Diener, E. D., Emmons, R. A., Larsen, R. J., & Griffin, S. (1985). The satisfaction with life scale. *Journal of Personality Assessment, 49*(1), 71–75. doi: 10.1207/s15327752jpa4901_13

Diener, E., & Chan, M. Y. (2011). Happy people live longer: Subjective well-being contributes to health and longevity. *Applied Psychology: Health and Well-Being, 3*(1), 1–43. doi: 10.1111/j.1758-0854.2010.01045.x

Diener, E., & Seligman, M. E. (2002). Very happy people. *Psychological Science, 13*(1), 81–84. doi: 10.1111/1467-9280.00415

Diener, E., Inglehart, R., & Tay, L. (2013). Theory and validity of life satisfaction scales. *Social Indicators Research, 112*(3), 497–527.

Diener, E., Lucas, R. E., & Oshi, S. (2002). Subjective well-being: The science of happiness and life satisfaction. In C. R. Snyder & S. J. Lopez (Eds.), *Handbook of positive psychology.* (pp. 463–473). Oxford University Press.

Dijkers, M. (1997). Quality of life after spinal cord injury: A meta analysis of the effects of disablement components. *Spinal Cord, 35*(12), 829–840. doi: 10.1038/sj.sc.3100571

Dirth, T. P., & Branscombe, N. R. (2018). The social identity approach to disability: Bridging disability studies and psychological science. *Psychological Bulletin, 144*(12), 1300–1324. doi: 10.1037/bul0000156

Dirth, T. P., & Branscombe, N. R. (2019). Recognizing ableism: A social identity analysis of disabled people perceiving discrimination as illegitimate. *Journal of Social Issues*, 75(3), 786–813. doi: 10.1111/josi.12345

Dirth, T., & Nario-Redmond, M. R. (2019). Disability advocacy for a new era: Leveraging social psychology and a sociopolitical approach to change. In D. Dunn (Ed.), *Disability: Social psychological perspectives*. Academy of Rehabilitation Psychology Series, Oxford Press.

Eid, M., & Diener, E. (2004). Global judgments of subjective well-being: Situational variability and long-term stability. *Social Indicators Research*, 65(3), 245–277. doi: 10.1023/B:SOCI.0000003801.89195.bc

Elavsky, S., & McAuley, E. (2005). Physical activity, symptoms, esteem, and life satisfaction during menopause. *Maturitas*, 52(3–4), 374–385. doi: 10.1016/j.maturitas.2004.07.014

Elgar, F. J., Davis, C. G., Wohl, M. J., Trites, S. J., Zelenski, J. M., & Martin, M. S. (2011). Social capital, health and life satisfaction in 50 countries. *Health & Place*, 17(5), 1044–1053. doi: 10.1016/j.healthplace.2011.06.010

Ellemers, N., van Knippenberg, A., de Vries, K, & Wilke, H. (1988). Social identification and permeability of group boundaries. *European Journal of Social Psychology*, 18, 497–513. doi: 10.1002/ejsp.2420180604

Emmons, R. A., & Diener, E. (1985). Factors predicting satisfaction judgments: A comparative examination. *Social Indicators Research*, 16(2), 157–167. doi: 10.1007/BF00574615

Erdogan, B., Bauer, T. N., Truxillo, D. M., & Mansfield, L. R. (2012). Whistle while you work: A review of the life satisfaction literature. *Journal of Management*, 38(4), 1038–1083. doi: 10.1177/0149206311429379

Fellinghauer, B., Reinhardt, J. D., Stucki, G., & Bickenbach, J. (2012). Explaining the disability paradox: a cross-sectional analysis of the Swiss general population. *BMC Public Health*, 12(1), 1–9. doi: 10.1186/1471-2458-12-655

Fernández, S., Branscombe, N. R., Gómez, A., & Morales, J. F. (2012). Influence of the social context on use of surgical-lengthening and group-empowering coping strategies among people with dwarfism. *Rehabilitation Psychology*, 57, 224–235. doi: 10.1037/a0029280

Fleischer, D. Z., Zames, F. D., & Zames, F. (2012). *The disability rights movement: From charity to confrontation*. Temple University Press.

Fujita, F., & Diener, E. (2005). Life satisfaction set point: stability and change. *Journal of Personality and Social Psychology*, 88(1), 158–164. doi: 10.1037/0022-3514.88.1.158

Gilman, R., Easterbrooks, S. R., & Frey, M. (2004). A preliminary study of multidimensional life satisfaction among deaf/hard of hearing youth across environmental settings. *Social Indicators Research*, 66(1), 143–164. doi: 10.1023/B:SOCI.0000007495.40790.85

Glenn, N. D., & Weaver, C. N. (1979). A note on family situation and global happiness. *Social Forces*, 57, 960–967. doi: 10.2307/2577364

Greenaway, K. H., Cruwys, T., Haslam, S. A., & Jetten, J. (2016). Social identities promote well-being because they satisfy global psychological needs. *European Journal of Social Psychology, 46*(3), 294–307. doi: 10.1002/ejsp.2169

Greenaway, K. H., Haslam, S. A., Cruwys, T., Branscombe, N. R., Ysseldyk, R., & Heldreth, C. (2015). From "we" to "me": Group identification enhances perceived personal control with consequences for health and well-being. *Journal of Personality and Social Psychology, 109*(1), 53–74. doi: 10.1037/pspi0000019

Greenspoon, P. J., & Saklofske, D. H. (2001). Toward an integration of subjective well-being and psychopathology. *Social Indicators Research, 54*(1), 81–108. doi: 10.1023/A:1007219227883

Hahn, H. D., & Belt, T. L. (2004). Disability identity and attitudes toward cure in a sample of disabled activists. *Journal of Health and Social Behavior, 45*, 453–464. doi: 10.1177/002214650404500407

Haslam, C., Cruwys, T., Haslam, S. A., Dingle, G., & Chang, M. X. L. (2016). Groups 4 Health: Evidence that a social-identity intervention that builds and strengthens social group membership improves mental health. *Journal of Affective Disorders, 194*, 188–195. doi: 10.1016/j.jad.2016.01.010

Haslam, C., Jetten, J., Cruwys, T., Dingle, G. A., & Haslam, S. A. (2018a.). *The new psychology of health: Unlocking the social cure*. Routledge.

Haslam, S. A., Jetten, J., Postmes, T., & Haslam, C. (2008). Social identity, health and well-being: An emerging agenda for applied psychology. *Applied Psychology, 58*(1), 1–23. doi: 10.1111/j.1464-0597.2008.00379.x

Haslam, S. A., McMahon, C., Cruwys, T., Haslam, C., Jetten, J., & Steffens, N. K. (2018b.). Social cure, what social cure? The propensity to underestimate the importance of social factors for health. *Social Science & Medicine, 198*, 14–21. doi: 10.1016/j.socscimed.2017.12.020

Haslam, S. A., Reicher, S. D., & Levine, M. (2012). When other people are heaven, when other people are hell: How social identity determines the nature and impact of social support. In J. Jetten, C. Haslam, & S. A. Haslam (Eds.), *The social cure: Identity, health and well-being* (pp. 157–174). Psychology Press.

Heckman, T. G. (2003). The chronic illness quality of life (CIQOL) model: Explaining life satisfaction in people living with HIV disease. *Health Psychology, 22*(2), 140–147. doi: 10.1037/0278-6133.22.2.140

Heisel, M. J., & Flett, G. L. (2004). Purpose in life, satisfaction with life, and suicide ideation in a clinical sample. *Journal of Psychopathology and Behavioral Assessment, 26*(2), 127–135. doi: 10.1023/B:JOBA.0000013660.22413.e0

Helliwell, J. F. (2007). Well-being and social capital: Does suicide pose a puzzle? *Social Indicators Research, 81*(3), 455–496. doi: 10.1007/s11205-006-0022-y

Hirschi, A. (2009). Career adaptability development in adolescence: Multiple predictors and effect on sense of power and life satisfaction. *Journal of Vocational Behavior, 74*, 145–155. doi: 10.1016/j.jvb.2009.01.002

Hogg, M. A., & Abrams, D. (1990). Social motivation, self-esteem and social identity. In D. Abrams & M. A. Hogg (Eds.), *Social identity theory: Constructive and critical advances* (pp. 28–47). Harvester Wheatsheaf.

Hopkins, N., Reicher, S. D., Khan, S. S., Tewari, S., Srinivasan, N., & Stevenson, C. (2016). Explaining effervescence: Investigating the relationship between shared social identity and positive experience in crowds. *Cognition and Emotion, 30*(1), 20–32. doi: 10.1080/02699931.2015.1015969

Huebner, E. S. (2004). Research on assessment of life satisfaction of children and adolescents. *Social Indicators Research, 66*(1), 3–33. doi: 10.1023/B:SOCI.0000007497.57754.e3

Huebner, E. S., Drane, W., & Valois, R. F. (2000). Levels and demographic correlates of adolescent life satisfaction reports. *School Psychology International, 21*(3), 281–292. doi: 10.1177/0143034300213005

Ingledew, D. K., & Brunning, S. (1999). Personality, preventive health behaviour and comparative optimism about health problems. *Journal of Health Psychology, 4*(2), 193–208. doi: 10.1177/0143034300213005

Inoue, Y., Funk, D. C., Wann, D. L., Yoshida, M., & Nakazawa, M. (2015). Team identification and postdisaster social well-being: The mediating role of social support. *Group Dynamics: Theory, Research, and Practice, 19*(1), 31. doi: 10.1037/gdn0000019

Iyer, A., Jetten, J., Tsivrikos, D., Postmes, T., & Haslam, S. A. (2009). The more (and the more compatible) the merrier: Multiple group memberships and identity compatibility as predictors of adjustment after life transitions. *British Journal of Social Psychology, 48*(4), 707–733. doi: 10.1348/014466608X397628

Jamal, R., Komal, M. W., & Ahmad, M. S. (2021). Comparison of life satisfaction and attitude towards disability between congenital and acquired physical disabilities. *Sir Syed Journal of Education & Social Research, 4*(2), 71–81. doi: 10.36902/sjesr-vol4-iss2-2021(71-81)

Jetten, J., Haslam, C., & Alexander, S. H. (Eds.). (2012). *The social cure: Identity, health and well-being.* Psychology Press.

Jetten, J., Haslam, C., Haslam, S. A., Dingle, G., & Jones, J. M. (2014). How groups affect our health and well-being: The path from theory to policy. *Social Issues and Policy Review, 8*(1), 103–130. doi: 10.1111/sipr.12003

Jetten, J., Haslam, S. A., Cruwys, T., Greenaway, K. H., Haslam, C., & Steffens, N. K. (2017). Advancing the social identity approach to health and well-being: Progressing the social cure research agenda. *European Journal of Social Psychology, 47*(7), 789–802. doi: 10.1002/ejsp.2333

Jones, J. M. (2021, February 3). *Personal satisfaction drops from 2020 record U.S. high.* Gallup, Inc. https://news.gallup.com/poll/329213/personal-satisfaction-drops-2020-record-high.aspx

Jones, J. M., Haslam, S. A., Jetten, J., Williams, W. H., Morris, R., & Saroyan, S. (2011). That which doesn't kill us can make us stronger (and more satisfied with life): The contribution of personal and social changes to well-being after acquired brain injury. *Psychology and Health, 26*(3), 353–369. doi: 10.1080/08870440903440699

Kafer, A. (2013). *Feminist, queer, crip.* Indiana University Press.

Klar, M., & Kasser, T. (2009). Some benefits of being an activist: Measuring activism and its role in psychological well-being. *Political Psychology, 30*(5), 755–777. doi: 10.1111/j.1467-9221.2009.00724.x

Knies, G., Nandi, A., & Platt, L. (2016). Life satisfaction, ethnicity and neighbour-hoods: Is there an effect of neighbourhood ethnic composition on life satisfaction? *Social Science Research, 60*, 110–124. doi: 10.1016/j.ssresearch.2016.01.010

Kocman, A., & Weber, G. (2018). Job satisfaction, quality of work life and work motivation in employees with intellectual disability: A systematic review. *Journal of Applied Research in Intellectual Disabilities, 31*(1), 1–22. doi: 10.1111/jar.12319

Koivumaa-Honkanen, H., Honkanen, R., Viinamaeki, H., Heikkilae, K., Kaprio, J., & Koskenvuo, M. (2001). Life satisfaction and suicide: A 20-year follow-up study. *American Journal of Psychiatry, 158*(3), 433–439. doi: 10.1176/appi.ajp.158.3.433

Labbé, D., Miller, W. C., & Ng, R. (2019). Participating more, participating better: Health benefits of adaptive leisure for people with disabilities. *Disability and Health Journal, 12*(2), 287–295. doi: 10.1016/j.dhjo.2018.11.007

LABS (2021, November). *Adapted sport LABS: Economic impact of the adapted sport industry* [Video]. Vimeo. https://vimeo.com/470007695

Lape, E. C., Katz, J. N., Losina, E., Kerman, H. M., Gedman, M. A., & Blauwet, C. A. (2018). Participant-reported benefits of involvement in an adaptive sports program: A qualitative study. *PM&R, 10*(5), 507–515. doi: 10.1016/j.pmrj.2017.10.008

Lewis, V. (2015). Crip. In R. Adams, B. Reiss, & D. Serlin (Eds.), *Keywords for disability studies* (pp. 46–48). University Press.

Lindly, O. J., Nario-Redmond, M. R., & Noel, J. G. (2014). Creatively re-defining fat: Identification predicts strategic responses to stigma, ingroup attitudes, and well-being, *Fat Studies, 3*(2), 179–195. doi: 10.1080/21604851.2014.865968

Linton, S. (2005). What is disability studies? *PMLA/Publications of the Modern Language Association of America, 120*(2), 518–522. doi: 10.1632/S0030812900167823

Little, D. L. (2010). Identity, efficacy, and disability rights movement recruitment. *Disability Studies Quarterly, 30*(1), 1–17.

Loewe, N., Bagherzadeh, M., Araya-Castillo, L., Thieme, C., & Batista-Foguet, J. M. (2014). Life domain satisfactions as predictors of overall life satisfaction among workers: Evidence from Chile. *Social Indicators Research, 118*(1), 71–86. doi: 10.1007/s11205-013-0408-6

Longmore, P. K. (2003). *Why I burned my book and other essays on disability*. Temple University Press.

Lucas, R. E. (2007). Long-term disability is associated with lasting changes in subjective well-being: Evidence from two nationally representative longitudinal studies. *Journal of Personality and Social Psychology, 92*, 717–730. doi: 10.1037/0022-3514.92.4.717

Lucas, R. E., Clark, A. E., Georgellis, Y., & Diener, E. (2003). Reexamining adaptation and the set point model of happiness: Reactions to changes in marital status. *Journal of Personality and Social Psychology, 84*(3), 527–539. doi: 10.1037/0022-3514.84.3.527

Luhmann, M., Hofmann, W., Eid, M., & Lucas, R. E. (2012). Subjective well-being and adaptation to life events: A meta-analysis. *Journal of Personality and Social Psychology, 102*(3), 592–615. doi: 10.1037/a0025948

Lundberg, N. R., Taniguchi, S., McCormick, B. P., & Tibbs, C. (2011). Identity negotiating: Redefining stigmatized identities through adaptive sports and recreation participation among individuals with a disability. *Journal of Leisure Research, 43*(2), 205–225. doi: 10.1080/00222216.2011.11950233

Lyubomirsky, S., King, L., & Diener, E. (2005). The benefits of frequent positive affect: Does happiness lead to success? *Psychological Bulletin, 131*(6), 803–855. doi: 10.1037/0033-2909.131.6.803

Major, B., & O'Brien, L. T. (2005). The social psychology of stigma. *Annual Review of Psychology, 56,* 393–421. doi: 10.1146/annurev.psych.56.091103.0 70137

Major, B., Kaiser, C.R., & McCoy, S.K. (2003). It's not my fault: When and why attributions to prejudice protect self-esteem. *Personality and Social Psychology Bulletin 29*(6), 772–781. doi: 10.1177/0146167203029006009

Major, B., Quinton, W.J., & McCoy, S.K. (2002). Antecedents and consequences of attributions to discrimination: Theoretical and empirical advances. In M. P. Zanna (Ed.), *Advances in experimental social psychology* (pp. 251–330). Academic Press.

Martin, K. M., & Huebner, E. S. (2007). Peer victimization and prosocial experiences and emotional well-being of middle school students. *Psychology in the Schools, 44*(2), 199–208. doi: 10.1002/pits.20216

McCarthy, J. (2020, February 6). *New high of 90% of Americans satisfied with personal life.* Gallup, Inc. https://news.gallup.com/poll/284285/new-high-americans-satisfied-personal-life.aspx

McCullough, G., & Huebner, E. S. (2003). Life satisfaction reports of adolescents with learning disabilities and normally achieving adolescents. *Journal of Psychoeducational Assessment, 21*(4), 311–324. doi: 10.1177/073428290302100401

McKnight, C. G., Huebner, E. S., & Suldo, S. (2002). Relationships among stressful life events, temperament, problem behavior, and global life satisfaction in adolescents. *Psychology in the Schools, 39*(6), 677–687. doi: 10.1002/pits.10062

McRuer, R. (2006). *Crip theory: Cultural signs of queerness and disability.* University Press.

Mejias, N. J., Gill, C. J., & Shpigelman, C. N. (2014). Influence of a support group for young women with disabilities on sense of belonging. *Journal of Counseling Psychology, 61*(2), 208–220. doi: 10.1037/a0035462

Meyer, C., Rumpf, H. J., Hapke, U., & John, U. (2004). Impact of psychiatric disorders in the general population: Satisfaction with life and the influence of comorbidity and disorder duration. *Social Psychiatry and Psychiatric Epidemiology, 39*(6), 435–441. doi: 10.1007/s00127-004-0755-3

Müller, R., & Geyh, S. (2015). Lessons learned from different approaches towards classifying personal factors. *Disability and Rehabilitation, 37*(5), 430–438. doi: 10.3109/09638288.2014.923527

Nakazato, N., Nakashima, K. I., & Morinaga, Y. (2017). The importance of freedom in the East and the West over time: A meta-analytic study of predictors of well-being. *Social Indicators Research, 130*(1), 371–388. doi: 10.1007/s11205-015-1180-6

Nario-Redmond, M. R. (2019). *Ableism: The causes and consequences of disability prejudice.* John Wiley & Sons.

Nario-Redmond, M. R., & Oleson, K. C. (2016). Disability group identification and disability-rights advocacy: Contingencies among emerging and other adults. *Emerging Adulthood, 4*(3), 207–218. doi: 10.1177/2167696815579830

Nario-Redmond, M. R., Kemerling, A. A., & Silverman, A. (2019). Hostile, benevolent, and ambivalent ableism: Contemporary manifestations. *Journal of Social Issues, 75*(3), 726–756. doi: 10.1111/josi.12337

Nario-Redmond, M. R., Noel, J. G., & Fern, E. (2013). Redefining disability, reimagining the self: Disability identification predicts self-esteem and strategic responses to stigma. *Self and Identity, 12*, 468–488. doi: 10.1080/15298868.2012.681118

National Council on Independent Living. (2020, April 3). *About NCIL.* https://ncil.org/about/

Ng, Z. J., Huebner, S. E., & Hills, K. J. (2015). Life satisfaction and academic performance in early adolescents: Evidence for reciprocal association. *Journal of School Psychology, 53*(6), 479–491. doi: 10.1016/j.jsp.2015.09.004

Ngamaba, K. H., Panagioti, M., & Armitage, C. J. (2018). Income inequality and subjective well-being: a systematic review and meta-analysis. *Quality of Life Research, 27*(3), 577–596. doi: 10.1007/s11136-017-1719-x

Nota, L., Ferrari, L., Soresi, S., & Wehmeyer, M. (2007). Self-determination, social abilities and the quality of life of people with intellectual disability. *Journal of Intellectual Disability Research, 51*(11), 850–865. doi: 10.1111/j.1365-2788.2006.00939.x

Okun, M. A., Stock, W. A., Haring, M. J., & Witter, R. A. (1984). The social activity/subjective well-being relation: A quantitative synthesis. *Research on Aging, 6*(1), 45–65. doi: 10.1177/0164027584006001003

Oswald, A. J., & Powdthavee, N. (2008). Does happiness adapt? A longitudinal study of disability with implications for economists and judges. *Journal of Public Economics, 92*(5–6), 1061–1077. doi: 10.1016/j.jpubeco.2008.01.002

Pagan, R. (2018) Disability, life satisfaction and participation in sports. In L. Rodriguez de la Vega & W. Toscano (Eds.), *Handbook of leisure, physical activity, sports, recreation and quality of life. International handbooks of quality-of-life.* Cham: Springer.

Pascoe, E. A., & Smart Richman, L. (2009). Perceived discrimination and health: a meta-analytic review. *Psychological Bulletin, 135*(4), 531–554. doi: 10.1037/a0016059

Patten, S. B., Williams, J. V., Lavorato, D. H., Berzins, S., Metz, L. M., & Bulloch, A. G. (2012). Health status, stress and life satisfaction in a community population with MS. *Canadian Journal of Neurological Sciences, 39*(2), 206–212.

Pavot, W., & Diener, E. (2008). The satisfaction with life scale and the emerging construct of life satisfaction. *The Journal of Positive Psychology, 3*(2), 137–152. doi: 10.1080/17439760701756946

Piliavin, J. A., & Siegl, E. (2007). Health benefits of volunteering in the Wisconsin longitudinal study. *Journal of Health and Social Behavior, 48*(4), 450–464. doi: 10.1177/002214650704800408

Powell, J., & Clarke, A. (2006). Information in mental health: Qualitative study of mental health service users. *Health Expectations, 9*, 359–365. doi: 10.1111/j.1369-7625.2006.00403.x

Powell, T., Gilson, R., & Collin, C. (2012). TBI 13 years on: Factors associated with post-traumatic growth. *Disability and Rehabilitation, 34*(17), 1461–1467. doi: 10.3109/09638288.2011.644384

Proctor, C., Linley, P. A., & Maltby, J. (2017). Life satisfaction. In *Encyclopedia of adolescence* (1- 12). Springer International Publishing.

Putzke, J. D., Elliott, T. R., & Richards, J. S. (2001). Marital status and adjustment 1 year post-spinal-cord-injury. *Journal of Clinical Psychology in Medical Settings, 8*(2), 101–107. doi: 10.1023/A:1009555910604

Ramos, M. R., Cassidy, C., Reicher, S., & Haslam, S. A. (2012). A longitudinal investigation of the rejection–identification hypothesis. *British Journal of Social Psychology, 51*(4), 642–660. doi: 10.1111/j.2044-8309.2011.02029.x

Rapport, F., Clay-Williams, R., Churruca, K., Shih, P., Hogden, A., & Braithewaite, J. (2017). The struggle of translating science into action: Foundational concepts of implementation science. *Journal of Evaluation in Clinical Practice, 24*, 117–126. doi: 10.1111/jep.12741

Reich, J. W., & Zautra, A. (1981). Life events and personal causation: Some relationships with satisfaction and distress. *Journal of Personality and Social Psychology, 41*(5), 1002–1012. doi: 10.1037/0022-3514.41.5.1002

Reicher, S., & Haslam, S. A. (2006). Rethinking the psychology of tyranny: The BBC prison study. *British Journal of Social Psychology, 45*(1), 1–40. doi: 10.1348/014466605X48998

Reicher, S., Spears, R., & Haslam, S. A. (2010). The social identity approach in social psychology. In M. S. Wetherell & C. T. Mohanty (Eds.), *Sage identities handbook* (pp. 45–62). London, UK: Sage.

Rey, L., Extremera, N., Durán, A., & Ortiz-Tallo, M. (2013). Subjective quality of life of people with intellectual disabilities: The role of emotional competence on their subjective well-being. *Journal of Applied Research in Intellectual Disabilities, 26*(2), 146–156. doi: 10.1111/jar.12015

Roy, A. W., & MacKay, G. F. (2002). Self-perception and locus of control in visually impaired college students with different types of vision loss. *Journal of Visual Impairment and Blindness, 96*(4), 254–266. doi: 10.1177/0145482X0209600407

Ryan, R. (1999, February 2). Quoted by Alfie Kohn, In pursuit of affluence, at a high price. *The New Your Times.*

Santilli, S., Nota, L., Ginevra, M. C., & Soresi, S. (2014). Career adaptability, hope and life satisfaction in workers with intellectual disability. *Journal of Vocational Behavior, 85*(1), 67–74. doi: 10.1016/j.jvb.2014.02.011

Schimmack, U., Diener, E., & Oishi, S. (2002). Life-satisfaction is a momentary judgment and a stable personality characteristic: The use of chronically accessible and stable sources. *Journal of Personality, 70,* 345–384. doi: 10.1111/1467-6494.05008

Schmitt, M. T., Branscombe, N. R., Kobrynowicz, D., & Owen, S. (2002). Perceiving discrimination against one's gender group has different implications for well-being in women and men. *Personality and Social Psychology Bulletin, 28*(2), 197–210. doi: 10.1177/0146167202282006

Schmitt, M. T., Branscombe, N. R., Postmes, T., & Garcia, A. (2014). The consequences of perceived discrimination for psychological well-being: A meta-analytic review. *Psychological Bulletin, 140*(4), 1–27. doi: 10.1037/a0035754

Schmitt, M. T., Spears, R., & Branscombe, N. R. (2003). Constructing a minority group identity out of shared rejection: The case of international students. *European Journal of Social Psychology, 33*(1), 1–12. doi: 10.1002/ejsp.131

Seaton, E. K., Caldwell, C. H., Sellers, R. M., & Jackson, J. S. (2010). An intersectional approach for understanding perceived discrimination and psychological well-being among African American and Caribbean Black youth. *Developmental Psychology, 46*(5), 1372–1379. doi: 10.1037/a0019869

Seery, M. D., Holman, E. A., & Silver, R. C. (2010). Whatever does not kill us: cumulative lifetime adversity, vulnerability, and resilience. *Journal of Personality and Social Psychology, 99*(6), 1025–1041. doi: 10.1037/a0021344

Seligman, M. E. P., & Csikszentmihalyi, M. (2000). Happiness, excellence, and optimal human functioning [Special issue]. *American Psychologist, 55*(1), 5–183.

Seligman, M., & Darling, R. B. (2009). *Ordinary families, special children: A system approach to childhood disability.* Guilford Press.

Seligson, J. L., Huebner, E. S., & Valois, R. F. (2003). Preliminary validation of the brief multidimensional students' life satisfaction scale (BMSLSS). *Social Indicators Research, 61*(2), 121–145. doi: 10.1007/s12187-014-9295-x

Shandra, C. L. (2017). Disability and social participation: The case of formal and informal volunteering. *Social Science Research, 68,* 195–213. doi: 10.1016/j.ssresearch.2017.02.006

Shapiro, J. P. (1993). *No pity.* Times Books.

Sherman, J. E., DeVinney, D. J., & Sperling, K. B. (2004). Social support and adjustment after spinal cord injury: Influence of past peer-mentoring experiences and current live-in partner. *Rehabilitation Psychology, 49*(2), 140–149. doi: 10.1037/0090-5550.49.2.140

Sheth, A. J., McDonald, K. E., Fogg, L., Conroy, N. E., Elms, E. H., Kraus, L. E., ... & Hammel, J. (2019). Satisfaction, safety, and supports: Comparing people with disabilities' insider experiences about participation in institutional and community living. *Disability and Health Journal, 12*(4), 712–717. doi: 10.1016/j.dhjo.2019.06.011

Shogren, K. A. (2013). A social–ecological analysis of the self-determination literature. *Mental Retardation, 51*(6), 496–511. doi: 10.1352/1934-9556-51.6.496

Shogren, K. A., Lopez, S. J., Wehmeyer, M. L., Little, T. D., & Pressgrove, C. L. (2006). The role of positive psychology constructs in predicting life satisfaction in adolescents with and without cognitive disabilities: An exploratory study. *The Journal of Positive Psychology, 1*(1), 37–52. doi: 10.1080/17439760500373174

Silván-Ferrero, P., Recio, P., Molero, F., & Nouvilas-Pallejà, E. (2020). Psychological quality of life in people with physical disability: The effect of internalized stigma, collective action and resilience. *International Journal of Environmental Research and Public Health, 17*(5), 1802. doi: 10.3390/ijerph17051802

Silverman, A. M. & Cohen, G.L. (2012). Correlates of well-being and employment among blind and partially sighted adults in the United States. *Unpublished raw data.*

Silverman, A. M., Molton, I. R., Smith, A. E., Jensen, M. P., & Cohen, G. L. (2017). Solace in solidarity: Disability friendship networks buffer well-being. *Rehabilitation Psychology, 62*(4), 525–533. doi: 10.1037/rep0000128

Smedema, S. M., Chan, F., Yaghmaian, R. A., Cardoso, E. D., Muller, V., Keegan, J., ... & Ebener, D. J. (2015). The relationship of core self-evaluations and life satisfaction in college students with disabilities: Evaluation of a mediator model. *Journal of Postsecondary Education and Disability, 28*(3), 341–358.

Smith, P., & Routel, C. (2009). Transition failure: The cultural bias of self-determination and the journey to adulthood for people with disabilities. *Disability Studies Quarterly, 30*(1). https://dsq-sds.org/article/view/1012/1224

Soorenian, A. (2005). An Investigation into the Impact of "Disability Arts" on Disabled Community At Large. [Unpublished Masters Thesis, Leeds University]

Steffens, D., Maher, C. G., Pereira, L. S., Stevens, M. L., Oliveira, V. C., Chapple, M., ... & Hancock, M. J. (2016). Prevention of low back pain: a systematic review and meta-analysis. *JAMA Internal Medicine, 176*(2), 199–208. doi: 10.1001/jamainternmed.2015.7431

Steffens, N. K., Jetten, J., Haslam, C., Cruwys, T., & Haslam, S. A. (2016). Multiple social identities enhance health post-retirement because they are a basis for giving social support. *Frontiers in Psychology, 7*, 1519. doi: 10.3389/fpsyg.2016.01519

Stock, W. A., Okun, M. A., Haring, M. J., & Witter, R. A. (1983). Age and subjective well-being: A meta-analysis. In R. J. Light (Ed.), *Evaluation studies: Review annual* (Vol. 8, pp. 279–302). Sage Foundation.

Stubbe, J. H., Posthuma, D., Boomsma, D. I., & De Geus, E. J. (2005). Heritability of life satisfaction in adults: A twin-family study. *Psychological Medicine, 35*(11), 1581–1588. doi: 10.1017/S0033291705005374

Sugarman, J. (2015). Neoliberalism and psychological ethics. *Journal of theoretical and Philosophical Psychology, 35*(2), 103–116. doi: 10.1037/a0038960

Suldo, S. M., & Huebner, E. S. (2004). Does life satisfaction moderate the effects of stressful life events on psychopathological behavior during adolescence? *School Psychology Quarterly, 19*(2), 93–105. doi: 10.1521/scpq.19.2.93.33313

Tajfel, H., & Turner, J. C. (1979). An integrative theory of intergroup conflict. In W. A. Austin & S. Worschel (Eds.). *The social psychology of intergroup relations.* (pp. 33–47). Brooks Cole.

Thoits, P. A., & Hewitt, L. N. (2001). Volunteer work and well-being. *Journal of Health and Social Behavior, 42*, 115–131. doi: 10.2307/3090173

Turner, J. C. (1985). Social categorization and the self-concept: A social cognitive theory of group behavior. In E. J. Lawler (Ed.), *Advances in group processes: Theory and research* (Vol. 2, pp. 77–121). JAI Press.

Turner, J. C. (2006). Tyranny, freedom and social structure: Escaping our theoretical prisons. *British Journal of Social Psychology, 45,* 41–46. doi: 10.1348/014466605X79840

Turner, J. C., & Oakes, P. J. (1986). The significance of the social identity concept for social psychology with reference to individualism, interactionism, and social influence. *British Journal of Social Psychology, 25,* 237–252. doi: 10.1111/j.2044-8309.1986.tb00732.x

Turner, J. C., Hogg, M. A., Reicher, S. D., & Wetherell, M. (1987). *Rediscovering the social group: A self-categorization theory.* Blackwell Publishing.

Valois, R. F., Zullig, K. J., Huebner, E. S., & Drane, J. W. (2003). Dieting behaviors, weight perceptions, and life satisfaction among public high school adolescents. *Eating Disorders, 11*(4), 271–288. doi: 10.1080/10640260390242506

Van Zomeren, M., Spears, R., & Leach, C. W. (2008). Exploring psychological mechanisms of collective action: Does relevance of group identity influence how people cope with collective disadvantage? *British Journal of Social Psychology, 47*(2), 353–372. doi: 10.1348/014466607X231091

Ville, I., & Ravaud, J. F. (2001). Subjective well-being and severe motor impairments: the Tetrafigap survey on the long-term outcome of tetraplegic spinal cord injured persons. *Social Science & Medicine, 52*(3), 369–384. doi: 10.1016/S0277-9536(00)00140-4

Wehmeyer, M. L. (2013). Beyond pathology: Positive psychology and disability. In M. Wehmeyer (Ed.), *The Oxford handbook of positive psychology and disability* (pp. 3–6). Oxford University Press.

Wehmeyer, M., & Schwartz, M. (1998). The relationship between self-determination and quality of life for adults with mental retardation. *Education and Training in Mental Retardation and Developmental Disabilities, 33*(1), 3–12.

World Health Organization. (2011). *World report on disability.* World Health Organization and World Bank. http://www.who.int/disabilities/world_report/2011/report.pdf

Zullig, K. J., Valois, R. F., Huebner, E. S., & Drane, J. W. (2005). Adolescent health-related quality of life and perceived satisfaction with life. *Quality of Life Research, 14*(6), 1573–1584. doi: 10.1007/s11136-004-7707-y

Index

About the Authors

Erin E. Andrews, PsyD, ABPP, is the Psychology Program manager for the nationally designated Veterans Health Administration VISN 17 Telemental Health Clinical Resource Hub. She is associate professor (affiliated) in the Department of Psychiatry at Dell Medical School, the University of Texas at Austin. She is Board Certified in Rehabilitation Psychology. Dr. Andrews's areas of clinical and research interest include disability identity and cultural competence, disability inclusion in psychology training, sexual and reproductive rights of people with disabilities, disabled parenting, and reducing bias in disability language. She is the author of *Disability as Diversity: Developing Cultural Competence* published in 2019 by Oxford University Press.

Kathleen R. Bogart, PhD, is associate professor of psychology at Oregon State University. She is a social/health psychologist specializing in ableism and rare disease. She has received grants from the National Institutes of Health and Good Samaritan Hospital. In 2021, Dr. Bogart was awarded the Social Personality and Health Network Diversity in Research Award. She is associate editor of *Orphanet Journal of Rare Diseases*. She identifies disabled and is involved in advocacy work as cochair of the American Psychological Association Committee on Disability Issues in Psychology. Her research has been featured in the *New York Times*, *Time*, and *Inside Higher Ed*.

Brandon L. Boring, MA, is a graduate student in the Department of Psychological and Brain Sciences at Texas A&M University. He has received a BA in Biochemistry from McDaniel College and a MA in Experimental Psychology from Towson University. He is interested in psychosocial factors that contribute to and are affected by pain experiences.

Brooke Bryson, MS, is a fourth-year PhD student in Oregon State University's School of Psychological Science. She received her master's degree in health psychology in 2019 with her thesis, "Stress, Social Support, and Life Satisfaction among Adults with Rare Diseases," which won the Western Association of Graduate Schools-Proquest Distinguished Master's Thesis Award. Broadly, her research evaluates—both quantitatively and qualitatively—ways to improve well-being for adults with diverse rare diseases, with an emphasis on the role of social support. Along with her mentor, she has published her rare disease research in top psychology journals and presented her findings at multiple national conferences.

Katherine Budge, MEd, MPH, is a doctoral student in the Counseling Psychology program at Texas A&M University. She received her Master of Public Health in Health Policy & Management from Columbia University. Her professional interests include issues of equitable access to health care, especially through telehealth and integrated care systems. She currently works and provides services at Texas A&M's Telebehavioral Care Program.

Thomas P. Dirth, PhD, is assistant professor of Psychology at Bemidji State University in Bemidji, Minnesota. As a disabled person in the academy, he centers diverse disabled perspectives to teach an array of multicultural psychological topics including the Psychology of Ableism and Disability. His research integrates disability studies perspectives with cultural psychology and the social identity approach to combat ableism and generate possibilities for more sustainable futures for everyone. Finally, he is an advocate and activist for equitable outcomes for disabled students and faculty in higher education. He received his PhD in Social Psychology from the University of Kansas.

Sidai Dong, MA, MEd, is a doctoral student in Counseling Psychology program at Texas A&M University, and a Psychology Intern at Texas A&M Counseling & Psychological Services. Her research interests focus on understanding the intersections among cognitive, behavioral, emotional development, and mental health outcomes for emerging adults, people with disabilities, and their caregivers. Sidai is passionate about promoting mental health care for minority and underserved populations, helping people navigate the health care system, accepting and celebrating diversity, and supporting them through critical life events.

Dana S. Dunn, PhD, is professor and chair of Psychology and director of Academic Assessment at Moravian University in Bethlehem, PA. He earned his PhD in experimental social psychology from the University of

Virginia and his BA in psychology from Carnegie Mellon University. Dunn is a Fellow of the American Psychological Association (APA Divisions 1, 2, 8, and 22), the Association for Psychological Science, and the Eastern Psychological Association. Dunn served as President of the Society for the Teaching of Psychology (APA Division 2) in 2010. In 2013, he received the Charles L. Brewer Distinguished Teaching of Psychology Award from the American Psychological Foundation, and in 2015 he was the APA's Harry Kirke Wolfe lecturer. He is the editor of the APA journal *Scholarship of Teaching and Learning in Psychology* and serves on the editorial board of *Rehabilitation Psychology.*

Michal Einav, PhD, is clinical psychologist and head of the MA program in Educational Psychology. She is senior lecturer at the Peres Academic Center, Rehovot, Israel, and also lectures at the MA program in child clinical psychology, the Tel Aviv-Yafo Academic College, Israel. The focus of Dr. Einav's research is on family relationships, couples, and parental interactions as well as on personal strengths such as hope theory, loneliness, self-efficacy, and sense of coherence. In her research she focuses on sources of strengths among individuals and families, with and without special needs, mothers in early intervention programs, and bereaved families.

Timothy R. Elliott, PhD, ABPP, is a university distinguished professor in the Department of Educational Psychology at Texas A&M University. Throughout his career he has studied adjustment processes among people living with debilitating conditions, resulting in over 280 professional publications. He co-edited the first (2000) and third (2019) editions of the *Handbook of Rehabilitation Psychology®.* He has received several awards including the Lifetime Achievement Award (2018) and the Wright-Dembo Award (2021) from the Division of Rehabilitation Psychology, the Auburn University College of Education Outstanding Educator Alumni Award (2017), and the Best Science Award from the Society of Counseling Psychology (2009).

Elisa S. M. Fattoracci, BA, earned her BA in Psychology from U.C. Berkeley in 2014. Currently, she is a second-year doctoral student in the Industrial-Organizational Psychology program at Rice University. Her research interests revolve around identity-based adversity. Current projects include researching workplace microaggressions, employees with invisible chronic illnesses, anti-racist educational practices, and resilience measurement, among others.

Anjali J. Forber-Pratt, PhD, is a disability activist, a two-time Paralympian and the director of the National Institute on Disability, Independent Living and

Rehabilitation Research (NIDILRR) in the Administration for Community Living. The work contributed to this book was completed when she was a faculty member at Vanderbilt University. As a researcher, her primary area of work relates to disability identity development. As a wheelchair-user for over 35 years, Dr. Forber-Pratt is nationally and internationally recognized as a disability leader and mentor. She was a White House Champion of Change in 2013 and the American Psychological Association awarded her the 2020 Citizen Psychologist Award for Advancing Disability as a Human Rights and Social Justice Issue Award.

Hannah Fry, MS, is a doctoral student in the Rehabilitation Counselor Education program at the University of Wisconsin—Madison. She completed her MS in Clinical Rehabilitation Counseling at the University of Wisconsin—Madison, during which time she completed practicum and internship at a community mental health counseling and state vocational rehabilitation agencies, working with the Spanish-speaking population in Madison, WI. Before returning to the UW for her PhD studies, she worked at a clubhouse for people with mental illness and substance use disorders. She has research experience in trauma-informed interventions in Latin America and vocational self-efficacy.

Devin Guthrie, BS, is a third-year Clinical Psychology PhD student with disabilities studying at Texas A&M University. They research existential and narrative psychology and are particularly interested in applying their research to the existential dimensions of issues surrounding disability, mental health, and climate change. Devin also writes creatively. Their poetry and creative nonfiction can be found in publications such as *PRISM International*, *The Notre Dame Review*, *The Wire's Dream*, and others.

Mikki Hebl, PhD, graduated with her BA from Smith College and PhD from Dartmouth College. She joined the faculty at Rice University in 1998 and is currently the Martha and Henry Malcolm Lovett Professor of Psychology with a joint appointment in the Jones School. Mikki's research focuses on workplace discrimination and the ways both individuals and organizations can remediate such discrimination and successfully manage diversity. She has approximately 200 publications, 21 teaching awards (including the most prestigious national award called the Cherry Award), research grants from NSF and NIH, and several gender-related research awards.

Joshua A. Hicks, PhD, is professor in the Department of Psychological and Brain Sciences at Texas A&M University. His research focuses on understanding the antecedents and consequences of the experience of meaning in life, authenticity, self-alienation, perceptions of free-will, and mortality awareness.

Yunzhen Huang, MS, is a doctoral student in Rehabilitation Counselor Education at the University of Wisconsin-Madison. She received her bachelor's degree in Psychology at Peking University in China and her master's degree in Clinical Rehabilitation and Mental Health Counseling at the University of North Carolina at Chapel Hill. Her research interests include (a) coping and positive psychology, and how these factors and interventions could improve psychosocial adjustment and health outcomes in individuals with disabilities; (b) equity and justice in counseling; and (c) effective interventions in federal-state vocational rehabilitation programs.

Joseph Maffly-Kipp, MS, is a third-year graduate student in Clinical Psychology at Texas A&M University. He grew up in North Carolina and attended Bates College for his undergraduate degree. His research interests lie at the intersection of existential psychology and mental health/illness, particularly surrounding concerns about mortality, meaning, and identity.

Alexandra M. Kriofske Mainella, PhD, has been working with individuals with disabilities for the past 25 years as an educator, advocate, youth developer, and rehabilitation counselor. She received her PhD in Rehabilitation Counselor Education from the University of Wisconsin Madison and now serves as a clinical assistant professor in the Counselor Education program at Marquette University. Dr. Kriofske Mainella researches disability and sexuality, disability and positive psychology and mindfulness, and continues to work as an advocate in the disability rights movement.

Malka Margalit, PhD, is educational and rehabilitation psychology professor, dean, School of Behavior Sciences, Peres Academic Center, Rehovot, Israel. She is professor emeritus, Tel-Aviv University. She is a laureate of the Israel prize in educational research (2017), on the Coordinating Board of the International Society for Research in Early Intervention, was vice president, International Academy of Research in Learning Disabilities, and chairperson of the Israeli Council of Psychologists. She published her research in 5 books, more than 175 articles in international peer-reviewed journals, and several chapters in professional books. Her research is focused on hope theory, loneliness, social-support, salutogenesis, and learning disorders.

Vani A. Mathur, PhD, is assistant professor of Diversity Science and Well-Being and director of the Social Neuroscience of Pain Disparities Laboratory at Texas A&M University. Her research focus is on pain and, in particular, on the social modulation of pain experience and physiological pain-related processes that leads to inequitable suffering and pain burden.

Megan McSpedon, BA, is a doctoral student in Industrial/Organizational Psychology at Rice University. Her research sits at the intersection of work and education, focusing on (1) the impact that educational experiences have on career outcomes and (2) learning in the workplace. Prior to graduate school, Megan was on the founding team of the Rice Emerging Scholars Program, a comprehensive STEM-retention and student-success initiative. Megan holds a BA from Rice University.

Michelle R. Nario-Redmond, PhD, is professor of Psychology and Biomedical Humanities specializing in stereotyping, prejudice, and disability studies. As a Ford Fellow, she graduated from the University of Kansas with a PhD in social psychology. Her research focuses on group identification, wellness, political advocacy, and social change. In 2019, she published *Ableism: The Causes and Consequences of Disability Prejudice for the Society for the Psychological Study of Social Issues* and is the 2021 recipient of the Society for the Teaching of Psychology's Promoting Diversity, Equity, and Inclusion Award. She is passionate about increasing access and reducing disparities in higher education.

Jeffrey G. Noel, PhD, is research assistant professor at the Missouri Institute of Mental Health, a research and evaluation center at the University of Missouri-Saint Louis. Collaborating with community-based service providers, he evaluates federally funded substance use treatment and substance use/HIV prevention programs, assessing implementation and outcomes of evidence-based programs to reduce health disparities for populations ranging from minority youth to pregnant and postpartum women experiencing substance use disorders. He has also conducted research investigating the relationship between drinking motives and alcohol-approach bias among college students who drink. He received his PhD in Social Psychology from the University of Kansas.

Timothy Oxendahl, BS, is a doctoral student in Industrial/Organizational Psychology at Rice University. He studies individual differences and team dynamics. Prior to graduate school, he conducted research with organizations including Oregon Health and Science University, U.S. Center for SafeSport, and Portland State University. Timothy holds a BS from Portland State University.

Kevin L. Rand, PhD, is associate professor of psychology at Indiana University-Purdue University, Indianapolis. His research focuses on how people think about the future (e.g., hope and optimism), pursue important goals, and cope when their goal pursuits are disrupted. He is particularly interested in how health-related stressors (e.g., pain, cancer, menopause) affect people's pursuit of life goals and the relationship between their most valued goals and treatment preferences. His clinical work is informed by existential principles in conjunction with cognitive-behavioral techniques.

Tomer Schmidt-Barad, PhD, is lecturer in psychology at the School of Behavioural Science, Peres Academic Center, Rehovot, Israel. His research is focused on risk and resilience processes in relation to personal and interpersonal resources. His studies are focused on power-incongruence, compliance to soft and harsh influence tactics within person–environment interactions and their expressions in social behavior. His research is also involved in studies of personal strengths such as self-control and personal sense of power.

Mackenzie L. Shanahan, MS, is a doctoral candidate in clinical psychology at Indiana University-Purdue University Indianapolis. Generally, her research focuses on the connections among expectancies (e.g., hope and optimism), coping behaviors, and health outcomes (e.g., pain and mental health). Specifically, her work aims to describe and identify the mechanisms driving these associations.

Elisabeth R. Silver, BS, is a doctoral student in Industrial/Organizational Psychology at Rice University. She studies workplace diversity and discrimination using computational and experimental methods. Prior to entering graduate school, Elisabeth served as a research analyst at Columbia University Medical Center. She holds a BS from the University of Michigan.

Susan Miller Smedema, PhD, CRC, LPC, is professor and current chair in the Clinical Rehabilitation Counseling/Rehabilitation Counselor Education program at the University of Wisconsin–Madison. Prior to working at UW-Madison, she taught at Florida State University and the University of Northern Iowa. She is a four-time winner of the American Rehabilitation Counseling Association Research Award, serves on the editorial board of Rehabilitation Counseling Bulletin, and is a board member for the National Council on Rehabilitation Education. Her research interests include psychosocial adaptation to disability with an emphasis on positive psychology, well-being, the PERMA model, and character strengths interventions.

Laurel Wade, MEd, is a doctoral student in the Texas A&M University Counseling Psychology program. Currently, she is a predoctoral intern with American University's Student Counseling Services. Her research and clinical interests include positive psychology and the application of personal resilience factors to facilitate development and optimal adjustment to life changes, including chronic illness and disability. She is currently pursuing these interests through her dissertation project chaired by Dr. Timothy Elliott, which examines mechanisms of resilience among veterans with spinal cord injuries.

Michael L. Wehmeyer, PhD, is the Ross and Marianna Beach Distinguished Professor; chairperson, Department of Special Education; and senior scientist and director, Beach Center on Disability, all at the University of Kansas. His scholarly work has focused on understanding and promoting self-determination and self-determined learning, creating and evaluating autonomy-supportive interventions, and the application of positive psychology to the disability context. He has published extensively in these areas and is an author or editor on more than 40 books and more than 460 scholarly articles and book chapters.

About the Editors

Michael L. Wehmeyer, PhD, is the Ross and Marianna Beach Distinguished Professor; chairperson, Department of Special Education; and senior scientist and director, Beach Center on Disability, all at the University of Kansas. His scholarly work has focused on understanding and promoting self-determination and self-determined learning, creating and evaluating autonomy-supportive interventions, and the application of positive psychology to the disability context. He has published extensively in these areas and is an author or editor on more than 40 books and more than 460 scholarly articles and book chapters. Dr. Wehmeyer is ex-president and a Fellow of the American Association on Intellectual and Developmental Disabilities; a Fellow of the American Psychological Association (APA), Intellectual and Developmental Disabilities he was/Autism Spectrum Disorders Division (Div. 33); and a Fellow of the International Association for the Scientific Study of Intellectual and Developmental Disabilities. He is a member of Phi Beta Delta Honor Society for International Scholars-Alpha Pi chapter (University of Kansas) and an honorary alumni inductee of Phi Beta Kappa Arts and Sciences Honor Society-Beta of Oklahoma chapter (University of Tulsa). Dr. Wehmeyer has been recognized for his research and service with awards from numerous associations and organizations, including, recently, the American Psychological Association Distinguished Contributions to the Advancement of Disability Issues in Psychology Award, the American Association on Intellectual and Developmental Disabilities Research Award for significant contributions to the body of scientific knowledge in the field of intellectual and developmental disabilities, the Distinguished Researcher Award for lifetime contributions to research in intellectual disability by The Arc of the United States, and the Burton Blatt Humanitarian Award from the Council for Exceptional Children, Division on Autism and Developmental Disabilities, and he was the Council for Exceptional Children Special Education Research Award recipient for 2016. Dr. Wehmeyer holds graduate degrees in special education and experimental psychology from the University of Tulsa and the University of Sussex in Brighton, England, respectively, and earned his PhD in Human Development and Communication Sciences from the University of Texas at Dallas, where he received a 2014 Distinguished Alumni Award.

Dana S. Dunn, PhD, is professor and chair of Psychology and director of Academic Assessment at Moravian University in Bethlehem, PA. He earned his PhD in experimental social psychology from the University of Virginia and his BA in psychology from Carnegie Mellon University. Dunn is a fellow of the American Psychological Association (APA Divisions 1, 2, 8, and 22), the Association for Psychological Science, and the Eastern Psychological Association. Dunn served as president of the Society for the Teaching of Psychology (APA Division 2) in 2010. In 2013, he received the Charles L. Brewer Distinguished Teaching of Psychology Award from the American Psychological Foundation, and in 2015 he was the APA's Harry Kirke Wolfe lecturer. He is the editor of the APA journal *Scholarship of Teaching and Learning in Psychology* and serves on the editorial board of *Rehabilitation Psychology*. Dunn served as president of the Eastern Psychological Association in 2018–2019 and as president of APA Division 22 (Rehabilitation Psychology) in 2019–2020. He is currently a member of the Board of the Foundation for Rehabilitation Psychology and APA's Board of Convention Affairs. Dunn is a former member of APA's Committee on Disability Issues in Psychology and the Board of Educational Affairs. The author of over 180 articles, chapters, and book reviews, Dunn writes about the social psychology of disability, the teaching of psychology, and liberal education. He is the author or editor of 35 books and writes a blog on the teaching psychology called "Head of the Class" for Psychology Today. Dunn is currently editor-in-chief of the Oxford Bibliographies (OB): Psychology. His recent books include T*he Social Psychology of Disability* (2015), *Positive Psychology: Established and Emerging Issues* (2017), and *Understanding the Experience of Disability: Perspectives from Social and Rehabilitation Psychology* (2019). Dunn has received the Wright-Dembo Lecture Award from APA Division 22 twice (in 2009 and 2019) and the Distinguished Contributions Award from APA's Committee on Disability Issues in Psychology in 2019.